THE SELECTED LETTERS OF
Anthony Hecht

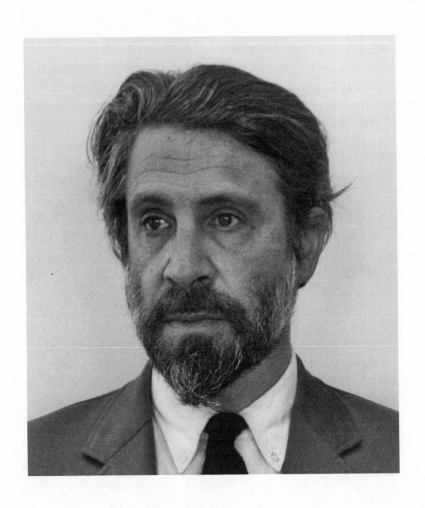

THE SELECTED LETTERS OF

Anthony Hecht

Edited with an introduction by

JONATHAN F. S. POST

THE JOHNS HOPKINS UNIVERSITY PRESS

Baltimore

© 2013 The Johns Hopkins University Press
All rights reserved. Published 2013
Printed in the United States of America on acid-free paper
9 8 7 6 5 4 3 2 1

All letters by Anthony Hecht © 2013 The estate of Anthony Hecht.

The Johns Hopkins University Press
2715 North Charles Street
Baltimore, Maryland 21218-4363
www.press.jhu.edu

Library of Congress Cataloging-in-Publication Data
Hecht, Anthony, 1923–2004.
  [Correspondence. Selections]
  The selected letters of Anthony Hecht / edited with an introduction by Jonathan F. S. Post.
      p. cm.
  Includes bibliographical references and index.
  ISBN 978-1-4214-0730-2 (hdbk. : alk. paper) — ISBN 978-1-4214-0785-2 (electronic) —
ISBN 1-4214-0730-2 (hdbk. : alk. paper) — ISBN 1-4214-0785-X (electronic)
  1. Hecht, Anthony, 1923–2004—Correspondence.   2. Poets, American—20th century—
Correspondence.   I. Post, Jonathan F. S., 1947–   II. Title.
  PS3558.E28Z48 2013
  811'.54—dc23
  [B]   2012012914

A catalog record for this book is available from the British Library.

Frontispiece. Anthony Hecht, late 1960s, around the time that he received the Pulitzer Prize for *The Hard Hours.* (Courtesy of Helen Hecht)

Special discounts are available for bulk purchases of this book. For more information, please contact Special Sales at 410-516-6936 or specialsales@press.jhu.edu.

The Johns Hopkins University Press uses environmentally friendly book materials, including recycled text paper that is composed of at least 30 percent post-consumer waste, whenever possible.

CONTENTS

ILLUSTRATIONS

Following page 128

INTRODUCTION

IN ONE OF THE CHARACTERISTICALLY AMUSING OBSERVATIONS
that makes reading his letters so enjoyable, Anthony Hecht remarked to his
friend and English editor, the poet Jon Stallworthy:

> It occurs to me that in the murky future, when it has been at length de-
> termined that I am a poet of sufficient interest to merit the publication of
> a volume of "Selected Letters," the editor of that book will be at a loss to
> convey what may, in the last analysis, be the most sprightly, various, and
> original part of my correspondence: my letter paper.   (December 22, 1976)

What is characteristic about the humor here is the note of self-deprecation in
Hecht's gradually, tellingly unfolding syntax. Initially imagining, with some
small effort, a time in the murky future when his letters might be deemed worth
collecting, the author manages to prick the puffery of this thought—although
not before nicely amplifying it with three well-chosen adjectives—with the
admission that the most valuable thing about his letters is the stock they are
written on. How seriously are we meant to take the claim, we wonder? Not
terribly. After all, Hecht only says what "may" be the case in the future. But
the momentarily modest gesture has done its work. It disarms the passage
of its potentially heavy freight involving posterity and lets us enjoy the airy
possibility that his stationery is more valuable than his thinking, even as we
smile over the sprightly claim that thought on paper has produced.

Hecht was speaking in this letter about nothing less than a duel to the fin-
ish with his friend and arch epistolary rival William MacDonald, the Roman
architectural historian. The subject involved which of the two could come up
with the rarest letterhead; and while MacDonald had an initial professional
advantage, his work taking him to many distant lands, the more geographi-
cally circumscribed Hecht still had some tricks up his sleeve. He employed
friends ("spies" as he calls them) to bring back stationery from all sorts of
exotic and unusual places, even the White House. At one point, Hecht sur-

mised that the most valued of all such heists "would be the paper of the Warden of the Regina Coeli Prison in Rome" (March 30, 1983). A Google search reveals that there is such a place and office, although I don't believe Hecht ever succeeded in this particular venture. But Hecht could be a persuasive fabricator of his whereabouts. So cleverly matched, in one instance, is the stationery from the Imperial Hotel in Japan with the description of a view of Mt. Fugi from the balcony in a letter written in 1979 that I had to check the biographical record to see if Hecht had ever returned to Japan after the time he spent there as a solder in the 1940s. He hadn't. And part of the joke, I quickly saw, was that the stationery itself had somehow survived as a relic from an earlier era. The Imperial Hotel had been torn down in 1968.

There is a great deal of this kind of mischievous fun in Hecht's letters, which will not be surprising to readers of "The Dover Bitch" and "The Ghost in the Martini," as well as much serious thought, as readers of "Rites and Ceremonies" and "The Venetian Vespers" might rightly expect. But his comment to Stallworthy also contains an important editorial truth. A published book of letters cannot perfectly represent the material conditions of their original epistolary circumstances. Whether as handwritten letters sent from camp or v-mails written from the military front or choice stationery bearing letterheads of the most elaborate and unusual order—often artwork in itself—the technology of book reproduction can only selectively hint at these visual features.

But equally to the point, we should remember (although the fact is often forgotten) that there is always a gap between the "life" and the faithful representation of that "life" that letters are assumed to convey. There is always a rhetorical context operating, even one as encompassing as a world war, and to read an author's letters only to arrive at a record of the self—how devious that phrase is?—performs a disservice of another kind. It is to miss the artfulness of letter writing, something Hecht seems to have understood instinctively. Or at least he came to understand it at a very early age, as the youthful letters written from summer camp suggest, with their penchant for reporting the odd detail or humorous event, in usually grammatically complete sentences, often in combination with a drawing or two to make the meaning graphically present. Hecht grew up in a cultured household on the Upper East Side of Manhattan, we're reminded, where lettered expectations were the norm.

As one of the pre-eminent poets of his generation, the generation of poets who came of age immediately after World War II—a generation that includes his contemporaries and friends Richard Wilbur, James Merrill, and John Hollander—Hecht was not just a spirited but also a prolific correspondent. He took occasional days off, to be sure. The Fire Island summer sun, in particular, sapped his epistolary strength, and there are a few dark years from which no letters survive. But for the most part Hecht was a willing correspondent. He almost always replied to the many who sent him manuscripts or books to read, for instance, although his patience could be tested by those who gave no advance warning or by random inquiries that presumed on a sense of professional generosity. Such was the case of one Mr. Johnson, a lawyer, who sent a tome to Hecht in which he sought to disprove the assumption that the Stratford-born Shakespeare was the author of the plays, and received nearly a tome in return.

So far, about four thousand letters, postcards, and v-mails have surfaced. What is unusual about the collection as a whole, as distinct from the revelatory merits of any one letter, is both the chronological range of the correspondence and the variety of moods and material they comprise. The earliest letters date from 1935, when Hecht went away to summer camp, and with a few exceptions, his letter writing continued until his death in 2004. Not only do Hecht's letters provide, for example, a vivid record of one person's response to war, they also afford a continual commentary on the literary scene of the second half of the century.

Most significant of all, the letters offer an understanding of the life that created the art. They are not the only windows onto the poet's past, it should be said. In his *Conversation with Philip Hoy*, Hecht provided readers with a richly meditated account of his life and poetry, and even before this extended exchange first appeared in print in 1999, he had given several valuable shorter interviews. But the letters allow a more immediate, often more detailed account of events, sometimes correcting errors that have crept into the biographical record. They also allow us to hear, as best we can, what Hecht sounded like at many different points in his life between the ages of twelve and eighty-one; and in this sense, the letters have their own important original story to tell about Hecht's growth as a person, poet, and critic.

I have organized the selection into separate sections, each with a brief introduction of its own. Tailored to the letters that follow, these prefatory comments seek to give some basic biographical information and to suggest a few connections to the poetry. I have done so in part for the convenience of readers less familiar with the overall shape of Hecht's career. But I have proceeded also in the hope that those who already possess a general overview of Hecht's poetry will be encouraged to read not only broadly but deeply in whatever portion of his life that most interests them. The fact that there are seven sections, I might add, does not necessarily suggest any special affinity with Jaques's famous "seven ages of man" speech in *As You Like It*, although the idea is intriguing, given Hecht's love of Shakespeare as well as possible similarities between Jaques's staunchly saturnine character and Hecht himself, clever satirist that he was. Although Hecht experienced melancholy at times, admitting at one point to "sharing many of the views and feelings of those" whom William James, in *Varieties of Religious Experience*, "calls sick souls" (February 16, 2002), the life that emerges in the letters is everywhere too complex, sociable, and various, indeed too loving and eagerly inquisitive, for this author to have traveled long in Jaques's company, even when, near the end of his life, Hecht could become positively and movingly Solomonic about the subject of aging. (See his letter to Francine du Plessix Gray, September 6, 2000.)

The seven sections seemed like logical markers in a busy and full career. In part the divisions are conventional enough. The first two focus on camp, student, and military life. But after these two, the subsequent chapters are meant to highlight major events and shifts particular to Hecht's biography, although it is hard to think that World War II did not constitute a major event in his life. But in the years following the war, Hecht had more freedom to cultivate his talents as a writer in directions of his own choosing, until, that is, he assumed his first regular teaching position at Bard in 1952. From the time of his appointment at Bard to his retirement from Georgetown University some forty years later, Hecht led the life of an academic poet, as was the case with many who emerged in the post-Ransom-Tate era. University employment for poets had replaced the earlier patronage system, and time off to write was often restricted to summers and to release from teaching duties thanks to either sabbatical leave or a major grant, of which Hecht received a goodly number. Folded into these busy years, then, was much writing: books of poems, essays, and several volumes of literary criticism. Some publications, such as the appearance of his first collection of verse, *A Summoning of Stones* (1954), followed by *The Hard Hours* (1967), also coincided with important shifts in his career and help to highlight several of the chapter divisions.

Given the manifest variety, is it possible to describe what a typical Hecht letter looks and sounds like? It might begin with a polite or snappy salutation, move to an occasional apology or joke to smooth the way for some commentary and analysis, in which, if Hecht were responding to a person's written work, he would usually (although not always) mix praise with some points of personal disagreement. He could be scrupulous about the truth as he saw it. He might then approach a conclusion with an anecdote in hand plucked from some unusual source. Hecht particularly enjoyed the story of Sir John Denham's plea to King Charles I, made during the English civil war, not to hang George Wither, "because so long as Wither lived, Denham would not be accounted the worst poet in England." My personal favorite in this vein, although it occurs near the beginning of a letter rather than the end, is the story of Grinling Gibbons, taken from John Evelyn's *Diary* and offered to Dana Gioia as a parable of the solitary life of the artist, or in this case, the translator of Seneca, since Gioia had been translating the Roman writer, followed by the abrupt comment, "you probably know all this." It's the last line that makes the anecdote Hecht's and not just Evelyn's. Hecht would then sign off, signature near the center of the page, not to be missed, with the tail of the *y* in "Tony" often extending under the whole name. Occasionally, he concluded the letter with an invented or forged name if the recipients were members of his family or the appreciatively witty MacDonald. And as with signatures, so with salutations: to those to whom he wrote frequently, Hecht possessed a deep pocket of possible openers. Here are just a few to his parents:

Eh bien:
Well, my old:
Dear kids:
Mes petits chous:
To all you fine people, greetings:
Festive greetings:
Saluté!
Alors!
Hallo.
Little ones.
You-all:
Hear ye:

Various and spritely indeed, and sometimes unbuttoned to boot in their comical salutes. Although Hecht's letters, especially the later ones, often have a dignified ring to them, the above addresses don't comport with the conventional view of Hecht the formalist in verse and garb—the poet wearing a gray flannel suit, as early reviewers sometimes charged. Rather, they speak of someone often familiar in address (and not just to his family) with a keen desire to capture and keep his reader's attention. Hecht was a natural storyteller we discover (but without surprise given the strong narrative element in his poetry), especially in some of the long letters back home reporting on his life and adventures in Paris and elsewhere after World War II. But there were plenty of smaller sagas to recount at home, too. These are occasionally of a slightly off color but amusing sort, such as the story he told James Merrill about sharing a limousine with a hooker on the way to the Bollingen Prize selection meeting. A bit rarefied to be sure, but that was part of the point of telling the story, as readers of the letter will discover. The more casual Hecht also comes into view in the generous support he gave to many younger poets, unexpectedly so in the case of Gary Metras, whom Hecht admitted barely remembering and whose work he apparently had sternly criticized one summer at the Bread Loaf Writers' Conference. After Metras revised his poems, however, Hecht thought enough of them to offer the surprised but grateful Metras further advice for graduate study. And more unbuttoned still, Hecht speaks with remarkable directness to Anne Sexton on many topics, including his painful first marriage.

To exchange variety for constancy for a moment, there are no letters to Hecht's second wife Helen D'Alessandro. This absence is not surprising. Their meeting was serendipitous, their courtship brief, their marriage lasting, and its harmonious effects everywhere resounding in the letters and the poetry. They were rarely ever apart, in observance of which I note that one of Hecht's favorite poems was Shakespeare's mysteriously beautiful poem about constancy in love, "The Phoenix and the Turtle," a sentiment repeated even more emphatically in the final couplet of Sonnet 53, the poem whose opening lines supplied Hecht with the title of his third collection of verse, *Millions of Strange Shadows*, and that he quoted at the end of his verse celebrating his wife's birthday.

Another act of constancy involved his teaching. Initially Hecht taught introductory courses in literature and courses in creative writing, to which he added, in time, Shakespeare and modern poetry, the latter at the graduate level; and this time-consuming activity, in conjunction with a native curiosity about all things literary, gave rise to a number of fascinating letters. Some amount to small essays in literary criticism, reminding us that the origin of the personal essay is itself epistolary, dating back to Seneca through

Montaigne and Francis Bacon. These letters, moreover, ought to be seen as complementing his many published essays and poems. They are sometimes written in defense of his own habits and practices. More often, however, they explore and report his thinking about others: W. H. Auden, Robert Frost, T. S. Eliot, Walter Pater, George Herbert, Elizabeth Bishop, and Dante Alighieri, for instance; and they are usually based on extensive and sensitive reading but occasionally on personal knowledge or anecdotal history. Or they present questions that have surfaced in the process of writing a poem, such as the letter to MacDonald querying the correct depiction of the Pierre-Auguste Renoir painting that serves as the basis for "The Deodand."

To describe one example of this more academically directed inquiry: a 1981 letter to Timothy Healy, then president of Georgetown University and a notable John Donne scholar, was written on the eve of Hecht's teaching Gerard Manley Hopkins's "The Wreck of the Deutschland." It worries at some length the suitability and meaning of a single phrase from the poem, a line borrowed, Hecht discovers by way of another scholar, from an article in *The Times* reporting the wreck. The letter is impressive in its mix of erudition and elegance, but it merits inclusion not for this reason alone, but for what it reveals about both Hopkins and Hecht. Thinking about that small phrase as it might appeal to a poet, Hecht goes on to illuminate its larger place in the poem, particularly as it relates to the central role of the spiritual exercises held dear by Hopkins with regard to the Passion and to the representation of human suffering more generally, a topic readers of Hecht will readily recognize as one of paramount importance to his own verse.

Occasionally Hecht's erudite eye can be so fine that I have felt comfortable including a letter only after calling on the help of specialists in the field to verify his speculations. I was gratified by the interest shown even to some of the more esoteric conundrums that Hecht addressed, such as the proper ordering of stanzas in a poem attributed to Sir Walter Ralegh. I have also tried to ensure that Hecht's more scholarly comments did not repeat observations made in his published works. But even in the case of Auden, where the probability of overlap is perhaps the highest, the letters almost always show some new angle of thought.

With a person as indefatigably literary as Hecht, it is hardly surprising to discover that he was a frequent reader of the letters of others: Lord Byron and John Keats early on for literary matters, of course; G. K. Chesterton as well as George Lyttelton and Rupert Hart-Davis for lighter, more convivial fare; and then for heavier mettle, Dietrich Bonhoeffer, Reinhold Niebuhr, the apostle Paul, in particular his Letter to the Galatians, about which Hecht wrote a trenchant essay, and Robert Frost, one of whose letters occasioned a response by his sister Jeanie that provided Hecht with an incident for a late poem of considerable pathos, "Sisters." Hecht also had a fondness for the genre of the formal verse epistle, dating back to Horace and continuing through Alexander Pope, an interest further reflected in his own splendid chapter on Auden's *Letter to Lord Byron* in *The Hidden Law: The Poetry of W. H. Auden* (1993). But however interested he was as a reader of the correspondence of others, Hecht never went so far in his epistolary enthusiasms (unlike his admired friend Elizabeth Bishop) to offer a class based on letters. No doubt, too, he didn't think writing a good letter as important as writing a good poem, but the activities were not in competition with each other, and one only has to think of the occasional place the letter occupies in his poetry, beginning with "A Roman Holiday" in *A Summoning of Stones*, to recognize that the format could in fact be readily transformed—in other words and usually with the help of rhyme.

I suspect that Hecht felt that, along with thought, his letters reveal something essential about character, *character* being what binds the distinctive formation of a letter (whether as a letter in the alphabet or a piece of correspondence) to the larger, complex matter of personal identity, the style of the handwriting to the person thinking. In his late poem, "Proust on Skates," in fact, Hecht gives this idea of style exquisite rendering in verse near the end of the poem. The skate's steel, incisory edge firmly reminds us that style derives from the Latin *stilus*, indicating a sharp writing instrument:

He glides with a gaining confidence, inscribes
Tentative passages, thinks again, backtracks,
    Comes to a minute point,
Then wheels about in widening sweeps and lobes,
Large Palmer cursives and smooth *entrelacs*,
    Preoccupied, intent

On a subtle, long-drawn style and pliant script
Incised with twin steel blades and qualified
    Perfectly to express,
With arms flung wide or gloved hands firmly gripped
Behind his back, attentively, clear-eyed,
    A glancing happiness.

Hecht's letters are in a less intricate mode, of course, but no less interesting for being so. In the poem about Marcel Proust, Hecht has discovered, through the metaphor of skating, a gradually emergent, triumphant image to describe the distinctive and meritorious complexities of Proust's style, which in turn serves as a metaphor to express perfectly the author's—Proust's—thought in its "glancing happiness." In turn again (so pivotally mimetic is this poem), the poet inscribes on the white page, as Proust does on the frozen lake, a reflection of his own thinking, right down to the fine use made of slant or "glancing" rhymes. A triumphant image because style, as presented in the poem, is an achievement set against an otherwise bleak landscape and evident mortality. In Hecht's letters, there is more matter and less art, for sure. And yet, complexities aside, images of triumph, too, in all the thought they unfold. Might we not also regard the letters then, as not just "spritely" in manner but as carrying something of the author's original "spirit," and perhaps just a little closer to the surface? It's hard to think that the author of "The Ghost in the Martini" didn't have this earlier meaning of spirit in mind as well, in what turns out to be that string of well-chosen adjectives to describe his handiwork.

Much of the pleasure in putting together a collection of letters is in re-creating the social world, the network of connections between and among people that locates the author in time and space. For Hecht this process can be especially illuminating, in part because he was always reluctant to comment on his person and poetry outside of arranged settings, and in part because his poems often assume, through a variety of literary devices, a measured distance between speaker and author. One takes away from the letters a keen sense of how deeply circumstanced Hecht's poetry is. But limitations of space and time also work to prevent viewing an epistolary exchange in its fullness, as a circulation of ideas that has a beginning at one end, and that along the way often incorporates references and allusions that only come to light when we see how the game is played at the other end as well. Along with the brief introductions for each chapter, I have therefore lightly annotated individual letters as circumstances require and information allows. But the wealth of detailed information now available on the internet has made largely unnecessary extensive glosses, especially of the many poets with whom Hecht was in contact.

An exception is the Hecht family household, the recipients of almost all Hecht's correspondence in the first three chapters, and yet known, if at all, to only a few readers today. A brief sketch put together from several sources, including the letters, tells us that Hecht was born into a nonobservant Jewish family. At the time of his birth, they resided on the Upper East Side of Manhattan in a large apartment at 140 East 89th Street until 1936 (the setting for his poem "Apprehensions"). Then, following their fortunes downward in the Depression, the family moved to 40 East 83rd Street in 1936, and once more in 1942, this time to the apartment on 163 East 81st Street, which the couple at some point purchased and in which Hecht's brother Roger lived until his death in 1990. All Hecht's later letters, from the time of his induction into the army, are to this last address. When, as in the case of one letter, he asks a favor of his younger brother Roger to check out a painting at the Metropolitan Museum of Art, we know that geographically speaking this is a small request. The museum is only a few blocks away.

In his *Conversation with Philip Hoy*, Hecht tells us that his parents Melvyn Hahlo Hecht (1893–1978) and Dorothea Holzman Hecht (1894–1979) were of German-Jewish descent. Their respective families emigrated to the United States in the middle of the nineteenth century, his father's family from Bamberg in Bavaria. Hecht doesn't specify the ancestral location of his mother's side of his family, but his parents, who were born and died within a year of each other, were married on January 19, 1920, at the Ritz-Carlton Hotel in New York City. They would have been thirty and twenty-nine, respectively, when Hecht was born in 1923. A second son, Roger, was born three years later, in 1926. Hecht has described in some detail his father's poor business aptitude and fortunes (and his several attempts at suicide) and his own misgivings about his mother, who, like his father, was from a family of considerable financial means and cultural aspirations. Her uncle on her mother's side, Hecht notes, along with being a collector of paintings, owned for many years "a thriving clothing wholesale business, Cohen, Goldman & Co., as well as a retail chain of men's clothing stores called Broadstreets," until "the business went under after WWII." At one point in his letters, Hecht makes a shadowy reference to her working for the War Department and speaks more generally about "the midnight aura of secrecy [. . .] in which our whole family seems to dwell from time to time" (April 26, 1945). And, indeed, the biographical record indicates that Dorothea was much involved with the Censorship Bureau during the war. Much later, Hecht also recalled in a 1995 letter to his editor Harry Ford the curious fact that she was once wooed by one Paul Brach, "a minor poet. She used to own a volume of his poems, inscribed to her with love from the author, and she seemed proud of his courtship. I suspect she chose my father instead because he came from a much wealthier family."

Hecht's younger brother Roger (1926–1990) suffered from epilepsy and a number of physical afflictions from childhood, including poor eyesight, a limp, and a semi-paralyzed right hand. He was never able to hold a steady job and was dependent on his parents and the family estate for support. The brothers were close in their younger days, attending the same schools (Bard and Kenyon College), with Roger following in his brother's literary footsteps, which necessarily included a number of common friends. The most important for Roger was probably his friendship with James and Anne Wright, as Hecht suggests in a letter to Robert Fitzgerald (February 21, 1980). Roger was the author of five books of poems published by small presses: 27 *Poems* (1966), *Signposts* (1970), *Parade of Ghosts* (1976), *Burnt Offerings* (1979), and a selection from these, *A Quarrelling of Dust* (1986). At his memorial service in April 1990, Hecht read a eulogy that touched on many of Roger's difficulties, habits, and enthusiasms.

Hecht's complicated relationship with his immediate family is the subject of a number of the later poems, but it is material more properly left for a full biography. A few other names associated with the household, however, merit brief mention here. Paula was the family cook, for whom the young Hecht felt great affection and whom he liked to tease. Bully was part of the household but in what capacity remains unclear, and Peppy, who put his paw print on letters to Tony, was their dog.

In 1987, when Hecht's editor and longtime friend Harry Ford was moving offices from Atheneum to Knopf, Ford sent to Hecht a copy of their many correspondences over the years. Hecht thanked him and remarked, "I have glanced through a few of the letters, and observe that they contain some juicy indiscretions regarding my opinions of certain poets and critics. Just the sort of thing that, judiciously edited, could make for a scandalously successful book. I vaguely regret the fact that I won't be around to read the reviews." Although letters of this kind constitute only a small percentage of the whole, I have tried to observe the author's wishes here, judiciously editing some letters but leaving in a few juicy indiscretions, perhaps the sort of thing that would please the author at least, were he to be around to read the reviews.

As for the overall selection, I have tried to follow the criteria implied in his letter to Jon Stallworthy: that they be spritely, various, and original. Many letters have been excluded—exchanges about poetry readings, thank-you notes, letters of appraisal that presume confidentiality in the first place, and narratives too long and detailed to survive reducing, including several written while Hecht was in Ischia and others that involve highly detailed criticisms of poems by former students and friends that are of interest to these authors. Also excluded are letters to Hecht's children, for reasons of family privacy. Still, cuts entail lingering regrets. The loss of a phrase or of an event or sometimes of an acquaintance can seem at times a diminishment of the subject and the life. The only compensation, a large one, is to be found in the superlative letters that remain.

Hecht's letters present few textual problems. His handwriting is generally clear, even when he was a young boy, and the typed letters, which constitute the majority of his correspondence, rarely involve corrections and crossed-out phrases. In this regard, they are quite different from the multiple revi-sionary efforts that went into the crafting of his poems. Once in a while, a letter may invite some small act of editorial intrusion. When these intrusions involve matters of spelling and punctuation, the corrections have been made silently. Anything more interpretive is signaled by the presence of brackets. At certain points, Hecht would use an asterisk to indicate the inclusion of a phrase written at the bottom of the letter or in the margin. These phrases have been inserted in parentheses in the proper place. All ellipses in brackets are editorial, although every effort has been made to preserve the sense and integrity of the epistolary format. Hecht also liked to add or try out a foreign phrase, especially in the army letters. These have been glossed in English, but the occasional grammatical lapses in the original have not been corrected since these are features of their epistolary circumstance. In some cases, I have split up some of the longer paragraphs for ease of reading. I have also retained, while standardizing, Hecht's typographical practice in the letters of underlining titles of works. Where Hecht might have put "Harmonium," for instance, in quotation marks, I have underlined the title of Stevens's book of poems. With regard to Shakespeare, whom Hecht quoted often from memory, I have keyed line references to *The Riverside Shakespeare* (Boston: Houghton Mifflin Co., 1974).

BRIEF CHRONOLOGY

1923 Anthony Evan Hecht is born in New York City, on January 16, to Melvyn Hahlo Hecht (1893–1978) and Dorothea Grace Holzman (1894–1979).

1926 Brother Roger is born.

1927–1940 Attends the Dalton School (1927–1930), the Collegiate School in Manhattan (1930–1936), and the Horace Mann School for Boys in Riverdale.

1935–1939 Spends summers at Camp Kennebec, Maine.

1940–1943 Attends Bard College, Annandale-on-Hudson, New York.

1943–1946 Serves in U.S. Army in the 386th Infantry Regiment, C Company, 3rd Platoon. Sees action on the German front, April 1945; stationed in Japan in fall–winter 1946. Discharged from the army on March 12, 1946.

1946–1947 Attends Kenyon College as a "special student," where he studies with John Crowe Ransom.

1947–1948 Briefly attends University of Iowa; has nervous breakdown in the fall but returns after Christmas to finish out the academic year. Meets Robert Lowell, Jean Stafford, and Flannery O'Connor.

1948 Attends Kenyon School of English in summer, where he studies with William Empson, F. O. Matthiessen, and Austin Warren. Studies privately with Allen Tate in New York City.

1949 Spends summer traveling in France and Italy; enters Columbia University as candidate for a master's degree in English literature.

1950 Receives M.A. from Columbia University. Returns in summer to Europe; in fall moves to Ischia, where he will meet W. H. Auden.

1951	May: awarded the first Rome Fellowship in Literature by the American Academy of Arts and Letters. Begins year-long fellowship in October.
1952–1954	Instructor, Bard College; colleagues include Saul Bellow, Irma Brandeis, and Henrich Blücher (whose wife Hannah Arendt also became a friend).
1954	Hecht's first book of poems, *A Summoning of Stones*, is published by Macmillan.
1954–1955	Marries Patricia Anne Harris, February 27. Returns in the fall of 1954 to the American Academy in Rome on Guggenheim Fellowship.
1956–1962	Teaches at Smith College, first as an instructor, then as an assistant professor, with several years off for fellowships: a second Guggenheim, a Hudson Review Fellowship, and a Ford Foundation Fellowship. Meets Sylvia Plath, Ted Hughes, Daniel Aaron, Leonard Baskin, and Helen Bacon.
1956	Son Jason is born.
1958	Son Adam is born.
1959	Files for legal separation from Patricia Harris in August.
1961	Divorce is finalized. Meets and begins corresponding with the poet Anne Sexton. Hospitalized for depression.
1962–1966	Returns to Bard College as an associate professor; then professor.
1967	Publishes *The Hard Hours* (Atheneum), and with John Hollander, *Jiggery Pokery: A Compendium of Double Dactyls* (Atheneum). Moves to the University of Rochester as a professor of English, where he will remain on the faculty until 1985.
1968	Receives the Pulitzer Prize for *The Hard Hours*, and also the Russell Loines Award, presented by the National Institute of Arts and Letters, and the Miles Poetry Prize. Named John H. Deane Professor of Rhetoric and Poetry at the University of Rochester. On leave at the American Academy in Rome, translating Aeschylus's *Seven Against Thebes* with Helen Bacon.
1970	Awarded honorary degree by Bard; elected to the National Institute of Arts and Letters.

1971	Appointed a chancellor of the Academy of American Poets; served until 1995. Marries Helen D'Alessandro, June 12.
1972	Son Evan Alexander is born.
1973	Visiting professor, Harvard University. *Seven Against Thebes* (Oxford).
1975	Elected to the American Academy of Arts and Science.
1977	Visiting professor, Yale University. *Millions of Strange Shadows* (Atheneum).
1979	*The Venetian Vespers* (Atheneum).
1981	Receives honorary degree from Georgetown University.
1982–1984	Named Consultant in Poetry to the Library of Congress.
1983	Shares with John Hollander the Bollingen Prize for Poetry.
1984	Receives the Librex-Guggenheim Eugenio Montale Award for Poetry.
1985–1993	Named University Professor at Georgetown University.
1986	*Obbligati: Essays in Criticism* (Atheneum).
1987	Honorary degree from University of Rochester. Receives Harriet Monroe Award by *Poetry* magazine.
1988	Awarded the Ruth B. Lilly Poetry Prize by *Poetry* magazine.
1989	Receives the Aiken-Taylor Award for Modern American Poetry by the University of the South.
1990	*The Transparent Man* (Knopf); *Collected Earlier Poems* (Knopf). Roger Hecht dies.
1992	Delivers the A. W. Mellon Lectures in the Fine Arts at the National Gallery of Art, Washington, D.C.
1993	*The Hidden Law: The Poetry of W. H. Auden* (Harvard). Retires from teaching at Georgetown University.
1995	*On the Laws of the Poetic Art: The A. W. Mellon Lectures in the Fine Arts* (Princeton).
1996	*Flight Among the Tombs* (Knopf).
1997	Awarded the Dorothea Tanning (now the Wallace Stevens) Prize by the Academy of American Poets.
2000	Awarded the Robert Frost Medal by the Poetry Society of America
2001	*The Darkness and the Light* (Knopf).
2002	Hecht Archive established at the Robert H. Woodruff Library, Emory University.

2003   *Collected Later Poems* (Knopf); *Melodies Unheard: Essays on the Mysteries of Poetry* (Johns Hopkins University Press).

2004   Awarded the Los Angeles Times Book Prize for *Collected Later Poems*. Dies, October 20.

2004–2005   Posthumously awarded the National Medal for the Arts and an honorary degree by Ohio Wesleyan University.

THE SELECTED LETTERS OF

Anthony Hecht

Anthony Hecht, age 13, at Camp Kennebec, Maine, 1936
Courtesy of Crista and Joel Lavenson

ONE

Childhood and College
1935–1943

Letters from Summer Camp, 1935–1938?

ALTHOUGH HECHT WAS LATER TO DESCRIBE HIS CHILDHOOD AS unhappy, the letters written to his parents during the five summers he spent at Camp Kennebec in Maine, from 1935 to 1939, offer an altogether sunnier picture. For the most part, they are filled with good-spirited fun. The young Hecht clearly enjoyed the camaraderie of his fellow campers, some of whom he knew from home, and the occasional pranks they pulled on one another, the physical stand-offs, tussles, and small triumphs that formed part of the socialization into the lightly masculine culture of camp life. He liked to include visual testimony of his activities: a paper bull's eye target used in shooting practice, for instance, carrying his score. He also created sample charts to show his daily schedule, passed along jokes he had heard, especially to his father, drew a box representing a special space he had kissed, and asked for a paw print of their pet dog Peppy. Very little figures into these letters that might reflect the family problems recounted in his powerfully autobiographical poem "Apprehensions," published some forty years later in *Millions of Strange Shadows* (1977).

Much of the charm of these letters is their simple emotional availability, a frankness made more graphically immediate by the boldly penciled hand-writing, in concert with the quickly maturing persona. "Love from your best pal," he concludes one letter to his father in 1936. He begins another the next summer addressed to both parents: "I am terribly sorry I didn't write to you this past week. I had no idea you were going away and was very much surprised and slightly frightened when I received your letter from Rhode Island. I thought perhaps someone was sick." In another, from 1938, he comments: "since you gave me an idea of what you do everyday, Dad, I'll give you about the same thing except I don't know the time as everything goes by bells." Then appears a vertical-spaced list of the day's events, including the ritual "daily trip to the House of Lords."

Childhood, children, auguries of innocence shadowed by a world of experience are huge themes in Hecht's poetry. Many years later, in response to a question by Norman Williams, Hecht spoke about his camp years in relation to his sestina, "The Book of Yolek." "As for whether I ever actually camped out as in the opening stanza of 'Yolek,' the truth is that as a very young boy I was sent to a summer camp, where they did all those things: fishing, canoeing, hiking, etc. It affected me much as you suspect it may have affected your son, and turned me into a confirmed reader." Hecht's remark, with its concluding whiff of humor, points to how his experience at summer camp occasionally served as a potential resource for a number of his poems: not only "Yolek," but "Third Avenue in Sunlight," with its description of strange tribal behavior, or the elegant athleticism recorded in "Swan Dive," to say nothing about the general sifting and redirection of these innocent pastimes—the ceremonies and rituals—as filtered through World War II experiences. In part because these letters form a striking contrast to Hecht's later, more meditative person, the person who became "a confirmed reader," but also because they intimate important connections to that same person and his poetry—the camp yearbook for 1935 identifies him as the "quiet but witty boy of the cabin," more drawn to the cultural than athletic side of camp, and in 1939 it lists him receiving the award for "best actor"—I have included here a small selection of the fifty-five surviving letters written from camp.

Camp Kennebec was founded in 1907 as an all-boys camp. It is still in business today but as a golf and tennis academy and is located in North Belgrade, about seventy-five miles north of Portland, Maine. In the 1930s, it was reached by an overnight train ride from New York City. "Mike and Meyer" were the characters played by the turn-of-the-twentieth-century comic team Lew Fields and Joe Weber, popular in Hecht's parents' lifetime and based on immigrant stereotypes. "Trapped" was probably based on the film version of the 1931 crime drama. "Uncles" refers to camp counselors. "Ted" referred to in the letter of July 17, 1938, is Ted Geisel, better known as Dr. Seuss, a family friend, who will reappear in the army letters, and was perhaps a source of inspiration for Hecht's early interest in light verse.

1935

Dear Mom,

I am sorry I made that mistake about the socks. Mike and Meyer went over with a bang and Alan acted as Mike. I am learning to swim and as I am a freshman the boys are pouncing on me. I wanted to tell you that it has been raining here for two days and it is necessary to wear boots. I am very sorry I have to ask for these things and I don't care if you don't want to send them but all the other boys are using them. We have an art teacher with hair on his chest. To night all the new uncles are giving a show. We made such a hit with Mike and Meyer that I am in the dramatic club. [. . .]

Love

Tony

Dear Mom

I am having a swell time up at camp. The other night we had grand council. We were dressed with blankets and walked slowly down to the council ring. Mr. Fleisher dressed as an Indian Chief was beating a drum. Uncle Mac who was medicine man blew the pipe of peace and the chieftains of each tribe were chosen, and then we were awarded feathers and wrestled for championship. Yesterday morning Schwabacher and [I] were fishing with my line because his busted and after catching some fish Schwaby caught a large white perch. He was pulling it in when we saw a pickerel over two feet long. He put it back and the pickerel half swallowed it but the line broke.

Love

Tony

Dear Mom,

I just received the uke and I have been playing and learning new songs on it. Fishing is great and I've caught very many fish. I am in three plays. Trapped; The Mello Drama and another. This is all because of the big success with Mike and Meyer. All the boys brought gum and our cabin has a spook house that boys pay gum to go in. In nature we have studied trees. We have a ousyla [pig Latin for lousy?] uncle.

Love

Tony

P.S. Tell Dad to write his letters to Roger because I don't go over there [Camp Androscoggin].

Dear Mom,

Today I got a postcard from Grandpa and I got a French stamp from Dad. Sunday afternoon we had a swimming meet and I almost made twenty-five yards. Uncle Ski and Dusty did some funny dive.

Sometimes Schwabacher and I go out and catch frogs. This afternoon we are going fishing. I was in a play last night and tonight I will play the uke in lodge. Dicky and Buddy and I want to thank you very much for the gum. The shoes have not arrived yet.

Love

Tony

Dear Mom:

I am out of the infirmary and feeling fine again. The other day, we had a corn roast and Mrs. Fleisher sent me to bed as soon as I came out. The last few days are pretty busy, packing, Grand Councils, etc. I hope you were not worried when Mr. Fleisher wrote to you that I was sick. We won the base ball game from Senior and also won the war canoe race from Senior. I'll be seeing you very soon and so till we see each again

Love

Tony Hecht

1936

July 2, 1936

Dear Dad,

I had a swell trip up here. I didn't sleep all night but I had a swell time. Cohen woke up Deutch with a cold glass of water about 2 hours before we got to camp and said he had 10 minutes to get dressed. When we got up to camp we had breakfast, made our beds and unpacked our trunks. I am very glad I changed cabins. I like this one much better. I have a Big Brother. He is one of the older boys who helps me. He explains things to me and helps me. I make his bed for him every morning at 20¢ per week. One Big Brother has two Little Brothers who he helps. The Little Brothers are always freshmen. Dicky Cohen and I have a swell Big Brother and also a swell uncle. I think I will like Senior just as much as Junior if not more. I got your letter and Mom's too. I hope she has a pleasant time and a good trip. I hope your business is coming along okay. I also think your typewriting is <u>TERRIBLE</u>. I like living in a tent. It's fun.

Love to you and Mom,
Tony

July 5, 1936

Dear Dad:

Freshman night went over swell. I did Mike and Meyer again with Shwabacher. It rained on the Fourth but we had a swell time. I am getting along this year so much better than last it isn't funny. My baseball has improved a lot. The older boys are swell to me and Cohen and Klingenstein never bother me. I can't exaggerate on what a good time I am having. On the Fourth it cleared for a few hours and we had races. It was lots of fun. I miss you so much it hurts. Ouch!! I hope you had a good trip. Let me know when you're coming up.

Dear Dad

At first I thought you didn't get my letters but when you asked me about my Big Brother in your last letter I knew you did. He is Robert Graham. I am getting along in swimming so nicely you would be very glad. By the end of the summer I expect to be able to go out in a row-boat by myself.

A Big Surprise! ! ! ! ! ! ! ! !

Hecht Recovers From Habit [drawing of finger and mouth]

I have been so excited I never think about this [arrow pointing to the drawing.] Nobody teased me but I am so busy doing things I forget all about it. There is nothing but good news for me to tell you. I rate very high in our baseball team. More good news. I had a fight with Klingenstein and I didn't win but was far from lost. I can beat up Cohen and both of them are beginning to respect me.

All the love I have to you, Mom and Roger,
Tony

Sunday, July 11, 1936

Dear Dad:

I just got my first air mail letter across the country from Mom. How about the canteen? It's not necessary but very useful. [. . .] I need pencils though to write my letters. I learned how to dive the other day and I am starting tennis. Every Tuesday we have talking movies. There's not much to say except that I'm having the time of my life and you're crazier than I am.

Love

Tony

Sunday, July 26, 1936

Dear Dad:

Every year there is a big fight between the camps and the first section. On Friday we had this fight and it was swell fun. All the campers wore white jerseys and the first section was supposed to rip them off. I borrowed one and lost it in the fight. The winning team in Dream Baseball game got a treat and I was official Duster of the catcher's mask so I got the treat too. It was lobster and I liked it very much. That night we had boxing and I fought Cohen and beat him even though I had a bad finger. I am having as good a time as ever and love you more than you love me.

Love

Tony

1937

Dear Mom and Dad:

I just received the letter you wrote on the 5th saying you hadn't received my first letter yet. This is my third and I can't explain the disappearance of the others. Swimming and tennis are coming along fine. The tennis teacher told me I would make a very good player. Last night there was a memorial service for Mr. Foxx. I don't think they should have done that because Charlie Foxx, his son, was in camp. The water is nice and warm up here and the fishing is pretty good. We will probably have movies tonight. [. . .] I am having a swell time. Tell Paula she's a nut.

Love

Tony

July 11, 1937

Dear Mom and Dad:

This year, a little later on, when visitors are allowed to come, the camp will present "H.M.S Pinafore," in which I will play the role of "Buttercup." I would probably have played Sir Joseph Porter except I am one of the few boys in camp that can still sing soprano. I'll let you know when it is to be given so you will know when to come up. This afternoon while Tishman was visiting the doctor the rest of the section hid his trunk in the bushes with his shoes and all his clothes. Then we took his bed out of the tent into a rowboat and left it on a raft in the middle of the lake and "pied" it. Dad ought to know what a "pie bed" is. Tishman quickly followed in another boat. Then came a fight between Tishman and us. We took his oars away. Then Tishman jumped in our boat and we rowed back then. Mr. Friedman and Mr. Fleisher walked past the dock and saw the result of our noble deed. I don't know what's going to happen to me so if you don't get another letter from me, you'll know I'm dead. [...]

Lots of Love,
Tony

[n.d., 1937?]

Dear Mom and Dad,

Being that I can't go on my trip Mr. Friedman is trying to make it as pleasant for me as he possibly can. We went out to shore once for a shore dinner. I had clam chowder, stewed clams, clam fritters, and boiled lobster, and pie a la mode for lunch. For supper that day I had fried chicken and ice cream. We have had the best food that anybody has had all season. I have had a pretty good time lately though I have had to stay in bed the last few days and read a Sherlock Holmes book. I got the cake long ago but forgot to write about it. It was swell, thanks a lot. I don't think Mr. Friedman wants me to have another though so you had better not send it.

The weather has been pretty good so far. Usually cool but sunny. Today it looks like rain. After being in bed for so long it is necessary for me to use a cane when I walk about. Mrs. Wiener and Mrs. Rothchild, Tommy Wiener's and Eddie Rothchild's mothers respectively, came up to camp to take Tommy home because he was sick. They brought him a basket of fruit and when he said he didn't want it, they gave it to me. Mrs. Friedman came over to visit me twice and brought me some ice cream. Dicky will be back from his long canoe trip on Sunday. I feel pretty good. I have a sore throat and a cold. Hope to be with you all soon.

Love
Tony

Sat. July 3, 1938

Dear Gang:

I had more fun than ever going up on the train this year. Had a real bath. Had another one when we got here 'cause it started raining. Things have been happening so fast I can't keep track of them. I was elected to the camp council and appointed dramatic commissioner. I've made out my program and will send it to you as soon as possible. I'm taking swimming, shooting, tennis, mechanics, wrestling, photography, etc. Our uncle isn't here yet so we have another. [. . .] In case Mom is interested we had steak for lunch today, but don't you write me what you had.

Freshman night was a success. There was a general slaughter and all the freshmen have to wear their pants inside out and backwards for three days.

I've been doing so much these past few days and am going to do so much more I don't know when I'll have time to write to you. I've been practicing for the play, which is to be given tonight and I think I'll be in another Gilbert and Sullivan, although I don't know which. They have a swell victrola up in the lodge with both popular and classical recordings and they have a set of about 12 records with music and songs from the "Mikado," besides having the "Nutcracker Suite," "Sheherazade," "Lohengrin," "Tannhauser," and millions of others.

Will you please send up a pair of rubbers, a good mystery book and some gum. Tell Paula she's a nut.

Love and kisses,
Tony

July 7, 1938

Dear Mob,

Got all your letters. Thanks! It has rained a little almost every day but today it was swell and I went in swimming for the first time. Last night we had a pretty rotten movie, but either next week or the week after, we get "Showboat."

By the way, the play was swell and I'm going to be in another one soon.

I had so much to tell you in my first letter I couldn't tell you what happened on the train. I got to my car with malice aforethought, put away my bags and filled my water pistol. Deutch, Bacharach and Cohen (the Irishman) had a compartment all to themselves. So we attacked and were repulsed and then were attacked again. During the course of the evening, Tishman's pants and bed were mysteriously drenched with water. How this came about I have no idea.

While this attacking and repulsing was going on, a couple of uncles came along trying to get the addresses of the "old folks at home" so they could send a telegram, which you should have received, reporting my safe arrival. They knocked on the door of the compartment and when it was opened, they were immediately greeted by a glass of cold water. I remained reasonably dry that night although after we arrived in camp it rained quite a bit and I got soaked right through. The Fourth was quite a success with everything being run off except a baseball game with Junior and that was postponed because someone had a case of mumps. I haven't taken any pictures yet because I haven't any film. Please send up <u>six or seven</u> films. Get <u>"Panchromatic" no. 127</u>. How is Peppy? Has he caught any more birds? Tell Paula she's a nut.

Love,

Tony

Sunday, July 17, 1938

Dear People,

Am I having fun? We won an Indoor game yesterday and I masterfully filled the position of second base and also bringing my batting average up to above 500.

I've been so busy I haven't had time to go fishing but once and I didn't catch anything then. I am going to try out for a play this evening or tomorrow which will be given next Saturday.

One of our uncles had a pair of red silk pajamas. And when I say <u>red</u>, I mean it. It occurred to me the other day how nice those pajamas would look at the top of the flagpole. So a bunch of us hoisted them up in the evening after the flag was down. However, a couple of waiters who found out whose pajamas they were, took them down and threw them in the lake. Well, we managed to get out of it.

I have been taking plenty of pictures and will need some more film soon.

Mom, motors is a period in which we learn how outboard motors work and run and are allowed to take out a motorboat.

How is Ted's book coming? Can Mom ride a bike or drive yet? How are Mary, Paula, and Bully?

Come up soon.

Love,

Tony

Private: To Dad

Dear Dad –

Story –

Two men were going to a masquerade ball as a cow, one to be the front, the other back. They were walking across a field when suddenly a real bull started chasing them. The back man said "Can you run?"

Front man: "I'll be fucked if I can"

Back man: "Well, you'll be fucked if you can't"

End –

Tony

Letters from Bard College, 1940–1943

Only eleven letters survive from Hecht's time as an undergraduate at Bard College. The relative dearth can be attributed to several factors. Hecht's time at Bard was foreshortened because of the war. Faced with being drafted, Hecht enlisted in the Reserve Corps of the Army on November 21, 1942, and began basic training by late spring 1943. He would receive his B.A. from Bard in absentia as a consequence of having qualified for the Army Specialized Training Program (ASTP), which involved twenty-six weeks of study at Carleton College, in Northfield, Minnesota, beginning in the fall of 1943. Hecht also found life at Bard challenging and full of intellectual and artistic discovery. Most letters come bearing an apology of one kind or another, the prose more often dutiful than spontaneous, mannered in its casual address, especially when compared to the camp letters, with their lively reports of daily activities. At this point in Hecht's life, home was clearly less interesting than college. And, of course, it was a simple thing to communicate by telephone.

Still, a picture of Hecht emerges as a serious student eager to participate in the school's extracurricular activities, including writing for the *Bardian*, the school's literary magazine, where he began publishing poems. Thought enters into these letters, along with self-analysis, admissions of insecurity, and a corresponding affirmation of self-worth—attitudes hardly unusual for a seventeen-year-old entering college but in Hecht's case more pointed for his having been, with the exception of geometry, an indifferent student in high school. In his first week at Bard, he was required to read the first volume of Oswald Spengler's *Decline and Fall of the West* for his "Problems in Philosophy" course. He would also take courses in contemporary poetry as well as in Shakespeare in this first semester, and, as his induction into the army approached, he took classes in math and physics in light of the qualifying exams for ASTP. But as the letters reveal, it was the variety of courses in the liberal and performing arts, as well as the school's emphasis on individual instruction, that distinguished the curriculum at Bard from that of its parent institution Columbia University and that left an important mark on his future thinking and writing, often moving, as it does, among the various arts and even occasionally the sciences. Indeed, evidence of the latter can be glimpsed in one of his last poems, "Aubade," with its rich pun on "Galilean laws."

Hecht clearly responded to the stimulation and encouragement he found on this small campus of around two hundred students, and he would later characterize his years at Bard as among his happiest. His attachment would grow to include as well two stints on the faculty, from 1952 to 1954 and again from 1961 to 1967, during which he would forge a number of valuable literary and academic friendships. Many of his classmates, however, were killed in the war. There were a few notable exceptions. Danny Ransohoff (1922–1993), mentioned in the first letter from Bard (and occasionally later), would become a significant contributor to the Cincinnati community and the University of Cincinnati. (A letter from Allen Tate to Hecht, dated July 8, 1960, speaks of Ransohoff recommending Hecht to give the Elliston Lectures at the University of Cincinnati.) Another classmate, Al Sapinsley, became a screenplay writer in Hollywood, and the two struck up a correspondence in the late 1990s. (See Hecht's letter of December 11, 1998.)

1940

Tuesday, September 10,
1940 Annandale-on-Hudson, New York

[To his parents]
Dear Folks—

I guess it's about time I took my pen in hand and wrote you a long delayed description of the life at Bard. Perhaps it is just as well that I didn't write any sooner because the first week was all rather confusing and puzzling to me. That first week was also quite an overwhelming emotional experience. I was extremely happy and very depressed within the same hour.

At first I felt quite self-conscious; I thought everyone was laughing at me behind my back. However, I found consolation in the splendid impressions I made on several of my teachers.

Right now I am very happy I have overcome all the fears of my first week. I have picked the courses I enjoy the most and which I can do best. I think that it is best for me to do this in my freshman year so as to establish myself in my own eyes and also in the eyes of my teachers.

As I told you before on the telephone, I am taking Art, Music, English and Drama.

Mr. Grossi was very much impressed by the drawing I showed him and consequently I am majoring in Art.

I wanted to take a course called the Art of Writing, with Mr. Harris, as my English course, but it isn't open to Freshmen. I was told by Mr. Harris to take the regular Freshman course, English 1–2 with Dr. Genzmer. So I went to Dr. Genzmer and told him what Mr. Harris had said and I showed him some of the stuff I had written. He liked the "Cardinal's False Teeth" very much, and said that if I didn't like the regular 1–2 course, after about 2 weeks, I could take a tutorial course with him, in writing.

The class I had today was Music. I think I will enjoy it very much. Besides the regular class in music I will be taking piano, voice, and Glee Club (I am practically Librarian of the Glee Club already).

The class was very enjoyable and very informal. There were eight of us including the teacher. It lasted for two hours with an intermission for walking around, stretching and general relaxation. I was asked to play the piano, so I gave out with a Bach Double Piano Concerto in C Major (last movement) which was very well received.

There seem to be very few really intelligent boys that I have met so far. Danny Ransohoff is the nicest and smartest although he and I differ greatly on several things. I have asked him to come to the city with me when I come in, since he lives way out in Cincinnati.

I told you on the phone that I bought one fifth of a car. I'm not sure you could exactly call it a car. It does, I admit, have the earmarks of a car (four wheels, motor, [I hope] etc.) but it must have been made in a time of deep despondency in the Ford family; at a time when Henry just didn't give a damn. Perhaps I'm exaggerating slightly! The car will take us where we want to go and back again which is all you can ask for seventeen dollars.

An amazing number of boys up here own cars. (Please don't consider this a hint because I don't want a car.) There is even one boy up here who owns a Rolls Royce. I have heard some weird tales about driving around Redhook [New York] at two o'clock in the morning, about inebriated professors and married students. You may be sure that I saturate each one of these stories thoroughly in a salt solution before digesting them.

You may want to know that I have not afforded myself of the opportunity of going to town every night. As a matter of fact, with the exception of last night when I had a bull session with Danny, I have gone to bed early every night.

It seems that the nervous tension of the trip up to college was too much for my victrola which is not in working order. I am afraid to fool with it for fear of causing further complications. What do you think I should do?

The dean's speech welcoming us to college was simply wonderful. I wish you could have heard it. When he was discussing the various aspects of life at Bard, he said that he hoped the library would come to mean more to us than merely "an unfortunate episode in American architectural culture."

I would like you to send me my copy of "Men of Music." It will help me very much in my music classes.

Everyone is extremely friendly. People simply flock to your room and introduce themselves and sit around and bull for hours on end. None of the conversations is particularly lofty, but it's lots of fun.

That's about all the news I can think of, except that the night before last "Pride and Prejudice" was given in the theatre.

Having a swell time!

All my Love,
Tony

1941

[March 15, 1941] Annandale-on-Hudson, New York
[To his parents]
Dear Folks—

Well, I guess I have no excuse. It's just that I don't like writing letters. I've had plenty of material for them, I must say. We started on our string of four performances of "Thunder Rock" last night [no doubt the play of that name by Robert Ardrey, later made into a movie]. I am sound man and am responsible for the effective and important wind, surf, airplane, radio jazz music, news commentator, etc. I also have a very small part in the end of the play.

However, I shall have the lead in "Aria da Capo," a one act play by Edna St. V[incent Millay]. Things are going along well enough. I wrote a couple of sonnets which I like very much. I haven't had a chance to do much work on my book of light verse called "Pigs Have Wings." Right now I am working on one about the king of Tibet who has a pet Yak named "John" and John is very conceited because he had a part in "Lost Horizon." John falls in love with an Ibex who was in "Marco Polo" and she got better reviews than he did so she snubs him. He goes away to live in a monastery and that's as far as I [have] gotten with the plot.

I have been drawing several portraits of students which have come out very nicely. I am also writing a musical composition about Bard, so you can see I'm busy as hell.

I am in need of money and a haircut. If you send the money, I think I can take care of the haircut.

I am writing regularly for the Bardian, now, bylines and everything. Sort of light verse commentaries on campus and current events. I have had two poems in each of the past two issues.

Your friend Mrs. Whitehill is certainly not a very observant person for the passage which "For Whom the Bell Tolls" is printed in front of each copy [sic]. However I will enclose it here. [. . .]

> All my love,
> Tony

[November 10, 1941] Annandale-on-Hudson, New York
[To Dorothea and Roger Hecht]
Dear Mom and Rog—

The reason I haven't written to you for such a long time is that I've been very busy preparing my talk for Philosophy—by the way, it went off very well—and trying to catch up on my Shakespeare.

Now that I have a little time, there isn't very much to say. I got my poem back from the New Yorker with the usual little printed slip. But this time somebody added in pencil—"Sorry, a nice sentiment." I immediately framed the slip and put the poem in the Bardian. [. . .]

> All my love,
> Tony

1942

[July 7, 1942] Annandale-on-Hudson, New York
[To his parents]
Dear Folks—

There's not very much I can say by way of apology. I've exhausted all the old ones. It may console you slightly to know that I have been working hard. My roommate—Bob Sazalyn—has been drafted, and now I have another one, a freshman from Cincinnati, a wonderful fellow named Mat Lawson, whom I hope you will meet shortly. He's only been to New York once so it will be very interesting for him . . . No information about the Army Reserve yet . . . but I have been taking the regular physical training course that all the regular Reserves are taking for the Navy etc. Every afternoon for two hours, we run and drill and exercise like crazy, and believe it or not, I like it and feel better for it. . . .

I'll come down to New York as soon as possible and I'll bring Mat, my roommate, along.

All my love,
Tony

1943

March 10, 1943 Annandale-on-Hudson, New York

[To his parents]

Dear Folks—

One might suppose that this sudden burst of epistolary prose on my part shows an inner dissatisfaction with things where I am, and a consequent desire to associate myself with another locale and a different situation. (You must excuse the analyses which have prefaced these last two letters to you. It is, generally speaking, the fault of my roommate, who is studying Freud just now. We argue over psychology almost every night.) This impression (mentioned before) would be entirely wrong, although I have no other suitable explanation for the phenomenon.

The fact is everything is going very well. Calculus has its fascinating facets, and Physics is rather a pleasure. What strange transformation has come over me! My poetry is coming slowly. Producing it, even in small quantities has always been for me a painful and laborious process. (I mean painful here not in the sense of unpleasant to do, but only difficult in the extreme.) I have picked a particularly hard job for myself in deciding to write a sestina—which is a very strict and old verse form dating back to the 12th century.

I have received all your messages and gifts in order, and thank you for them. I have already made use of the tobacco, the shaving-brush and the letter-paper. Quod Est Demonstrandum.

I have not yet partaken of the cake, though I have admired it from a distance of about two and a half inches. My thanks to Paula for the cake, cookies, and her splendid little note. It is indeed comforting to know that her culinary thoughts will be with me when I'm in the Army. [. . .]

Love,
Tony

Ninety-seventh Regiment in Czechoslovakia, spring 1945
Courtesy of Emory University Libraries Rare Books and Manuscripts Division

TWO

World War II
1943–1946

NINETY-THREE LETTERS, INCLUDING A FEW V-MAILS, POSTCARDS, and telegrams, survive from Anthony Hecht's nearly three years in the army. These constitute a continuous and remarkable record of his activities during and immediately after the war. The only major gap in the epistolary record, from October 1943 through March 1944, roughly coincides with his time as an ASTP (Army Specialized Training Program) candidate at Carleton College. This lacuna notwithstanding, his correspondence can be usefully divided into three phases. About one-third, or thirty-four letters, were written between June 1943 and December 1944 while Hecht was undergoing basic training in the United States in preparation for deployment abroad—although whether to Japan or to Europe was shrouded in mystery and a matter of ongoing concern for Hecht as it was for others. Another seventeen letters survive from his brief time serving on the European front—in France, Czechoslovakia, and Germany, from early March to late June 1945. He participated in what turned out to be, in April, the final campaign by the Allied powers against the German forces along the Rhine and in the Ruhr Valley. The remaining forty-two letters, dating from roughly the end of August 1945 to late January 1946, cover his time in the United States, which included several furloughs, and his subsequent deployment to Japan.

On March 12, 1946, having spent thirty-three months in the army, Hecht would be discharged as Private First-Class in the 3rd Platoon, C Company, 386 Regiment, 97th Division.

There has been much published correspondence by World War II veterans, including some by American poets, the most notable being those by Randall Jarrell and James Dickey. Most collections are fervently patriotic, involving the dangerous exploits of a celebrated fighting force or of a previously un-represented group. More unusual are collections of letters that involve the reader in an extended personal saga, frequently given to matters of survival. While Hecht's letters belong in this second category, their drama is of an altogether different kind, more reminiscent of Hamlet (an alter ego whom he frequently quotes) than Homer. These letters are, by turns, humorous, anecdotal, moody, given to self-analysis and abrupt turns of thought, laced with literary quotations and allusions, and yet often intimate and direct. By contrast, those written from Japan, when Hecht's life was no longer in dan-ger and he worked on stories for *Stars and Stripes*, are full of reportorial zeal.

Hecht's audience (variously addressed as "Dear Kids," "Dear Folks," "Mes Chers") was the Hecht household at 163 East 81st Street in Manhattan—his main link to the civilized world in those years. While these salutations referred specifically to his parents, he knew that his letters would be shared with his brother Roger, Paula, the cook, and occasionally others close to the "clan." Most notable was Kathryn Swift, a family friend who knew German and with whom Hecht shared literary interests. As much as the letters re-count the unfolding saga of Hecht's life in a world over which (like Hamlet) he could exert little direct control, they also, by the very nature of their often fraught circumstances, insist on a significant role for the recipient; in this sense the letters are not so much about their author only as they are about the per-sons addressed and the needed circuit of exchange that accompanies extreme conditions. Along with epistolary flair was a palpable wish to receive in turn.

The pitch and timbre of the letters differ according to their underlying circumstances. Those written while Hecht was in basic training are often crafted out of a sense of boredom and ennui; those from the front, from a sense of purposeful activity; and those from the final phase of his service, though initially fraught with postwar depression and uncertainty over his future, are characterized by exhilaration over the favorable turn in occupa-tion duties in Japan. Throughout his many moods, one quality is constant: Hecht's concern for his immediate readers—the Hecht household. Letters were often written to spare anxiety, allay fears of his whereabouts, or apologize for occasional moodiness or depression. When he was at or near the front, his letters home did not dwell on the details of war or depict military actions.

In their reticence, an element of official wartime censorship is operating, as he sometimes reminds his readers. But while the letters of other World War II soldiers routinely allude to military maneuvers, gunfire, tanks, and the like, Hecht is conspicuously silent on these topics. "The exigencies of combat have made writing impossible for the last few days," begins one letter, with characteristic reserve. We sense the proximity of danger only indirectly. In the immediate aftermath of one of his platoon's most heated battles, for instance, the only sign Hecht gives of having endured action in the extreme is a reference to his "getting a short, much needed rest yesterday and today" and then manifesting an unusually keen sense of relief and joy in the most recent batch of mail: "Your letters, as always, are a blessing. Keep writing them just as you have been. Dad's peerless Baedeker of Europe—(although you ought to shift the locale to Germany) and Roger's fabulous discourses on sundry things, and mom's reporting of the tastes, smells, fashions and talk of home. They do wonders for me." He then follows this expression of gratitude with a characteristic expression of concern: "At the same time, do not be alarmed by the irregularity of mail from this end. I know that long periods of silence will not reassure you, but I'm sure you understand that I'm not always in a position to write letters" (April 20, 1945).

Along with this saga of survival, the letters reveal two further stories unfolding during this period of Hecht's life. The more immediate one, beginning in basic training, was his ongoing search for intellectually stimulating employment. He feared the dulling reduction of his mental faculties more than body fatigue, injury, or perhaps even death from action on the front lines. Within the first year, in a letter of May 1944, he recognized that his initial plan to write something every day was futile, even though prompted to do so by William Shawn at *The New Yorker*. He enlisted the help of family friend Ted Geisel (better known as Dr. Seuss) for a transfer to work in the studios in Los Angeles on military and recruitment movies.[1] Failing at that, Hecht repeatedly applied for transfer to the Counter Intelligence Corp (CIC). While in Germany, he eventually succeeded in this effort, though it was only a temporary assignment, announcing his good fortune through a cryptically resonant quotation from Isaiah 52:7: "How beautiful upon the

[1]Geoffrey Lindsay, "Anthony Hecht, Private First Class," *Yale Review* 96 (2008): 10.

mountains are the feet of him who bringeth tidings of great joy" (April 26, 1945). During this time, he met Robie Macauley, wonderfully described in his letter of May 24, 1945. In this new role, as his sobering letter of May 14, 1945, makes clear, his duties included interrogating Germans in the wake of his Division's liberation of the concentration camp at Flossenbürg on April 23. But he was returned to his original outfit with "the cessation of hostilities," a reference, presumably, to the German surrender on May 7.

Only after Hecht was sent to Japan, following a month-long furlough home and a further, hugely depressing month waiting to be shipped out, did he escape from the life of a foot soldier by assuming a position in the Public Relations Office (October 9, 1945). This quickly eventuated in sleuthing out stories to write for *Stars and Stripes*. He also produced several radio dramas to entertain the troops, and on one occasion, navigated the shady parts of Kumagaya, the town where he was stationed, in search of a piano for a concert. Not that these activities satisfactorily resolved the increasing anxieties he felt over a delayed literary career (January 16, 1946). Nor did he altogether forgo his wish to be transferred to CIC. But the relief, indeed exuberance, discovered in his newfound employment clearly distinguishes these later letters as a group from the earlier army letters, and the change produced some fascinating accounts of the immediate postwar political and cultural life in Japan: both its more insidious side, as a haven for Nazis (October 30, 1945), and its more cultivated side, as a refuge for Jewish musicians (November 7, 1945).

The other story is more complex and bears on Hecht's development as a writer. For the most part, the letters are highly literate, indeed highly literary affairs. Hecht never assumed in them the masculine slang of a wartime demotic associated with soldiering. Often the letters are peppered with a significant range of quotations or utterances in French, German, and English, the first two being the languages that he was practicing. And they usually carry references to many books and authors—Thomas Hardy, Elizabeth Bowen, William Wordsworth, Marianne Moore, and the odd allusion to his current reading, such as Jean Malaquais's *War Diary* (September 18, 1944) and various literary journals and magazines. There are also significant stretches of parody, especially when writing to Roger, most often with echoes of James Joyce and Shakespeare. It is doubtful Hecht had a single epistolary model in mind. For all their allusiveness, the letters are characterized by spontaneity and improvisation, but he was happy to acknowledge (and often to follow) his own recognition that letters should carry "witty digressions, after the fashion of Byron" (March 5, 1945). So, too, the many different salutations and assumed names (often geographically appropriate) are part of their flair. They keep Hecht humming along seemingly slightly above, if not far from, the madding crowd of military life.

There's humor here, of course, but also amplitude, the beginning orchestration of significant speech no longer constrained by classroom decorum and further fueled in Japan by a sense of journalistic immediacy. Letters written from Bard are one thing, but here was a special platform, unique with regard to his family (Roger went to summer camp and on to college, but never to war), and burgeoning with authorial potentiality. "This shall be the first of my letters to undergo the rigors of censorship—a fact which makes me feel as though I were addressing a vast 'reading public'" (March 16, 1945). A joke to be sure, but one that also reminds us of the wider urgency forced on the author by the present occasion, who now feels "as if I'd added a millennium to my age" (June 12, 1944). Here is Hecht, in yet another mood, opening a letter in the manner of Hamlet in the fifth act: "Opportunities present themselves in droves, it seems, and my pen is equal to all of them" (August 23, 1944). This kind of brash self-assurance was unthinkable in the earlier letters from Bard, as are the often startling juxtapositions of incident and information: reporting in one sentence on reading *King Lear*, then telling his family that it is "a fine play by William Shakespeare" who "used to write sonnets for high school anthologies"; then writing a paragraph describing his depression, followed by an admission that he will not be reading his books "for quite a while," but then concluding with the witty query, adapted from epic, "Seen any rosy-fingered dawns lately?" (March ?, 1944). These are vigorous letters, catching at many thoughts and portending in their reach and rhythms a writer to be.

For all Hecht's later reluctance to speak about his wartime years, there can be little question that the experience, shaped and colored by much further reading, deeply affected his poetry. To name but a few poems, the list would include "Japan," "A Deep Breath at Dawn," "Behold, the Lilies of the Field," "Rites and Ceremonies," "'More Light! More Light!'" "Apprehensions," "The Feast of Stephen," "The Deodand," "The Venetian Vespers," "Still Life," "Persistences," "The Book of Yolek," and "Sacrifice." The ample selections of letters from this period of Hecht's life set a context for understanding these later acts of creativity. Given the centrality of Germany and the Holocaust in his poetry, I have included most of the letters written from his time in Europe and chosen significant samplings from the other phases.

These are selected with an eye to their urgent variety and to tracing out the ongoing drama of one person's wartime saga.

1943

June 22, 1943

[postcard: view of county buildings and business center, Pittsburgh]
[To his parents]
Dear Kids:
En Route—
I don't know where[.] Only God and the General Staff know that, and God isn't too sure.

Will write[,]
T

[July 26, 1943, Fort McClellan, Alabama]

[To his parents]
Dear Kids—

"Variations on a theme by
William Wordsworth"

"—And oft, when on my couch I lie
In vacant, or in pensive mood,
They flash upon that inward eye
That is the bliss of solitude;
And then my heart with rapture fills
And dances with the daffodils."[2]
Also assorted garden weeds
Can make my ventricles rejoice.
The thought of cultivated seeds
May flash upon that inward voice
Which tells the sergeant that it's dawn
And sends me out to cut the lawn.

I think an account of all my fabulous military experiences is about due. You've been wondering, I suppose, whether I've been made a sergeant yet, and just how

[2]Wordsworth, "I wandered Lonely as a Cloud," 19–24.

many men I can order around. Well, the bald facts are these. After six days in the army I'm still a private. (Come now, don't despair.)

I reported to the proper authorities at Penn. Station, and I was lined up with about six other Bard students and the group from Stevens Institute [of Technology in New Jersey]. We were then dismissed for half an hour—and a more unprofitable furlough, I hope I never have. I made a short phone call home, and then wandered around the station till it was time to leave. Poor Paula seemed quite broken up about the whole thing.

The train took us to Trenton. When we arrived, there was nobody around to meet us, and the suggestion was made that we were not expected—consequently not wanted. Somebody shouted (one of the Stevens boys) "All those desiring to return to civilian life, line up by the ticket booth and prepare to purchase tickets for New York." This may give you a slight idea of what most people around here think of the army. Most of the people in my company are E.R.C. [Enlisted Reserve Corps] College Students so I don't know if their attitude is typical of the average draftee, but they seem to feel this way. —It's not so bad—so far; however they'd just as soon be back in civilian life. Getting up in the morning at 5:30 isn't so bad. Neither is making your bed, or mopping the floor. Even drilling for hours on end out in the drill field, in the hot sun, isn't as bad as it may sound. The most unpleasant thing I've encountered so far is standing endlessly at "Formations"— there are four each day—and not being able to take a crap whenever I want to; especially since there's no time for it till about 4:30 PM. [. . .]

(The above was written at Dix. I am continuing now after my first week at Fort McClellan)

At Dix we had a very remarkable sergeant. We were told that he served in the Polish Army in the last war, and also served in Spain and China "between wars." He is not what you might call intelligent. One day when he was complaining that too many men were just sitting around when they should have been working, he issued the orders—"The benches are put there for your convenience, so don't sit on them!" Sergeant Lidek had a definitely malevolent streak in him which he would display when picking K.P.'s for the following day. You see, you can't do K.P. until you've been processed—that is, gotten your uniform, had your I.Q. test and seen the movie on the Articles on War. Lidek had the time of his life singling out the eligible men.

Well one night I was among the eligible men and was all set to go on K.P. when Lidek said "I want about 20 husky men to volunteer for about an hour or an hour and a half of work tonight—and you get tomorrow morning off."

Now consider the situation—this would not only mean no K.P. but a free morning. On the other hand we were liberally warned upon our arrival at Dix not to volunteer for anything because its always much harder than they make it sound. And of course you must remember the qualifying adjective "husky." I shall not drag it out any longer—I volunteered—and this was the beginning of my first "Commando Raid."

Now I must return to Sergeant Lidek for a moment. The sergeant was in charge of Company C, and one of his many worries was to make sure the company area was kept neat and orderly. It was his special pride that almost all the sidewalks in the company area were made of cement instead of dirt, as was the case with every other company in the camp. The reason none of the other companies had cement sidewalks is because the government does not issue cement for that purpose. How did Company C get it? That's where I come in.

There was a private civilian construction company off the post limits about a half mile away. The twenty volunteers went out to pilfer the stuff, with Lidek himself doing the reconnaissance work. We were instructed to meet the sergeant half an hour after "lights out." When it was spread around what sort of work we were going to do, forty-three men showed up. We spent an exciting hour and a half swiping the stuff—throwing ourselves flat on the ground when the headlights of cars appeared.

Now I must tell you something about Camp McClellan. [. . .] The indoctrination process is very thorough. We received our rifles the second day we arrived, and also our bayonets. We are always addressed as "soldier" unless it is a personal conversation, and there are an infinite number of little things that conspire to make us forget we were ever civilians. The most important one is— when you wake up in the morning it's too early to think, during the day you're too busy to think, and at night you're too tired to think.

Yes, parts of this training have been pretty trying. The bayonet course which is almost finished now is very taxing at times. Also the "hand to hand fighting" more cheerfully called "dirty fighting." That course comes to a grand finale tomorrow with a "free for all."

The thing I most of all resent about the army is that you have no time to yourself. That's why I haven't written. In the evenings we have to take our rifles apart and clean them thoroughly, shave, shower, clean and polish our shoes. Then there is a good possibility that we will get some sort of detail like K.P. which keeps you working till 11:15 or Guard Duty—which lasts all night long. And then you must do regular duty the next day.

Right now we're on the Rifle Range, firing for record. We leave the Company area at 3:30 in the morning, spend the whole day at the range and come back about 5:30 or six. I'm doing well so far. I'm in the sharpshooter class—and just one point below the expert class. But we're only part way finished. We've only shot rapid fire so far. The day after tomorrow we short "slow fire," so I may still qualify as expert. [. . .]

All my love
Tony

1944

[late March/early April] 1944 Fort Leonard Wood, Missouri
[To his parents]
Dear Family—

I made several desperate attempts to get in touch with you, both by phone and telegraph, but things are so arranged at this post, that it is almost impossible to get to the right place at the right time.

To allay all your worries right away—I am well and among friends. In the past week I have done what it took 3 weeks to accomplish at [Fort] McClellan. I learned how to operate, aim and fire the MI rifle, and I fired it for record on the range. It was all very well for me, since I'd had it all before, in profusion, so it was merely redundant. But there are others here who never even saw a rifle before, and it rather rushed them. Our "basic training" here is supposed to last six weeks, but we came here when a group was just half way through their cycle. The plan is to finish us both up together, which means that we will be doing in 3 weeks what they do in six. All this haste is due to the fact that the division is going on maneuvers on the 23rd of April. Two weeks out in the field—and two weeks back here—then two weeks in the field again. This is liable to keep up for 2 or three months.

My morale is better than it was during my first few days here—but, on the other hand, I don't think it will ever be quite what it was at McClellan because I haven't got the A.S.T.P. to look forward to. There is nothing especially pleasant in the offing and the future ("zukunft" to you) bodes no particular good.

I do not choose to write about the present simply because it's routine boredom. I do not care to speculate on the future because it looks too ominous. This leaves only the past to think about, and I've thought about it so much, I'm already beginning to feel like Marcel Proust. [. . .]

I have been reading King Lear a fine play by William Shakespeare—I'm sure you've heard of him. He used to write sonnets for high-school anthologies.

I fear that I shall once again fall into that mental slump, which is so necessary to being a good soldier. After one week here, my thoughts have already become less coherent. This is liable to be the most depressing feature of army life again for me. Even on your own free time you cannot manage to think the thoughts you want to, and escape from the army for a while. Everywhere you look you see barracks, jeeps, rifles, soldiers, insignias and everything that pertains to the army. You can't get away from it. It's like a horrible obsession.

I sent Al [Millet, army friend from ASTP] a copy of one of Roger's poems, a sonnet. I'm sure he'll like it and I'm anxious to hear what he thinks of it. I'll let you know what he says.

I trust you received my books all in good condition. I'm afraid I shall not be reading them for quite a while.

Seen any rosy fingered dawns lately?

Love,

Tony

[June 12, 1944] Fort Leonard Wood, Missouri

[To his parents]

Dear Folks—

I regret to say that I am quite depressed about things in the offing. I think I told you once that, according to schedule, we were to be here till October—that next week I go off on a six day problem, that later on I go out in the field for five weeks straight. Radical changes have been wrought very recently which seem to throw this scheme somewhat askew. I have it on pretty good authority that something big is going to happen to us around the 23rd of July—the whole division will be affected. We may be going on maneuvers, or moving to a new camp, or shipping to a P.O.E. [Point of Embarkation]. I don't know—but the number of furloughs a company is now permitted to send out at one time has been raised from 7% of the personnel to 25%. In addition, all men will have to have physical exams before leaving on furlough. So I may (?) see you again. I certainly hope so. The 32 mile hike back from bivouac was rather rough. We started at 9 P.M. and arrived in camp at 6 A.M. I went into St. Louis with Jimmy, and had a few drinks, which served to lead me through a gamut of emotional variety, changing momentarily from rare exuberance to abysmal depression. It was strangely reminiscent of my younger days. I can say "younger days" in all seriousness because since I've been here, I feel as if I'd added a millennium to my age. [. . .]

I have enjoyed all your letters immensely, and look forward to them every day. I think I may have told you—I've started a sonnet sequence—a series of V mail letters to Al [Millet]. Have finished one and started two others.

Let me know what The New Yorker does with Roger's work—

The next day—

Further rumor and information seems to indicate our going to a P.O.E. and subsequently to a "staging area" overseas. (This is relative to the 23rd of July.) The training is becoming increasingly difficult and arduous.

There's not much more I can say. People aren't saying very much around here now. If there only were a light on the grubby horizon. Being neither the captain of my fate nor the master of my soul, it is hard to be bloody but unbowed.

"How weary, flat, stale and unprofitable

Seem to me all the uses of this world."[3]

> Gloomily,
> Tony

August 23, 1944 Santa Monica, California

[To his parents]

Dear Folks—

Opportunities present themselves in droves, it seems, and my pen is equal to all of them. When I last wrote, I told you we were going south to Camp Callan, near San Diego. We are "en route." We have stopped overnight at an army recreation camp (for soldiers returning from fighting overseas), a very comfortable camp, in Santa Monica. I phoned the Geisels this evening; Ted wasn't home, but I spoke to Helen, and I shall call back later and speak to Ted. So far things are going well.

The fact that I am already on my way to Callan pretty well precludes the possibility that I am on any of the many "shipping lists" that were rampant about the division on my return. People were, and still are, leaving for all over.

> And thus do we of wisdom and of reach,
> With windlasses, and with assays of bias
> By indirections find directions out.
> Hamlet [2.1.61–63]

It occurs to me that my next letter may reach you before this one, since my next will be air mail again—(I'll be able to get at my envelopes). Please excuse the non-sequitur.

> All my love,
> Tony

[3]*Hamlet* 1.2.133–134.

September 28, 1944 Camp Cooke, California

[To his parents]

Mes Chers:

Forgive whatever evasive or nebulous qualities you may encounter in this note, but I am now, for the first time, subject to censorship, of a sort. I trust I am not guilty of a breach of military reticence if I suggest that, were this ban to be lifted, I could report nothing that would give you cause for either worry or excitement. It is still, I regret to announce, the same dull routine, but the powers that be, with their odd taste for melodrama, have decided to enliven the situation by shrouding it in mystery. You can't win a war without secrets, you know.

Last night I got rather potted on 3.2 beer, and one of my manifestations of this condition is the advent of extraordinary mental lucidity, together with an unusual and scintillating eloquence. So I wrote a letter to Pres. Gray [of Bard College]. I'm afraid I can't describe it other than to say that it deviated to some considerable degree from the established precedent of letter-writing. I'd like to see his face when he reads it. Don't get me wrong; my words did not reek of liquor, but instead they were vivid and free, unhindered by the servile bondage of logic and grammar.

I must confess that the cause of this rather conservative orgy last night, was a keen but misdirected desire to release myself from the fit of utter depression which has been blunting the edge of things for me for the past several weeks. [. . .]

This note is doubtless far from cogent, or anything mildly pertaining thereto. My next one will be composed with great, soaring flights of imagination. I'd like to think it might resemble Alice in Wonderland, but present circumstances tend to confirm the suspicion that it will be more like The Fall of the House of Usher.

Love,

Tony

[October 11, 1944] Camp Callan Hospital, San Diego, California

[To his parents]

Dear Folks—

October Fool! You thought I'd be at Camp Cooke now, as previously advertised, didn't you? Ha, ha! Well you're wrong—wrong as hell. I'm back at Callan. It is a long and relatively uneventful story. I took off on my cruise of the Pacific and environs; altogether we made four landings, securing, against almost no opposition except cactus, small portions of the California Coast and adjacent island. It will doubtless give you great satisfaction to know that these strategic spots are in safe hands. We made our last landing on Saturday morning. The tactical problem was to last all day and then we were to camp there, set up tents etc. and move into Camp Cooke on Monday. All went according to schedule till the problem was over. Then the barracks bags didn't arrive. They contained the tents and blankets and additional warm clothes. In fact, they didn't arrive till very late that night, by which time I had contracted quite a cold. To break it off, they took me to the hospital at Callan (because it is much nearer to where I was, than Cooke) where the doctor pronounced me in great danger of living. I subsist on a diet of liquids and sulfur drugs. I must admit I don't feel too good, but my temperature has gone down to about 99 so I guess it's not too serious any more.

Write same old address Camp Callan Hospital.

Love,

Tony

[October 12, 1944] Camp Callan Hospital, San Diego

[To his parents]

Dear Folks

Excuse sloppy writing but I'm in bed, with only a small hand-mirror behind this paper to keep it flat, so that everything slides around as I write.

The first diagnosis of my condition is that I have gout, which I contracted from eating too much of those rich, tasty, field rations which the army offers us every so often.

Matter of fact, I have pneumonia. Don't be scared. Comparatively speaking, I'm leading a much happier life here in the hospital with my own private little illness, than I did when I was with the company, sharing the great public woe. For the past four days I have been living in a little oxygen tent, which has many advantages over the little tent I used to live in. First of all, it's indoors. Then, it's air-cooled. It also has windows, so that I can look out and watch all the silly people playing doctors and nurses. —can see them stalking down the halls with a mesmerized look in their eye and a bottle of urine in their hand. I do not yet know when I shall emerge from my little home of calico and eisinglass. "They" don't seem to know either. They seem to be taking everything into consideration, however. They are, if nothing else, thoroughgoing. They have taken x-ray pictures of me, they have taken my blood count; they have also taken samples of my blood (more than I personally thought I could spare)—and they are trying to destroy the evil that lurks in my body and soul, by drowning it in fruit juices and water. The idea and spirit behind this treatment is not unlike that which spread through New Salem at the time of the famous "witch-dunkings." Both come from the same malevolent natures. It's just a bit more refined in the hospital, that's all. Doctors have to keep up appearances. You should be delighted to know that I only have pneumonia. With things as they are today, any number of other things could have happened to me to give you more cause for alarm.

Write and tell me how glad you are that I'm ill.

Love,

Tony

[October 26, 1944]

[To his parents]

Dear Folks—

Yesterday I got your telegram and today your letter of the 21st, forwarded from this hospital. In the letter you ask "will you go to a recuperation camp? Will you get a furlough? May there be a chance for reclassification?" I'm afraid you overestimate either the severity of my illness or the generosity of the army. I was in the hospital for two weeks, in the oxygen tent for about four or five days, and under sulfur drug treatment for two days. During the last week I was permitted to get up and walk around, eat at the hospital mess, go to the Red Cross Recreation hall etc. In the course of the treatment they took three blood tests and an x-ray of my chest. I'm telling you all this to assure you that I had the best possible treatment. I am back with my outfit, still feeling a little weak, and I shall see if I can't get a 'Light Duty' slip for the next few days. That's about as much as I could hope for in the line of furloughs or recuperation camps. You have to be on the very point of death before you get a furlough. As for reclassification, I could duly get it with a permanent disability, or else the fact that I were prone to a particular illness. One mild case of pneumonia won't do it. I wish just as much as you that there were something in it for me, but it doesn't look that way. I shall try to phone & let you know this information before this letter reaches you, but the facilities here are pretty bad. I hope I have dispelled most of your worries concerning my health. I had hoped to do that through my letters to Roger—to show you that I was feeling well & in good humor.

This camp is a horrible place—a very "waste land," barren, nothing but sand & fog, and blighted with the seventh plague—the presence of soldiers. I do not think we shall be here very long—possibly till the middle of November. Then? To another camp somewhere in Calif. No one seems to know for sure.

My return from the hospital brought on a fit of despondency which threatens to linger a while. Seldom have I felt such a keen desire to escape completely from all features of reality. If you have an extra box of cocaine in the closet, ship it to me, will you? I must stop before I become maudlin.

I hope Roger had the best time it was possible for him to have on his birthday. Shall try to phone.

Sonst nicht[s] neues,[4]

All my love,
Tony

[October 28, 1944] Camp Cooke, California
[To his parents]
Dear Folks—

The morale has taken a new plunge, the reckless extravagance of which is unparalleled. I am plumbing the depths of a fathomless sea—beginning to feel like an emotional William Beebe [the naturalist and explorer who set a deep-sea dive record in 1934]. Today I embarked upon a venture which, under ordinary circumstances, would prove stimulating and exciting. I offered to write a Regimental show to be put on in about 5 or six weeks. This, of course, in addition to my regular training—which, incidentally, I have not yet started, since I'm still weak, and have been allowed to rest a while. Nevertheless, I came away from my interview with the Special Service Officer in a fit of abysmal despair. Don't ask why. You've asked why before and I told you the truth when I said I didn't know. It is partly due, no doubt, to my return to my original status. But that's not all. I have been here long enough to get over the initial shock.

> "I have that within me which passeth show
> These but the trappings [and] the suits of woe."
> Hamlet [1.2.85–86]

You understand, I know, that I am not trying to cause you concern—this is evidently a perfectly normal thing with me. I've had it all along through high school and college—and I shall come out of it sooner or later as I always do.

So much for the nausea. Sonst nichts neues. There is never news, of course. Not even as much as you are able to garner from the menus of our relatives. I have been reading a bit—there's a good library here. An anthology of long

[4]Otherwise nothing new.

poems and a book of short stories by Elizabeth Bowen, an Englishwoman who is very good. By the way, you might mention to Roger that the esoteric quotation which I carelessly attributed to Michael Drayton over the telephone, was really, I think, Andrew Marvell. I must say a few words to Roger.

Dear old goat—

How's the old petty pace coming along? From day to day? Well, Hercus Civis Eblaneusis, I always say. Leopold Bloom thought that the keys gag was very clever, but he failed to see the wheels within wheels of the situation. No wonder his friend spurned him—he was a faux pas? But not us—no sir. Not by the beard of my aunt in which many a dog hath died and if the sun breed maggots in a dead dog, well, you know what happens as well as I. Look at your aunt. Awful, isn't it. Ship her off to a nunnery. Say it, if you like—weary, flat, stale, and unprofitable, but if we cease to bear fardels, the genus is liable to become extinct. In which case we are bereft of the toads with gems in their heads. But then, I never thought of these as appropriate wedding gifts. —Ship her off to a nunnery. We'll meet again. We'll part once more. The place I'll seek, if the hour you'll find.

Yours ever, whilst this machine is to him,
Tony

December 26 [1944] Camp Cooke, California

[To his parents]
Dear People—

Since the last time you heard from me, I've made more efforts than I can recall to get in touch with you. All to no avail. Tried to phone Christmas eve but there was a 12 to 14 hour delay in getting calls through. Tonight the delay is 4 to 5 hrs. Je suis désollé, mais qu'est ce qu'on peut faire?[5] [. . .]

Now to the main news. I shall not be home on furlough at the time I stated. The division is leaving for maneuvers in California on about the 21 of January. The maneuvers will last about a month. I shall be one of [the] first to leave after they are over. Which makes it about the end of February. Sorry. I know how you counted [on] celebrating all those occasions. But, after all, this only means that we'll be here in the U.S. that much longer. I understand our division has dropped from second to ninth on the shipping priority list. We were seventh when we were in Missouri. Of course this ninth place is the position we were

---

[5] I am desolate but what can one do.

in before the German Offensive started. I don't know where we are now. Still, it looks good.

I had a long talk with a German prisoner (auf Deutsch, naturlich). But don't spread that around. It's a Court Martial offense. He was 22 years old, and it has been five years since he has seen Christmas at home. He was in a Panzer Outfit in Africa. Thinks very highly of America and Americans. Doesn't, for instance, think Germans are better. Thinks Nazism would never work in this country, because people prize their individual liberty too highly, whereas they don't in Germany. He seemed quite intelligent.

Now, there's a job I'd really like to have—reeducating German prisoners of war with an eye to anticipating the problems that will arise in Germany after the war. Ah, well.

Hoping this reaches you in time to allay whatever fears you may have conjured up since you last heard from me,

Love,
Tony

1945

February 27, 1945 At Sea [v-mail]

[To his parents]

Dear Kids—

The present jaunt upon which I am engaged in no way resembles any previous ones I enjoyed in your company. [The Hecht family sailed to Europe on several occasions in the late 1920s and 1930s.] People look upon this trip from a totally different perspective from the one we were familiar with. For example, I distinctly remember the bar on the ship—the table-tops were done in red linoleum or plastic with a playing-card motif decorating the border. The bar proper was a semi-circular affair against the forward bulkhead, arranged with bottles and indirect lighting—altogether a very charming hang-out. Now, as far as I can determine, this vessel has no bar at all, and was obviously constructed to carry miscreants from the Venetian Doge's Palace to the prison, in the event that the Bridge of Sighs broke down. The chief steward does not have that suave continental air, and they do not serve bouillabaisse at 11 o'clock every morning. All in all, this voyage falls quite short of the previous ones, and though I appreciate being sent on the Grande Tour, if you paid more than 75 cents for the passage ticket you were stuck.

The trip, I may add, has been singularly uneventful. I expected to see the First

Mate pipe the ship's company on deck every morning to witness punishment. As a matter of fact, nobody has been keel-hauled—not even suspended by his thumbs from the yard-arm. And I doubt if the crew can sing anything more closely resembling a "chanty" than "The Beer-Barrel Polka."

Seriously, though, we have had an exceptionally calm time of it—and it has not been nearly as bad as I anticipated. I eagerly await your first letters with all the addresses of friends and relatives abroad, and any helpful suggestions on continental etiquette that you'd care to make. Send me voluminous letters and I shall try to reply in kind—Hold off with the books, however, till I give you word. And let me know about the college extension courses.

Je vous embrace,
Antoine

March 5, 1945 Somewhere in France

[To his parents]

Dear Kids—

It has suddenly occurred to me that I neglected to tell you what steps to take apropos of those books of mine which are languishing in the hands of Lois [Montgomery]. Repair, then, to the nearest Los Angeles Telephone Directory, and find the address of Martindale's Book Store (Beverly Hills branch—approximate address 113? Santa Monica Blvd.) This is where she works and they can forward your letter to her. The books included Auden, Marianne Moore, Huxley, Euclid (I think), Shapiro etc. Can't remember them all—but my names are in them so she'll know. I have with me <u>Finnegans Wake</u>, <u>The Pocket Book of Sonnets</u>, <u>Five Shakespeare Tragedies</u>, a <u>Pocket Anthology of Short Stories</u>, and copies of <u>The New Yorker</u>, <u>The Atlantic Monthly</u>, <u>The Partisan Review</u> and <u>Horizon</u>—so you see I am not without literary means.

What I have seen of France so [far:]

This is an abridged version of the first draft of this letter. Abridged in the sense that the original second page has been entirely omitted. I have done this myself because, as I was in the very midst of writing this letter, I was called away to a security and censorship lecture, and found out that everything I had said was censorable. It was, of course, a matchless page of eloquence, rich with powerful metaphors, sparkling with ~~eloquence~~ (oops) witty digressions, after the fashion of Byron. But, what ho! The army, being essentially an illiterate organization, cares not a whit for the flights of my fancy, nor the purity of my prose—the hell with them. It simply means that you and posterity will miss out on one more beauty which might have been a joy forever.

I have just thought of a book I might like to have, but if you have any difficulty locating it, don't bother. It's a paper bound edition of André Gide's "Journal" published in French by some Canadian Press. See if you can locate it, but don't rush all over town.

I look forward with great eagerness to your first letter, and hope that you will have included "Maddy's" address. I would very much like to write to her, and I more or less expect to get one from her soon. That was a splendid concert, that one. Really.

If I pick up any cheap Daumiers or Matisses over here, I'll ship 'em right home for that big bald spot between the bookcases in the living room.

Je vous embrace de tou[t] mon coeur,
Antoine

P.S. If you have any pride in the reputation of the family, for God's sake don't let Anne [Stern] embroil us [in] any sort of mess with the Schwabachers. It would be an ineradicable blot on the old eschutcheon.

Rabelais

Herewith are appended brief instructions on what to write about in your letters. Describe in full the good books which may make their appearance from time to time, plus any remarks the critics have to make. Keep me posted on any news of my friends you may come across. Brief opinions of any new shows as they appear—and if you have a particularly good meal now and then, send lush descriptions. Any news of exhibits at the Modern Museum or the Metropolitan, with your own criticisms if you go. Describe any renovations at home, to the minutest detail, floral decorations, new clothes you might buy, additions to the library. Let me know when the cherry blossoms and dogwood and forsythia bloom in Central Park. Let me know how Paula makes out with Schopenhauer.

As for me, I have no reason for complaint. Things are neither better nor worse than I expected—which in fact is saying a great deal.

March 7, 1945 Somewhere in France [v-mail]
[To his parents]
Dear Kids—

Today your first letters arrived, the third and the ninth, oddly enough, and as a result my morale has jumped to almost fever pitch. The idea of numbering your letters is a splendid one, and though I have already written several to you (I can't remember how many) I'll start numbering from now on. [. . .]

—Mon Dieu, a great change has occurred. I am continuing this letter the following day, (March 8), and I am no longer where I was, but am instead somewhere else. (That's about all one can say about location over here.)

However, the great blessing has come. Just what I had hoped for. There is always a marked paucity of polyglots in any army. I'm afraid I can do nothing but revel in my good fortune without giving you any details. It must suffice to say that I'm well pleased with the turn of events. There are some absolutely wonderful aspects to the present set-up, all of which fall under the "restricted" category. It annoys me just as much as it must bother you, this veil of mystery, but "que peut-on faire?"[6] [. . .]

Je vous assure que tu [tout] va bien ici, et j'espère que cette bon[ne] chance va duré pour la durée.[7]

Je vous embrace,
Antoine

March 19, 1945 Somewhere in France

[To his parents]
Dear Kids—

I've written you a V Mail letter this evening but because I feel verbose and poly-lingual, I choose the old fashioned epic in preference to the "sonnet-space" allotted by the V-Mail letters. In addition, I am trying to irritate my Platoon Leader who has to read all these letters, and work him up to the point where [he] arranges to have me discharged from the army in order to save himself the work of reading these pages.

I'm writing by candle light, and would feel rather like Martin Luther in his dark little cell, writing the translation of the Bible into German—were it not for the fact that a radio amplifier just above my left ear is blaring forth popular music, and there's a motion picture playing just around the corner. As you may guess from this, I am not yet in the thick of battle. The news looks good and I continue to have high hopes[. . . .]

[Tony]

[6]What can one do.
[7]Things are going well here. I hope this good luck will be long lasting.

[To his parents]

Dear Kids

Today I stand in receipt of eleven letters, including one from Kathryn, that priceless one from Paula, and a "Bard Newsletter." I am delighted to receive the info that my letters to you are arriving "en fin," and I was afraid that you might be unduly concerned over the delay, or perhaps think I might lapse into a periodic "blackout" in my literary commerce with you. Your own mail has been coming through steadily, and with blissful regularity, with such fidelity that if a day passes which fails to bring me at least one letter, I curse all the subalterns in the Post Office Dept.

I admit to a certain laxness in the past few days which have elapsed without my writing a word. My explanation (which I do not proffer as an excuse) can be, as usual, nothing but vague at best. Something big for me was in the offing—but unfortunately it did not come off. I was waiting to write you a letter of great rejoicing, which, of course would be anything but specific. There is still a chance, and in the event that the Fates don't knot up the yarn, I will write you:—"How beautiful upon the mountains are the feet of him who bringeth tidings of great joy."[8]

I'm afraid I cannot elaborate upon my precious good fortune, other than to say that it presented me with the opportunity to get some of the local brews, and do a bit of sightseeing. With the exception, however, of that brief period, all my letters have been written from the same place.

I'm writing again by candle light, this time feeling like Erasmus, so you can see that these minor discomforts provide good artistic discipline. I have not, however, managed to ferret out enough solitude to put out any distinguished prose, much less verse.

A brief word to Paula: Many thanks for your letter which I read without any difficulty. I must admit that I suspected that Schopenhauer's dislike for women would prejudice you against him. I appreciate the spirit in which you attempted the cookies, despite the results, and beg you not to be too downcast about it. All you need is practice. Seriously, though, the food here (unlike Johnie's outfit) is remarkably good—not, of course, like that meal you (Mom) described in one letter involving chicken and mushrooms and chocolate éclairs—but by all military standards, excellent. This does not mean that I would not appreciate food if sent. Thanks again for the letter.

[8]Isaiah 52:7.

A brief word to Roger—Dear old shoe, your peerless parchment on divers introspections served to revitalize an otherwise grubby horizon of noxious extroverts, with a bit of healthy neuroticism. It was an invaluable respite from the incessant monosyllabic balderdash which festers in all our minds for sheer lack of stimulus. I look back in awe and reverence to those days when I was intellectually acute and perceptive enough to be comfortably maladjusted. I reached the apex of that psychological luxury during my years at college, and those years will remain for me some of the most thwarted delights in my memory. By the same token, I look forward to the day when I can re-enter our living-room with a goodly supply of scotch, and just sit and wallow in my own pathologies. Write soon again.

A brief note to Kathryn:—(which I hope you will pass on to her.) My dear Kathryn, you may justly accuse me of both mental and physical laziness for not writing directly to you (you richly deserve at least one long letter—it may yet come), and for not replying in kind. I flatter myself that my fluency in both German and French has improved since I've been over here, but to offer you written proof makes me feel as if I were about to dash off a line to Bertolt Brecht, or some equally prominent literary figger. I am much interested in your plans to join me on the continent, and hope I shall not miss the chance of seeing you. I'll be sitting at the corner table of the Café de la Paix at 3 o'clock, when the war's over. I expect you to help me determine the authenticity of some Van Goghs and Cezannes for our bald spot in the living-room at home. Similarly, I expect you to have all necessary information concerning vintages, and full instructions for headwaiters on your own particular method of preparing "crepes suzette." I'll follow this gibberish with a letter less given to fripperies. Thank you ever so much for your polyglot letters, Sincerely, Tony.

As to the rest of you, cher famille, I continue to thank you for your letters which are my constant delight—for the copy of Gide you sent (which of course has not yet arrived) and for your excellent morale. Strangely enough, my own morale has been remarkably high since I've been here. May this be a harbinger of Fate, "Deo Volente" (Ovid). Many of the boys over here with me are pitifully homesick—to such a degree that it is with mixed pleasure and pain that they receive a letter. Do not think me an ingrate, but I am somehow weathering this difficulty handsomely. Perhaps it is because France is practically a second home to me now. I have found time to chat with some very pretty Mlles. Which brings to mind A. Planche. I've gotten two V Mails from her, neither of which take full advantage of the space offered. Let her know how much I appreciate them, nevertheless. Incidentally, don't include any cartoons etc. in V Mails. For some reason it is impossible to reproduce them. I got that one letter in its original form. Sonst nichts mehr.[9]

> Get potted a few times for me,
> Pascal

April 6, 1945 Somewhere in Germany

[To his parents]

Dear Kids

I sincerely hope that you have not allowed the gap in my letters to cause you any alarm. I'm sure you realize that moving around and various military idiosyncrasies of mine preclude the possibility of writing regularly anymore.

As you see, I have arrived in the "Vaterland." I came by way of Belgium and Holland, travelling in the traditional luxury of troop sleepers marked "40 hommes—8 Chevaux." I spoke to quite a number of civilians on the way here, and they are all most optimistic about the end of the war—much more so than I am. I may tell you now that my brief sojourn "elsewhere" was in Rouen, where I was working as an interpreter. It's a most remarkable city—absolutely full of history. Joan of Arc was imprisoned, tried and burned at the stake there; William the Conqueror and Richard, Coeur de Lion floated in and out from time to time; Corneille was born there, and the place is just glutted with sights. It was here, incidentally that I met O'Hara's ex-wife.

Your letters have been coming through more or less regularly, as the occasion permits, and I am very grateful for them. Since you press me to send requests, my primary need is woolen socks—I'd appreciate all you can send.

It will doubtless interest you to know that since we've been in Germany we've been billeted in German homes; so you can see that things could be a lot worse than they are for me. In fact, my only complaint right now is that my feet hurt. In the house I'm in now, there's a piano, and I've been having quite a time, though my fingers are very stiff from lack of practice.

I will write again as soon as I can. Give my best to Kathryn, Paula and whomever else you think deserves them.

> Sei immer herzlich gegrurst[10]
> Wilhelm II

[9]Otherwise nothing more.
[10]Always best wishes [or greetings]

April 20, 1945 Somewhere in Germany

[To his parents]

Dear Kids—

I have been getting a short, much needed rest yesterday and today—sleeping, eating, smoking and generally taking it easy. Mail has been coming through from all of you and A. Planche, Kathryn, Anne Stern (yes, I said Anne Stern) Mary Shaffer, and assorted sources—all coming through, as I say, much more frequently than I have time to answer. Your letters, as always, are a blessing. Keep writing them just as you have been. Dad's peerless Baedeker of Europe— (though you ought to shift the locale to Germany) and Roger's fabulous discourses on sundry things, and Mom's reporting of the tastes, smells, fashions and talk of home. They do wonders for me. At the same time, do not be alarmed by the irregularity of mail from this end. I know that long periods of silence will not reassure you, but I'm sure you understand that I'm not always in a position to write letters. From what I have seen of Germany, I can safely say that it is far better off than France. On the other hand, I think reconstruction in this country will be accomplished much more quickly than in France. The French just sit around in realms of self-pity, telling one atrocity story after another. No doubt the occupation was horrible—but who do they expect is going to rebuild France,—the Germans, perhaps?

For as long as I've been in this country, I've only slept on the ground one night (so far). In every other case I've slept on the floor, sofa, or bed in a German house. The inhabitants are told, (by me, of course) either to move to the cellar for the night, or to move out altogether. They generally prefer to stay in the cellar, an old habit of theirs for which our Air Force and Artillery are responsible. One night we slept in a school house which was on the H.Q. of a Hitler Jugend organization. I am naturally required to do all translating, to secure mattresses, hot water, and whatever accessories are necessary. On the whole the Germans we have "stayed with" have done their best to impress us with the idea that they were never Nazis, they hated the party, they're glad the war's almost over, they're delighted that we've come and assorted fairy tales of this kind. Every single family—and many prisoners that we took—told us the same story. The explanation of why they went to war (they admit they started the war) was that if they didn't fight and cooperate generally with the Nazis, they were shot. Now this argument, if pursued to its logical conclusion, ("reductio ad absurdum," as Aristotle would say) would mean that Hitler with one pistol at the back of two other men, etc. has completely terrorized every last person in Germany. A remarkable feat! These houses are frequently full of Nazi propaganda, most elaborate, and many have framed photographs of the members of the family who are in the service. As you see, we don't trust any of them.

I wrote a letter to Maddy a long time ago, while I was still in France, in fact, and never heard a word from her. Perhaps you could contact Ben and discover what the matter is. I have lost her address and cannot write her again. I remember your writing that you intended to have Ben, Mary and Maddy in for dinner some time. Did that ever happen? How was it? Perhaps you've already written to me about it and I haven't gotten the letters yet. (By the way, in answer to your constant query, air mail is faster than V mail.) You may or may not be interested to know that today I was awarded the "Combat Infantryman Medal," an award whose meaning I do not entirely understand myself.

Thank Anne Stern for her letter for me. I have lost her address. I cannot keep these little scraps of paper around all the time.

Things look good.

Wie immer[11]

Hohenzollern

Of the "friends" alluded to below, Tom Mack was a classmate from Bard and in ASTP at Carleton College. "Philips" was probably Laughlin Phillips. After an early career in the CIA, Phillips served as board chairman (1966–2001) and director (1979–1991) of the museum in Washington, D.C., that bears his family name.

April 26, 1945 Somewhere in Germany

[To his parents]

Dear Kids—

"How beautiful upon the mountains are the feet of him who bringeth tidings of great joy."

Do you recognize the quote? I can only refer you to a previous letter of mine [March 25, 1945], in which I whispered of the harbinger and vast portents of a wonderful future. I said if everything transpired as I hoped it would, I would open my first letter on the subject with the quote that appears above. At that time things fell through in the most dismal fashion imaginable, and my morale took a commensurate drop. However, yesterday, with a surprise element worthy of our best dramatists, I was whisked out of a "front-line" Infantry Co., and sent back to Battalion, then to Regiment, and finally to Division.

In case your exuberance to open my mail and taste of the fruit of first class

[11]As always

prose was such that you failed to notice the change in my return address on the envelope, I offer a recapitulation here:

Anthony E. Hecht

#12187656

97th C.I.C. Detachment

H.Q. 97th Inf. Div.

c/o Postmaster, New York City, N.Y.

A.P.O. 445

I must admit that I am not yet permanently situated here—I am working on a basis charmingly termed "detached service." I will, nevertheless, continue to have the highest hopes, for as you know, C.I.C. has been one of those inaccessible Nirvanas, which I've always hoped for, and [. . .] the dissatisfaction of not being in it was heightened by the number of friends I had who did make it. You yourselves know two of them—Philips and Tom Mack.

C.I.C. has that great, midnight aura of secrecy about it in which our whole family seems to dwell from time to time. You, Mom, were never very explicit about the nature of the work which the W.D. [War Department] asked you to do over here, but I somehow gathered that it might be in this line. And Kathryn, who is to all intents and purposes, a member of our clan, sounds, as she writes of her incumbent trip to Europe, like some neo-Romantic figure—possibly out of the "Count of Monte Cristo."

You can surely surely appreciate the beauty of my position when you consider that for the first time since I've been in the army, I am doing work that interests me. It is a more important phase of the war than I ever expected to be concerned with; it is a greater responsibility than I have ever been granted in my phenomenal military career. But what intrigues me most of all is that this is the first time the army has offered me anything in the way of an intellectual challenge (whose glove I am delighted to pick up). You remember how I complained, even during Basic Training of the stifling, retrogressive mental atmosphere. My sparkling mental acumen dwindled to a paltry remnant of what it was. O miserere nobis!

Last night I slept in quarters that were the very paragon of luxury. If the commanding general has any more comforts and conveniences than I had—by God, he is welcome to them. I begrudge him nothing. Though he walk on carpets of concubines, and drink of the nectar of gods, he is no more content than I. I slept in a feather bed of royal cherry wood, beneath a carved wood paneled ceiling. There was running water and electricity, a radio, the toilet functioned properly, and all the normal facilities of a house, such as walls, floors and a roof. (Do not be misled into thinking that I am happier here than I was at home.)

See if you can discover why Maddy never answered my letter to her. And send me her address again—I have lost it. Inform Ben, and any other friends of mine about town of the "exceeding great joy"—(and send me Al's address—I've not seen my duffle bag with all my addresses since I left France).

[Sei immer herzlich gegrusst und gebusst?][12]

J.S.Bach

May 14, 1945 Somewhere in Germany

[To his parents]

Dear Kids—

I sincerely trust that all your anxiety for my welfare was assuaged when you received my last letter, bearing the intelligence of my transfer. I am sure you must have been just as happy as I was. You will note (but not with alarm, I hope) that I have been returned to my original outfit. This was done at the cessation of hostilities and what will become of me is still a matter of some contention. Rest assured that I have "taken steps." It seems that the interim between this letter and my last was much greater than it should have been—if it should be commensurate with the luxury in which we live. For I must admit that while I was with C.I.C. I lived in regal style. If on the other hand, this lapse may in any way be explained by the comparative leisure I had, I feel that I am purged of sin—for I have been busy as hell, catching up with the Gestapo, the Sicherheitsdienst, the SS., S.A. u.s.w.[13]

This letter is written primarily to inform you that the war is over, and I have come through it unscathed. You had probably guessed as much by this time, but I am sure that my own confirmation can clinch the matter more firmly than anything else. Unscathed, of course, does not mean unaffected. What I have seen and heard here, in conversations with Germans, French, Czechs, & Russians—plus personal observations combine to make a story well beyond the limits of censorship regulation. You must wait till I can tell you personally of this beautiful country, and its demented people. The country really is beautiful, some of the most beautiful landscapes I have ever seen. It looks almost as though it had been created by Norman Bel Geddes [the famous theatrical and industrial designer] instead of by God (no blasphemy intended, just a plug for Norm).

A great batch of your letters arrived this evening, in which you mentioned

[12]Always best wishes and kisses

[13]u.s.w = und so weiter: "and so on." The list includes various organizations created under Hitler: Sicherheitsdienst (SD) was one of the oldest security organizations; SS = Schutzstaffel, the Nazi protection squad; S.A. = Sturm Abteilung, Storm Troopers or Brown Shirts.

purchasing replacements for all those books I left at Lois Montgomery's. I hope you don't do that—partly because of the expense, and partly because the listing I sent you was incomplete—and I cannot remember now just what books I did leave there. Perhaps another letter to her, with a slight note of impatience, will do the trick.

A letter from Maddy (and a very satisfactory one) arrived last night.

There is not much more I can say now. If you have postponed your V-day celebration in my behalf, stop postponing and get out the drinks for God knows when I'll be home. There is plenty to drink to, as this letter can testify—and that does not include all the hopes for the future. So invite Kathryn over, if she has not already left, and have a vast number of drinks on me.

Cum tuo in spiritum ero.[14]

> Love,
> Tony

May 24, 1945 Near Bamberg, Germany

[To his parents]

Dear Kids—

I must admit that I was surprised at what I took for a tone of painful naivete which I seem to have detected in your post V-day letters. Correct me if I'm wrong, but [I] felt that you had the idea that "the war is over—and Tony's on his way home." I hope I misconstrued your meaning, but according to a recent poll of Army personnel having 84 points or less, the consensus of opinion seems to indicate that the war is not yet over. Or, if you prefer, only one war is over. [. . .]

[To] quote directly from Stars and Stripes . . . [:] "Every man in the 4 divisions will receive a furlough of undisclosed length in the U.S., and the divisions will probably undergo additional training in the States before shipping to the Pacific."

Despite the anticipation of getting home again, I am nevertheless quite depressed by my inability to get into Military Government. I went up to Division H.Q. to see what could be done, and everyone was very discouraging. I insist on maintaining one hope, however. I think that while I was working at C.I.C. I managed to worm my way into the good graces of a few key men, who told me then that if there was ever again a call for more men, I would surely be one of them. One of these men was particularly interesting—I may have mentioned him in a letter before—his name was Robie Macauley, a descendant from

---

[14]Hecht's loose Latin might be translated as "I will be with you in spirit."

old T.B. Macauley. He majored in the classics at Kenyon College, and has studied under John Crowe Ransom and Ford Madox Ford (Roger should know the names). He has excellent taste in music (Mozart is his favorite composer) and, of course, in literature, and is fully acquainted with contemporary writing. His taste in art is similar to mine, genuine without too much cultivation. After college he worked for a while as an investigator for an Insurance Company. He has a sharp quiet sense of humor, is very soft-spoken and well mannered, and is very easily depressed—more easily—I think—than I. He's tall and lanky, very thin, with amazingly stooped shoulders, and it's a tribute to the strength of his personality that the army has never had any effect on his posture. We became very close friends while we were working together, and I hope to be able to introduce him to you some day.

For the present we have relapsed into the typical garrison "training schedule" with hikes, close-order-drill, physical training etc. It was amazing with what rapidity they rushed us from front line fighting, back to the same damned routine. As if they were afraid to let us profit in any way by the victory in Europe. We didn't expect anything more than a rest but apparently the feeling is that we're not even entitled to that.

By the way, if there's another world war in 30 or 40 years, don't go pointing any fingers at my generation. The news of the progress of the San Francisco Conference is very disheartening, but it has nothing to do with my generation, except insofar as we will be paying the penalty (together with our children) for the mistakes that are being made. This war, like the last, has accomplished nothing in a positive sense—only in the negative one of destroying an aggressor. I think I was fortunate in expecting no more than that from the beginning. It seems, in fact, that the time is pretty well past when war can have any positive value.

In Dad's blue-print of the house, he omitted two chairs in the living room—the one Peppy sleeps in and the one everyone stumbles over on the way to the bed rooms.

A bientot
Paul Claudel

August 3, 1945 Fort Bragg, North Carolina
[To his parents]
Dear Kids—

I am gradually becoming acclimated (that's a little too strong—resigned is better) to my status and surroundings, and have calmed down quite a bit—

although the great "questions" of my future are still uppermost in my mind every moment of the day. But being, as I said, somewhat more subdued than I was at any time during my furlough, I wish to offer a most sincere apology for my frequently irritable moods during those 30 days. Those things I said which bothered or saddened you, were said, as I'm sure you both realize, under considerable emotional pressure. You are, of course, entitled to speculate on the cause of the pressure (Dad attributes too much to <u>The New Yorker</u> situation) but personally, my theory has nothing to do with any single incident or event. I believe that I was so happy on my furlough, and managed to get so far away from the idea of the army, that the unalterable fact of my return assumed unduly large proportions, and hung, like the sword of Damocles, above me, almost from the time I arrived. Going back was not like previous goings back. I had been away from my company during my last month overseas, and I disassociated myself from it on the trip across. That I was away from the company so long, and had become, mentally, at least, autonomous, made return to this imbecilic, servile existence all the more difficult. Add to this, the beautiful Nirvanas that were flaunted in front of my face just before leaving, in the form of <u>Yank</u>, C.I.C. etc., the ultimate goal, which I was powerless to do anything about, and I think you have the essence of the difficulty. Suffice to say that this stage is at least partially past, that I never had a happier furlough, and that I very much regret those unpleasant moments.

Except for that letter from Gray, I've gotten no mail from anyone. I answered his letter immediately, with a long rambling letter. I wrote a short note to [William] Shawn, thanking him for his kindness to me during my sojourn in town, and wrote a long letter to Robie last night. This frenzy of activity is brought on by the fact that, up till this evening, I haven't done any work at all (nor has anyone else) and have spent all my time in the barracks reading the <u>Kenyon</u> and <u>Partisan Reviews</u>. I have exhausted them both, and would be grateful if you'd send Barzun's book, though by the time it arrives, I will probably have little time for reading. Could also use some more airmail stamps.

Most of the men in my barracks think I've changed since I came back from furlough. I'm quiet, I stay by myself, I don't go out to the P.X. and movies in evenings. Actually, I am waiting to be taken away from them. I keep imagining how the word will come—in a letter from <u>Yank</u>, a wire from Robie, an order to pack my bag and report to Regiment. I fully realize that I am building up hallucinations which, if totally destroyed, will leave me desperately depressed. But I cannot help it. I cannot be satisfied with this animal existence.

"The fault, dear Brutus, is not in our stars, but in ourselves, that we are underlings."[15]—This is only a half truth; theoretically splendid, but practically untrue.

In my leisure, I have had several ideas for poems, but have not been able to bring myself to write them. My rationalization is the constant interruption of lewd conversation which people try to drag me into. I have at least reached the point of detachment to create the following untitled verse, which I sent to Robie:

> An earnest young latter-day Pater
> Wrote a piece on the "Maps of Mercater,"
> But so cryptic his phrase
> And contextual maze,
> He was finally shot as a traitor.

A bit too obscure, perhaps, but the effort was there. Let me hear from you soon.
                                        Love,
                                        Tony

                                        August 9, 1945 Fort Bragg, North Carolina
[To his parents]
Dear Kids—

I started to write you a letter last night, but it's a good thing I didn't, because I was too depressed. I haven't heard anything definite from <u>Yank</u> or Robie yet, but our division schedule is being speeded up and we'll be leaving this camp on the 17th of this month. All this happened yesterday, a day of mixed blessings, which also brought the first Atomic Bomb and Russia's entrance into the war . . .

God grant that this may be the last day of war.
                                        Love,
                                        Tony

                                        August 13, 1945 Fort Bragg, North Carolina
[To his parents]
Dear Kids—

I stand in receipt of a number of your letters which are, so far, unanswered—mainly because I have been too depressed to answer them. This only goes to prove that I am essentially more optimistic than you are. The fact that Japan is

[15]*Julius Caesar*, 1.2.140–141.

on the point of defeat, that we are awaiting her acceptance of our terms, does not elate me as it should. I suppose I never really expected to see combat in the Pacific. But I am still scheduled to start a transcontinental journey in less than a week, and I am destined to go overseas from there. We continue to pack, draw equipment, and behave generally as if the war were going to last at least another year. The New Yorker has not come through; Yank hasn't said a word, and the whole aspect is rather grim. Nothing substantial from Robie, either. Though the homefront seems to be able to see the rosy-fingered dawn even though it's still midnight, I'm not that clairvoyant. I do not relish the idea of wandering about some typhus-infected island, occupying swamp land and sand dunes. If this is what you meant in your letter by "red tape," I don't like it.

Barzun arrived, and many thanks. Glad to hear about Roger and Bard.

It looks as though I'll live through this war, but what concerns me is what will happen to me before I get out of the army.

Love,
Tony

August 14, 1945 Fort Bragg, North Carolina

[To his parents]

Dear Kids—

The war ended this evening.

I was walking past the orderly room with Rike, a friend in Anti-Tank Co. We were on our way to visit Jim Ryan, and join him in some beer at the PX. Suddenly there was a terrific shout from one of the barracks, and instantly everyone seemed to be shouting. It was like spontaneous combustion, as though everyone had heard the news simultaneously. People rushed out of the buildings and stood around shouting, shaking each others hands and patting one another on the back. Then they began to feel silly and wandered back into the barracks.

I was affected in much the same way. As soon as I heard the shouting, there was no need to ask what was going on. We'd been waiting for this for too long. The Atomic bomb, Russia's entry, the Jap proposal, our counter-proposal, the false report of acceptance, the great delay of communication, made the final announcement seem very anti-climactic. Nevertheless, I was caught with the excitement of the great crowd around me, and I went over to one of the men in my company, and shook his hand warmly. We stood grinning at one another for some time and could think of nothing to say. So I went off with Rike to find Jim.

We wandered up by the Service Club, and the band was coming down the street, playing like hell. It was followed by a huge entourage of soldiers, many of them marching in step & formation. The band was in motley uniform, apparently having left whatever they were doing to come out and blow their heads off. Rike and I joined the great throng behind them, as they marched around the central area of the camp. Ordinarily I would not have done this (nor would Rike), but we both felt extremely calm about the news and thought that perhaps if we participated in this public demonstration, the contagion of the excitement, and possibly even the profound significance of its meaning, might be caught.

But it worked the other way. The people who were shouting themselves hoarse stopped shouting, the band got tired of playing after a few numbers, and the men started to wander back to their company areas with weak, puzzled smiles on their faces. They were wondering just what it meant to them. They didn't expect to see combat in the Pacific, particularly after the events of the previous days, but they were still destined for shipment overseas and people were still packing, and would continue to pack tomorrow, and the next day.

Everything goes on quite as usual, as if it were yesterday, or two weeks, or a month ago.

All I know is I've lived through the war. This should be enough, I guess.

I don't know what to think.

Love,

Tony

[October 6?, 1945] Japan

[To his parents]

Note: Paper supplied by Japanese Society for the Propagation of International Love

Dear Kids—

Since you have heard a report of the trip in Jim's letter, I will dispense with any further description. Suffice to say it was insufferably hot in the holds at night, and it smelled like an old gymnasium. We were onboard ship for thirty days, going to Cebu in the Philippines first—and apparently by mistake. Then we went to Leyte, thence to a weakness, thence to a sadness, and by this declension, into the madness wherein he now raves, and we all do mourn for—i.e. Japan. We landed at Yokohama, disembarking from the ship at about 3 AM. We drove through the darkened city in trucks, going a short distance to the railroad station. The city, even in the darkness, seemed extremely modern, and the damage done in no way compared with the wrecked cities of Europe. We arrived at our destination at 8 AM of a bright and pleasant morning. The trip was quite interesting, especially when going through the rural "districts" in which the architecture was typically Japanese. Those buildings seem to be made essentially of bamboo, paper, a few pieces of pine, and glass. There is much light in the room, a great part of the walls being devoted to windows, and a soft diffuse light coming through the paper walls between the strips of bamboo. This use of natural light, through the use of many and large windows to opaque walls, together with the tasteful simplicity of the furnishings (which are few, at best) have a remarkably "modernistic" appearance. Le dernier cri de Yokahama, so to speak. The roofs are heavily tiled or thatched, and shrines and monuments inscribed with Japanese characters occur as frequently as pissoirs in Paris. [. . .]

Keep writing, and thanks in advance for the books, the hair tonic [booze], caviar, etc.

Love,
Li Po

October 9, 1945 Kumagaya, Japan

[To his parents]
Dear Kids—

I am translated! How beautiful upon the mountains are the feet of him who bringeth tidings of great joy. I am bound in a nutshell, but count myself king of infinite space.[16] I have been assigned to the Public Relations Office of this division. My job will be to write feature stories about the division, its personnel, and its occupation sector for American newspapers and the <u>Stars and Stripes</u>. So far I have written nothing but the enclosed limerick:

> "L'Arte Moderne"
> Un homme nomme Gaston De Gaulle
> Est un artiste fantastiquement drole;
>   Sur un jolie collage
>   Il a fait un visage
> Avec c[h]apeaux et fillets de sole.[17]

Mail has not been coming through very well because of the weather conditions. It rains here almost constantly, and most planes have been grounded. So

---

[16]Isaiah 52:7; *Hamlet* 2.2.254–255.
[17]*Modern Art*

> A man called Gaston De Gaulle
> Is a fantastically funny artist;
>   On a pretty collage
>   He made a face
> With hats and fillets of sole.

far I have gotten about seven letters—but have gotten none in the last four days.

I am living most comfortably now, in barracks, with electric lights, so there is no point in sending any necessities—just luxuries—food, drink, books etc. And by the way, if you can get any <u>cheap</u> reproductions of the following artists, please send:

Van Gogh	Picasso
Rousseau	Mattise
Chirico	Cezanne

(This represents the collective choice of the whole P.R.O. staff, a very agreeable and intelligent group of men). Don't spend much money on them since I won't be able to bring them home without damaging 'em beyond repair. We would just like to liven up an otherwise drab office.

Love,

Kandinsky

[Note on back of envelope]: Improvisation is the soul of genius.

Stanislavski

[October 18, 1945] Kumagaya, Japan

[To his parents]

Dear Kids.

Just a note to tell you to remove the bar sinister from the old escutcheon, for I am now engaged in legitimate endeavors of a most interesting nature. I've been writing stories furiously for the <u>Stars and Stripes</u>. The stories are, of course about the 97th—but the work is fascinating, the company is delightful, the conversation is intelligent, witty, provocative, ribald, and thoroughly enjoyable.

Actually, I find less time to write you now than I did while I was back in the company. We frequently work till 11 or 12 at night, and if we don't work, we just sit around and talk about Plato, the moral basis of democracy, the effect of strikes on the war effort, food, the effect of the army upon individuals, the Defenestration of Prague, the receptivity to art of different people, the lack of German intellectual advancement in the last 50 years, drink, the comparative efficiency of various forms of propaganda, sex, or intimate notes on the lives of Picasso, Koussevitsky, Isadora Duncan, Frank Harris, Berlioz, Shakespeare, Taine, Dürer, and ourselves, of course.

As you can well imagine, this is almost the first time since I've been in the army that I've had access to such a fund of sensible and entertaining talk. [...]

Your letters are finally coming through at a gratifying rate, and I continue to take immense pleasure in reading them. I have tacked most of the articles and clippings you sent me on the wall of the office beside my desk. I eagerly await the arrival of all those packages which must be on their way to me in the mail, for I stand in great need of that mosquito repellent, despite the cold weather. Send on books, the more the better—they will receive a generous audience here.

I have been into Tokyo—specifically to Radio Tokyo, where the <u>Stars and Stripes</u> are located, and to the Imperial Hotel, Frank Lloyd Wright's monstrosity [demolished in 1968] which is restricted to field grade officers only (that means majors or above). However, down in a small cavern in the cellar, there's a sort of Peons Pavilion where Enlisted Men are served a pretty decent meal at a fair price. Next door to the Peons Pavilion is the Serfs Salon, where junior grade officers may eat.

There's really nothing extraordinary about the town. It's big, dirty, sprawling, crowded, and generally unpleasant.

Thank Kathryn for her wonderful letters, especially the one from Saratoga Springs, and keep writing yourselves,

La morale de cette histoire,
C'est de boire avant de mourir.[18]

Voltaire

October 24, 1945 [Kumagaya, Japan]
[To Roger Hecht, now at Bard College, a birthday letter]
DEAR BECKMESSER

The rose withers on the stalk, the woods decay, the woods decay and fall, after many a summer dies the swan, and your birthday passes into grey oblivion. The rollicking Geburtsfest [birthday party] is over, and there you are—an old man in a rented house, being read to by a professor of Middle English. The glory has faded from your eyes, the flush of triumph from your cheeks, and all in all, you're beginning to look like Ramses the second. Death and Transfiguration. People are starting to talk, you know. They say, "how he is growing old, how his hair is growing thin." Have you taken to wearing a necktie rich but modest, asserted with a simple pin? Fie! By the foul bowels of Klopstock, fie! Look to the lady, go and catch a falling star, but for God's sake <u>do something</u>—don't just stand there with that stupid expression on your face. [. . .]

[18]The moral of this story is to drink before you die. From the traditional "Chevalier de la table ronde."

How are things getting along in the Slough of Despond? Pretty slough? What are you reading these days? How is Dupee? What is Mary McCarthy like? Have you been writing? If so, what?

WRITE.

Herzlich,[19]

Hans Sachs.

The events reported here, with great excitement, eventually did appear in Yank *but not for another month and in a much "emasculated" version, as Hecht later reported to his parents.*

October 30, 1945 [Kumagaya, Japan]

[To his parents]

Mes Chers,

[. . .] I have been having a positively fabulous time these past few days, seeing a great deal of Robie [Macauley], and engaged in covering one of the most sensational and fantastic stories to come out of this war. You will no doubt read all about it in the papers some time soon, and even see it in the movies, for there were newsreel photographers up there. However, I was there, and I think I have more background material on it than any one else except the CIC men.

It all hinges around a small resort town about 50 or 60 miles from here. The name of the town is Karuizawa. It used to be a leading summer resort for foreign diplomats and businessmen in Japan. When war came in '41, a number of neutrals evacuated to the town, and after the defeat of Germany, and the bombings of Tokyo, there was a great influx of foreigners. These were mostly Germans, who had managed to form a veritable state within a state. It was a Germany in miniature. It was divided into party sections—Kreis, Gau, Ort, Block—just like Germany. It had its own food supply, its own rationing, its own semi-Nazi organizations, its own cultural societies, its own Geheimnis Staats Polizei, its own spy network. It was extremely powerful in the orient, and most of the significant personae in this drama have been living right in this town. And I was there. I spoke to some of them, and have the background on most of them. Their stories are fascinating.

Take Paul Wenneker, for example. Full Admiral in the German Navy. Former commander of the German pocket-battleship "Deutschland." Captured the American vessel "City of Flint." Was made naval attache to German Embassy in

---

[19] Warmly

Yokahama. Used to get most of his naval information at geisha parties, where Japanese naval officers would soften under the influence of women and drink, and consequently spill the beans. Once took Hitler on a Baltic cruise. He was in charge of German U-Boat activities in the Pacific.

Then there's Joseph Meisinger. He was known as the "Butcher of Warsaw." Was connected with the Criminal Investigation Division of the Bavarian Police in Munich. Later was Dept. Chief of the Berlin Gestapo, where he had a reputation for cruelty. He was transferred to Warsaw in '39 where he became notorious for atrocities against the Poles and Jews. Came to Japan in '41 as police attaché to the German Embassy, and it is suspected that he controlled the Ambassador. It is also suspected that his real mission in Japan was to provoke war between Japan and Russia, to relieve pressure on Germany's eastern front. He was supposed to be one of the most important men under Himmler.

Or there's Karl [Gustave] Kindermann, who studied classical philology under some of the best German professors, and immediately after finishing his doctor's thesis on the use of Latin terminology in medicine, became a spy for the German Government in Russia, where he was captured, and interned for a year, and upon his release, wrote the book, In The Toils of The O.G.P.U. [1933]. Did some more spying in Russia again in '39 and after getting out of the clink again, wrote Moscow Totenhauesern. Wrote a long treatise on the cultural heritage of the Red Sea basin. He is a Jew, but his German passport is not stamped with a "J" as it usually is in such cases. Was the only Jew admitted to the Embassy in Yokahama. Was in correspondence with Rabbi Stephen S. Wise of New York, and Wiedermann of San Francisco fame. Was interested in refugee problems, Moslems, philology, and Gestapo work, which he carried on here in Japan.

I can't give you the background on them all. There's Mosaner, an Olympic ski champion, and Gestapo man. Speringer, an SS man and former official at the Dachau Concentration Camp. Hammel, a former butcher who knows 50 languages and dialects. Count Duercheim, the "Goebbels of the East," propaganda minister.

They're not all bad characters that accumulate up here, either. Dr. Joseph Rosenstock, a German Jewish refugee, and present conductor of the Tokyo Philharmonic, and a number of other estimable characters.

THE ABOVE IS STILL EXTREMELY CONFIDENTIAL, AND IT IS MOST URGENTLY REQUESTED THAT YOU KEEP THIS TO YOURSELVES ENTIRELY, WITHOUT EXCEPTIONS. I will give you the word on when to release the info as soon as I can. [. . .]

Love to all,
Esterhazy

[To Kathryn Swift]

Oh, thou Kate, thou marvelous Kate—

(I wish I had my Shakespeare here. I'd be ready with an appropriate salutation.)

I shall not apologize for not having written to you since I've been overseas. Not a word from Germany, nor Japan. Any excuse I might proffer would be much too thin to be convincing. I have finally been "driven" to writing to you out of gratitude for your thoroughly delightful letters. Don't misunderstand me. This has not been due to any particular letter which happened to coincide with a great surge of energy on my part, but rather it is the cumulative effect of those splendid missives which were continuously sent out into a silent void, with not so much as a belch in response. Nor am I so presumptuous as to think that I can make up for this infinite silence in one letter, but I have recently met some people who, I think, would interest you greatly—some of the old "transition" crowd, so to speak—and I want to tell you about them.

One chap you'd like is Dr. Joseph Rosenstock, the conductor of the Tokyo Philharmonic Symphony Orchestra, classmate of Artur Rodzinski, friend of Adolph Busch, and a delightful little man. He looks a bit like Voltaire without a wig, if you can imagine that. He has piercing blue eyes, a handsome aquiline nose, a sharp, biting sense of humor, and a profound sense of responsibility as a conductor towards his orchestra and the public. He is a German Jewish refugee, and God know what he's doing in Japan. (But then there are a lot of unusual people here.) I had tea at his house yesterday (was introduced to him by Robie), and we have become fast friends. He has invited me to come to all of his concerts in Tokyo, and to meet him backstage after the concerts are over.

An even better friend of mine is a chap named [Leo] Sirota. Magnificent pianist. Ranks, so they tell me, among the six best in the world. I must admit I've never heard of him, but I heard him play Chopin, Liszt and Glinka the other night, and insofar as I am able to discern, he is incomparable. I had tea at his house too (one drinks a lot of tea in Japan), and he played for Robie and me. He is a good friend of Rudolph Serkin, Egon Petri, and a few others whose names I've forgotten. He's giving a concert in Tokyo with Rosenstock on the 15, 16, and 17 of this month, and he also cordially invited me to come and visit him backstage.

These are only two of a most remarkable group of people now living in the beautiful summer resort of Karuizawa, here in Japan. For further information about other folks of a more insidious nature, ask the folks to show you the last letter I sent them. I told them that the story was extremely confidential, but the secrecy has been lifted [. . .].

Will write again soon,

Love,
Tony

November 23 [1945] Kumagaya, Japan

[To his parents]
Well,

I have been reading, with a modicum of interest, the various suggestions which have been made as to what should be done with the formula for the atomic bomb. Should we deposit it in a "time capsule" along with some gifted interpreters, for the future use of posterity? Should we manufacture the stuff in a diluted form, and sell it commercially as a laxative? Every crack-pot in the world has an idea about this earth-shaking problem, and even some intelligent men have bothered their brains about it.

Actually, I don't think it makes any difference what the final decision is. The bomb was discovered in the first place because the cumulative knowledge of physical science, together with its accompanying theories, made such a discovery possible. All that was needed was a man with the imagination and correlative powers to add the sum of the theories and facts; the result was inevitable. But the theories and facts are common property, inasmuch as all knowledge is common property. And if one man can deduce the formula from a common body of information, another man can do it too. An American has done it; there is nothing to prevent a Russian, or a German, from doing it again. The raw materials, in the form of fact and theory, are readily available to anybody who is able to make use of them, and all that is lacking is the mind to grasp what is already implied. America has no monopoly on such minds. They crop up all over. This is one reason why so many of the most revolutionary scientific ideas have been conceived separately and simultaneously throughout history. Calculus, quinine, the theory of evolution (I wish I had my books with me; I could give you innumerable examples) are not to be attributed to certain men with the idea that had Leibniz not lived, or had Darwin never existed, these things would never have been known. Sooner or later all these things would have been discovered. This may sound a bit like Spengler, but don't be fooled. Spengler attributes these discoveries to an omnipotent Destiny. If Napoleon had not lived, if Galileo had never been born, other men would have fulfilled their functions, because destiny decreed it. I am not trying to say anything of the sort. I am simply suggesting that if there are two apples on the left, and two apples on the right, sooner or later somebody's going to come along and, being wise, recognize the fact that there are four apples. We cannot put knowledge away in a vault; it is much more lively than any of us.

These mental peregrinations were brought on mainly by a desire to keep the weary old mind in working condition by thrusting weighty problems before it at regular intervals—about once a year. And also of course, to let you know that I'm still capable of enfeebled comments upon the world at large. And though nothing spectacular has happened for the past two or three days, which is indeed unusual, I felt like writing to you. I wrote last night, a short note attached to my mss. about Karuizawa.

Keep writing.

Love,
Tony

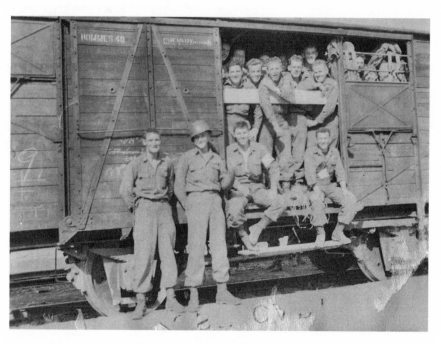

Troop train, postwar France, 1945
Courtesy of Emory University Libraries Rare Books and Manuscripts Division

November 25 [1945] Kumagaya, Japan
[To his parents]
Dear kids,

No long letter today. Nothing much going on. Just wanted to send you some photographs taken in various parts of the world. I am not in any of them. The picture of the troop train (40&8) was taken on the trip back to France after the war was over. It is offered simply as documentary evidence of the splendid travelling facilities and improvements that have been made since the last war.

The banquet scene was taken here in Japan at Thanksgiving. We had turkey, cranberry sauce, corn, fruit cake, apple pie, nuts, salad, fruit, coffee, and beer.

The post cards are of a huge Buddhist monument at Takasaki, about 30 miles away.

The photos of the Japanese garden and house were taken at Takasaki, too. It's the home of the sculptor who designed the statue on the post card. I was there, with an interpreter, of course, to get some information about the shrine for a story.

I have still not mailed the package of silk I was telling you about some time back. In the mean time another package of little items has accumulated, and I plan to send them both home very soon. One of them will contain the 75 yards of white silk I wrote you about, in addition to about 16 yards of striped, colored silk. Included in this box is the black lacquer cigarette box I mentioned in an earlier letter, and a handsome, white turtleneck sweater, which I plan to wear when I go back to college.

In the second box is a fur-lined Japanese aviators suit, which should come in handy if you ever decide to become a Japanese aviator. For aviators who have fixations about fur, I have also included a similar suit without fur. It ought to be good for groveling around the house. As a matter of fact, the jacket is rather nice.

Oh, I forgot to mention that in the first box there are some Japanese rifle sights, which we can use to spy on the neighbors.

tally ho
Chris. Marlowe

November 26 [1945] Kumagaya, Japan
[To his parents]
Well,

Went to an old whore house today. Pretty lousy looking place. The girls weren't so hot either. But I got what I was looking for.

I was looking for a piano.

I think that I may have mentioned in an earlier [letter] that I was trying to get Leo Sirota to come down to division for a recital. Well, the general approved the idea, and turned all the details over to me, and I've been searching high and low for a piano that's good enough for as excellent a musician as Sirota. The only pianos in the division area that are army property, are all spinets or uprights. However, an officer I know told me that there was a reasonably good grand piano at a particular whore house not far from here, and that's where I went this morning.

I had an interpreter with me, which solved what might otherwise have been a rather embarrassing situation. As it is, I'm sure the girls are still puzzled by our behavior. I dare say we're the first people who ever came in there, played the piano, talked to the owner, and then, without further delay, left. However, the deal was consummated. And, in passing, I think it's a rather amusing note that one of the greatest living pianists is to give a recital on a whore house piano.

Another piece of good luck. Some time ago, just for the hell of it, I started to write a radio script, satirizing the popular conception of "what we're fighting for." The little white house, and blueberry pie, etc. Well, I was just doing it for fun, and I didn't bother to finish it. It floated idly about the office for some time. In the meantime, the 97th division had gone on the air, with a weekly broadcast (every Sunday afternoon) from Radio Tokyo. The long and the short of it is that my script is to be incorporated into next Sunday's program. It's going to be typed tonight, and I'll send you a copy.

I was deluged with packages and mail today. Two parcels from Kathryn, a letter full of clippings, and two typewritten letters from you, as well as the prints, The Partisan Review, the Bard newsletter, and the Bardian which included an excellent poem by Roger. That's enough to last me for some time.

The prints are delightful. Just what I wanted. The Cezanne still life is the best reproduction, I think, and is a splendid piece. The other Cezanne, with the two figures, I was not familiar with, but I like it very much. The reproduction of the Gauguin was rather bad. The Picasso is one of my favorites, as is the Chirico, The Redon serves to bring back memories, though the color is very poor. All in all, they are wonderful, and I thank you immensely.

By the way, there's an ad in the issue of The Partisan Review you sent me for a small shop called "Books 'N Things" at 73–4th Ave. Tel. Gr. 5-8746. I pass this information along because the ad says they have volumes no. 3–4 of Verve, the magazine which had those handsome reproductions of primitive Italian paintings in one of the issues which I bought while on furlough. If you have time, I wish you'd look into it.

Love
Vincent

December 8 [1945] Kumagaya, Japan

[To Kathryn Swift]

Dear K.

(That looks sort of like Tchekov, doesn't it?)

I quote from your latest missive: "If you like my [translation of Rilke's] 'Cornet', then you must like [Amy Lowell's] 'Patterns'. . . ."

Madam, this follows not. This is most strange, a veritable non-sequitur. I am not trying to affront your predilections for the poem, particularly if it has a personal and heightened meaning for you, but I do not like it. In fact, I think the last line ("God, what are patterns for?") should be intoned with a feeling of exasperation. What for, indeed. What was Amy for? Now, there you have a question. Especially when you consider her size. As a matter of fact, her size has a lot to do with it. Gross wasn't the word. Mammoth. Gargantuan. A bloated behemoth. She lacked every physical quality of femininity—well, some of them, anyway. She must have been acutely aware that she was not "acceptable" as a woman when she started smoking cigars. The dame was frustrated. As a result, all this inhibited femininity was released in her poems. Now, I've got nothing against women, not even against Amy, whatever she was. But when she starts being so God-damned feminine all over the place, I turn to the wall. Dickinson can be feminine without becoming cloying. There is a strength and rigidity to some of her poems which balances the delicacy of feminine quality. But Amy's poems are like a Schrafft's dessert. Fudge and whipped cream, piled on top of candied fruit, and syrups, and molded into a very pinnacle of sweetness.

I am sorry you picked an Untermeyer anthology. He's an old fool with no taste, and didn't even start including Eliot in his anthologies til he was forced into it by the tremendous acclaim the poet got from all the best critics. Even now, his choices are frequently unrepresentative of a poet, and they often reflect the anthologist's bad taste. I would suggest, however, that the next time you visit chez Hecht, you borrow some books. I don't remember exactly what books we have, but I'm sure of the following: try Harmonium by Wallace Stevens. Particularly such poems as "Peter Quince at the Clavier," "Le Mononcle de mon Oncle," . . . memory fails. We also have a pamphlet of selections for Rilke's "Das Stundenbuch" with foul translations by Babette Deutsch. Eliot's Quartets. Several volumes of W.B. Yeats. Auden, et al.

Nevertheless, I eagerly look forward to the arrival of the Rilke, both original and translated versions. They are easily the finest Christmas present you could send.

Things are getting dull around here. We have descended into the maelstrom of conflicting personalities, and everyone seems to grate on everyone else. In addition, the brass is making our job doubly difficult by insisting on censoring every release from this office, and consequently cutting down our output to a mere shadow of its former self. The brightest part of my day is when the letters arrive. Yours are real gems, and I can't thank you enough.

Toujours gai

Tony

December 26 [1945] Kumagaya, Japan

[To his parents]

Dear kids,

[. . .] The usual military pall hung over Christmas again this year, but it was accentuated more than ever before by the untidy condition of the world. There may have been those who thought it ironic to celebrate the birth of the Prince of Peace in a time of war, but I think the newly-arrived peace has made the occasion much more paradoxical than it was before. When we were fighting, we were doing something which, despite its barbaric nature, was necessary to the people of the world. In a negative way, we were accomplishing something. With the peace at hand, we are rapidly losing everything which was gained in the fighting. I have written you about this before, about China, Indonesia, politics, pressure, reaction ad nauseam. Japan is still full of corruption. From men in the highest places down to the lowliest menial in the fascistic Japanese Police Force, politics and corruption are rampant. There is one particular incident which occurred this Yuletide which brings home my point very nicely. The bulk of the Japanese people, who have borne the expense of the war (I speak only of the financial expense) are for the most part very poor indeed. Besides this, the war has caused all sorts of shortages, much more severe than those in the States, particularly in housing, food, and coal. As a result, food rationing has been turned over to Japanese civil authorities, in order that the most equitable distribution of foodstuffs may be made. A few days before Christmas, it was discovered that the mother of a large and very poor family, driven to insanity by starvation, killed one of her step-children, cooked it, and fed it to her husband and children. It seems that she was not getting her due from the food rationing system, and being too poor to deal with the black market, was driven to cannibalism.

This is the story I mentioned in my last letter, referring to it simply as something big coming up. As you can see, it has its sensational angles, and will probably receive wide coverage in the states when we release it. The story should be ready in a few days.

The point, however, is this: people are starving all over the world, some in a more sensational manner than others, but they're starving nevertheless. Whether this condition can be rectified immediately I doubt very much, and some situations might even be considered beyond the realm of practical assistance, such as the feeding of entire nations. But where the starvation is the fault of political corruption, it is a sign of what by now has become altogether too clear—that in a certain and very important sense, we have ended this war in catastrophic defeat. It may seem ridiculous to you to exaggerate one incident into a "Decline of the West," but I have seen so much of this graft, corruption, and intrigue, both in and out of the army, in minor and major matters, affecting few and many, that I consider this story quite representative in many ways. [. . .]

Rien de plus.

Lots of Atomic Love,
Max Plank

December 27 [1945] Kumagaya, Japan

[To his parents]

Dear kids,

Just wrote you last night, so this will be a short note, but I just found out about a few things which I thought might interest you.

In last night's letter I mentioned the case of cannibalism which we're covering now. Well, I'm getting most of the information from a Captain Gottesman, a rather colorful gentleman from Brooklyn, who is the legal officer of the 77th Military Government Detachment. He's a very intelligent guy, has travelled all over the world, was sworn into his legal position at the Supreme Court in Washington when he was a civilian. I don't know much about his background, except that his father had something to do with the manufacture of silk in the States, but the Capt. is a good fellow, excellent company, a fine sense of humor, u.s.w.[20]

As legal officer, it is Capt. Gottesman's duty to investigate, among other things, the records and books of all large Japanese corporations within his Ken (Ken being the Japanese word for Prefecture, which is the limit of the MG [Military Government] authority for that area). In line with this work, Gottesman requested GHQ [General Head Quarters] to put out an order requiring all Japa-

[20]Und so weiter = and so on.

nese firms to show statements of ownership, etc. from before the war started, with periodic reports on all changes which would cover the entire period up to the present time. GHQ refused the request. Why they did this you may judge for yourself when you hear why the request was made.

All the Japanese industries which were involved in war production are beginning the reconversion program, just as is being done back home. For authorization they have to deal with the MG, of course, and it's usually Capt. Gottesman who takes care of them. In one particular case which he told me about, he asked the men who represented the particular corporation who had laid down the initial capital upon which the corporation had been established shortly before the war started. The Japanese replied quite simply, "The Goodyear Tire and Rubber Company." The Capt., thinking there had been some misunderstanding on the part of the Jap, rephrased his question and got the same answer. And how much of the corporation did Goodyear own? 450 out of the total 500 shares. And as the war proceeded, Goodyear bought up the other 50 shares. At the end of the war, the corporation was worth 30 million yen. So the Capt. asked, "Who owns the corporation now?" And the Jap answers, "I do." And Capt. Gottesman asked, "You mean you bought it from Goodyear for 30 million yen?" And the Jap said, "No." And Capt. asked how much he paid for it, and the Jap said "Nothing." So Gottesman asked how he could say he owned it, and the Japanese replied, "Very delicate question."

Now, Goodyear is far from the only American [corporation] which was actively involved in the Japanese war effort. Capt. Gottesman mentioned General Electric, Douglas Aircraft. Am going to try and find out more about this as soon as I can. Will let you know. If I can get documentary evidence, it would make a swell story for PM [*Picture Magazine,* a leftist New York City newspaper].

Love,

Tony

1946

January 5 [1946] Kumagaya, Japan

[To his parents]

Dear Kids,

[. . .] Got a letter from Robie [Macauley] this morning, and his parents need have no further worries about him. He's leaving for home on the 9th, that's four days from now. [. . .]

In his letter he mentioned that he had just heard from a friend of his, Peter

Taylor, a good short-story writer, who is teaching school in some place like Wilsbury Hants, Somersetshire. He's been able to get to small gatherings with T.S. Eliot and has had conversations with Gertrude in Paris. As Robie says, it makes me realize how far I've gone away from the "literary life." [...]

Love,

B. Croce

This letter was written the day after Hecht's twenty-third birthday. Hence the applicability of Milton's sonnet, "How Soon Hath Time," followed by lines stitched together, with some alteration, from Hamlet 2.2.565–578. *Milton wrote his "Hymn on the Morning of Christ's Nativity" not at nineteen but in the month he turned twenty-one.*

January 17, 1946 Kumagaya, Japan

[To his parents]

Dear Kids,

As I recall, Milton wrote a sonnet upon becoming twenty-three years old. Not only did he write a sonnet, but the damned thing has become immortal. Besides this, he'd written plenty of immortal stuff before he ever became twenty-three. Take the "Hymn on the Morning of Christ's Nativity," written, I believe, at the age of nineteen. Yet I, a dull and muddy-mettled rascal, peak like John a'dreams, unpregnant of my cause, and can write nothing, no, not for a world, upon whose property and most dear life a damn'd defeat was made. Ah, it cannot be but I am pigeon-livered, and lack the gall to make oppression bitter. For if I would, oh, what would come of it?

I have, in fact, begun a series of articles on the little faults and flaws which are barely discern[i]ble in the army system. Petty problems, of no consequence, yet it amuses me to invent banter and small talk on the subject with which I feel I am modestly acquainted. They are delicate pieces, almost fragile (commensurate with the subject), and the finicky might even call them precious. But to me they shall represent an achievement equal to a monograph on the Tasmanian business cycle; shallow on the surface, perhaps, but of great pitch and moment to the intelligent reader. [...]

Watch for the Ding an Sich,

E. Kant

January 21, 1946 Kumagaya, Japan

[To his parents]

Oh, joyful, joyful.

How beautiful upon the mountains are the feet of him who bringeth tidings of great joy. "If the present shipping schedule holds, enlisted men with 45 points or 30 months service . . . will be home or on their way home by mid-February, Col. L. B. Shaw, 8th Army G-1 announced Saturday."—Pacific Stars and Stripes, Jan 21, 1946.

That includes me. I have 31 months service, which means that I'll be among the last of the group to ship out [. . .]. Nevertheless, if I leave on the 15th of Feb. I'll be more than delighted. I hadn't expected to leave before April. [. . .]

Excitedly,
Petronius

Anthony Hecht, age 24, University of Iowa, 1947
Photograph © C. Cameron Macauley, courtesy of Cameron Macauley

THREE

Back Home and Abroad
1946–1952

A STRIKING SNAPSHOT OF HECHT IN 1947, NOW INCLUDED IN the *Wikipedia* entry for him, seems to capture the peripatetic spirit of the young poet in the years immediately following the war and leading up to the publication of his first volume of poetry, *A Summoning of Stones*, in 1954. Hecht is dressed in the casual fashion of the day: open-collar shirt, sports jacket, jeans rolled up. Hands in pockets, he rests comfortably on a trunk or footlocker, facing us but staring off into the distance, as if thinking about what? Where he has come from? Or where his next stop will be?

At the time, Hecht was briefly a student and instructor in the Iowa University Writer's Workshop. The photograph, taken by Charles, or "Chuck," Cameron Macauley, who became a celebrated photographer and filmmaker during the second half of the twentieth century, was Robie Macauley's younger brother. The photo hints at the literary circle that Hecht was drawn into immediately after the war. His army friend Robie Macauley, more than three years his senior and an aspiring fiction writer, had graduated from Kenyon in 1942 and urged Hecht to study there. At Kenyon, Hecht seriously pursued the study and writing of poetry, primarily under the tutelage of John Crowe Ransom (two poems of his would appear in the 1947 autumn issue of *The Kenyon Review*). He also took courses in Seventeenth-Century English

Poetry, Studio Art, and Moral Philosophy. This association, in turn, would lead to his meeting Allen Tate, William Empson, and young but already established poets like Robert Lowell.

Hecht's letters from this postwar period tell the story of a young man very much on the move—literally, and indeed exhaustingly so at one point for Hecht, and, in retrospect, complicated to piece together. After the year at Kenyon, Hecht spent the summer of 1947 on Cape Cod, with Robie Macauley, among others—"it's morning; I'm tight already. Beer & sunshine. All in excellent spirits," begins one postcard. Then on to Iowa for 1947–1948, in the company of Macauley and Peter and Eleanor Ross Taylor, where he would meet Flannery O'Connor and Paul Engle. Hecht's time at Iowa was also marked by his having to withdraw temporarily from school in early November. He suffered what he later described as a version of postwar traumatic stress, but he returned after Christmas to finish out the year. For the summer of 1948, he was again at Kenyon, this time affiliated with the newly founded Kenyon School of English. In the fall, he returned to New York City, where he studied informally with Allen Tate and also taught Tate's poetry workshop at New York University. In the academic year of 1949, Hecht enrolled in Columbia University's master's program in English, where he met Mark Van Doren, among other notable literary figures. (While at Columbia, he would also meet aspiring younger poets and later lifelong friends Richard Howard and John Hollander.) Hecht spent the summer of 1949 in Europe, mainly Paris, before he returned to New York to complete the degree. He then again set sail for Europe in July 1950 for what would turn out to be a two-year stay, mainly in Italy, his time abroad extended when, to his complete surprise, he was awarded the Prix de Rome at the American Academy in Rome, becoming the first Fellow in Literature. Hecht did not return home until the end of August 1952, when he assumed an instructorship at his alma mater, Bard College. In early 1954, *A Summoning of Stones* was published, dedicated to his brother Roger.

From one angle, the letters from this period tell a familiar postwar story of the itinerant American student/artist supported at home by the G.I. Bill and buoyed abroad by a robust dollar (and in Hecht's case by occasional financial help from parents and grandparents). Lowell and Richard Wilbur, both living in Europe, figure into Hecht's letters, and the traffic of familiar faces flowing through Paris, including former classmates, family friends, army acquaintances—or appearing along the remoter shores of Ischia, off Naples—makes it seem, as it must have appeared to Hecht, that he had never quite left the United States. While living in Ischia, Hecht met W. H. Auden, their paths crossing on a number of social occasions. One memorable meeting, as reported separately to both his parents and Allen Tate, gave rise to the most extended discussion of Hecht's poetry to appear in the letters from this period. Other persons in the Ischian community include Elsa and Ray Rosenthal and Anne and Irving Weiss.

From a biographical perspective, these letters describe Hecht's increasingly intellectual and emotional independence from his parents. Hecht could speak with marked frankness about the self-discipline required to improve upon his present achievements by seeking to surpass others he especially esteemed, as he notes in a letter to his parents about Robie Macauley and his family. A key phrase here is the reference to his assuming "constant and rather painful apprenticeships" (September 10, 1947). Hecht could also sharply address, or redress, his parents on old family subjects—his mother's meddling in his personal life, for instance—the most sensitive involving Roger's upbringing. The two boys were, in most regards, opposites, and yet during this period brotherly affection and a common interest in literature bound them together, as the letters reveal. Tony clearly looked out for his younger, less able sibling, indeed, wanted what he thought best for Roger: greater independence, particularly from his parents. Roger, with Tony's encouragement, wished to be more like Tony, a writer; however, in reality this only meant exchanging one form of dependence for another. Their relationship is touching and was never to be closer than during these years.

The letters from abroad, several of short-story length, reveal something else: the emergence of Hecht's narrative and descriptive powers. The war letters are largely written from depressed circumstances, both visual and psychological. But the travel letters, especially those from France and Italy, clearly delight in reporting adventurous tales and exotic sights from afar—and of chance encounters with newsworthy people along the way, such as Marlon Brando, Orson Welles, and Ernest Hemingway's son Jack. We glimpse here, too, Hecht's increasing fascination with observing the world—Paris and Venice in particular—as well as his growing appreciation for art and music. The latter interest is especially apparent in his collaborations with the distinguished composers Lukas Foss and Leo Smit, both of whom Hecht met at the American Academy in Rome. These twin interests in the arts, moreover, form important features of his verse that will continue throughout his career: from the early Audenesque "At the Frick" in *A Summoning of Stones*, which also features several musically inspired poems, to the later deeply meditated "Matisse: Blue Interior with Two Girls—1947," published in *Flight Among the Tombs* (1996), and the vocally exuberant "An Orphic Calling," which appeared in *The Darkness and the Light* (2001).

From these years of Hecht's apprenticeship, I have selected letters that not only illuminate his mental and physical itinerary but also bear directly on the composition of Hecht's first and still least known volume of poems. "Seascape with Figures," for example, is quite explicitly based on events recounted in his letter of June 25, 1949. "Samuel Sewall" seems prompted, in part, by a wig-wearing charade in Paris described in a letter of August 22, 1950. A completed version of the poem is included in a letter to Roger dated November 18, 1950. And "Alceste in the Wilderness," on its way to publication in *Poetry*, is perhaps more than amply glossed, as Hecht realized, in a letter to the editor, Karl Shapiro. A sub-story involving this first collection of verse is the long time it took to complete. As it turned out, the final version excluded a number of poems that had appeared in journals as well as a few unpublished poems tucked into letters home. There is also no poem in the volume that corresponds to the "long" poem that Hecht was trying to finish at the end of his stay at the American Academy. It is possible that the reference is to an early version of "Rites and Ceremonies." Many years later, details of the slow process of assembling this first volume, in which "each new poem was, as it were, the death of an earlier one," come to the fore in a letter of encouragement written to the poet B. H. Fairchild (June 7, 1993).

1946

October 13 [1946] Gambier, Ohio

[To his parents]

Dear kids,

[. . .] Received your letter and wire, and also a letter from Roger, which I answered immediately. He asked me for a contribution to the <u>Bard Review</u>, so I sent him the following limerick:

Observations on The Futility of Incessant
and Devoted Labor.

A saint by the name of Jerome
Translated the Biblical Tome
From Hebrew and Greek,

Which no one could speak,
To the obsolete language of Rome.

[. . .]

Love
Tony

John Crowe Ransom (1888–1974), influential poet and critic, was founder of The Kenyon Review. *Hecht wrote appreciations of his teacher in* The American Scholar 49 *(1980) and* The Wilson Quarterly 18 *(1994). C. M. Coffin was the author of a number of studies related to John Donne, including* John Donne and the New Philosophy *(1937), the study referred to by Hecht below. Philip Blair Rice (1904–1956) taught philosophy at Kenyon and was associate editor of* The Kenyon Review. *His major publication was* On the Knowledge of Good and Evil *(1955). Rice also wrote a foreword to George Santayana's* The Sense of Beauty *(1955). Hecht published an elegy on Santayana in* The Hard Hours.

Saturday [October 26, 1946] Gambier OH

[To his parents]

Dear kids,

Things are going along beautifully. I am now wearing my navy blue (formerly olive drab) shirt and trousers with a chartreuse tie. Very striking indeed. [. . .]

I have had a class in each of my subjects, the last one was just this morning, and they all look fairly promising. In my first class with Mr. Ransom, he brought up some material that had been submitted to the <u>Review,</u> and read it aloud to the class (about ten students). Then we analyzed it and tore it apart, put it back together, etc. The whole thing was highly entertaining; Ransom has a magnificent sense of humor. I have had several long conversations with him in private, and he has continued to be extremely cordial to me.

For my course, which is actually a conference, in 17th Cent. poetry, I prepared a few notes on the poetry of John Donne, and spoke for an hour and a half, almost sans interruption. My teacher, Dr. Charles Coffin, has himself written a book on the background of Donne's philosophy and was apparently quite impressed with my peroration, told me that he enjoyed the class immensely, and that he had learned a lot from my remarks.

My art class, which does not threaten to be nearly as stimulating as these others, will nevertheless be pleasant and enjoyable. We will spend six hours a week in the studio painting (I have done a preliminary sketch for a still-life) and will write a certain number of papers (which I shall try to get out of, if possible).

I am also sitting in on a philosophy class (not for credit) on the theory of value, taught by Phil Rice, and I expect that it will be very exciting.

I have made a great number of friends among the students here, and together with the ones I had met before, like Chuck Macauley, I feel fairly well established. I suspect that my prose style still betrays a certain feeling of unrest, and anxiety—however, I have not had to take any Pheno-barbitol since the first night I was here—and as a matter of fact, a few things are still hanging in the air. But on the whole, things are working out as well as they possibly could.

The cognac is gone. It was really fine stuff, and I made the mistake of offering it to one person who did not fully appreciate its merit, but drank it for the effect. Nevertheless, there was enough for me to enjoy and to offer to various discriminating friends. The Scotch Blend will probably go tomorrow, since it's Macauley's birthday. [. . .]

Love
Tony

[December 10, 1946], Gambier OH

[To his parents]

Dear Mom and Dad—

I didn't know anything about Dad's illness till the morning of the day I phoned. Your letters were held up about ten days by the coal strike. In fact, they were the first letters I'd gotten from you in several weeks. I've been very upset about it, especially since you must have thought that I wasn't even interested enough to write. I hope that Dad will be up and out of bed when I get home for Christmas.

There is hardly any news from out here. Classes are going along in a fairly monotonous way, and I have decided to ask Ransom point-blank this evening whether he's going to use my poem in the <u>Review</u>. I don't think he'll say "yes," and I'm sort of annoyed at the idea of him having kept it this long without coming to any decision. I gave it to him when I first arrived at Kenyon, and he's been holding me off ever since then.

Got a letter from Robie [Macauley], explaining about his plans to go to Switzerland this summer & wondering if I wanted to go with him. He said that you would both come over and visit us at Zurich. We could have a big party at the Dolder Hotel. I haven't answered his letter yet, but it sounds like a good idea.

On the other hand, do you remember my telling you about a graduate school in writing and criticism that Phil Rice wanted to start? He once asked Robie and me to write letters about it, during the furlough we had between Europe and Japan. Well, it seems that the school will actually begin this summer—here at Kenyon. [The Kenyon School of English actually got under way in the following summer of 1948.] Aside from its being located here, and making use of the college buildings, it will have nothing to do with Kenyon. The Rockefeller Foundation is sponsoring the whole thing. Ransom will be head of it, Lionel Trilling and F.O. Matthiessen of Harvard will be here. This is all still strictly confidential, since the Rockefeller people have not yet actually signed on the dotted line—so don't mention it to Roger, or the first thing you know it will be all over Bard and everywhere. Ransom told me not to tell anybody about it, and at the same time suggested that he'd like Robie and me to be here, possibly even as instructors. So my plans for the summer will hinge on that, and on what Robie decides about it. [. . .]

Love

Tony

1947

Tuesday [September 10, 1947]

Pine Springs Ranch, Hudsonville, Michigan

[To his parents]

Well,

Your letters (two of them) arrived this morning, for which my thanks. I was a little disappointed that you congratulated me for "spilling my guts," as though I had properly performed some bodily function. Please do not think that writing letters serves me as a watered-down kind of confession or therapy; I don't think of it as an opportunity to discourse on my woes in the hope of receiving in return the appropriate sympathy and praise. I write to you to let you know what's going on, and because the business of writing helps me to objectify and remove myself from the very stuff I'm writing about. I guess, if you like, this is a kind of therapy, but I prefer not to think of it in this way. [. . .]

For a good long time I have had the unfortunate habit of selecting someone whose achievements and intelligence (not personality, please note) I admire, and of trying to persuade myself that I am his equal. These experiences have always been painful, but in every case I have managed to come through to my own satisfaction. Whether this is merely a slow process of rationalization I have no idea, but I have convinced myself that I have advanced beyond Al Sapinsley

or Ben Snyder, for instance, both of whom at one time made my life rather un-
pleasant through my insistence on such a comparison. Please understand that
this has not been a process of emulation; I do not desire to be like them but
better than them, and it has only been through constant and rather painful ap-
prenticeships that I have been able to come forward with any degree of satis-
faction. The people I have selected to fulfill this function have not been chosen
solely upon my own admiration for their abilities, but because they have also
received the admiration and approval of other people whose opinions I respect.
This applies to Robie, for instance. No matter what I should like to think of him
I cannot discount the fact that Ransom thinks well of him, that he was offered a
full-time teaching job at $3000 while I was offered an assistantship at $360, that
he was offered the same amount by the U. of Tennessee, where he was invited
to teach any courses he wanted to teach, etc. etc. The fact that he is four or five
years older than I am does not signify. So much for this. In a week we'll leave for
Iowa, and perhaps things will change for the better. In the meantime, I manage
to lose myself completely in reading to be done for my course.

Send Roger my regards.

Love

Tony

1949

*Among the rich cast of identifiable characters in the next few letters are two of
Hecht's army friends: Al Millet, from ASTP, in 1949 attending Cranbrook Academy
of Art in Bloomfield, Michigan, and Paul Henissart, from CIC, author of* Wolves in
the City: The Death of French Algeria *(1970) and several spy novels. The "sculptor
friend" alluded to in the first letter was probably Ivan Majdrakoff, the dedicatee of
"Seascape with Figures." His wife was the artist Julia Pearl, the person addressed in
"To Julia." Paul Scott Mowrer and Edgar Ansell Mowrer were prominent, midcen-
tury news correspondents, each receiving a Pulitzer prize for reporting.*

June 25, 1949 Paris, France

[To his parents]

Dear ones:

I'm sorry to be so late about writing, but things have been absolutely hectic
since our arrival, and today, out of fatigue and a desire to let you know what's
been going on, I have turned down an invitation to attend the marriage of Er-
nest Hemingway's son, Jack (by his first marriage—Ernest's, that is—to Hadley

Richardson), to some girl from San Francisco [Byra L. "Puck" Whittlesey]. Went to a cocktail party for them the other night, given by Paul Scott Mowrer, father of Edgar Ansell Mowrer, and Jack's stepfather. Party started at 6:30 and went on till 11:30. [. . .]

The trip was superb. We had no sooner gotten over the initial excitement of getting aboard, the frantic search for Al's passport, and the perfunctory fare-wells (for which I feel very contrite), than Al discovered a sculptor friend of his from Cranbrook who was traveling over in the company of a very effeminate person named John Newberry, who, as it turned out, owns and directs the larg-est and most important art museum in Detroit. They immediately invited us forward to the first-class bar for cocktails that night, and the next night again, on which occasions Newberry produced a large jar of imported black caviar, melba toast, chopped egg whites and yolks, and sour cream, all of which set off the taste of an infinite number of martinis to fine advantage. [. . .]

To return to my sheep. [. . .] Ate like a hog. Picked up a great sunburn. Swam in the pool. Observed retreat every evening by firing off a series of martinis. We had two very rough days, which Al and I weathered with magnificent hauteur, while everyone was vomiting all around us. We were almost the only ones in the dining room for a while. [. . .] Completely floored our waiter by the amount of food we ate; had two complete breakfasts (including creamed chicken, eggs and bacon) before leaving ship at France. Stayed up all night for arrival at Le Havre, and well worth it. Came tooting in at about 4 in the morning, and it was the most beautiful sight in the world. Lights on the water, sky red in the east, blending to ultra-marine just above, very clear, stars all over the goddammed place, and then, when it got a little lighter, all the Frenchmen came out in their blue denims and berets and bicycles. [. . .]

There's much more to tell, and at present I'm at a loss to describe my general state of intoxication with Paris. Walking along the Seine or the Boulevards at night is nothing but himmlich.[1] [. . .]

Love to all,

Tony

P.S. Have gotten two of your letters. You seem to have a very confused idea of American geography. Schweitzer is going to lecture at the Goethe bicenten-nial in Colorado, whereas Ransom and Ted will be teaching at the University of Utah. These are not the same place.

[1]heavenly

[July 10, 1949] St. Guenole, Brittany, France

[To his parents]

Well,

The most extraordinary series of events has taken place since I last wrote. I finished that letter in the morning, and then started to wander around the area of St. Germain des Près, looking for a place to eat. Al, of course, after much groaning and swearing, and pledging his eternal fealty to France, and Paris in particular, had taken off for Sweden the day before. Marian had gone off on a bicycle tour of the continent with some friends, and Paul was too far away to get hold of easily, so I was feeling a bit lonely for the first time since my arrival. However, Al had departed with the understanding that Paul and I would go down to the Côte d'Azur, and wire him from there, so that in the event he didn't like Sweden, he'd come down and join us. Mulling these thoughts over, I wandered idly past a restaurant (it was about two o'clock—this is for Paula's benefit) and looked in to see if there was any room to eat. It looked fairly crowded, and just as I was about to move on, I saw a figure rise from the cavernous darkness within, flailing its arms about in an attitude of semi-recognition.

It was Tony Petrina. He was just about finishing his meal, but there was a free place beside him and I sat down and ordered. We hashed over all our old Bard friends, etc. He has just finished a dramatic version of Richard Wright's <u>Black Boy</u>, has translated it into play form, that is. He said his mother was coming to Italy in about a week or so, and he was driving down to meet her in a jeep, with his friend, whose name he mumbled, and I didn't catch, and who was sitting across the table from us, silently auditing the conversation. This friend was a hulking sort of guy, with a Charles Atlas torso, of which he was obviously proud, and wore a tight-fitting cerise T-shirt with almost no sleeves to show himself off to best advantage. His hair was rather too long, and curled up in front of the ears, like Spanish side-burns. He sat sullenly, offering only an occasional grunt, or dull remark. Tony explained that he (the friend) was on his way down to play in an Italian movie. I asked him if he'd done any movie work before, and there followed a long and embarrassed silence, and then Tony explained somewhat confusedly that this was Marlon Brando, who had the lead in <u>A Streetcar Named Desire</u>.

The tension was quickly cleared up, and we got into a very pleasant conversation, when I noticed a girl named Cici Grace, to whom I had given a carton of cigarettes to smuggle into France for me, since she was bringing in only 4 cartons herself, and the limit is 5. I went over to ask her about the cigarettes, and as soon as I came back both Tony and Marlon asked me about her. She's an extremely beautiful girl, who will be modeling for <u>Vogue</u> next month, when she comes back from Brittany with me. But I get ahead of myself. When Cici finished lunch she stopped by the table to speak to me, and Tony and Marlon both jumped to invite her to have coffee with us. She declared she had to go off to the bank, but returned in ten minutes since the bank was closed. She had coffee with us, and then Marlon suggested that she go over to the American Express Office with him if she wanted to cash her checks. Having no intention of being cut out, I said I'd go along, and Cici and I were the last two people admitted to the bus, leaving Tony and Marlon in the street, waving farewell. We cashed her checks, and then went to a nearby café for a drink, when who should come strolling down the street to join us but Marlon Brando.

However, after finishing our drinks, Cici said she wanted to see Sacré Coeur, and Marlon, having other appointments, was obliged to leave us, promising, nevertheless, that he and Tony would get in touch with me before they left for Italy. (They didn't.) Cici and I went up to Sacré Coeur by bus, and while walking around from the back saw them shooting a scene from a French movie in front of a little chapel just behind the cathedral. Then we went through the cathedral, and sat for a while in the park in front of it, watching the children play and swim in the fountain. I got her back to the American Embassy where she has some friends who were planning to take her to Brittany the next day for ten days. I had already invited her to come down to the Côte d'Azur with me when she came back, and she had agreed.

The next day I moved out of the [Hotel] d'Isly and in with Paul and Jay Sheers to their new and lavish apartment, which has two bedrooms, an incredibly large living room and drinking room, a kitchen, two bathrooms (with baths) etc. I lived there until I left Paris, paying no rent, and eating in for the most part, at a great saving to myself. I spent that day getting settled in the apartment, and at about 6 p.m. Cici phoned and said the trip had been delayed by the arrival of Secretary Snyder of the Treasury, so would I like to take her out to supper. Jay, and his girl friend, Gin, and Paul had already gotten the ingredients for supper, including steaks, so they urged me to bring Cici up to the apartment for supper, which I did. From then on I saw her as often as possible—she did finally go away on a short trip, but couldn't go to Brittany (they went to Chartres instead), for lack of time. In the meantime Paul and I inquired about prices in the south, and they were a bit too high for either of our budgets.

When she came back it was agreed we should go to Brittany together. She was quite satisfied with that arrangement, and so after a few days in Paris after her return, during which we wandered about the city, sat in the parks and made love, we went off to Brittany together by train—Paul and Gin were to follow a few days later by car. We had been directed how to get here, and two friends of Paul's, Frank and Paula Amy, were here to greet us upon arrival and had already reserved rooms for us. The place is superb. A splendid beach, no tourists at all, rooms and meals for 700 fr[ancs] per day, and the meals, except breakfast, involve about six or seven courses. Fish, langoustines, shrimp, crabs, and meat, generally veal, at about every meal.

The night before we left [Paris] Cici phoned to say that she'd just been hired by <u>Vogue</u>, and they wanted her to start the next day, but I told her I'd already gotten the tickets, so she told <u>Vogue</u> that she'd be back in August. We have really fallen in love with each other, though not deeply. She's 22, went to Smith, her full name is Gertrude Keating Grace Jr., her father is a surgeon and diagnostician, who works at times at St. John's hospital in Brooklyn, she has three sisters, one older and married, two younger, the family lives in Greenlawn Long Island, which is near Huntington.

She's very gentle and unaffected, and very feminine, dresses beautifully, and is an absolute paragon of beauty. [. . .] Have gotten a terrific sunburn, the water is cool but pleasant for swimming, we bring a bottle of wine to the beach every afternoon. There's no room for more in this letter.

Love to all,

Tony

August 6, 1949 Paris, France

[To his parents]

Et bien,

I am very much surprised that I haven't heard from any of you for some long time now, since you have my Paris address, which is to remain permanent till the time of my departure. I admit, of course, that it's been some time since I wrote myself, but, mirabile dictu, I have a legitimate excuse for once. I must begin, however, by going back to St. Guenole, and explaining that shortly after I last wrote you, the girls, Cici and Gin, decided to motor (Gin had her own car) leisurely back to Paris, hitting every watering spot where there was even so much as a sign of moisture. The girls are both inveterate tourists, both majored in art history at college, and both swoon at the sight of anything out of the 11th century, no matter what it is. Speculate ad lib. Frank and Paula Amy, and Paul and I remained. [. . .] I read lots of Proust and got incredibly sunburned, and I'm already turning pale again. I should have explained a bit earlier, perhaps, that the reason Cici left early was not to get away from me—our parting was quite tender and heart-rending—but to get back to Paris and find out about this job modeling for Vogue. (Incidentally, she began today.) To confuse the narrative sequence a little bit more, when she arrived in Paris from St. Guenole, Vogue seemed quite uncertain about their plans, and were very hedgy about what they'd pay her, finally telling her to come back the following week, when they'd be more settled. So she and Gin drove off on another sightseeing tour, this time to Luxembourg. When she came back this time, they told her they definitely wanted to use her, but they wouldn't be able to start photographing till a week later. Nothing daunted, the girls took off again like big-assed birds to do the chateau region of the Loire. By the time they had returned from the tour before this last, Paul and I were back in Paris ourselves, but properly to represent my role in this rat-race, I must return for a moment to St. Guenole. During the last week there, I felt rather weary and exhausted most of the time, but I attributed this to the effects of the sun. However, upon returning to Paris, the weariness persisted and was eventually joined by other discomforts[. . . .] One evening, just as the girls returned from stuffing themselves with culture, I realized that I had a fever of some kind, took some aspirins, and went to bed without sup-per. The next day, before leaving on another Kunstreise,[2] the girls drove me to the American Hospital in Neuilly, where, for 1500 fr[ancs], a very pleasant American doctor told me that I had infectious mononucleosis, and should take sulfadiazine . . . remain in bed for three days, and eat lightly. All of which I have done, and am now cured. [. . .]

The last I heard from you were the letters telling me I'd been accepted by Columbia. Has The Hudson Review come out with my stuff yet? Any word from Kenyon about those other poems? [. . .]

Love

Tony

August 18 [1949] Venice, Italy

[To his parents]

Dear Household:

I shall spend no time at the beginning in explaining how I happen to be here in Venice instead of in the French Alps, where, according to my last letter to you, Paul and I were planning to spend some time before coming back to Paris. I'll come back to that later. Right now it is necessary to say that Venice is beyond

---

[2]Art trip

doubt one of the most enchanting cities in the world. From the window of our room we look out upon the basin of St. Mark's, with the Doge's Palace and the famous tower, together with the entrance to the Grand Canal off to the right. Across the basin, and directly in front of us, is the Justinian Palace. We have an impeccable view of the Venetian sunset.

Coming here was the most extraordinarily lucky choice we made the whole trip, and we made our decision on the basis of a tip from an Italian journalist in Turino. The day we arrived, we saw a vast and magnificent exhibit of the paintings of Giovanni Bellini in the Doge's Palace. Danny [Ransohoff] would give both arms and his mother to see it; not only to see it, but to be here. He would be captivated by the idea of an American destroyer tied right up at the sidewalk just a few hundred yards from our hotel. The basin is very deep so that even heavy liners can come right into the midst of town. But most of the boats one sees are the traditional gondolas, and beautifully polished sailboats and motor boats. We have done very little sight seeing, in fact, none, save the Bellini exhibit and a visit to the famous Verrocchio equestrian statue, and the worst part of it all is that we must leave tomorrow, after having been here only a week. But owing to Paul's limited financial resources, and the fact that I am supposed to meet Al in Paris in a few days, we leave tomorrow morning on the Orient-Simplon Express, which will get us into Paris, by way of Switzerland, on the following morning.

However, despite this rush the time has been well spent. We have eaten well: good Italian cheeses and wine, wonderful fruit, and pastry that far surpasses the French. And instead of sight-seeing as such, we have wandered about town, down little side streets and over lovely little bridges, as well as having taken several boat trips up and down the Grand Canal, or having sat at a café on its bank on a warm evening, drinking Tom Collins' in full view of the Rialto. We have met an Italian aviator who is stationed here, and speaks excellent French, and with whom we have spent as much time as possible. Yesterday we had lunch with him at the airport just at the moment that Paul Hoffman arrived by plane to confer with [Italian] Premier [Alcide] De Gasperi.

The town is swarming with celebrities just now, since the International Motion Picture Film Festival is taking place here this month. We went to see one of the German entries the other night, Madchen Hinter Gittern (fairly good, but not extraordinary), and the next day, walking along the Lido, we saw the very attractive girl who played the lead, sitting at a café. Orson Welles is in town, though not for the festival, but to make a movie of Othello, and is to be seen about with a huge and well tonsured beard. But most extraordinary of all, yesterday, as Paul and I were on our way to buy our railroad tickets back to Paris, walking along towards the Piazza San Marco, who should go by in the opposite direction but Tony Petrina. We had a coffee with him, and it appears that he left Marlon Brando somewhere in France, went down to the Côte d'Azur and sold his jeep, and then came to Venice to meet his mother[. . . .]

I have really not told you enough about Venice to make clear how thoroughly delighted I am by it. Whenever I come to Europe again I am determined to come here. It is the only European city I have ever been in, besides Paris, that has a distinctive and totally individual character and atmosphere all of its own, and in some ways, though certainly not in all, it is more charming. Paris has a heavy, sometimes even lugubrious quality to it; the buildings are consistently grey, and all the principal landmarks are massive in their impressiveness—places like The Louvre, the Opera, even Notre Dame. Venice is full of color, and unlike Paris, is not especially beautiful at night, except the lights along St. Marks' basin, and perhaps the Piazza. But the buildings are all in delicate pastel colors, deep grape reds, olive yellows, and even the least imposing of them has a charm and loveliness. And the large palaces, like the Doge's, are light in feeling and color, being made for the most part of Greek and Italian marble, sometimes streaked, and sometimes of white porphyry. There is a greater variety of architectural style, including Byzantine (as in St. Marks' Cathedral), Romanesque, Moorish, Gothic and Baroque. Paris inclines to be more grandiose, its most impressive sights being the great vistas of avenues and boulevards, the monumental arches, buildings and churches with parks before them, etc. There are no real vistas in Venice. Both the streets and canals are devious, and therefore, because one sees much less of it at a glance, it has a much more intimate feeling. I am sorry to have made all these comparisons to the detriment of Paris, lest it give you the impression that I don't like it there. That is hardly the case, as you must have guessed from my earlier letters. Mais Venise est quelque chôse d'autre.[3] The effect of the masts of the sailboats tied up to the quays in the evening with the sunset behind them is quite beyond anything [J. M. W.] Turner was able to arrive at. One more comparison with Paris is necessary. Paris for all its beauty, has some very regrettable sections, whereas Venice, even in its most remote and secretive parts, all of which, it seems to me, we must have walked through at one time or another, is never quite undistinguished. One evening, as we were walking home to supper by way of the Piazza, an orchestra at one of the chic cafes in that area was playing Eine kleine Nachtmusik. The effect was indescribable. Even in Paris

[3]But Venice is really something else.

one cannot stand in the most beautiful part of town with a view of the sea at sunset, and listen to Mozart. [. . .]

Love

Tony

Hecht's reference to the "test" family below is to August Von Wassermann, who discovered the early test for the detection of syphilis still in use today.

September 1 [1949] Paris, France

[To his parents]

Kinderlein:

When Paul [Henissart] and I returned to Paris, none of the people we knew and expected to see was here. Jay Sheers, his girl friend, Gin, and Cici and a few other people had gone off to Spain to see some bull-fights and a fiesta of some kind. [. . .] Marian Spearman had not returned from her bicycle tour of 77 (count 'em, 77) different countries. Etc., etc. So Paul and I spent most of our time together. One afternoon, [. . .] we were sitting at Weber's café and restaurant, thinking about Marcel Proust, who mentions the place in "Within a Budding Grove" [from *Remembrance of Things Past*]. We were both lost in thought when who should present herself but Gloria Wasserman of the test family [. . .]. She was just driving by in a bus and happened to see me from the window. We had some beers together, [. . .] went to the Gauguin show, and after supper went to a splendid Bach concert, which included the 4th Brandenburg concerto, the concerto for two violins and orchestra, the concerto for one violin and orchestra, the suite in B and a chorale and Fugue for orchestra in B minor.

The next day she came around to the d'Isly to get me, because she wanted to go shopping for prints, and I had expressed the intention of picking up a few as presents before I left Paris. So we went around to a little art shop that had been recommended to me, and started looking through portfolio after portfolio of etchings, lithographs, woodcuts, dry-points, and watercolors of a tremendous and catholic variety of artists. [. . .] When we finished we were too exhausted to make objective judgments, so we decided to come back again in a few days.

The next day Gloria was busy, and nothing much transpired, except that I bumped into Marlon Brando on the street. I told him I had just seen Tony Petrina in Venice, and asked him what had become of his plans to go down there and do an Italian movie. He said that he had been receiving all sorts of tantalizing offers of jobs in the States, and since the Italian movie people were not able to pay him much, and were ill-organized, and didn't know when they'd start shooting, he was planning to fly back to the States in a few days. The next day Gloria came around and we went back to the art shop. This time I was able to narrow things down to three prints—2 Rouaults and a Braque. The Braque was an original signed wood-cut in three colors, limited to 50 copies, of which I had the 40th. The Rouaults were black and white, unnumbered and unsigned. The main thing, however, was that the whole thing came to 50,000 francs, or about $140. [. . .]

Love to all,
Tony

1950

Karl Shapiro (1913–2000), poet and essayist, was the editor of Poetry *magazine from 1948 to 1950. The poem referred to below, "Alceste in the Wilderness," appeared in the magazine's September 1950 issue, and was later included in* A Summoning of Stones.

June 19, 1950 New York NY

Dear Mr. Shapiro:

Thanks very much for your note. I'm taking advantage of the invitation to send the poem back with an "explanation"—which is not meant to be a justification of obscurity. If you think the poem doesn't stand up without the help of this appendix, you might either use the following as a note or else disregard the whole thing. I will send along some other work when I get it done.

The poem is based on Molière's <u>The Misanthrope</u>, wherein, you may recall, Alceste, the protagonist, cannot reconcile the forms and morals of society with his own notion of what is honest and real, and he goes into voluntary exile at the end of the play. He leaves behind him the girl he loves, Célimène (to whom the poem refers only through pronouns: her underthings, her laces—because her presence is recalled to him only vaguely by the agency of the pastel tones of the snuff-box, his only souvenir of life in society), and it is likely that Philinte, formerly his best friend, will become his most important rival for Célimène's affections after Alceste leaves. So much for the characters. The point of the thing would be something like this: having renounced the "artificial" ways and convictions of society, Alceste finds himself nevertheless unable to assimilate reality simply by stepping into its midst; it is too full of unaccountable violences. "He could distill no essence out of this," as opposed, for example, to Samson, who in a similar situation (when he saw the lion's carcass full of bees and honey) came up with an observation about sweetness rising out of strength, which he put to his fiancée's family in the form of a puzzle. The point here, I should think, would be that sweetness is due to come out of Samson's strength when, at the end of his life, he works God's Will. In my poem, the monkey is a symbol of lust, as the lion was of strength, and Alceste's difficulty is that he does not understand how sweetness might issue from this, and is appalled to see them instantaneously linked. Though the heat and vague memories of Célimène arouse lust in him, he prefers to think that the monkey looks like Philinte, his present rival, rather than like the girl or himself, who would suit the occasion equally well. Unable as he is, then, to assimilate reality in its rough state, he is presented with the alternative of accepting it at the "aesthetic distance" of a pastoral version, such as the design of Daphnis represents on his snuff-box. A pastoral version of nature is of course a partial one, an "artificial" one, and is particularly favored in the courtly society which Alceste has just renounced. It is, if you please, what Eliot and Tate might call a "lower mythology," very low, perhaps, but a mythology in that it serves to reconcile human beings to reality and nature. If it is artificial, it is no more so than the society that accepts it, and without its help, or the help of a "higher mythology" no essence is likely to be distilled. This is why Alceste goes back. There is a deliberate ambiguity in the line, "In the pale shade of France's foremost daughter," which is not too important, but I might as well throw it in while I'm at it. If shade is read as tint or color the line would refer to Célimène, who might well be France's foremost daughter in the estimation of Alceste, and who is always recalled to him in terms of tints and colors (as in the second stanza about the snuff-box). But if shade is read as ghost, it cannot refer to Célimène, who is still alive as far as this fiction is concerned, but refers to the more objective notion of France's foremost daughter, Joan of Arc. Not only is she France's patron saint (if there can be a feminine patron saint) but she represents a purity and sweetness that Alceste misses in his present situation, and she is able to reconcile the violences of reality at the remove, this time, of a "higher mythology." This is not likely to occur to Alceste, who, I take it, is not a religious man, but it might occur to the reader. The pun is really not very important, and I'm afraid I've labored it too much.

I'm embarrassed at having gone on at such length about my poem, for I suspect that a poem should not need this much exegesis on the poet's part, at least. The main difficulty might be resolved, perhaps, by a note to the effect that Alceste, Philinte, and the nameless "she" are persons in the Molière comedy, and that Daphnis is merely a pastoral swain appearing in the design of Alceste's snuff-box. But I cannot remember that any poem appearing in <u>Poetry</u> has ever needed notes before (except "The Waste Land") and it may well be an important weakness in this one.

Let me thank you again for your interest in my work. I hope to send you more in the future, but I'd be glad to know what you think of the enclosed.

Yours,

Anthony Hecht

Polly and Oscar Williams were friends from Kenyon, the latter not to be confused with his namesake, the anthologist Oscar Williams, mentioned in the following letter, who was to include several Hecht poems in his New Pocket Anthology of American Poetry from Colonial Days to the Present *(1955). Paul Radin was the younger brother of Max Radin, the author of the 1916 work* The Jews among the Greeks and Romans, *cited in Hecht's letter below of November 1951.*

August 22, 1950 Amsterdam, Holland

[To his parents]

Ha, there—

[. . .] I was able to lead a relatively tranquil life in Paris, and to see a lot of my old friends. One of them was Paul Radin and his wife, for whom Polly and Oscar and I prepared a rather spectacular welcome to Paris. We rode in the Metro from the Pantheon, which is near Oscar's home, to the Gare St. Lazare, immaculately clothed, clean white shirts, bow ties, and all necessary finery, including gloves. However Oscar and I were both wearing wigs.

Oscar had one which looked sort of like Henry V's hair, from the movie of the same name, and I had one with a bald pate, and blond hair around the edges down to my shoulders. Oscar carried a copy of <u>Pravda</u> [the official communist newspaper of the Soviet Union] and I carried the complete works of Molière. We created quite a stir in the subway and at the station. Mothers could not drag their children from the sight of us. When we got to the station we had to wait about twenty minutes for the train, and were a source of almost unendurable curiosity to the general plebs. Paul was delighted, however, and we saw him several times in Paris. [. . .]

What news of <u>Furioso</u> and New Directions? Let me hear from you and I will write again in a few days.

Love to all,

Tony

Richard Wilbur (1921–), a longtime friend of Hecht's, is a poet and translator. The poems in Poetry *to which Wilbur refers are "Alceste in the Wilderness" and "To Phyllis." The latter appears without title as the final section of "Songs for the Air or Several Attitudes about Breathing" in* A Summoning of Stones.

November 15, 1950 Forio d'Ischia, Italy

Dear Dick:

Forgive the long delay in answering your kind note, which was forwarded to me here in Ischia, along with a copy of <u>Poetry</u>. It was good of you to write, and I am very happy that you should have liked the poems. I was rather pleased with them myself, but in their present context, coming, as they do, immediately after yours, they do not show to their best advantage. I would be sorry if this should seem merely the polite thing to say, since it comes in answer to your spontaneous compliments, but I confess to being exceptionally lazy, and have, up till now, been able to win out over the occasional temptation to write to someone when I am especially delighted with his work. Feeling somewhat guilty for not having taken the initiative myself, I can only disregard the fact that compliments returned are suspect, or poor form, or mildly contemptible, or whatever they are, and tell you quite sincerely how much I admired your poems in <u>Poetry</u>, particularly "Castles and Distances" and "Sensible Emptiness." Both of these seem to me extraordinarily fine.

I have been in Europe since spring, mostly in Paris and Amsterdam, the latter being a very charming city, but having more dog turds on its streets and sidewalks than any other place I have ever been to. The city was redeemed largely by its people, who are very agreeable, its good cigars and gin. Have come down here to Ischia for the winter, hoping to work hard and get a book of poems finished by spring. Ischia, you may know, is a little island just outside the bay of Naples and north of Capri. During the summer a bizarre little "literary" group, including Auden and Truman Capote, has its headquarters here, but these have all fled to the limelight somewhere, which is just as well. It is sort of primitive but pleasant here; the weather is rather raw just now, but winter ends in February. Pomegranates, figs, dates, tremendous quantities of grapes (very good local wine), good cheeses, and tiny, brilliantly red tomatoes, the size of ping-pong balls. Lots of olive and palm trees, flowers, especially some strange vine with a violent purple blossom, are still in bloom. We make our own vodka by mixing equal amounts of straight alcohol and water, passing this through powdered charcoal several times to remove impurities, and adding a bit of sugar and lemon rind for flavor. Extremely potent stuff. Living is very cheap here, and there is really nothing to do but eat, work, sleep, and read. I plan to return to the States in spring, unless a war should crop up, and I hope to get a chance to see you again under less poisonous circumstances than that binge at Oscar Williams'. Please get in touch with me if you should come to New York,

With best wishes,
Tony Hecht

1951

January 18 or 19 or something [1951]
Forio d'Ischia, Italy

[To Roger Hecht]

Dear Roger:

You have a right to be surprised at the arrival of this letter so fast upon the heels of the last one, but don't jump to the conclusion that I have decided to reform my character and write home every few days. Nothing of the sort. The fact is that I have begun a poem which looks as though it might turn out pretty well, but being without books here (or at least without the particular book I want), I have to ask you to copy the necessary information and ship it off to me in a letter as soon as possible. What I want is a little anecdote in Vasari's "Life of Michelangelo." It's the one in which some subaltern or menial in the Vatican takes a strong objection to the nudity of all the figures in The Last Judgment, and Mike, in a fit of righteous indignation, immediately paints his portrait in among the damned in Hell. The poor blister goes to the Pope to complain, but the Pope, who is a witty old bastard, remarks (in Latin): "If Michelangelo put you in Hell, all the spiritual forces of the Church are not enough to get you out," or words to that effect. Now what I would like to have is an accurate account of the incident, including the Pope's incisive comment in the original. I'm sorry to give you all this trouble, but I hope it will be worth your labor and my patience—since it will be some time before I get your reply, and I don't want to do any further work till I have all the material assembled. Here is what I've done so far; the first stanza [of "To Julia" is quoted].

Sort of Yeatsean, I suppose, but what the hell. The painting ["Young Woman with a Pink," now attributed to Hans Memling and described in the stanza] is in the Bache Collection in the Met in the same room with the two Holbein portraits. The woman is dressed in dark red, and I'm not sure that she's actually wimpled. In addition, I invented the landscape through the window, but then I suppose Memling did too. [...]

Let me know all the latest poop, and please send that stuff from Vasari off as soon as possible.

Thine,
George Selwyn

In 1951, Hecht was selected by the American Academy of Arts and Letters to be the first Fellow in Literature at the American Academy in Rome. His twelve-month residence began in October 1951. Allen Tate (1899–1979), poet and critic, was the generous and influential mentor to a number of important poets, including Robert Lowell, Randall Jarrell, and John Berryman.

April 3, 1951 Forio d'Ischia, Italy

Dear Mr. Tate:

I have just gotten a letter from Roger, telling me that I've been awarded, by the American Academy of Arts and Letters, a grant to stay in Rome for a year to write poetry and represent American writers at the American Academy in Rome. I am writing to offer you my happiest and most profound thanks for the part you played in my nomination and election, to tell you that I am deeply conscious of the confidence you have placed in me, and that I hope to deserve it. I have not yet received official notification from the committee, but I have sent Roger, as requested, a wire stating my joyful and grateful acceptance of the award.

I fear these are very poor thanks: I'm at a loss to know what to say. The first notice I had of this came in the form of two telegrams from home; one from my mother, composed of obscure and hysterical congratulations, and the other from Roger, which was fairly informative, but mystified me by stating that I had "won a poetry prize," although I hadn't entered any competition, and I was certain that my family wouldn't undertake to enter my work in something of that sort without my authority. The wires arrived on the 31st of March, and a thoughtful friend suggested that the whole thing might be an ill-timed April Fool's joke. This struck me as a remarkably brutal observation, which I dismissed, but not without a certain uneasiness. I was sure that my family would never play a joke of that sort, and I thought I could detect, amid the obscurity and hysteria of my mother's wire, a genuinely maternal note. I gathered that she was very proud of me. All this was substantiated by Roger's letter, which gave a very lucid account of the conditions of the award, and of his several conversations with you about it. It has made me inexpressibly happy, and I can only clumsily repeat how deep is my sense of satisfaction and gratitude.

Most sincerely,

Tony

April 26, 1951 Florence, Italy

[To his parents]

Dear old Omnes:—

This will be just a note—to keep in touch with you—and let you know why you haven't heard from me recently. Up till about 4 days ago I still had not heard from the committee officially, though I had gotten a very kind letter of confirmation from Allen Tate. Then a telegram arrived from someone named [Laurance] Roberts, sent from Rome, and inviting me to come there to see him concerning the appointment to the Academy. I came up with some friends of mine from Ischia, and we spent about 3 days in Rome. Roberts, it turned out, knew very little more than I did about the whole business, since this is the first time the appointment has been made for poetry. He did tell me about living conditions, etc., and said that I did not have to stay at the Academy, though there were definite economic advantages in doing so.

The Academy is located in an unbelievably sumptuous palace in one of the most beautiful parts of Rome, called the Geniculam [Janiculum] (or that's the way it sounds, anyway). It is on the same bank of the Tiber as St. Peter's and located among beautiful parks that are said to be full of nightingales at night. [. . .]

While in Rome we got in as much sight-seeing as we could bear—including St. Peter's, the Roman Forum, the Colisseum, the Marcellus Theater, St. Clement's (where there are some magnificent Masaccios, including the "Expulsion of Adam and Eve from the Garden of Eden" [Hecht is probably fusing here recollections of the Masaccios from the Brancacci Chapel in Florence]) and an untold number of churches. Then we came to Florence the day before yesterday, and have been sight-seeing ever since we got here, with time out one evening to visit Robert Lowell and his wife, Elizabeth Hardwick. (I am going to see them again this evening. They are leaving Florence next week, where they have been living since October, for a short trip to Greece and Turkey, and then are going to Paris to meet Robie and Anne Macauley, who are coming over for 6 weeks this summer. Robie has been teaching at North Carolina.) In Florence, so far, we have seen the Uffizi and Pitti Palaces, the Palazzo Vecchio, a great number of churches, most of them magnificent, and from where I am sitting now, at a café on the south side of the Piazza of the Republic, I can see the top of the Giotto tower, done in white, pink, and dark blue-green marble. I am sitting at a marble-topped table, writing and drinking Martell cognac, and feeling quite pleased about things in general. My friends left yesterday to go to Venice for a few days, and they will pick me up on their way back.

I enclose a photo "con barba." It's not a very good one, so I shall send some others—I am having a lot taken to immortalize the Thing, because I think I shall cut it off when I get back to Ischia. (You may be interested to know that there was no surprise or object[ion] to it on the part of Roberts). Met Auden in Ischia, and was invited up for drinks with some friends. He seemed very nice—I was surprised. I will write a fuller, more detailed letter when I get back to the machine.

Love to all,

Tony

June 5, 1951 Forio d'Ischia, Italy

[To his parents]

Dear old Omnes:

Roger arrived safe and sound the day before yesterday. He was in wonderful spirits. While we were getting his bags through customs, all sorts of people he'd met during the trip over came up to say goodbye to him and wish him a pleasant stay in Italy. I was really delighted to see him again. He'd picked up a fine sunburn on the way over, and was very excited and happy about being here. We got finished at the dock at 8:30 a.m. and by 9:30 we were on our way to Ischia. We got to the house around noon, had lunch, sat around and talked for a while, and went swimming in the afternoon. For supper, I prepared my unparalleled spaghetti dish, (a friend, Elsa Rosenthal, came up to have dinner with us), and last night I made dolma. So you can see that I'm letting Roger have the works. Last night Elsa was supposed to take us up to Auden's for cocktails, but the weather was bad and she didn't want to come all the way into town, so perhaps we'll go tonight or the next night. The weather has been sort of gloomy the last two days (though, happily, it was splendid the day Roger arrived) and we had a little rain yesterday and today, but it ought to clear up soon. [. . .]

Love,

Asst. Pope

Although the two letters recounting Hecht's meeting with Auden repeat some of the same information, there are enough differences to warrant including both. Raymond

Rosenthal (1915–1995), essayist, literary critic, and translator, lived in Italy in the 1950s. "Thekie," Thekla Clark, was a family friend and eventual author of the 1996 Wystan and Chester: A Personal Memoir of W. H. Auden, *in which Hecht makes a cameo appearance.*

October 4, 1951 American Academy Rome, Italy

Dear Parents:

Well, I'm here. Ray Rosenthal made the trip with me, as had been planned, and as Thekie told you. He wanted to come up anyway, for his own reasons: he's writing an article on Roman archeology for <u>The New Yorker</u>. The whole trip was made without any difficulty; even the cat caused no particular trouble (she lives in my rooms, and I take her for a walk in the garden every day), although she was pretty scared by the trip, and by being carried in a box the whole way. We left Ischia at 5 in the morning, spent some time in Naples, where Ray had some chores to do, and took the train for Rome at 2 in the afternoon, arriving at the Academy at about 5:30. There was nobody here to greet us, Mr. Roberts, the director, and his staff having gone down to Naples the same day to greet the new Fellows arriving on the boat from America. They just got here last night and I have really not met anyone much yet.

I have two large rooms, a bedroom and study, that look out on a beautiful courtyard designed like a cloister, with a garden designed around four beautiful and immense cypress trees which stand at the four corners of a pool, fed by a lazy fountain, and sustaining an immense goldfish. The furnishings are practical, though not especially beautiful: there are two very comfortable beds, one of which is being used by Ray, and it will be removed after he leaves, two large <u>armoires</u>, a large bureau, table, bed-table, fine old-fashioned academic desk right out of an American university professor's nightmare, three arm-chairs, two ordinary chairs, two lamps in the bedroom, a desk-lamp, and a large book-case. The walls are completely bare, and are painted white, so that although the rooms are very bright most of the day, they have a certain chill and monastic cast to them. I hope to get some reproductions to put up in order to relieve the asceticism of the place a bit. [. . .]

Let me tell you about my interview with Auden. It lasted two and a half hours, and he went over each one of my poems very carefully with me. It was a slightly tense business, as I had anticipated, because he was naturally concerned that I shouldn't take offense at any critical comment he made, and at the same time he wanted to be as honest and scrupulous as he could be. I took no offense at anything, of course, but when I tried to defend certain things I had done, he behaved as if he thought I resented his criticism, and he would modify his position and qualify his comments into oblivion. He told me he liked the poems very much, though I don't know what that really means, since I think he would have said that in any case, providing he didn't actually dislike them. Some of his comments about details were very apt and helpful, but he has a totally different way of conceiving a poem from the way I have, and he feels that I've been too much influenced by Ransom and Tate not in style but in theory. He feels that details are an ornamental embellishment to verse and should never be allowed to distract the reader's attention from the main line of discourse, whereas I believe that the details should be made to subsume, to contain, to embody, to incarnate the point and meaning of the poem. In a way, I think we're working towards the same goal from opposite directions, but my way is better suited to me than his. He said of the "Aubade" for example (the one coming out in <u>Kenyon</u>) that there was too much detail, that the poem could have been written in the same number of stanzas, but with each stanza of four lines instead of ten. He liked best of all the poem I sent to <u>Poetry</u> called "La Condition Botanique." And he told Ray and Elsa Rosenthal the next day, that he thought my poetry was better than most of the younger poets, specifically Wilbur's and Shapiro's—though, I don't see how Shapiro gets into the "younger" category any more. You must not misunderstand me; the whole interview was carried on in the most cordial terms; it's just that there was a difference of opinion on some points which we sensed more strongly than we declared. And now, upon reflection, I feel that there's much in Auden's point of view that's valuable; which is what I mean when I say that we are working towards the same goal from opposite directions. And I think he may be right most of all in saying (as he said to the Rosenthals but not to me) that my verse was perhaps too formal—not in the metrical sense, but in being somewhat impersonal in tone, disengaged from the central emotions of the poems. This is mainly what he has against Ransom and Tate, and with many qualifications, he's right. In any case, it has given me something to think about, and that's a good thing. [. . .]

Love,
Tony

P.S. Any word from Oscar Williams about any further anthologies?

October 16, 1951 American Academy Rome, Italy

[To Allen Tate]

Dear Mr. Tate:

[. . .] Perhaps you may remember a rather long poem of mine that Roger showed you last spring, which started out about a Memling painting. Well, Auden remarked that the stories of the Michelangelo incident (about painting his critic's face into Hell), and the business about the Defenestration of Prague were both so familiar as to require only casual reference or allusion in order to recall the whole story, whereas I had devoted an eighteen line stanza to each one. The point here was a little different, though, because it had to do with what might properly be expected of a reader, and tied in with a point he raised concerning an item in another poem called "La Condition Botanique," which should be out shortly in Poetry. There is a reference in this last poem to Simeon Pyrites as the patron saint of Fool's Paradise. Auden recognized the play on Stylites, of course, and knew, in addition, that pyrites was iron disulphide, but could not see what bearing that had on the poem, whereas he apparently didn't know, what I might have expected, that pyrites is fool's gold. What's more, it seems less demanding on the reader to ask him to look up pyrites in the dictionary, where he will immediately come across the familiar nickname, than to ask him to read through the life of Michelangelo for the details of this little incident, which Vasari records, but others may not have bothered with; or to read through a history of the Holy Roman Empire for an account of the defenestration, which I don't believe is even mentioned in the Encyclopedia. But more important than all this is the fact that it shouldn't really make any difference how familiar the story is. The botanical poem, which was the lightest of the group I showed him, he liked the best. Of two poems that had appeared some while back in Kenyon, he said nothing about "Hallowe'en" and remarked about "Springtime," a little translation from Charles of Orléans, that I should make sure I have the archaic spelling right, because it's the sort of thing that scholars will jump on me for. After going over all the poems one by one, (except "Hallowe'en"), he repeated his comment about the danger of allowing detail to distract the reader's attention from the poems argument or topic. By way of example, he quoted these lines of Yeats, from "A Prayer For My Daughter":

"I have walked and prayed for this young child an hour . . ." and went on to ask, "Why an hour? Why not twenty minutes or forty-six?" I think I said something about the use of a conventional language, and the way it gives the feeling of a distinct, and eventually an individual voice. But he stuck to his point, and felt that "an hour" was just stuck in to fill out the line, or rhyme, or something. Anyway, when I objected, he dropped the point, and turned to something else. It was only very much later that I recalled his mentioning very favorably Wyatt's "Rememberance" ["They flee from me"] and wondered how he would justify, "Thanked be fortune it hath been otherwise / Twenty times better." [. . .]

I want again to send you my most sincere and grateful thanks for your part in my nomination and election to this Fellowship. I'm afraid that when I wrote you saying that my first reaction to the news that I had won was that the whole thing might be a joke, you perhaps thought I was not taking the prize as seriously as it deserved to be taken. Let me assure you that I meant to express only incredulity; I have never had such a complete and happy surprise in my life. And I feel very grateful.

> With sincere good wishes,
> Tony

> November 1951 American Academy, Rome, Italy

Dear Parents:
[. . .] I am going back to Forio for Thanksgiving, having received a special invitation to partake of turkey, pumpkin pie, chestnut dressing, etc., with the Rosenthals, the Weisses, and other friends of mine down there. As for work, the songs (seven in all) that I have been writing with Leo Smit are all done, and most of the music has been written. I think they're wonderful, and can't wait to hear them performed. The scoring calls for four mixed voices, ten instrumentalists (winds and strings). I have finished the first part of the long poem, which will probably have three more parts (at least three more) when finished. I am working on it slowly since it's an entirely new kind of thing for me, and if it comes off, should be quite fine. In the mean time I am also working on smaller poems, began one the other day, and have been doing a lot of reading: Philo, Josephus, Livy, Suetonius, some Roman archeology, Pound's letters, Richard Wilbur's second book of poems (very good), Max Radin (Paul's brother) on the Jews among the Greeks and Romans, and some German poetry. (I think I may try some translations of some early things: Walther von der Vogelweide, or something like that. By the way, you could really do me a great favor, which I would appreciate very much. Would you copy out and send me a poem of Ronsard's called "Contre Denise, Sorcière," which you will find in my library in a little anthology of French poetry edited by André Gide, and published by

Pantheon. I have wanted to try doing that one for some time, and they don't have a copy of it here.)[. . .]⁴

Love,
Tony

1952

[To Allen Tate]

Dear Mr. Tate:

[. . .] At last I think I have got enough for a book. It's about time, I suppose, but I'm rather glad I've taken this long. The book will represent quite a variety of style and development, and if this is good for nothing else, it may keep me from being "typed" as a poet with a specialized talent, and who must be expected to fail if he tries anything outside his own little province. I think, or at least I hope that the book may come to an impressive total, and I feel quite satisfied with at least a few of the poems. [. . .]

I will be back in the States in October, when I plan to get the mss. together, make all the final revisions, and show it to you, if I may, before sending it to a publisher. And this is something else I'd like to ask you about: we spoke about publishers once in New York, and I told you about the agreement I had with Macmillan to let them have first look at the poems. [. . .] In any case, I know that there are several other houses that are interested (I had a letter from Knopf this summer, and Random House; New Directions and some others had gotten in touch with me previously), so there will be no trouble finding a publisher. [. . .] I should like very much to know what you think of all this, and what suggestions you care to make. With best regards and good wishes for a very happy New Year.

Sincerely,
Tony

July 1, 1952 American Academy, Rome, Italy

Dear Parents:

Forgive my not writing for so long, but I've been working hard. Just finished a new, and fairly long (150 lines) poem. It's not the Big one; that still has to be finished, and I want to add a couple of shorter ones before I leave here. So

---

⁴"Invective against Denise, a Witch," eventually appeared in *The Venetian Vespers*.

I'll be pretty busy for the rest of the summer. The Greek trip is off, for economy reasons. A letter from Bard informs me that they would like me to offer (1) Ambiguity and Symbolism, (2) a writers' workshop in prose and poetry, (3) an introductory course to literary forms, i.e., novel, drama, poem, short-story, etc., using whatever examples I like. So that gives me as much latitude as I could ask for. Got a letter from that Poetry Awards outfit, whose previous message you forwarded to me. As I think I wrote you before, I revised "Aubade" and changed its title [to "A Deep Breath at Dawn"] before sending it to them. They wrote back, explaining the complications that would arise if they permitted everyone to revise his work after it had been judged (all very understandable) but then went on to say, "Furthermore, if your poem were to be reconsidered, some of the Editors might score your new version lower than the original one and your poem might be displaced by some one of the excellent poems which were barely eliminated." I have answered them as follows:

> I have just received your letter concerning the revisions I have made in my poem. The practical difficulties you face in having to reconsider so many poems, with such a widely scattered editorial board, are quite clear to me. But there are some other matters I find puzzling.
>
> In revising a poem, as well as in writing it, I do the best I can; and though any changes from the original may strike an audience, or a board of editors, as being all for the worse, I incline, insofar as I write them at all, to regard them as improvements. And I cannot be persuaded that a work, having undergone such improvements, should give place to any less perfect version of itself with which I am manifestly dissatisfied, no matter how charitably disposed towards its imperfections your editors may be.
>
> I should be sorry to eliminate myself from the anthology you are publishing, and from the competition you are sponsoring; but if the problems of revaluating my revised poem against the excellence of its competitors should seem prohibitively complicated, I will have to content myself with the kindly interest you have taken in my work.

As for further plans, I sail from France on the 21 of Aug., and will try to finish my work here as soon as I can so that I can spend a little time in Paris before coming home. [. . .]

Love

Tony

Lukas Foss (1922–2009) was a German-born, American composer. His many works include "Time Cycle" (songs with orchestra after texts by W. H. Auden, A. E. Hous-man, Franz Kafka, and Friedrich Nietzsche). A Columbia recording exists of the Louisville performance of Ein Märchen vom Tod (A Parable of Death). *Leo Smit (1921–1999) was a prolific American composer and pianist. His early career in-cluded collaborating with the dancer Valerie Bettis. A "Choir of Starlings" was first performed on February 25, 1955, at the Metropolitan Museum of Art.* Caedmon *premiered with the Buffalo Philharmonic on December 10, 1972.*

Sept. 12, [19]52 Annandale-on-Hudson, New York

[To Allen Tate]

Dear Allen—

I've been back in America a week, and have already taught my first class up here [Bard College]. I'm really not quite used to it yet; I feel a little foreign. [. . .]

This is to thank you again for my year in Italy. I plan to write at greater length and elaboration later on about the Academy and the other people there. Among other things, I collaborated with a couple of the composers there: Lukas Foss and Leo Smit. For the first, I translated a very short story, really a parable, called "Ein Märchen vom Tod" by Rilke, with strophes from the poems interspersed here and there for the chorus to sing. The work has been commissioned by the Louisville symphony orchestra, who will perform it in March, with Vera Zorina [the famous actress and ballet dancer] as narrator—with chorus and orchestra. For Leo, I wrote a group of seven songs in the English madrigal tradition, which are scored for four mixed voices and ten instruments ["A Choir of Starlings"], and which may be done this year in New York as a ballet, by Valerie Bettis. And finally, most ambitious of all, I wrote the text of a cantata, based on the story of Caedmon—for soloists, chorus, and orchestra, music again by Leo.

Aside from all this, I'm within an ace of finishing the book—in fact, there is one unfinished poem to clear up, and I'll be done. This poem, which will be the largest and most ambitious in the book—about 500 lines—I hope to finish up very soon, and after polishing up a few earlier things, I want to type up the whole business, and send it to you, for any comments or criticisms you might care to make—if I may. [. . .]

Most sincerely,
Tony

Anthony Hecht, in his study at the American Academy in Rome, 1954–1955
Courtesy of Adam Hecht

FOUR

Marriage and Single Life
1954–1967

THIRTEEN YEARS SEPARATE THE PUBLICATION OF *A Summoning of Stones* in 1954 and *The Hard Hours*, Hecht's second collection of poems, published in 1967. Their respective critical receptions could hardly have been more different, however. *Stones* garnered a few reviews, some good, including a short notice by Richard Wilbur in *The New York Times* (April 4, 1954). *The Hard Hours* received the Pulitzer Prize for Poetry in 1968. By 1990, it had gone through nine printings in the United States alone. The award, and, in Hecht's case, the recognition accompanying it, radically increased his visibility in the wider world of poetry.

The letters that survive from this period are fewer in number than at any other point in Hecht's life. No doubt this is largely because, with the exception of one fourteen-month sojourn abroad (October 1954–December 1955), Hecht was located in the States, busy teaching first at Bard College (1952–1954), then at Smith College (1956–1962), and then back at Bard (1962–1967). As a letter to Allen Tate reminds us, rather frustratingly, since we can only surmise what their conversation was about, the telephone was also an easy, alternative means of communication.

In contrast to the previous period in his life, Hecht's peregrinations, now geographically narrower and of an academic sort, are only the occasional subjects of his correspondence. Rather, the letters of greatest moment, indeed those describing events central to *The Hard Hours*, are of a decidedly domestic and private nature. These cluster primarily around two periods. The first, dating from his 1954 stay in Italy, involves Hecht's marriage to Patricia ("Pat") Harris on February 27, 1954, a marriage candidly, if optimistically, described in "The Vow" as a union of "Jewish diligence and Irish jest." At age twenty-one, nearly ten years younger than her husband, Pat was an aspiring model and by all counts remarkably attractive. She would soon succeed in appearing in *Vogue*, as one of the letters indicates. But the marriage also seems to have encountered difficulties almost from the outset. (Hecht's later characterization of these years forms the subject of his December 26, 1984, letter to J. D. McClatchy.) The two separated in 1959 and divorced in 1961, although not before having two children and enduring much emotional turbulence, memories of which ripple outward in Hecht's poetry to include "The Venetian Vespers" and continuing on to the final volume of verse, *The Darkness and the Light* in the Dantesque poem called "Circles." (Pat's subsequent marriage to Baron Philippe Lambert von Rothschild, in February 1962, referred to in the letters, ended in divorce in 1973.)

Seven months into their marriage, the couple traveled to Italy, where, supported by a Guggenheim Fellowship, they planned to spend a year. But soon after arriving, difficulties emerged when Pat became pregnant. The immediate problem resolved itself through a miscarriage, but their relationship continued to be stressful, and Pat returned home by boat in June 1955. Tony followed some six months later, having accomplished little work in the interim. Besides providing an immediate context for "A Vow," the letters from this period shed some general light on other poems in *The Hard Hours*, including "Ostia Antica" and "Clair de Lune." As Hecht was to remark much later, in a 1968 letter to L. E. Sissman, "the writing of both, and even more, the prolonged thinking about them before writing, was a sort of therapy for me during a troubled time." "Ostia" settles, without joy, for a version of sacrificial love "bearing heavy articles of blood/And symbols of endurance," and "Clair de Lune" registers, with Symbolist indirection, the painful consequences of separation and departure.[1] And in the final poem in the collection, "'It Out-Herods Herod. Pray You, Avoid It,'" the speaker is clearly a single parent.

[1]Further illuminating comments on "Clair de Lune" can be found in Hecht's brief essay "Missing the Boat," in *Night Errands: How Poets Use Dreams*, ed. Roderick Townley (Pittsburgh: University of Pittsburgh Press, 1998), pp. 51–56.

The second group of letters dates from the early 1960s when the solitary Hecht, eager for female companionship, was in frequent and occasionally boozy correspondence with the poet Anne Sexton. The relationship between the two was brief but complicated, covering about eighteen months. It is enough to note here that in these letters and postcards—sixteen in all, of which I have included seven—Hecht speaks often about his unhappy domestic and emotional life, which included taking antidepressants and a three-month stay at Gracie Square Hospital in New York, or "Crazy Square Hospital (as it is affectionately called by its inmates)," as Hecht noted in one letter. His letters allude, moreover, to other amatory entanglements and longings that would ultimately go into the making of *The Hard Hours*, in particular "A Letter" and "A Message from the City," epistolary love poems, it should be noted, in part generated out of this newly intimate world of letters he was exploring (and somewhat resisting) with Sexton. As the letters suggest, especially the letter of May 23, 1961, their relationship was not a sexual one. And, of course, the two shared poems—Hecht was also drinking deeply from Charles Baudelaire's well in this period of his life—and thoughts on their poetry and their respective, different careers. Sexton had recently achieved celebrity status, with an appearance in *Newsweek*. Hecht had not, although in the view of Sexton's biographer Diane Middlebrook Hecht's reputation as an intellectually gifted poet, who had received a number of distinguished prizes, greatly appealed to the academically insecure Sexton.[2] After 1962, their relationship dwindled to occasional meetings and a few shared poetry readings.

Along with prizes won, which included a second Guggenheim in 1959, followed by a Ford Foundation Fellowship, these years did provide some bright moments: the birth of Tony and Pat's two sons Jason and Adam on November 4, 1956, and October 26, 1958. Poems about each boy, in very different moods, appear in *The Hard Hours*, with "Adam" being composed after the divorce, when the children were living abroad with their mother. As a letter to Allen Tate, probably written in late 1959, reveals, Hecht could find moments of dark humor in his dissolving, complicated, and deceptive domestic scenario.

During this period, Hecht also made some valued acquaintances. These included an extended friendship, dating from his stay in Italy, with the Roman architectural historian William MacDonald, with whom he would

[2] *Anne Sexton, A Biography* (Boston: Houghton Mifflin, 1991), pp. 146–148.

enjoy an especially lively and often comical epistolary relationship for nearly four decades. He also initiated a friendship with William Arrowsmith, the classicist and translator, during his time in Rome. A little later, much fun was shared with John Hollander in the sudden buzz surrounding double dactyls, noted in a 1965 letter to Donald Hall. And, of course, the comical riff on Mathew Arnold, "The Dover Bitch," also appeared during these years, although it left no explicit footprint in any of the surviving letters, except for Hecht's reference that its title was inspired by his Smith colleague Daniel Aaron (October 4, 1992).

Professionally speaking, Hecht was finding his way into *The New Yorker*, first with "The Gift of Song" in 1954, a poem that appears in *A Summoning of Stones* as "Imitation." Encouraged by Howard Moss to sign a first-read contract with the magazine in the early 1960s, Hecht began to appear more frequently, with "Clair de Lune" in 1960, "A Letter" in 1962, and "A Hill" in 1964, and many more times thereafter. Rejections occurred, to be sure, including what now seems the head-scratching decision by the magazine to turn down "'More Light! More Light!'" but Hecht handled them with equanimity. Hecht also reviewed frequently for *The Hudson Review* in the late 1950s and 1960s, serving on the editorial board from 1966 to 1968, and he was repeatedly invited to submit poems to journals and anthologies, of which his appearance in the *New Poets of England and America* (1957), edited by Donald Hall, Robert Pack, and Louis Simpson, is probably the most noteworthy. The poems selected for inclusion were, in order of appearance, "The Vow," "La Condition Botanique," "Samuel Sewall," and "The Origin of Centaurs."

Along with Hecht's more personal correspondence, I have included a few letters that throw occasional light on his poetic views and on some of the poems themselves. A letter to Donald Hall, for instance, briefly illuminates Hecht's sequence on "The Seven Deadly Sins," composed in collaboration with the artist Leonard Baskin. Their friendship began during Hecht's years at Smith, and it would ripen and continue to bear fruit until Baskin's death in 2000.

I've concluded this period of Hecht's life with a letter to Jon Stallworthy, then poetry editor for Oxford University Press. Along with helping to initiate a long friendship with Stallworthy, the letter is the first surviving instance, I believe, of a charming story about John Crowe Ransom that Hecht was fond of repeating. It would appear verbatim in an essay he published in a book called *Masters: Portraits of Great Teachers* (1981), which he would later quote in his *Conversation with Philip Hoy* (1999). The story is a good one and bears repeating. Its place in this letter, delivered with gracious wit and self-deprecating modesty of its own, suggests a poet also becoming at ease with an image of himself in the larger world of letters, and while it does not predict Hecht's turn to the more explicitly autobiographical poems of the next volume, it certainly anticipates some of their concerns.

1954

Sunday (?), October 3, 1954 American Academy, Rome, Italy

[To his parents]

Dear Friends,

I must cover a lot of ground briefly in this, but let me say at the beginning that we are now comfortably and happily established at the Academy, our trunk has arrived, and all goes well.

Though there was little sun on the voyage over, the weather was reasonable as far as the sea was concerned. Not only did neither of us feel ill, but we gorged ourselves with food and wine. We had a highly social life on board ship, going to all the galas, in First and Tourist classes, as well as our own, and meeting some very nice people, among them a man named Hans Motz, formerly a colleague of Oppenheimer's, who was on his way to a full and permanent professorship of physics at Magdalen College, Oxford, and who invited us to come to visit him there on our way back to the States, and offered to take us with him on a trip to the west coast of Ireland.

Paris at first was pretty dismal. [. . .] However, we ran into a former student of mine, now in the army and on leave in Paris, who was staying with his aunt at the George V, and in spite of the fact that I flunked him in Freshman English at Bard, he seemed very glad to see us. It was arranged that the next day he would take us in his aunt's Cadillac (with chauffeur) to Chartres and Versailles, which was done. When we returned to Paris we met the aunt, who took quite a liking to us both, and from that moment on continued to ply us both with champagne till the moment we left Paris two or three days later. She took us to a very gaudy night-club in Montmartre, and to dinner, and to various little dives that she particularly liked, and in order that we should be able to drink champagne with her to the last possible minute, had us driven to the station with our luggage by her chauffeur.

The train trip to Rome was, as you might imagine, exhausting; especially after all that champagne. [. . .] Though it was either terribly overcast or actually raining every day we were in Paris, as soon as we crossed the Italian border we had sunshine and warm weather. Though we had no sleep during the night trip through France, we had no trouble staying awake to look at the Italian countryside on the way down. Pat didn't care for Paris at all, but is enchanted with Italy. Moreover, Paris was far too expensive. Though we didn't eat at any of the few expensive places I thought we might be able to squeeze into our budget by living cheaply, we still spent much more than I had planned; and this in spite of the fact that we were almost completely in the hands of a lavish aunt for the last three days.

We arrived at the Academy, ate, and went straight to bed. The next day I got the trunk at the station, and in the evening after dinner took Pat for a walk to see the Campidoglio, the Roman Forum, the Piazza S. Ignazio, the Pantheon. We met [Laurance] Roberts and his wife as soon as we arrived; they were cordial and friendly, as usual. I saw [the archeologist] Frank Brown for just a moment before he left for England and America, and there are two people back again (as I am) who were here when I was here. They were not particularly close friends of mine, and on the whole the group here now is a lot more solemn and less lively than the one I knew before. Of course, these people don't know one another well yet, but it doesn't look too promising. The one exception is the Wilburs, who are living in an apartment away from the Academy but nearby, with their three kids.

Our plans at present are to stay at the Academy for about a month, during which time I plan to do some work and Pat will be taking Italian lessons. After that, we will look around for a cheap place to live. We are both happy and well, and once we get back into a normal routine of eating and sleeping, will be feeling on top of the world.

> . . . with love from us both,
> Tony

> [Late October/Early November 1954]
> American Academy, Rome, Italy

[To his parents]

Dear Folks,

I'm sorry that it should have been so long since you heard from me, and I hope you haven't worried too much; but it has not been out of negligence or laziness that I have delayed. I simply felt very uncertain about a lot of things, and thought it best not to write until I had made up my mind what to do.

Let me put this as briefly as possible. In spite of all precautions to the contrary, Pat is pregnant, and I am planning to send her back to New York by plane next week to have something done about it. She will not come to you. She will stay with a friend of hers until she can get a job and find an apartment of her own. I plan to return myself by ship (as I shall have to, what with the trunk and all) as soon as I can. I have not been able to get any work done, and in the frame of mind I'm in, staying here with Pat gone and with other people around me who are and have been working successfully, would only add to my sense of defeat and frustration. The tenure of my Guggenheim is already half gone, and I have nothing to show for it; and the contemplation of this alone is enough to make me feel terrible.

I have told Pat that our return does not mean any alteration in our relationship, though I think that if I had not said this, she would have refused to go home or to have anything done about her pregnancy. I am chiefly concerned that this should be taken care of first.

You can help me in the following ways. First, I shall need some more money transferred to my checking account. I have only just gotten my first bill from the Academy, and will have to pay that and whatever else accrues till the time I leave; plus Pat's passage and mine. Please transfer $300. Next, when you write, please keep your letters as neutral as possible, because I am telling Pat that I shall write you only that we are coming back to the States, and though I hope I can get her to leave next week, I can never be sure. Third, I suspect that my return may have a devastating effect on Roger, and I hope this can somehow be taken into account. In fact, I will plan not to leave here until I hear what you think ought to be done about this. It is Pat's plan to go back and find an apartment for us, but I am at last certain this is not the solution. However, I can't say this to her while she's pregnant.

I'm sorry to have to write this sort of letter.

Love,
Tony

[November 1954] American Academy, Rome, Italy
[To his parents]
Dear Folks,

I'm afraid the last letter I sent you was pretty hysterical, but I've calmed down a bit now, and can think a little better. It's not that the situation has changed very much; in fact, for a few days it was worse. Just after I wrote to you, Pat changed her mind, and declared she refused to have an abortion. Her reason, (aside from the instinctive and maternal one) was that she was sure I was asking this of her as a preliminary to leaving her. We have both calmed down a good deal since then and she has now consented. Tomorrow she has an appointment with a doctor, and we will have a test made. The plans, as we have talked it over, are that if she is pregnant, she is to fly home to stay with her mother and have the abortion done in N.Y. by the doctor who operated on her last spring. If she must tell her mother about it, she will say that the doctor says it is too soon after her operation to have a baby. However, after thinking it over, I have decided on a different and better plan. I am not sure it would be a good thing to let Pat go home, pregnant and alone, to her mother. She might change her mind about the abortion again, or her mother might change it for her. So I have decided that if the test is positive, I shall tell her that we are going to have it done in Switzerland, because it's cheaper there, and I can be with her. After it is done, she can fly back in order to get a job and a place to live; and I suppose I will tell her that I'll follow by boat, though I'm not sure I will—and I'm not even sure I'll tell her that.

The chief thing is this—that I, and you, must be absolutely circumspect. If Pat supposes for an instant that I plan to separate from her, she will refuse to go through with the abortion. Moreover, as I think I wrote you in my last letter, I have told Pat that I have not written to you about any of our difficulties. So that I must ask you again to be very careful. It occurred to me that you might even take it into your heads to fly over, but I don't think this would help matters at all, and it would be sure to do a great deal of harm. Pat still resents me for having confided in you about our previous difficulties. And you must be careful in your letters to give no clue as to what I've written you. For example, if I can manage it, I shall not even tell her I am sending this, so do not acknowledge its receipt. Not even in letters addressed only to me; since if she sees they come from you, she feels entitled to open them. And I can't ask her not to, now, without arousing her suspicion. In case you may have sent something off right after getting my last letter, without taking account of these precautions, I am trying to get to the mailbox every day before she does. But I can't be sure I always will.

If the test tomorrow is negative, I shall ask the doctor to give her something to start menstruation again. If it's positive, we shall leave for Switzerland as soon as possible.

The thing I want to ask you to do is to make sure that Pat is now on my Blue Cross policy. When we go I shall give the number on my own policy, and shall assume that it now covers her. I have no idea how much this will cost, but I do believe that it's cheaper in Switzerland, and moreover, it's legal there.

Hope to be able to write you more cheerful news, though right now things look pretty gloomy.

Oh, I almost forgot. The <u>Partisan Review</u> was very nice.

Love,
Tony

[December 2, 1954] American Academy, Rome, Italy

[To his parents]

Dear Folks,

Just a note to set your minds at rest; I should have written this a few days ago, but things have been too hectic, and I've been too exhausted.

Pat has had a miscarriage. It was a God sent solution to our problems, because even though she had consented to an abortion, it would have been dangerous so soon after her last operation, and in fact the doctors might have decided against it on just those grounds. She had her menstrual period about a week ago, and this was followed by an inflammation and infection of her tubes, etc., and she has been ordered to stay in bed for five days, and to have shots every 12 hrs. All this is going forward; she is quite well, and of course we are both immensely pleased and relieved that things have worked out this way. The Doctor has told her to see a gynecologist after her five days of shots and rest, and what will be said then—aside from laying off sex for some time to come—I can't guess.

For a few days after I wrote to you that Pat had consented to go to Switzerland, she became a little more apprehensive of the medical skill of Europe (not without reason, since we saw several doctors and each said something different) and she thought the wisest plan might be to fly home and have Dr. Kesseler take care of her. I still think that the best solution for us now is that as soon as she's well enough, she ought to go back and get a job in the States, and I ought to stay on here and try to get some work done. Her plan is for me to follow her back, and for her to support me so that I can go on writing and won't be under the pressure of the Guggenheim finances and time limit. I don't know how I can get her to consent to my plan, since this medical crisis, like the last one, has brought us sort of together again. Nevertheless, it is a crisis, and I have still gotten no work done. And I feel somehow that if I could get myself away from the emotional complexities that her presence entails, I might be able to get down to work. When she's well, I will try to explain this to her so as not to hurt her feelings, and see if she will consent to go back for the remaining time.

I am sorry to have worried you with all this, but I thought you'd be glad to know that the immediate problem is solved.
                                    Love,
                                    Tony

1955

Dear Dad,

I am writing to you alone, instead of to the family as a group, because I think it will be easier for everyone if you can explain matters, and avoid upsetting Mom and Roger. I would have written to you at your office, for even greater privacy, but I can't find the address. The first thing I have to tell you is that Pat sailed two days ago (the 13th) on the Cristoforo Columbo for New York; by common agreement between us. She will be staying with some girlfriends of hers in New York (at least till she finds a place for herself and has found a job) and her friends will pick her up at the dock with a car.

This would have been a very difficult letter to write if I had written it when I first intended, but I am feeling a good deal better now, and have some friends from the Academy staying here with me, and am settling down to a calmer view of things. We have had rather difficult times since coming to Europe, and one result has been that in the whole year I have written only one poem. Pat feels very responsible about this, and has consented to go back to America for this reason. About a month or a month and a half ago things were beginning to go well and peaceably with us, and we both knew that I had not done much work, and that the Guggenheim money had run out, and that we were living on savings, and that there was perhaps a little more than a thousand dollars in savings in my second account. So Pat suggested that we try to live as cheaply as possible and stretch the savings through another winter (perhaps by staying at Mary's farm in Austria during the winter) so as to make up for all the work not done on the Guggenheim. I thought it worth the risk, so I wrote to Bard, giving up my job; ostensibly, because I had not gotten a promotion or even a raise. But shortly after this there followed a period of extreme difficulty, and Pat became convinced that what she ought to do was to return to the States and try to find some psychiatric help, which she now intends to do.

I am writing this to let you know more or less what has happened, but also to try to make things as easy for all of you as I can. This means above all to try to avoid any contact, even by telephone, between Pat and Mom. I know she means well, and she sometimes lets things go unconsciously and without malice, but Mom is very capable of hurting Pat, and that's just what I want to avoid. In a recent and otherwise cheerful letter she said, apropos of the death of Harry Weiss, "Pat, I don't suppose you'll miss him much, but he was a very great friend of mine, etc." It's all very well to say that it was meant as a sort of joke (which I know is what you'll say) but if it is, it's a joke in very bad taste, suggesting as it does that Pat is nasty enough to rejoice over the death of somebody who was not her friend. It seems to me all this care ought to be taken because Pat will have to have a certain amount of contact with you. First of all, there are some things of hers still in the house, and things of both of ours up at Bard. Then, she is travelling home with the trunk and Roger's suitcase, and is bringing home a few things of mine. I have asked her to get in touch with you at Parke, Benziger [an import company] by phone soon after she gets in, but it seems just as well to let you know that her temporary address will be care of Dolores Del Vita, 1025 Third Avenue, so that if she fails to reach you, you can reach her by mail. I have told her that she may have whatever gramophone records of mine she wants till I get back, save those which Roger wants.

As for myself, and my own plans, I am still rather undecided. Since I have rented this place till the end of August, and it's very nice and cheap, I think I'll stay here; and I think it would be good for me to be far away from Pat for a while to think things over. I am not sure how earnest she will be about trying to straighten herself out. Moreover, I need a little rest. And maybe, with some luck, I can get some work done. However, the money is getting short, and I would appreciate the transfer of $500 to my checking account. What I shall do in August, I don't know yet. If I should by any chance be working furiously and well, I may try to stay on as long as the good work continues. But I suspect that after a year of not writing and after what has happened over here, it may take me some time to get back into my stride. In that case, I would come back to the states in the fall, and get a job of any sort to see me through the winter. As you know, I have some fairly good teaching prospects for next year.

Please try to be gentle with Pat when you see her. She is very sick, and knows it, but tries hard to forget it most of the time. I hope she will want to try to do something about it. If not, something will have to be worked out. And don't worry about me. The worst of it is over now.

Love

Tony

[To his parents]

Dear Folks,

I have been back from my trip for some time, and should have written before, but didn't, and for reasons that I shall try to explain. For one thing, I wanted very much to get back to work, and didn't want any excuse for not working to get in the way of it. But the work has been going forward with the greatest difficulty, chiefly because I cannot concentrate. I have no feeling about whether what I am writing is good or bad, and the whole business is totally without excitement and pleasure for me. And I am sure I know the reason. It's that I can't stand leaving unresolved my situation with Pat. I hear from her fairly frequently, asking when I plan to come back, and she knows that I am supposed to appear at the poetry reading in the middle of January. It is not mainly loneliness I feel, though I feel it; but I have been lonely before. It is quite frankly the fact that nothing is really settled between us, and that in the mean time I worry about how things are going to work out. This has made my work more difficult than it has ever been before. And there has been no lack of encouragement. I don't know whether I told you, but there was a quite talented and successful young German composer [Hans Werner Henze] down in Ischia who has been commissioned to write five songs for Benjamin Britten and Peter Pears, and which they will take on a world tour of recitals, and the composer wants me to do the texts. I have only been able to turn out one short one so far, and he needs them soon, and not being able to work panics me and makes writing even more difficult. And there have been other requests for work.

Anyway, the point is that I am feeling very tense and uncomfortable here, and am not really having a good time, and am not getting much work done, and since the chance to work was the original excuse for staying here, it seems to me pointless now. So I plan to go down today or tomorrow and pick up reservations on a ship coming back. There's one that sails from here on the 11th of Dec. and gets in in time for Christmas, and I'll try to get on that. Unless you have any reason to suppose that this is a bad idea, I should like to try to get back as soon as possible. If you have reasons to recommend to the contrary, please let me know. But be assured that I am not doing this merely because I have been getting a lot of affectionate letters from Pat. The effect would have been the same, perhaps even more violent, if she had never written at all.

If you are really convinced that it would be bad for me to come back, it will not be too late for me to change my plans if you write right away. But on the other hand, do not forget that I am supposed to appear at the poetry reading pretty soon after Christmas anyway. Under either circumstance, I will need some more money. There is now $214.50 in my account, which is not enough to go home or to stay here long on. So I would appreciate your transferring $500 to my checking account.

Please be assured that I have not made this decision lightly, it seems to me the only sensible thing to do.

Love

Tony

1957

William Arrowsmith (1924–1992) was a distinguished classicist, literary critic, translator, and editor. He was the general editor of the multivolume Oxford series of Greek plays, for which Hecht translated (with Helen Bacon) Seven Against Thebes *(1973).*

[January? 1957] Northampton MA

[To William Arrowsmith]

Dear Bill,

Thanks for your fine letter [from Rome]. It brings back so vividly the intoxicating cologne of the fairies, the piercing screams of the beaten wives, that one could almost believe one was there, in the presence of the infant Hercules, so cunningly wrought (so rudely forced) by America's leading sculptor. Did you know that nightingales sing in the <u>cortile</u> in spring? They work themselves into the inmost parts of those great cypress, and let go for all they are worth, attracted, no doubt, by the creative atmosphere of the place. Nevertheless, we wish we were there with you, in the midst of all that baroque and classic splendor.

How is old Mason Hammond [Harvard professor in charge of classical studies at the American Academy in Rome]? And what was [John] Ciardi's reaction to my review of his book [of poems, *As If*, in the autumn issue of *The Hudson Review*]? But none of that is important. What <u>is</u> important is that unto us a son was given on November 4th, and he is called Jason, and is well and happy and weighs 15 ½ lbs. And I am not complaining when I go on to remark that that's all the news from here. Or at least all the news that can be committed to a letter. Other than this we are all well and happy, and find Smith a pleasant but indifferent place. There has been no word from Texas or Blackmur, but I send my unstinted thanks for all you have done in pleading my case. I also enclose a poem, a new one, hoping that you will like it. I feel pleased but disconcerted by the company I keep in your library; chumming about with Yeats, I am liable to start smelling roses in winter and get into involved conversations with the dead.

We think of you often as ones who have fresh basil in their salads, and who can walk in the Piazza S. Ignazio if they choose. And we trust it will not be too long before we can introduce Jason to his rightful classical heritage.

With warmest greetings to you all,
Tony Hecht

1959

Donald Hall (1928–) is a poet, critic, essayist, and anthologist.

[1959?] [Northampton, Massachusetts]

Dear Don:

[. . .] I'm not sure what you want in terms of biographical data. Just the bald facts? Born: 1923 in New York City. B.A. Bard College, M.A. Columbia. Three years as rifleman in 97th Infantry division, in Germany, Czechoslovakia, during European campaign and then occupation duty in Japan. Teach English at Smith (previously at Kenyon, N.Y.U., Bard, State University of Iowa). Smoke, drink, write dirty limericks. Married five years, two children. Am about half-way through a new volume of poems which I hope to finish on my year off from Smith next year. Have collaborated with composers in writing texts for cantatas, and for songs, and just finished a collaboration with an artist here, a wood engraver named Leonard Baskin, on a small emblem book called The Seven Deadly Sins (the poems intend to justify the sins, not by making them attractive, but by showing that the alternatives are perhaps just as sinful or pointless; the rationale behind this being that the sins are not really deadly till they're really persuasive). If this goes well, (it's being privately printed in a limited edition at a fine press), we may go on to expand it into a full-fledged emblem book with about 25 or 30 emblems.

If you want more personal stuff, let me know.

Best
Tony

[October 1959?] New York NY

[To Allen Tate]

Dear Allen,

I am delighted that you liked my little piece in Sewanee, and very proud that they asked me to contribute. I waited to answer your warm and affectionate letter until I could get a look at the issue itself (it just got to me) and I must say that I find myself in luminous and distinguished company, though given the occasion, this is not surprising. I hope there was a party, and that Katherine Anne [Porter] made it, and that you are as happy in your honors as these many acts of homage intended[. . . .]

Your suspicions about my affairs are well grounded; I daresay word of this sort does get around. Pat and I are separated; she is living in New York too, and I have the older boy [Jason] with me on weekends. This seems like a rather messy way to live, but there are messier ones. Curiously enough, we had arrived at this understanding early in spring, just before John Ransom came to give some readings at Amherst and Mt. Holyoke, and I had already moved into a small apartment in Northampton. I picked Ransom up at the airport, it had been years since I had last seen him, and our meeting again was as cordial and warm as I could have hoped for. It's about an hour's drive from the airport to the college, and most of that time he spent bringing me up to date about old friends who were at Kenyon when I was there. It had been my plan gently to inform him sometime during the trip of my new status, but his chronicle was so filled with sorrow at premature deaths, catastrophic marriages and sensational divorces, that I couldn't bring myself to add anything to it. I took him to his hotel, and then phoned Pat, who likes nothing better than to play a misleading role, and she was delighted to agree to deceive him. Before lunch I brought him back to what was now her house, where she made us a little appetizer and served us drinks in the most domestic way, and where Jason, then 2 1/2, crawled amiably all over the guest, asked him about his eyeglasses and his tie, and lent to the whole scene its last authentic touch of bliss. Our little play lasted through the whole weekend, or at least as often as we saw Ransom, and it was the only grounds upon which Pat and I had been able to meet amiably for some time. I suppose, however, that word does get around, and that Ransom must know or suspect whatever you knew or suspected. And there's no point in trying to conceal an accomplished fact.

The worst of it is over, I have survived, am relatively cheerful, hard at work (just now on an endless omnibus review for <u>Hudson</u>) and look forward to getting a lot done this year, and to seeing you whenever you come this way.

With all affection,

Tony

Newton Arvin (1900–1963) was a literary critic and professor of English at Smith College. Shortly after Hecht wrote his letter, Arvin would be arrested in September and find himself at the center of a notorious scandal at Smith College involving several male colleagues, including William Spofford and Joel Dorius, both of whom were fired. Hecht would later write on Dorius's behalf for a teaching position at the University of Rochester. As it turned out, Hecht did receive a Ford Foundation Fellowship and was able to take another leave of absence from Smith.

February 1, 1960 New York NY

Dear Newton,

[...] [T]hough I know pretty clearly how generously and sympathetically you will read these words, I'm not sure what I expect you to be able to do about the matter, or indeed whether there's anything at all to be done. Perhaps by the time I get to the end, something practical will occur to me.

Seen in remote and judicious perspective (from 450 miles away, and eight months after the fact) my career as a teacher at Smith seems anything but auspicious, and you know better than I what difficulties have arisen in my case. I am well aware that my first year was a disaster. Jason was born on the 28th of Sept. [November 4?], and a week later Pat came down with a breast-fever that kept her in bed for a month and a half, and prevented nursing. Since we couldn't afford very much help, I spent all my free days and every night taking care of her and the baby. Unhappily, because the marriage was already disintegrating by leaps and bounds, things did not get much better when Pat's health improved, and she took little or no care of the baby all that year. (I ought to say that I'm telling you this now to explain, not to justify, my academic performance. The college hired me to teach, and is not expected to concern itself with the complications of my private life. For this reason, I made no attempt at the time to excuse myself on these grounds.) Oddly enough (or perhaps not so oddly, when you think of it) the same thing happened again when Adam was born two years later at about the same time of year. Within two weeks of her return from the hospital, Pat broke her leg skating and was in a cast for two months, but this time we had some money saved from a <u>Hudson Review</u> fellowship that I had been awarded the previous year, and which we had planned to add to the Guggenheim. Needless to say, it all went into nurses and baby sitters, and I was at least free to do my teaching job. So much for the domestic and medical background.

After that first year, I felt that my academic work was without blemish and enjoyable, and particularly last year, I believed that my students liked the classes. [. . .] Nevertheless, the department must have felt that the elimination of the failures charged to me in my first year was a triumph of a rather negative order, and you have more reason than most to know of the curious difficulties and hesitations involved in my promotion. I know I need hardly tell you how grateful I was then and still am for all the concern you took in this matter[. . . .]

I had some hope that when I returned to Smith I should have earned enough confidence in the eyes of the department to be given some course of my own such as I had petitioned the Curriculum Committee for several years ago. When I came to visit Northampton shortly before Christmas, I spoke to Elizabeth [Drew], and she told me, not without some genuine embarrassment, that I was scheduled to teach, when I began my fourth year at Smith and ninth year of teaching in the fall of '60, the same courses (freshman English and creative writing) that I had been given when I first arrived. [. . .] It takes no ghost from the grave, no seventh son of a seventh son, to read these signs aright. And it has seemed to me for some time that the handwriting on the wall could hardly be more legible. Nevertheless, what seems to me so clear, some consoling friends insist is no true reading of the fact. [. . .]

I have gone into this gloomy chronicle because the Ford Foundation seems very strongly inclined to offer me a fellowship for next year. It is one for which I was nominated; I did not apply. It will be offered to only about ten poets and novelists throughout the country, and therefore carries with it a genuine sort of distinction. I would very much like to accept it, both for the time it would offer me to work, and for the honor. The Foundation asked me if Smith would be likely to grant me a second and consecutive leave of absence, and I told them, probably not. They suggested that I inquire before making up my mind whether to accept the fellowship or not. I should add that I am being offered an appointment at the University of Delaware, about which I have not made up my mind either; but I shall certainly ask them if I can postpone acceptance of the appointment for a year in order to take the Ford. Clearly you can see some of the questions posed by this situation. Will Smith offer me a leave again next year, and perhaps a more interesting teaching program when I return? Are my hopes and prospects attractive enough at Smith to make it seem worth turning down the Ford and the Delaware offer (which involved the same rank, a higher salary, and freedom to teach any courses in poetry I want to)? I hardly expect you to be able to give me all the answers, and I'm sure you know I'm not writing merely for reassurance. What I would really like is your opinion as to whether Smith will give me another leave to take the Ford (understanding that some pleasant publicity will attach to the college as a result, and they will not be paying me any salary for the year) and whether you believe that if the college refuses leave, it would still be worth my while, in the long run, to turn down the Ford and come back. [. . .] I gather that there are some who are convinced that since I have no PhD, I am not qualified to teach anything save elementary courses and creative writing. [. . .] I do not think I belong on campus as "a poet," a sort of cultural and decorative embellishment to the place, rather like a bronze statue of Sophia Smith, to be noticed in passing with brief homage which is good for the soul. [. . .]

I'm sure you understand that I am asking you for your personal opinions and feelings[. . . .] And please forgive my imposing on you in this way.

> With all good wishes,
>
> Tony

[July 1960] New York NY

[To Allen Tate]

Dear Allen:

I will thank you properly for <u>The Fathers</u> when I see you in September; and for your kind words about the translations.[3] This is meant mainly to reassure you that you did not "let me down" the night I phoned, though indeed I was distressed, and I still am. I am sure that there was nothing clear and careful I could have said on the phone, and nothing very certain that I can say now, except that it is a religious problem, though very impure and unclear, complicated not only by personal uncertainty but by outside pressure and circumstance.

I think it's better that I venture no more than that for now, and hope that in September I shall stand a little more firmly wherever I stand; or at least to be able to explain myself better, and be certain that this is not due to a local moment of "disorientation."

As for your kindness (and Danny Ransohoff's) in thinking of me and recommending me for the University of Cincinnati Lectures, I can just hint at how flattered and pleased I am. I have no idea at all whether Smith would take kindly to the idea of giving me a third year of leave—though from every practical point

---

[3]Tate's early novel, *The Fathers* (1938), was reprinted in 1960 with a revised introduction by Arthur Mizener. The translations probably include: from Baudelaire, "To a Madonna, Ex-Voto in the Spanish Style," which is dedicated to Tate in *The Hard Hours*, "The Swan," and "Je n'ai pas Oublie"; and from Apollinaire, "The Bells." The latter three translations, uncollected, were published in *The Hudson Review* (Autumn 1961).

of view there's no reason why they shouldn't. They are not losing any money by it, and yet it was difficult to persuade them that the glory and distinction of my fellowships devolved indirectly upon them. I did, of course, finally get my leave extended from one to two years, but it was a surly sort of concession from them, intended to make me feel that they were being wantonly generous, and that I had better have a very clear idea of my indebtedness to them. Even so, they might very well be impressed by so august an invitation.

Please give my warm greetings to Isabella [Gardiner, Tate's second wife], and unless complications of schedule arise, I'll be up there in Sept.

With all affectionate good wishes,

Tony

Howard Moss (1922–1987), poet and critic, was poetry editor of The New Yorker *from 1950 to 1987.*

[Late 1960] New York NY

Dear Howard:

You've been the soul of patience, or perhaps you've given up any hope of hearing from me. Anyway, I enclose, after all this time, a couple of poems which I hope might win me a contract. But I ought to admit that even now I have a dim sense of hesitation.

I think both the poems are good, you understand; I wouldn't have sent them along otherwise. But I have a feeling that the one called "More Light! More Light!" is not the sort of thing The New Yorker is famous for publishing. And I feel a little dubious about what the reaction is likely to be—a bit too explicit and ruthless, perhaps. I don't mean to accuse the exalted powers of squeamishness; after all, they put everything aside for [the 1946 publication of John] Hersey's "Hiroshima." But I have a feeling that they think this sort of brutally straightforward stuff is all very proper in reportage, and possibly even in a story, but that poetry is expected to exhibit the more fragile delicacies of the soul, etc. You, of course, will be able to make a better guess than I as to whether there is any dim bias along these lines. If you feel there is, and that my situation would not be advanced by showing this poem, perhaps it would be best to withhold both of them until I come up with a new one. I'm sure you'll know best what to do. [...]

As for the other poem ["A Hill"], it seems more the sort of thing that the magazine is in the habit of printing. I haven't been able to think of any sort of title for it, so I suppose it might just be called "Poem." But if you happen to think of something pithy and apt, I'd be grateful. Anyway, quite aside from whatever the gods decide, I hope you like these poems yourself, and I send my thanks in advance for your efforts in my behalf.

All best wishes,

Tony

1961

This is the first of Hecht's letters to the poet Anne Sexton (1928–1974). The Wannings were close friends of Hecht's. "The Dover Bitch" was dedicated to Andrews Wanning, and Hecht composed an Epithalamion in honor of their daughter Margaret's marriage. (See letter of March 19, 1971.)

April 14, 1961 New York NY

Dear Anne,

I just got your letter—both your letters, the one on the cocktail napkin too. They got here a little earlier than is usual for the mail, and I found them on my way out to the post office to send the government its pound of flesh. (When they get enough of this flesh together, they'll stitch it up and shoot it into orbit.) If your letters had come at the regular time, I would have missed them, because I'm going away for the weekend—up No'th, to Saugerties, across the river from Bard College, to visit some old friends, Pat & Andrews Wanning. Do you know them? It seems possible that you might because they have a house in Maine, at East Blue Hill, I think; and then perhaps you might have given a reading at Bard and met them there, where Andy teaches. Philip Booth [the poet] and his wife will also be guests there this weekend, though Booth has a practical purpose in mind—he's coming to be interviewed for a job at the college. I remember your mentioning his name, so I guess you know him, and I'll take the liberty of giving him your regards.

Except for little weekend skirmishes like this, I don't plan to be away from New York much at all until August, when I will take my children to Fire Island for a month. After that, God knows. I have so set my heart on this next year of work (my own work, writing) that I'm not going to give it up without a good fight. Right now I'm not even thinking about it, because I can't really make any plans till I talk to my ex-wife. She is by no means the soul of candor, so I don't know how much good the talk will do, but we'll see.

Those are the details of life. And now, what do I say? I love you? Yes, I guess I do. But I feel sort of foolish writing a love letter to a happily married woman. Still, it was a wonderful time we spent together, and in ways that I can scarcely put my finger on, you made me very happy. I hope that by the time this reaches you, the wine glasses will have arrived, and I should like you and Kayo [Sexton's husband] to drink a toast to each other first, and then one to me. I take it there'll be something around the house to put in the glasses; there's no reason why they can't be used for good dry martinis, for that matter.

From here, a moment before I run for the bus, I wish you every happiness. You are an astonishingly gifted and accomplished poet, and an unbelievably lovely human being. Every one who knows you is lucky.

Love
Tony

[Early May 1961] New York NY

[To Anne Sexton]

Anne, dear Anne:

This will be a curious letter. Not at all like me. I am sad. Because I am in love. But not with you, or, not entirely with you. Anyway, you have a man of your own. The trouble is, so does she. And she feels a kind of mute, Thomas Hardy loyalty to him. But she loves me. I know it. I have written her a poem ["A Letter"]. I think it is good, but I don't know; I just finished it an hour ago. I'd send it to you, but the stanzas are too complicated for me to manage just now. I'm a little bit drunk. Which reminds me, I think you drink too much. Though perhaps no more than I do; which is too much.

To answer all the questions in your letters: Yes. I don't mind your spelling mistakes. I put them down to haste and bad spelling, which covers my errors in this line. I envy your kelly greenery. Here, in the late afternoon, the bricks of the building across from my back window are lit for half an hour with rusty evening light. Still, I was up in the country last week (I gave a reading at Bard College) and it was almost like being born. Which reminds me: I would love to read on a program with you. The trouble is, I am really not terribly well known, I am not on any lists and my name doesn't ring enough bells. So the only readings I give are generally arranged by friends: Betty Kray at the [Poetry Center, 92nd Street] Y, Bill Meredith at Connecticut, and some old colleagues at Bard. O yes, and I shall be reading next week at Columbia, again through an old acquaintance, Robert Pack. (You see what happens to me when I get tight? Even my letters turn out to be blank verse.) So what I suggest, if this seems all right to you, is that you mention me as a possible co-reader when you are asked somewhere to read. I think you must have many more such engagements than I do, and if you would not mind, I would be terribly pleased. [. . .]

[. . .] I am proud to be one who can make you feel at home in the world. I'm sure Kayo can, too. Anyway, I had better remain your loving but erring swain,

Tony

May 9, 1961 New York NY

[To Howard Moss]
Dear Howard,

Here is something hot off the typewriter ["A Letter"]. It'll give us something to talk about on Tuesday, unless by that time you find it a subject you would rather avoid. I hope there will be no objection to the fact that I have deliberately left a few loose ends by way of insisting upon the anonymity of the person being addressed, and the various personal entanglements that set these two people apart. The intention is not to be obscure, but rather, I should hope, to lend a curious excitement by indicating that there are some things that cannot safely be said. Still, I suppose it's a bad policy to offer explanations beforehand; plunk it in the laps of your Olympians, and let them decide.

Yours,
Tony

May 23, 1961 New York NYC

[To Anne Sexton]
Dear Anne, dear,

It was only a moment ago I finished talking to you on the phone from Newark; you put in an extra 25¢ for a little moment more of talking, and I told you that I had just delivered the surplus diapers and an overlooked sweater to the apartment where my children live with my ex-wife. Well, here I am, quietly euphoric, after a very happy day with you. Even so, with a natural aptitude in this direction, I find myself, even a little drunkenly, marshalling all that I can to bear against you. I don't want Florence Nightingale to take care of me. In fact, I'm sure she had a deep resentment of men. Anyway, I don't need that kind of help; I can take care of myself. Moreover, I have come to think that the best thing about our relationship is precisely that there is a "safety factor" and that we have really, without ever having told each other any lies about ourselves, managed to maintain a certain privacy, which is not lack of candor or trust, but an instinctive knowledge. Of lots of things. That we could hurt each other, that we could hurt others. That whatever payoff there is isn't worth it. Other things too, which my potted intelligence can't manage on a typewriter. Or perhaps it can, but not tonight. Anyway, I think we can continue to understand each other perfectly (or at least seem to, enough to make ourselves happy) as long as we observe the terms of the truce. I'm not quite sure what the terms are, and neither are you; they haven't been written down. This is where instinct comes in. [. . .]

Love,
Tony

[September 1961?] New York NY

[To Anne Sexton]
Dear Anne:

[. . .] I am enclosing "Message From the City" in reasonably final form. As you see, I have used your discovery about how to end it. But I had to put other things in. I know you were trying to pare it down, and I have not stuck things in to make it longer or out of attachment to any lines or details. But I have never tried before, by shifting the order of the parts of a poem, to discover a new emotional sequence for them, and I found it very difficult. The problem was to arrive at the last lines with clarity and restraint, and still have an emotional logic to the little shifts in tone. I don't know whether it works or not. Let me know what you think.

Love,
Tony

[October 28, 1961] New York NY

[To Anne Sexton]
Dear Anne,

I put off writing till I had engaged and successfully defeated a lousy head cold, and now I feel a little more human. [. . .] As for the melancholy, it's quite simple. Pat has finally come to terms with her Belgian boyfriend [Philippe Lambert] and they are to be married in February, at which time she will be taking the children to Europe. I faced this crisis once before, and weathered it, and it really should be no harder the second time; and she told me about this final arrangement (I suppose it's final) several weeks ago. But yesterday was Adam's birthday (he was three) and next Saturday is Jason's birthday (he'll be five) and very soon Christmas will be here, which means a lot to both of them and of course to me too, and all these events conspire to force themselves upon my consciousness; and then they'll be gone. You understand that in the long run I am glad that Pat is getting married, and I think it is all for the best for the children. Still, it is hard to be simply rational about these things, and I'm feeling pretty low.

Later. You phoned, and then I went out to the New School to do my stint on the panel, came home as soon as possible, and went to bed. It's Saturday morning now. I have arranged not to take the children this weekend, or only for a little while tomorrow, if I'm better. You see, I was being premature in my first sentence, above. I still have a fever and a cold. I wish I could write poems when I feel like this—it would cheer me up—but I can't.

Forgive the moody aimlessness of this letter.

Tony

1962

[To Anne Sexton]

Dear Anne,

I guess by now you figure that I have collapsed into the kindly institutional arms of Crazy Square Hospital (as it is affectionately called by its inmates). But no; you would be wrong. It is true that I am a shit, a bounder and an ingrate, and should have written long ago to thank you and Kayo for that wonderful weekend, but the fact that I didn't is to be set down wholly to my corrupt character, and you are to understand that I am still at large. I also realize that I might have answered at least one of the four or five letters you wrote since my visit, but then, when you're dealing with an ornery critter like me you've got to expect the worst. The truth is that I've been feeling rather aimless and vacant and incapable of any purposeful action at all. I know you've been concerned about me; Cal [Robert Lowell] phoned a few days ago (to invite me to a very pleasant dinner) and told me that he'd heard something about my situation from you. And I realize you may have worried at not hearing from me, and may have thought something bad had happened.

Well, nothing bad has happened; indeed, nothing had happened at all. It's partly the drugs of course, but it's mostly the continued effects of the depression that make me feel that I'm in a trance day in and day out, and that nothing is going either to annoy or please me very much at all. It's like the humming of a single sound in the ear—dull and monotonous yet soothing. But I feel sort of like a zombie, and nothing that happens seems important or interesting. So I have no news to report. Though I seem to do as many things as I used to, they all seem to me savorless and flat. I've been trying to write—without much success—but I suppose I must wait for things to clear up. The departure of the children has been slightly delayed again; this time till the middle of Feb. I'm seeing my Dr. four times a week and my intake of tofranil has been increased. Sonst nichts neues. O yes, one thing; I've definitely decided to quit Smith.

Please don't worry about me, I shall be back among the living after a while. And by the way, I'm not sure I like the idea of being given away to Maxine [Kumin] as if I were an old worn scarf. I think you girls are getting pretty frivolous about me.

Love

Tony

February 13, 1962 New York NY

[To Anne Sexton]

Dear Anne,

You cannot imagine how stunned I feel. It's not as if I hadn't had a year or more to prepare myself. But yesterday, I saw my children for the last time before they depart today for Belgium. Pat came in a taxi to pick them up; we waited for her downstairs in my apartment house, and by the time I got back upstairs to my apartment I felt as if I'd been hit with a club. I'm only slowly coming out of it now, but it absolutely killed the little spurt of writing energy that took me through the Baudelaire translations and one or two things of my own. Right now I feel as if I will never write again.

Pat got married on Saturday, she is pregnant, and plans to come back to have her baby in America in September. Moreover, in a phone conversation this morning, she suggested that nothing could be more convenient from her point of view than that I should take the children for a couple of months after the baby is born. It is altogether like her to expect everybody's schedule of life to conform to hers. I told her that I have no job at present, but that I expected to be teaching next fall, and that under those circumstances I didn't see how I could manage. But we both blithely agreed that it was too early to make definite plans. I had rather foolishly hoped that after she got married I would be able to settle down to a reasonable routine of life.

Anyway, here is something left over from translating Baudelaire.

Her only happiness comes to her in dreams
And watching wrestling on a friend's TV.
Her eyes bulge at the hammer-locks, and she
Feels her throat knotted with unuttered screams.

And the hooded torturer pulls her husband's eyes
Out of their sockets, which he fills with sand.
Her husband's feet are marked with an iron brand.
But whatever happens to him, he never dies.

Consider the grey roots of her tinted hair,
Her teeth and the sour odor of her breath:
What should life be when it has come to this?

Is there not mercy in heaven enough to spare
Some uncorrupted glint of mortal bliss
Now, in the lingering hour of her death?

Love
Tony

1965

December 17, 1965 New York NY
[To Donald Hall]
Dear Donald,

A note in haste. First thanks for the Maimonides double dactyl. It is lovely. And in fact I am writing to ask you to send me RIGHT AWAY as many good ones as you have written. For publication. There's money in it.

Let me explain. A few weeks ago [John] Hollander came into town, and one evening in a bar I explained the form to him. Since then he's been carried away; endless postcards keep arriving from Yale. Anyway, a few other people have heard about it, and some others have done some composing, now Esquire wants to publish two pages of them. So will you please send me your best. I'll keep in touch and let you know when they're coming out. (Nota Bene: the editor there with whom I am dealing feels they cannot reasonably print anything with "fuck" or "shit" in it, but they have no scruples [about] very much else).

It was fine seeing you all at Ann Arbor. You were very hospitable and I enjoyed myself enormously. Give my best to Kirby.

Tony

1966

Claire Nicolas White (1925–) is a poet, author, memoirist, translator, and editor. She and her husband, the sculptor Robert White, were at the American Academy in Rome with the Hechts. Hecht dedicated to her his translation of Du Bellay's "Heureux qui, comme Ulysse" in The Hard Hours.

Dear Claire:

Thanks for your letter, and for sending the poems. I'm glad you liked the reading, though a little regretful that you should feel that one of the poems, "The Room,"[4] in your words, "demands an answer." I feel I had read most of the official "answers" to it before writing the poem. In any case, it is not meant, as I hope you know, as an attack upon anything you or I or any decent person believes in; I agree that it is a very bitter poem, but it still seems to me, after thinking about the situation for more than twenty years, and about the poem for about 12 before actually writing it—I had notes for it when we were all in Italy in 1954—that the bitterness is not unjustified. [. . .]

Love to you, and to the whole family,

Tony

P.S. I notice that you swipe your envelopes from the Smithtown Bank. It is, of course, only a short step from envelopes to stock certificates and hard cash. If I read of anything of the sort in the papers, I shall know what to think.

1967

Jon Stallworthy (1935–) poet, critic, and biographer, was poetry editor for Oxford University Press, the English publisher of The Hard Hours. *On the occasion of a poetry reading excursion to England, a venture he shared, by happenstance, with Anne Sexton, Hecht was asked to provide a brief autobiographical summary for possible inclusion in* The Poetry Book Society's Bulletin.

September 12, 1967 [Rochester, New York]

Dear Jon:

[. . .] I was born in New York City in 1923, and for many complicated reasons, my childhood was a rather bitter and lonely one. Things picked up when I went to college, but not for long: in the middle of my junior year I enlisted in the army in order to be able to finish out that college year, and then was called up. After an infantry basic training, I was sent to a special language training program, presumably to prepare for intelligence work overseas. The program was to last 28 weeks; in my 24th week the whole thing was abandoned by Con-

---

[4]From "Rites and Ceremonies," in *The Hard Hours.*

gress because it was an election year, and the program seemed to favor college educated men and the sons of immigrant parents who had an edge in languages on the rest of the population. I returned to the infantry, and served in France, Germany, Czechoslovakia, and finally on occupation duty in Japan. In Germany, I was briefly attached to the Counterintelligence Corps.

My first encouragement in poetry came from John Crowe Ransom, under whom I studied after the war at Kenyon College, where I also taught for a while. I used to offer Mr. Ransom specimens of my work from time to time. He would harbor them somewhere and never say a word, and I was much too shy to ask his opinion outright. I was hoping of course that he would like something of mine well enough to publish it in The Kenyon Review, which he then edited. One day I went to call upon him in his office for some help and advice about a class I was teaching. It had something to do with Shakespeare, as I remember, and we were deeply and hectically into it, when I looked past his head to the blackboard where he habitually wrote down the names of the contributors to the next issue of the Review, in the order in which they would appear, and with the number of pages they would occupy. And there, to my astonishment, high on the list, and right between Lionel Trilling and Eric Bentley, was my name. At this point Mr. Ransom was being very animated about Macbeth, and all for my benefit, but I overcame my good manners and interrupted him to ask whether this meant that I was to appear in the next issue. He turned around to look at the blackboard, smiled, and in his very gentle Southern voice said, "I seem to have made a slight mistake," whereupon he rose, went to the blackboard and erased the H in front of my name, and put down Br instead. He was apparently going to publish a Brecht story with a commentary by Bentley. He did in fact publish a poem of mine in the next issue, but I have often wondered whether his liking for that poem might not have been tinged with embarrassment. [. . .]

Best wishes,
Tony

Melvyn and Dorothy Hecht, ca. mid-1950s
Courtesy of Helen Hecht

Roger Hecht, late 1930s
Courtesy of Helen Hecht

Left to right: Anthony Hecht, Ingrid North (wife of the artist Philip North), and Robie Macauley, University of Iowa, 1947
Courtesy of Cameron Macauley

Ischia, 1951. Anne Weiss (*second from left*), Elsa Rosenthal (*center*), Irving Weiss (*front center*), and Hecht (*far right, with beard*).
Courtesy of Emory University Libraries Rare Books and Manuscripts Division

Patricia Harris Hecht, Ischia, 1954–1955
Courtesy of Adam Hecht

Anthony Hecht, at a café in Europe, late 1960s
Courtesy of Adam Hecht

Evan Alexander Hecht, age 5, and father, 1977, Rochester, New York
Courtesy of Helen Hecht

With sculptor friend Dimitri Hadzi, in the Hecht back yard,
Washington, D.C., ca. early 2000s
Courtesy of Helen Hecht

Left to right: Chip Kidd, J. D. McClatchy, Anthony Hecht, and Kathleen Ford,
1998, on the occasion of his 75th birthday
Photograph © Dorothy Alexander

Left to right: Anthony Hecht, Nicholas Christopher, Edward Hirsch, and
Joel Conarroe, 92nd St. Y, 2003. Photo of W. H. Auden
on the back wall by Nancy Crampton
Photograph © Nancy Crampton

Helen and Tony Hecht, New York City, 1998, on the occasion of
his 75th birthday

Photograph © Dorothy Alexander

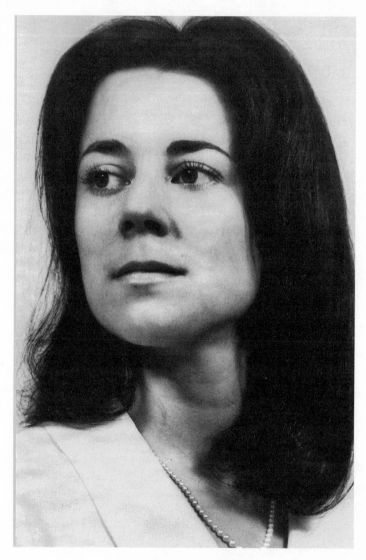

Helen D'Alessandro, 1971
Courtesy of Emily Boland

FIVE

A Second Life
1968–1982

IN 1967, ONLY MONTHS SHY OF RECEIVING THE PULITZER PRIZE
for Poetry for *The Hard Hours*, Hecht was appointed the John H. Deane
Professor of Rhetoric and Poetry at the University of Rochester. His eigh-
teen-year tenure at Rochester proved to be the longest appointment of his
academic career. Hecht was forty-four years old when he arrived and sixty-
two when he left. Despite the city's pewter gray skies, as he recalled in one
letter, the years there were also among his brightest and most productive.
After the lengthy hiatus between his first two books of poetry, Hecht pub-
lished two volumes within two years: *Millions of Strange Shadows* in 1977,
followed by *The Venetian Vespers* in 1979. As he remarked, somewhat to his
own astonishment, in a 1978 letter to Robert Fitzgerald: "For someone who
in the past has taken twelve or thirteen years over a book, this is a very heart-
ening and intoxicating experience." He was referring to the newly found
fluency of *The Venetian Vespers*, with its several long dramatic monologues;
but the experience of heightened creativity could fairly, if not intoxicatingly,
be extended to the decade as a whole. During these years, his poems ap-
peared with regularity in many of the familiar places—*The New Yorker*, of
course—but also in other journals and magazines new to Hecht, reflecting
a wider appreciation of his poetry both in England (*The New Statesman*

and the *Times Literary Supplement*) and in the United States (*The Georgia Review* and *Ploughshares*).

How do we explain this long decade of productivity? For one thing, winning a major award brought with it neither paralyzing anxiety nor simple lethargy. Letters written immediately following the award inform us that, along with working with Helen Bacon on their translation of Aeschylus's *Seven Against Thebes*, Hecht was busy on two very different fronts with his own verse. He was composing the high-spirited comedy of "The Ghost in the Martini," written in Rome in late 1968, in which a graying, still single, and now successful poet is enjoying the attentions of a young female admirer, while trying to suppress his earlier, sniveling alter ego. And he was soon to forge a new direction in the complex, dark, deeply self-involved dramatic monologue, "Green: An Epistle," a poem Hecht amusingly described at one point as being "lightly frosted," thus hinting at the role Robert Frost was coming to have in his imagination. In that poem, Hecht sensed he had struck a new vein, writing in a letter of September 1970 to his editor Harry Ford: "I've just received from Allen Tate a letter so head-swellingly flattering about 'Green' that I quote it *in toto*, shamelessly."

But Hecht's life was about to take a more dramatic and sustaining turn. In March 1971, at the National Book Award ceremony, the forty-eight-year-old poet briefly encountered Helen D'Alessandro, a former student from Smith. They were engaged ten days later and married in June. In separate letters written in March, Hecht would liken his happy plight to Bottom's being "translated" in *A Midsummer Night's Dream*—a comparison that anticipates the more elaborately described marvel of transformation that is the subject of "Peripeteia," published in *The New Yorker* (February 11, 1974) three years after their meeting. Describing this turn in events in a letter written in March 1971, he invoked a code-phrase for good fortune, dormant since his war years: "How beautiful upon the mountains are the feet of him who bringeth tidings of great joy" (Isaiah 52:7).

In almost every regard, Hecht's second marriage was the mirror opposite of his first. One of its immediate consequences for his poetry, with a long-term effect, was the emotional stability it brought to his personal life. He would often speak of being unable to write poetry unless he felt free from duress, a truth borne out painfully and in some detail in the letters from 1954 to 1955 when under the stress of his first marriage. And while the decade of the 1970s was hardly free of anxiety—his father's attempted suicide coincided with a pummeling Hecht received in the same week at the hands of Denis Donoghue in *The New York Times Book Review*—Hecht's hardest hours, although not altogether forgotten, belonged to his more solitary past. The dedication to *Millions of Strange Shadows* leaves little question about Hecht's changed personal fortunes: "For Helen *of whom I have / Receiv'd a second life,*" a line from *The Tempest* spoken by Ferdinand of Miranda— "miraculous Miranda."

The letters from this period, more than eight hundred, are among the richest and most varied in his career. No longer addressed to his parents (although Hecht's disquieting family circumstances emerge, like a Piranesian maze, in the densely autobiographical "Apprehensions"), the letters now embrace a wider audience, often on a more concentrated set of topics focusing on the subject and world of poetry. Those addressed include, most notably and with new emphasis, other now-established, albeit sometimes embattled, poets of the new "old guard": W. D. Snodgrass, Richard Wilbur, James Merrill, John Hollander, and Richard Howard, for instance. (Where W. S. Merwin fits in the mix is the topic of some interesting letters.) 1968 was not just the year of Hecht's Pulitzer, we must remember. It was also the year of the Tet Offensive in Vietnam, much campus unrest and sit-ins, Lyndon Johnson's determination not to seek re-election, the Paris uprisings, Richard Nixon's decision to run for president, and, in narrower but more immediate circles, of wide-open rifts in the poetry world—especially on the subject of political poetry, on which Hecht always cast a wary eye. (His own poetic response to political concerns of the time is best seen in *Shadows* in "Black Boy in the Dark" and "The Odds.")

A particular bête noir for Hecht in this period was Robert Bly, as a humorous letter to Harry Ford indicated (February 16, 1978). But not far behind (and rarely left behind) was Louis Simpson, who figures into many letters but most comically perhaps in the literary parable Hecht sent to Mona Van Duyn and Jarvis Thurston (March 31, 1976). A catalogue of Hecht's amused disdain for the current literary scene would find its way into one of his wittiest satires, "A Lot of Night Music," published in *Ploughshares* in 1975. "Poor, poxed Diana, laid open to the charge / Of social Actaeons"—an image (and pun) for the age, if not for all time. In the poem, the names of the gross offenders are politely left out.

The tenure of Hecht's appointment at Rochester produced notable exchanges with colleagues, particularly Joseph Summers, the Herbert scholar and friend of Elizabeth Bishop. (Like both Elizabeth Bishop and James Merrill, Hecht was an heir to Herbert's influence, evident in his poem, "Gladness of the Best.") As their friendship evolved, Summers became a trusted reader of Hecht's poetry, as his letter of June 16, 1978, suggests. Lost from this period, unfortunately, are all the letters but one to Cyrus Hoy, the delightful and formidable textual scholar and Shakespearean, to whom Hecht dedicated "Dichtung und Wahrheit." Hoy's influence can perhaps still be felt, however, in Hecht's increasingly more scholarly interest in Shakespeare during these years.

Although Hecht would often complain of being snowbound in Rochester (the weather inspired an amusing sestina) he still managed a few escapes, *en famille*. In the fall of 1973 he spent a semester as a visiting professor at Harvard; at Yale in the spring of 1977; and parts of several summers in Italy. The rewards were different in each case. Time spent at other universities widened his circle of friends among a younger generation of poets to include, among others, Brad Leithauser, Mary Jo Salter, and J. D. McClatchy, friendships that deepened over the years until the end of Hecht's life. The return to Europe was a return not only to Bellinis and gorgonzola, but to a primal source of inspiration, to which *The Venetian Vespers* and several other poems testify.

As Hecht's poetry began to receive greater attention beyond the reviews, he was brought into contact with scholars elsewhere, such as Ashley Brown, whose essay on Hecht inspired the poet to write to him about some of the books that mattered most to him. These years required an increasing number of ceremonies to attend, prizes to bestow (and occasionally lament), and poetry juries on which to serve—and some from which to resign, which Hecht could do with considerable force.

The letters from this period underscore Hecht's deeper immersion into the world of poetry. Some do so in a rather off-hand but still illuminating way. His brief note to W. D. Snodgrass points to the inspiration he found for "After the Rain" in Snodgrass's "The Marsh." More ample and complex, as the letters suggest, is Hecht's admiration for James Merrill's long poems, and the quiet challenge they posed and which Hecht answered in "The Venetian Vespers." As the letters from late 1977 reveal, no poem of his caused greater excitement in the making than this. And, for once, he left an extended record of his thoughts about the process and his intent. On the basis of his unstinting admiration for Bishop's poems, especially "In the Waiting Room," and for Merrill's "Lost in Translation," I suspect that Hecht was able to see his way into altogether new territory for him: writing an autobiographical poem of his own in "Apprehensions." So, too, his ongoing friendship with Richard Howard perhaps helped to further his interest in writing dramatic monologues.

Still, for all the seriousness of purpose found in the letters from this period—as in the one to Ira Sadoff, in which Hecht defends his use of diction in "The Grapes"—there continue to be many strains of Hechtian humor, not just in the letters to William MacDonald, to be sure, where, in one instance, he fabricates a version of himself for posterity, but also in the occasional limericks and little anecdotes sprinkled about. Along with letters of this sort, I have included a few curiosities: a response to one John Benson—"o rare John Benson"—who had requested lapidary verse inscriptions for a field of seafront monuments in Newport, Rhode Island (a project that never got off the ground). Another belongs to the burgeoning genre of responses to known and unknown poets hoping for criticism. Hecht received many such requests, which he always tried to answer. One from a person identifiable now by name only—Phyllis Siegrist—clearly touched a nerve.

Toward the end of the 1970s, Hecht's thoughts were turning increasingly toward literary criticism, especially of Auden and Shakespeare, and I've concluded this section with letters indicating this intensification in interest. But as the final letter to MacDonald indicates, the underlying psychic wounds brooded over in "Green: an Epistle" were, to Hecht's surprise, still not completely in the past.

1968

Philip Booth (1925–2007) was a poet and one of the founders of the graduate program in creative writing at Syracuse University, where W. D. Snodgrass, Donald Justice, and George P. Elliott also taught in the late 1960s. Hecht's friendship with Booth dates back to 1961.

May 2, 1968 Rochester NY

Dear Phil:

[. . .] I had a dream last night that you were right about what you have been hinting to me—that is about the Pulitzer. It made me feel very good indeed. But thinking back on it this morning I remembered that there was another part of the dream in which it was revealed that one of my colleagues here, a very nice guy, but very small, slight, frail and frightened, had an unsuspected and terrific record as a former professional football player. [. . .]

Best,

Tony

The Hard Hours *was published by Atheneum, where, for twenty-eight years Harry Ford (1919–1999) was poetry editor and responsible for creating a distinguished list of poets that included John Hollander, Richard Howard, James Merrill, W. S. Merwin, Mark Strand, and Mona Van Duyn, among others. In 1987, with the dissolution of Atheneum, Ford went to Alfred A. Knopf, taking many of his poets, including Hecht, with him.*

July 11, 1968 Saltaire, Fire Island NY

Dear Harry:

[. . .] I am just beginning a book that Richard [Howard] translated, and am exasperated with it because it is so fucking French. Perhaps you've read it: <u>Madness & Civilization</u> by Michel Foucault. I was put on to it by Donald Finkel. I confess I have not got very far, but I am already enraged. Why should it be that the French, who like to point with pride to the luminous clarity of the prose of Descartes and Pascal, should then proceed to write expository prose as if history or ontology were governed by the nice antitheses and parallels of prose discourse, and conceive that a metaphor, gracefully introduced at the beginning of a paragraph, and worked as hard as possible throughout it, should end by demonstrating an unambiguous and irrefutable fact? I ask, as Dr. Chausable [a character from Oscar Wilde's *Importance of Being Earnest*] said, merely for information[. . . .] The prose performs dexterous little mathematical feats of addition, subtraction, multiplication, and division such as a grade school child might surpass in, and having demonstrated its great precision and elegance in performance of these elementary disciplines, it asks the reader to take for granted that the subject about which it is discoursing must necessarily be suited to these functions and categories. [. . .] for example, the first half of page 23 sets up categories which it proceeds to invalidate in the most carefree way in the world, and that so eager is the author to arrive at the conclusion which he has set his heart upon, that he hopes to float there upon the bosom of inflated prose which is not meant to bear too careful an inspection.

I follow this little outburst with a little domestic, Dickensian one. A few days ago I found myself chiding my children for too ad lib. use of the word "fuck." Yesterday morning my older son (eleven and a half, going on twelve) had a genial chat with me in the morning when he woke up, and before breakfast. The chat wandered aimlessly, as it should have done at that time of day, and under the dazed conditions we were both in, not having quite come awake, when presently he said to me, "Daddy, what does 'fuck' mean?" Much struck by this question, I answered in the coolest and most surgical tones that it pertained to sexual relations between men and women. "I know," he said. "Then why did you ask?" said I. "Oh, I just wanted to see if you knew," he replied.

Affectionately,

Tony

Richard Howard (1929–), poet, critic, translator, reviewer, and editor of The Paris Review *and* The Western Humanities Review, *has taught at a number of universities, most recently, since 1997, in the* Writing Division *at Columbia University. His long friendship with Hecht dates back to 1950–1951, when Howard was an undergraduate at Columbia and Hecht a graduate student.*

July 27, 1968 Saltaire, Fire Island NY

Dear Richard:

I promise, I feel sure, to be a grave disappointment to you. First of all, I am by nature and training a rotten correspondent, lax and of weak character; whereas it is equally clear that you belong to the great epistolary tradition, full of flourish, style and promptness. I shall not be able to keep this up; I already feel my powers growing feeble. But more grave than even this, I am obliged to confess that I have not pursued Foucault; and for several reasons. Of these, one is my deep and inflexible conviction that originally the man's name was simply Fou, and that as a consequence of being teased by schoolmates, his whole mental life was so colored as to account for his entire career. Adding a second syllable to his name was a particularly unconvincing disguise, and he stands confessed as the very incarnation of his own topic [*Madness and Civilization*]. Secondly, the whole business has given me bad dreams. For several nights running now I have dreamed that I have been forced to attend a huge symposium on the subject of "Structuralism, Existenz, and Pop," the participants being Susan Sontag, Esther Montag, Eleanor Dienstag, Mildred Donnerstag, Betsey Freitag, Mitzie Samstag, and Herman Mitwoch, who is the moderator, but who is hopelessly unable to bring any moderation whatever to the proceedings, which never seem to proceed.

[. . .] I should like to take advantage of the kindness of your offer to let me read <u>Painting in Florence and Siena After the Black Death</u>. Millard Meiss does not sound French enough to scare me, and the title suggests a plentiful supply of dirty pictures to balance the offending footnotes. [. . .]

Best,

Tony

George Starbuck (1931–1996) was a poet and the director of the University of Iowa's Writer's Workshop (1967–1970) and the Graduate Program in Creative Writing at Boston University (1971–1996). Many years later Hecht would encourage the University of Alabama Press to publish Starbuck's Works: Poems Selected from Five Decades. *He wrote a brief introduction to Starbuck's poetry for* The Wilson Quarterly *19 (Summer 1995) and the foreword to the* Works. *The events described below pertain to the World Poetry Festival at Stony Brook, New York.*

August 4, 1968 Saltaire, Fire Island, NY

Dear George,

[...] The phone communication you had from Jim Tate had a certain spiritual kernel of truth in it. He did not behave very rudely to me, but it's true that he was very drunk and rather hostile. The hostility arose largely from the fact that he was so drunk that when he ventured to read some of his poetry to a small group of us, he was almost completely unable to do it. This was the general tenor of the whole weekend. Needless to say, you missed nothing. I left on the second day, but a letter from Snodgrass told me what I missed. [Louis] Simpson undertook to entertain the entire group of invited poets (more than 90) at his home. One of them sat on, and fell through, a glass table of his. Ed Sanders sufficiently provoked a visiting South American poet to swing at him, upon which one of Sanders' long haired friends attacked the visitor with a bottle in hand. (I have not heard how that came out, but I know that the South American had been invited by the State Department.) Denise Levertov was to introduce [Eugène] Guillevic, the visiting French poet, whose appearance was to end the whole weekend. She did not venture to appear till five or ten minutes beforehand (she skipped the rest of the conference) and then proceeded to take over very officiously and high-handedly, offending Louis as well as another woman who, along with Denise, was to read the English translations of the French. When Guillevic was finally done, she said, "My husband [Mitchell Goodman] has just been arrested, and I have written a long poem about it, and since you are such an appreciative audience, I'll read it to you." Someone remarked, quietly, "Her husband was arrested, and she is suffering from subpoena envy."

Best,

Tony

The "clipping" was from an August 2, New York Times article, bearing the title "Body of NYU Student is Frozen," about the Cryonic Society of New York, which advocates freezing the body at death in the hope of its being thawed back to life when an appropriate cure can be found for the cause of death. The article, and Hecht's response, served as stimulus for Richard Howard's poem, "The Failure of Nerve, an Epoch," dedicated to Hecht in Howard's Findings. (See also Hecht's letter to Howard of February 5, 1971.)

August 6, 1968 Saltaire, Fire Island, NY

Dear Richard,

Rotten correspondent though I be, I am not so poor as to fail to thank you for your letter and the Meiss book, and the clipping, which I return. My reaction to this last was a mild, familiar and historical sadness. You too may remember that early issue of <u>Partisan Review</u> that began a continuing symposium on what was called "The New Failure of Nerve." The title, as I recall, was taken from a book of Gilbert Murray's, perhaps from the <u>Five Stages of Greek Religion</u>. As it comes dimly back to me now, Murray was concerned to show that in a late and decadent period the Greeks, having lost all faith in religious, political and social orthodoxy, gave themselves over to cultish and fantastic practices and philosophies. The editors of <u>PR</u> saw an ominous return to this in the '40s; they might profitably have waited till now. This "freezing" business strikes me as scarcely more absurd than most of the other current cults including [Timothy] Leary and the hippies, the pseudo-religions and mind-cure movements, or even the student insurgents with their astonishing moral self-righteousness. I feel particularly puzzled and irritated by this last group because I find myself in some measure sympathetic with a number of their causes. But they are almost all like the son of Sir Andrew Undershaft [in George Bernard Shaw's *Major Barbara*], who confesses to his father that while, technically, he may be unqualified to hold any sort of job or do anything whatever, he at least knows the difference between right and wrong. This moral clarity, expressed with a remarkable shrillness, seems so simple and available to the young. I suppose I just sound elderly, and am obviously over 30, but I have come to think more and more of a poem by Simonides in which he says that it is not merely difficult to be good but very nearly impossible. [. . .]

All good wishes and many thanks,

Tony

Dickens scholar George H. Ford (1915–1994) was chair of the English Department at the University of Rochester when Hecht was hired.

October 20, 1968 American Academy, Rome, Italy

Dear George,

From the window of the living room in my luxurious suite on the grounds of the Villa Aurelia (which was the Corsini family's summer town residence, and which Bernard Berenson declared the finest villa in Rome) I can look out over my immediate private terrace, with geraniums in terra cotta pots and a quite large bay tree trimmed into the shape of a perfect dome, out through the pines to a clear view of the Basilica of Maxentius in the Roman Forum which appears in the middle distance, and much of the rest of the city, littered, as it were, between green branches, to the Alban hills beyond. Freshly cut flowers have been put on my dining room table, and tuberoses on the mantelpiece over the fireplace. I can smell them from here at my desk; they are mildly distracting.

I can afford to be mildly distracted, having arrived only a week ago; and I'm still giddy with excitement. I can see in the persons of the younger Fellows at the Academy the original dazzled awe at even being here at all, of having won the prize in the first place; not many of them have got their feet back on the ground, and some have been here over a year already. And their lovely delirium I first enjoyed in 1951, and again in 1954. So my return for a third visit seems all the more miraculous and unlooked for. I suspect it would be unkind of me in the extreme to spell out in any detail the sumptuousness of my circumstances and appointments. My immediate neighbor, besides the director of the Academy and his wife, is the composer Elliot Carter. We share more or less the same view; I don't grudge it to him.

Most satisfactory of all, I've gotten down to work. My collaborator [Helen Bacon] and I are 160 lines into a first draft of <u>The Seven Against Thebes</u>; and I am also working on a longish, vaguely comic thing of my own, tentatively called, "The Ghost in the Martini."[1] And I have material for several more poems at hand, so I have no excuse for not getting on, except the lure of the city, and the country beyond it. So far I've been puritanically self-denying; I don't know how long that will last. I've also undertaken to do a film script—a documentary about a work of sculpture by a friend of mine, Dimitri Hadzi, who was commissioned to do a huge piece by the federal govt. for the Kennedy Memorial Bldg. in Boston, which Gropius is designing. Other than this, I have almost nothing

[1] Included in *Millions of Strange Shadows* (1977).

to do except assimilate the ambience. And indeed though only here a week, I already feel at home. [. . .]

The other day, bright, clear and warm, I was with some friends in a rose garden at the top of the Palatine. This area was the property of the Farnese family in the 16th century, and they presently sold it to Napoleon III, who proceeded to louse up irreparably the remains of the imperial palaces beneath for his own gardening purposes. The gardens went to seed after a while, and Napoleon sold out, but much has been restored since (not the palaces, of course) and the roses were full blown, and the trees, ilex and cypress, marvelous dark and subtle shades of green against the bone-white brilliance of the Forum below. That was my only venture into town; except for visits to the foundry where the final sections of Hadzi's work are being cast and assembled. I suspect that if my present mood and resolve lasts, I won't get into town very much, or at least not enough to get a sense of its own life. This will be just as well. Esquire asked me to do a piece for them on Rome, but I've got enough to handle as it is. On the other hand, I have no illusions about the firmness of my character; for instance, I gave up smoking this summer, stopped dead, altogether. But three days out of New York on the Michelangelo the excitement got to me and I broke down. Still, I now manage on half a pack a day, which, for someone who smoked more than two is a sort of improvement. It also demonstrates, if such demonstration were needed, that I have managed to balance my strong puritan tendencies with a certain simple idiocy. [. . .]

Warm greetings to you and Pat,
Tony

1969

Melissa Frost was the two-year-old daughter of Lucy and Alan Frost in 1969. Both parents were in the Ph.D. program in English at the University of Rochester when Hecht arrived. Living in the same apartment complex, they helped to form a sort of surrogate family for Hecht and remained close friends until Alan, with family, returned to Australia to join the faculty at La Trobe University.

March 1, 1969 American Academy, Rome, Italy

Dear Melissa,

Will you still love me now that I've grown a beard? Personally, I think it looks rather distinguished, and here in Rome, where the people are pleasantly provincial in spite of the fact that this is Italy's Hollywood, I am regularly mistaken for somebody who is probably very important and famous, but who just can't be placed at the moment. It's really rather amusing to have people staring at you and conferring with a neighbor in whispers about who you might be. It happened to me years ago, when I had my first beard, and most amusingly in New York. I had taken a friend to see a new acquisition at the Met., an Aphrodite they had just copped. Having seen it carefully on an earlier visit, I stood back from the crowd and let my friend ogle from close up. Presently a very sweet old lady came up to me, and apparently mistaking me for a museum official or curator of some kind, asked me some highly technical questions about the statue and where it was found. I got out of that quite skillfully, I thought, and without showing my hand. Also in New York, and wearing the same beard, I told a cab driver to take me to the City Center, where the ballet was playing. Without further inquiry he left me at the stage door. So you see the sort of impression I am able to make. In case you're interested, my beard is the aristocratic, pointy kind that figures so often in the El Greco mural of the death of some Spanish saint. [. . .]

Love,

Tony

These comments, mainly about "More Light! More Light!" were for the revised edition of Twentieth-Century Poetry: American and British (1900–1970), *ed. John Malcolm Brinnin and Bill Read (New York: McGraw-Hill Book Company, 1970).*

June 11, 1969 American Academy, Rome, Italy.

Dear Bill Read,

There's a postal strike on here in Italy, so I have no way of knowing when or whether this will reach you, but I'll give it a try anyway. (Writing from Rome these days is a little like a seance with a peculiarly unreliable Indian spirit control. The reason I got your letter was that it happened to arrive during a brief visit of mine to the States.)

In answer to your questions (1) who is the martyr in the first two stanzas? No real person; the details are conflated from several executions, including [Hugh] Latimer and [Nicholas] Ridley whose deaths at the stake are described by Foxe in <u>Acts and Monuments</u>. But neither of them wrote poems just before their deaths, as others did. (2) Is the "shrine at Weimar" a reference to Goethe and is the title of the poem from Goethe? Yes to both. The title is what are reputed to be Goethe's last words. He stands, through them (and of course in other ways), as a representative of the German Enlightenment. Since there was no railroad station at Buchenwald, prisoners who were sent there were set down at the nearest station, which was Weimar, and then marched the rest of the way to the camp. (3) Is the incident with the Jews and the Pole an actual historical event? It is, though I have tampered with the ending by having the Pole shot on the spot. The event is reported in a book called <u>The Theory and Practice of Hell</u> by Eugen Kogen, who survived five years as a prisoner in Buchenwald, and who then helped draw up the indictments that were used at the Nuremberg Trials. (4) Is there anything further that might aid in presenting the poem? I don't think so; you seem to have asked the right questions and the rest of the poem is straight-forward enough. But since you are planning to use "Lizards and Snakes" I might as well point out (what you may already know and think obvious) that the last line comes from Milton's "On The Morning of Christ's Nativity." The intention, whether it succeeds or not, is not to be merely literary and high-fallutin. The woman who quotes it is supposed to be a certain kind of devout, Puritan mid-Westerner to whom the Bible and Milton are almost equally sacred texts, and who has most of both by heart. There are more such than one might think.

Thank you for your praise of <u>The Hard Hours</u>. I am back to writing poems again, after having spent much of this year doing a translation (in collaboration with a classicist) of <u>Seven Against Thebes</u>.

All good wishes,
Tony

William L. MacDonald (1921–2010), Roman architectural historian, taught at Smith College for many years. His friendship with Hecht dates from their stay at the American Academy in Rome, 1954–1955.

August 7, 1969 Saltaire, Fire Island NY

Dear Dodge Owner:

I hope, fer Cry Sakes, that you have kept my entire correspondence on file so that in due course you can make a mint of money by publishing my letters, you lucky bastard. I will even give you a few hints and guide-lines for the introduction, which, I think, might begin somewhat along these lines: "When I first knew Anthony Hecht he had not yet attained to the world-wide celebrity that was later to be his; he was a simple, charming, and modest young man—and all these qualities (except, possibly, his youth) he maintained throughout his career and despite his eminence." Something along that line, if you see what I mean. A few cheerful anecdotes to illustrate my natural wit and good nature might not be out of place, if judiciously chosen. But I suggest that if you must err, it be on the side of brevity, and that you let the letters speak for themselves.

I have just completed a poem on a touching, religious theme, which I send you forthwith:

> Said Mary to Gabriel, "Oi!
> Well, at least I am glad it's a boy.
> But what should I say
> When my waistline gives way?
> That I'm filled with elation and goy?"

I have an idea for some really filthy pictures for your book on Roman cities; I'm sure Mike Bessie will approve. After all, it will really sell the book.

Forever,
Jeremy Bentham

1970

January 19, 1970 Rochester NY

[To Harry Ford]
Dear Harry,

First of all, let me thank you for sending the [Perez] Zagorin book [*The Court and the Country: The Beginnings of the English Revolution*], which it looks as if I will not get around to reading for some time now, having in prospect instead a lot of god-damned exams and term papers to grade. Still, I look forward to a certain future leisure, when I can get down to it.

Meanwhile, and as a token of gratitude, I send you the following morsels.

> Said a model of Auguste Rodin
> As she rose from a pose for him, "Tiens!"
> So he ventured to seize
> On her "flowre delice,"
> As she gratefully murmured, "En fin!"

> Proust wrote in his "Recherché" one day:
> "There is nothing so cute, I must say,
> At least to my mind,
> As a young boy's behind
> If one's given to derrières pensées."

There was a young Gaul from the Somme
Whom sexual ennui made glum;
   At such moments he'd sigh
   With a tear in his eye,
"Il n'y a que des femmes et des hommes."

Scholars may some day inquire into the strong French influences here, and recall Eliot's debt to Laforgue. But only the most perceptive of them is likely to discover the "flowre delice" in its native home in [Spenser's] The Shepherd's Calender.

Best,

Tony

With Louis Simpson (as chair) and Lawrance Thompson, Hecht served on the 1970 selection committee for the Pulitzer Prize for Poetry, which W. S. Merwin received for The Carrier of Ladders.

July 29, 1970 Saltaire, Fire Island, NY

[To Harry Ford]
   Dear Harry,
   [. . .] Finally, I have just gotten your good, long letter, answering mine about the prize and the contenders. Let me say that for all my respect for Bill Meredith's work, it will not, for me, be "an agonizing choice" between him and Bill Merwin. I was one of those, as I think you know, who was doubtful about the "new style" when it first appeared in The Moving Target. I have slowly reversed myself on that. There is a lot of rather bad poetry that tries to fake the grand and bardic impersonal voice, and for a while I thought it both too easy and too self-serving, this desire to sound oracular. It is, of course, a style I have evaded. But in time I have finally caught the true lilt of Merwin's cadences and the tone of his voice, and I can tell now that his poems are not at all like the fake stuff I have seen so often. [. . .]

Yours,

Tony

L. E. Sissman (1928–1976), poet and advertising executive, received the National Book Critics Circle Award posthumously for Hello Darkness *(1978). His and Hecht's friendship dates back to 1967 when, serving on the Jury for the Lamont Prize, Hecht first encountered Sissman's poems. Hecht wrote a brief introduction to his poetry for* The Wilson Quarterly *19 (Winter 1995).*

August 14, 1970 Saltaire, Fire Island, NY

Dear Ed,

Thanks for your very heartening letter about "Green." I'm much indebted to you for your comments. I should like to know, further, if you think the second section should just be struck out, whether some other connective passage should replace it, or whether it should be rewritten, eliminating the "wry self-deprecation," but keeping those elements—the foreign room, the wobbly table—that are echoed in the last lines of the present version.

As for elucidation, I'm not sure I shall be much help. I'm still too close to the poem and therefore not quite reliable about what's in it. But I'll hazard a few words. It was a consuming paranoia that I had chiefly in mind (and, though this is scarcely relevant, and certainly not meant to be legible in the poem, I had in mind three different people only one of whom is a woman.) But with the appropriation of the evolutionary metaphor, the poem is really meant to work in a double way; that is, it presents a conception of nature as possibly malign. It has always seemed odd to me that so little notice is taken of the fact that all the current theories and commonplaces of evolution began along with nineteenth century ideas of progress; and that we unconsciously take for granted that any development of any species is a consequence of the survival of the fittest, which is in itself an assurance of the best. Best, at least, in the capacity either to outwit or overcome circumstance by brains or strength. But there is a certain naive optimism in this view which rests rather more on faith or on the heart's desire than on any proveable fact. Perhaps, when the terms of the poem are converted over to the psychic realm, the phrase "naive optimism" is unfair, and ought to be replaced by something like Santayana's "animal faith." I mean by this not only that man is born to sorrow as the sparks fly upward (and sufficient unto the day is the evil thereof) but that the whole of our psychic lives are given over to active and energetic motions toward some goal we esteem, or submission to what seems inexorable. We conceive these postures to be adequate and right, and we hope to be wiser or better or possibly even happier because of them. It would be dangerous for us to think otherwise. But the psychic life can be self destructive in even more camouflaged a way than nature. I suppose that the poem is also ambiguous in that it can be read as a self-accusatory statement by the speaker. That is to say, the reliability of the speaker may be questioned. Is <u>he</u> paranoid, and therefore given to seeing evil everywhere? There is, however, a sense of universal moral corruption that is intended to embrace the reader along with everyone else. How can we recognise evil if we are untainted with it ourselves? Who is not tainted with it; and who, in the end, can be a reliable witness?

I'm afraid I've sounded terribly pompous and inflated about the poem. No doubt not much of this comes through; and of course in the time of writing it, the thing worked itself out pretty unconsciously.

Warmest greetings,

Tony

1971

February 5, 1971 New York NY

[To Richard Howard]

Dear Richard,

Findings is really a splendid book, better, I think, than Untitled Subjects, though comparisons of this kind are foolish to make. Anyway, if the earlier book won a Pulitzer, Findings deserves at least as much. I've read it over with care and delight, and find myself deeply moved both by whole poems, and sometimes simply by certain little locutions, like the snake-swallower's "It isn't much different, what I do,/Except it's what I do." All of it seems genuine and admirable.

That is meant as tribute, and is sincere. What follows is comic gloss. You will observe how carefully I've read through the book by the following, as yet untitled, work:

"The beast is dying, will die, this year Of Gray's Elegy, . . ."[2]

A mild complaint of schoolboys, you would suppose.
But no. Marxists have long despised its smug
British condescension toward the poor,
    And as a medical man

Unpolitisch, trained at Hopkins and Zurich,
I can attest to divers mortal fevers
Brought on by a too careless text. Take Werther.
    A bloody epidemic.

[2]A line from Howard's poem "Scenes from the Life of Behemoth." A typescript version of Hecht's poem found in the archive does bear the title "Death and Literature."

I had a patient once who died of Boswell.
Not simple Boswell, mind you, but complications
Brought on by Clifford and the industry,
    Yale's eighteenth century

Machine without a God. It's not uncommon,
Though the A.M.A. will not inform the public.
What I don't understand is why the keeper
    Should read Gray to a rhinoceros.

                    With all good wishes,
                    Tony

                                            Feb. 24, 1971 NY

[To Richard Howard]
    Dear Richard,
    I have read through your new translation of the Gide [*The Immoralist*], a
book I had not read for years and years. So that while I cannot venture any
comparison of your translation with an earlier one, I take for granted your care
and fidelity to both the word and the spirit of the text. I hope you will forgive
me if I admit I found it an irritating book. I found my credulity taxed beyond
the demands of the wildest Gothic romance, both in general and in detail. For
example, it is very difficult for me to believe that Michel could possibly have
three friends who could endure to listen to such a protracted recitation with-
out interrupting him with a swift kick in the ass. These are not friends; they are
a species of saints. To put up with not only the sheer length of his discourse,
but his own blank uncomprehension of its meaning—Job should have had such
friends. As for detail, I quote: "I returned drunk with air, dazed with speed, my
limbs numb with a faint and voluptuous weariness, my spirits highly eager and
fresh. Marceline approved, encouraged my whim. Still in boots, I brought to the
bed where she lay expecting me a smell of wet leaves that she said she liked."
It seems to me impossible to believe that Gide ever went horse-back riding. [. . .]
After riding a horse to the point of "voluptous weariness" one smells of the
horse and the stable, not of "wet leaves," however many of them may have
hung pendulous in the Normandy air. Nor does it seem to me that this is defen-
sible on the grounds that it is a subtle authorial instance of Michel's blindness
about himself—if one may use blindness about a particularly insensitive sense
of smell. That would have been a good place in the narrative for one of them
to kick him.

I hope you will forgive my irritation; it is, after all, not with you. If it were, it would be a very brutal response to the kindness of your note. My quarrel is purely with Gide, who presumably has enough saintly friends to put up with him. [. . .]

Let me thank you again for the kindness, and the emphasis, of your response. It's very encouraging.

Gratefully,

Tony

Robert Fitzgerald (1910–1985), poet and translator, taught for many years at Harvard.

March 19, 1971 New York, NY

Dear Robert,

Burrowing through papers, I came across the poem I had written for the marriage of Andy Wanning's daughter and son-in-law. And since you asked to see it, I send it along. Let me also add that I had lunch with Andy in New York only a couple of weeks ago, and he has come to terms with his grief in a way that I find touching and heroic.

A Little Epithalamion for Margaret Wanning and Michael Sommer

Margaret, may the birched, beeched, the mapled and the firred
And bouldered woods of Maine
Echo and answer to you every word
Of Lasso's great refrain,
Which your young bridegroom will repeat again;
And may those joys for which the nations pray
Inaugurate today
A deep consent and concord, a clear peace
In an elect society of two,
Whose constant, dancing pulses shall not cease
To sing, "Mon Coeur Se Recommande A Vous."

And Michael, keep the music of this day
Dancing within her heart,
In which you bear the tenor, and must play
The instrumental part.
May all the wit of polyphonic art

And all its weaving grace so knit you twain
That the whole State of Maine
Shall echo Lasso in its lovely trees
As your own hill has echoed heaven's blue.
Organ and star, part upon part, agrees,
Singing, "Mon Coeur Se Recommande A Vous."

> Affectionately,
> Tony

March 24, 1971 New York NY

[To Alan Frost and family]

My dear (and numerous) Frosts,

[. . .] It may seem to you that I shall have nothing left to recount. But you shall be surprised.

[. . .] I am engaged to be married.

I leave a short space between paragraphs to allow for the calming of Melissa's hysterics. The girl is named Helen D'Alessandro; she is dark-haired, shining eyed, soft-spoken, gentle, intelligent and altogether lovely. She was a student of mine at Smith College. I was married at that time, and after that, of course, we had completely lost track of each other. But at this year's most crushingly crowded literary event, the National Book Award ceremonies on March 4th (to which I was invited only because the poetry prize went to a poet [Mona Van Duyn] published by my own publisher), we somehow contrived to bump into each other in a room the size of a grand ballroom, packed as densely as a loaded elevator. I wish I could continue this narrative with the sort of circumstantial detail it deserves, but the simple truth is that since I phoned her, four days later, I have been somewhat dazed, and my historical sense has somehow wasted away.

Rochester knows all about it. Rowland Collins came into New York for two days and saw a great deal of us while he was here. He, in turn, went back and reported to Amelia [Hicks, English Department administrative assistant] in great detail. And everyone now seems almost as giddy as I am. As for the two of us, we have not yet decided on a date or place; whether to have a big, little or no ceremony; or indeed any of the things that ought, I suppose, to loom large for us. We are virtually married anyway, and we will surely have gotten around to the perfunctory legalities before she comes back to Rochester with me next February. Meanwhile, she is continuing her job as an editor at a publishing house (not mine) and I, well, I am translated, like Bottom, in A Midsummer Night's Dream.

So, Alan, don't speak to me of work. What have I to do with work, man? I have no finished poems that I can give you, and though I have about four in progress, the progress has been completely arrested as of this month. And who shall say when I shall get with it again? But when I do, I promise you shall hear from me.

Meanwhile, it is wonderful to be able to exchange good news with you. How beautiful upon the mountains are the feet of him who bringeth tidings of great joy [Isaiah 52:7].

Love
Tony

May 12, 1971 New York NY

[To Allen Tate]
Dear Allen,

Helen and I have given serious and careful consideration to your extraordinarily kind suggestion that we get married in Sewanee. But out of solicitude mainly for her parents, who are rather old and do not like to travel, we have decided to do it "within convenient distance," to borrow a phrase from [John Donne's] "The Ecstasy." Helen's small apartment here in the city has a little garden in the back, and I have invited a Catholic priest whom I know at Loyola in Chicago to come in and marry us there (i.e. the garden). We expect to have on hand only her parents and mine, and possibly swell the ranks by the addition of her sister and my brother. I am sorry indeed to know that you have decided not to come up to New York for the Institute's and Academy's Ceremonial later this month, for I had particularly wanted to introduce Helen to you, and furthermore to tell you of my very recent visit with John Ransom during my swirling passage through the Ohio Poetry Circuit. "The old Gentleman," I think, "holds gallantly," and we spoke of you, and of his revisions of his work (some of which I ventured openly to regret) and of some new work I had never seen. His first remark to me, after greeting me warmly and studying me with a kind and considerate eye, was, "you're . . . more mature."

Affectionately
Tony

July 22, 1971 Saltaire, Fire Island, NY

[To Richard Wilbur]
Dear Dick,

Your publishers, at what I would guess was your own kind prompting, have sent me a copy of your translation of [Molière's] School for Wives. I had seen

it on Broadway, I'm delighted to say, with Helen, and with my visiting depart-
ment chairman from Rochester; and all of us so delighted in the fluency and
wit and style of the thing that I know I intended to write you about it, but
can't remember now whether I did so or not. That evening in the theater was
memorable in a number of ways, and in one particular that Helen and I still
cherish. A few nights later we were at a party at which two of the other guests
were John and Anne Hollander, and at which I found myself commending your
School for Wives in high and lavish terms. Presently Anne asked me to de-
scribe the costumes, and for the life of me I couldn't remember anything about
them, save that they seemed suitably "period" items, unassertive but fitting.
Anne, of course is something of a costume designer herself, and thought it a
primal weakness of intelligence to sit through a whole damn play without being
able to describe the costumes in the most minute detail. She adopted towards
me an attitude of elderly, psychoanalytic patience, saying that she was certain
that if I just dredged a bit in the foul waste and m[u]ddle of my unconscious, I
would doubtless come up with something to the point. The best I was able to
do was to recall a madonna-like blue dress that Agnes wore early in the play.
This merely proved to Anne that she was right about the essential feebleness
of my unconscious mind, along with my very faulty sense of priorities. During
the same evening John found it within himself to call Helen, who had just been
introduced to him as my fiancée, "a moral idiot." So what with one thing and
another, your version of Molière has a special and abiding place in our family,
which Helen and I think of from time to time with mirth and gratitude.

Best,
Tony

1972

---

*W. D. Snodgrass (1926–2009), poet and critic, was a friend of Hecht for more than
forty years.*

January 6, 1972 New York NY

Dear De,

I'm sending you the enclosed, nameless poem ["After The Rain"] because
it appears to me to be a remote relative—a second cousin several times
removed—of your own fine poem, "The Marsh." Also, in the hope that you
would not mind if I dedicated it to you. Needless to say, I would be grateful for
any critical comments you might be prompted to make.

My love to you and Camille, and I look forward to the time I can introduce Helen to you both.

Tony

Howard Nemerov (1920–1991), poet and critic, was Distinguished Poet in Residence at Washington University, St. Louis, from 1969 until his death.

April 20, 1972 Rochester NY

Dear Howard,

[. . .] As you must know—for Mona [Van Duyn] has written us that she has released the cat—Evan Alexander is amongst us, hearty of appetite and strong of lung. Too strong, if anything. In fact, sedatives have been recommended. And used. And though Helen and I are more or less constantly groggy, we are deeply happy and grateful, though there are moments when you would scarcely detect it from facial expression or passing expletive. We have also bought a house, a huge thing, and my first. I feel the mortgage hovering over me—at present no bigger than a man's hand, but the man is the Boston Strangler.

May all go well with you and yours,

Tony

1973

Hecht's friendship with the poet James Merrill (1926–1995) dates back to their first meeting in Rome in 1950. The occasion described below involved the deliberations of the Bollingen Prize committee, which selected Merrill as the 1973 recipient.

January 19, 1973 Rochester NY

Dear Jimmy,

I was delighted to get your note, but more delighted still to have had a part (one third) in the decision. Our deliberations were remarkable for their cordiality and friendliness, upon which we were all commended by the two Yale librarians who sat through our meeting, silent, like proctors at an exam. [. . .]

Helen and Evan and I flew from Rochester to Hartford, and then took a limousine to New Haven for the event. In the limousine with us was an indisputable hooker, redolent with the scents and gaudy with the embellishments of her trade. It appeared she was destined for the same hotel as we were. I made mention of this fact at the rather literary dinner party (Robert Penn Warren, Cleanth Brooks, Thornton Wilder, Pound's daughter, Stevens' daughter) and said that it occurred to me that she was very likely in the employ of one of the candidates for the [Bollingen] prize, and had been sent to New Haven to sway the jury. Thornton Wilder appeared doubtful, Norman Holmes Pearson seemed prepared to entertain the idea, the wife of the Yale librarian, Mrs. Rogers, was genuinely shocked. Only Eleanor Clark smiled.

We wish you all good things. We've not been in touch with Mona since the prize was announced, but we're sure that she must be as delighted as we are.

Yours,

Tony

Brad Leithauser (1953–), poet and novelist now on the faculty of the Writing Seminars at Johns Hopkins, studied with Hecht at Harvard in 1973.

July 19, 1973 Rochester NY

Dear Brad,

[. . .] It's hard for me to suggest good modern narrative poems to you because there aren't many of them. I don't think of things like Williams' <u>Paterson</u> or Pound's <u>Cantos</u> as narrative, and that also goes for long poems by people like Olson and Zukofsky. What I can actually suggest is a sort of heterogeneous, unorthodox mixture that fits into no comfortable category; but make of it what you will. Lowell's "Notebooks" has a sort of annual cycle and some personal history woven into it. Roethke's "The Lost Son" and "Praise To The End," I think you know. Robert Penn Warren has at least two books, one on Audubon (fairly recent) and <u>Brother to Dragons</u>, published in 1953. There is Ted Hughes's <u>Crow</u>. Two books by David Jones: <u>In Parenthesis</u> and <u>Anathemata</u>. There's W.D. Snodgrass's sequence, "Heart's Needle" in the book of that name. There's the title poem of James Merrill's "Nights and Days,"[3] as well as a poem called "From the Cupola" in the same book. There are several narrative poems in the books of L.E. Sissman, especially the volumes called <u>Dying: An Introduction</u>, and <u>Pursuit of Honor</u>. There are three volumes by Donald Finkel: <u>Answer Back</u>, <u>Adequate Earth</u>, and <u>Simeon</u>. Finally, there is Elizabeth Bishop's ballad, "The Burglar of Babylon." That's all that comes to mind, except for a lot of garbage. [. . .]

---

[3]Hecht must have been thinking of Merrill's lengthy "The Thousand and Second Night," since there is no title poem for *Nights and Days*.

I send you my affectionate good wishes, and all my warmest hopes for your poetry.

Yours,

Anthony Hecht

1974

April 17, 1974 Rochester NY

[To James Merrill]

Dear Jimmy,

[...] Evan has been allowed to tear up any copies of <u>The New Yorker</u> he has a mind to, except the one in which "Lost in Translation" appeared. I can't tell you how glad I am at last to see it before me and read it at leisure. It is every bit as stunning as when I first heard it, full of tact, splendor and perfectly controlled emotion. It seems to me, more and more, one of the finest poems of our time. I can't think of a poet alive who wouldn't be lucky to have written it.

We all send our love.

Tony

1975

For some years, Hecht and George Dimock (1912–2000), Smith College classicist, collaborated on an edition of Sophocles' Oedipus at Colonus *for the Oxford Series of Translations of Greek Plays under the general editorship of William Arrowsmith. All that remains of Hecht's efforts is "Praise for Kolonos" in* Millions of Strange Shadows *and "Chorus from Oedipus at Colonos" in* The Transparent Man.

May 2, 1975 Rochester NY

Dear George:

I should have written earlier, probably after our last phone conversation, but this is a rough time of year—classes ending, exams about to begin, and the lecture on Dickinson to polish and deliver. But however delayed this is, it is intended as a response to my "recollection" of that phone conversation, which may be very inaccurate; and I will be happy to stand corrected if I am wrong.

It was my impression that you felt the English text of the play as it now stands requires only minor and local revision. You spoke only briefly of the introduction, suggesting, as I recall, that perhaps it required more labors than the text. Let me set down my own feelings, as carefully as I can, and without any sense whatever of the tensions and confrontations that poisoned our earlier correspondence.

As you probably know, Arrowsmith gave some lectures at Cornell this term, and being so near at hand, came by to talk about the text. He has thoroughly convinced me that it is stilted and unnatural in its language, not merely in isolated passages but throughout. For this fault I should take the largest part of the blame; perhaps all of it. No doubt it is the result of my aim at rendering the play in blank verse, which has had, in more places than I can care to think of now, the effect of very inferior Shakespearean rhythms and dictions, and a certain amount of detectable padding. There are places where an elaborate and complex syntax, no doubt parallel to the Greek, but very "Shakespearean" for all that, is too much at odds with modern, or at least less stylized, rhetorical modes of address; and which would require such concentrated attention for the audience to follow as to become a serious irritation and an impediment to clarity and enjoyment. Please do not suppose I have been brain-washed by Arrowsmith into a desire to come up with a "pop" rendering—the chorus turned into young hippies, lots of electric guitar music, and the title changed to "Up Against The Wall." But I do think that to say, in a casual exchange, "My poor dear father, the towers behind which the city shelters, as far as I can see, are still far off," is, quite simply a language that does not ring true.

With regard to the introduction, it occurs to me that I have never actually written to you about your final draft. [. . .] Let me begin by acknowledging what you well know: I am no Greek scholar, and do not profess to be one. Yet I am disturbed by some things about your introduction. [. . .] Here I shall have to speak more bluntly. [. . .] I feel that your introduction as it stands greatly reduces the resonance, and indeed the importance, of the play. You seem to have chosen, for reasons of your own, to leave out or disregard all that is numinous in the text. I don't think that I am speaking as one with a pre-Raphaelite taste for softness, mysticism and foggy-mindedness. But the fact is, is it not, that Sophocles himself was an initiate in one of the cults whose rites were seriously concerned with the ideas of purification and rebirth, brought about through the strain of great trials, and with the assurance of a kind of immortality? As I read your introduction, it is my impression that you have turned the play into a rather simple and moralistic homily in which there are the good guys and bad guys, like a TV western; and if you persist in being a good guy despite all odds, things will work out for you in the end—as they do for Theseus, and as they will for Oedipus, who is to enjoy a posthumous revenge against his enemies.

[...] My discomfort arises, therefore, out of what I conceive to be an excessively "moralistic" reading of the play on your part, and a further sense of your own discomfort with what I call the numinous.

I hope this letter will not seem provoking; God knows, it is not intended to. [...] Still, it seems important [...] to let you know my own feelings about where I think we are.

With all good wishes,
Tony

1976

[To James Merrill]

Dear Jimmy,

I've been reading <u>Divine Comedies,</u> and while I am no longer absolutely speechless, it has taken me several days to find my voice among the keys I write with. The book is so breathtakingly fine that I am filled with the frankest envy, only barely overcome by delighted admiration. It is triumphant in ways so rich and complex, assembling so intricately so much of your life and your work, full of such deep, historical reverberations; so generous in its comedy, and so eloquent in its regrets, that to say merely that it is your finest book of poems is nothing. It is a work so richly satisfying, of such astute, mosaic beauty that I can think of no living poet whatever who could come near matching it. It arrived when I was in the midst of time-off from teaching and set aside to do my own work. But reading it, I confess, has stopped me dead in my tracks. I expect gradually to recover my self-esteem, and to go on; but for the moment I'm dazzled, and choose to do nothing but admire. Your work belongs completely in the company it has chosen: Yeats, Stevens and Pope.

Yours,
Tony

Mona Van Duyn (1921–2004), poet, taught for many years at Washington University with her husband Jarvis Thurston (1914–2008).

March 30, 1976 Rochester NY

Dear Mona and Jarvis:

Here is a little literary parable for you, taken more or less intact from <u>The Book of Knowledge</u>.

Fairies have more powers of magic than witches, and poets have more powers of magic than fairies. Poets can raise up mighty nations with their enchantments, and people the waste places with shining spirits. Thomas the Rhymer was one of these great poets. He could sing a man's soul out of his body and send it whither he willed.

One day the youngest daughter of the Queen of Scotland fell ill, and the Queen sent Thomas the Rhymer to get some magic ointment from the goblin hiding in the heart of Ailsa Craig.

Thomas the Rhymer came to Ailsa Craig and began to chant strange chants. He chanted the head of the goblin out of the great rock; he chanted its shoulders out. But just as he was chanting out its hand that held the magic ointment, a donkey brayed and spoiled the chant, and frightened the goblin clean out of the rock, and the goblin escaped with the magic ointment.

And so it is even unto this day. No sooner does a gifted poet (Jimmy Merrill, for example) begin to sing than some donkey (Louis Simpson, for example) begins to bray.

We delighted in our visit to St. Louis, and in nothing more than that we were able to see a great deal of you in our two brief days. The trip was in every way a success, and particularly from Evan's point of view. He had three girls (two Gasses and a MacDougal) to charm and to insult; a zoo to wander through and the weather to exult in. We all three are greatly pleased and very grateful. And we want to remind you to come visit us either on your approach to, or retreat from, Bread Loaf.

Love,
Tony

August 2, 1976 Rochester NY

[To Harry Ford]

Dear Harry,

I hope this will not come as too rude a shock, but I have a new book almost done. [. . .] I have even, in my enthusiasm, worked out the order in which the poems will appear, and there remains only to do the Brodsky and find a title for the book. It's not that I have no title; it's that I have two. One of them: <u>Apprehensions</u>—which is the title of a rather longish blank verse narrative poem. The other is: <u>Millions of Strange Shadows</u>, which is from a Shakespeare sonnet and is quoted in another poem in the book. You may not have any feelings on that topic till you see the whole works. [. . .]

All the best,
Tony

[To William MacDonald]

My dear young man,

It is, I think, salubrious and worthwhile for us all to meditate, from time to time, on the great theme of mutability and transience, to mortify our overweening vanity, and to say with the preacher, "What profit hath a man of all his labour, . . ." and so forth. What, after all, is Fame? And what, Celebrity? Fleeting evanescences, mere toys and illusions. I know you will think this simple modesty in me, and dismiss it with a casual wave of the hand. But when you attain to my age and gravity, you will know that some of those goals, which in your youth seemed the only possible or valuable target upon which attention could seriously be fixed, turn out in the end to be gossamer-frail or utterly illusory. What are we, after all, but a handful of dust, if I may thus express myself? I know you too well to doubt that you will protest, and point to the value of scholarship and the arts as in themselves conferring a sort of immortality. Ah, but we must chasten our hopes with a little dose of Sir Thomas Browne and Marcus Aurelius and Epictetus. Let me offer a salutary instance.

Remaindered books have their own humbling effect, of course, and no doubt this is truly beneficial to us all, but my instance only begins with that given datum. Browsing, as was my wont, in the university bookstore, I came upon a volume called Ancient Rome, by Georgina Masson, originally published in England under the title A Concise History of Republican Rome, and now (in a rough sense of that word) published in this country by Viking Press at $13.95, but reduced, when I encountered it in a sort of feverish clearance sale, to $3.48. You may not believe it, but I sighed the sigh of Heraclitean Flux, and a tear from the depths of some divine despair, of which Tennyson speaks, rose to my eye. But I bought it, and took it home. It is an interesting book, and perhaps it deserves its swift slippage toward oblivion, since it offers no acknowledgement to any other scholar in the field. Poetic justice, you may say; the cold, retributive force called up by vanity. But even this is not my instance. In the back of the book is what is called there a "Select bibliography." Not "selected" in the unpretentious sense merely of "chosen" or "picked out," but "Select" in the snobbish, patrician sense of the term. It must be admitted that some of the names that appear there are reasonably distinguished: Lanciani, Boethius, Rostovtzeff, L.R. Taylor. But, and here at last is my instance, one of the cited volumes was The Architecture of the Roman Empire Vol. I New Haven, 1965 by one L. Macdonald. These are the things, as I say, that instruct us.

St. Pelagia,
The Harlot

December 22, 1976 Rochester NY

[To Jon Stallworthy]

Dear Jon,

It occurs to me that in the murky future, when it has been at length determined that I am a poet of sufficient interest to merit the publication of a volume of "Selected Letters," the editor of that book will be at a loss to convey what may, in the last analysis, be the most sprightly, various, and original part of my correspondence: my letter paper. Indeed, I am engaged in a serious rivalry with a good friend of mine, one William MacDonald, an art historian, whose book on the Pantheon Penguin has published in your country—and our duel consists of trying to outdo one another in exotic letter paper. Since his profession calls for a good deal of travel, he has been able to pick up dandy stationery from hotels in Petra and Abydos and Mogador. I have not his same advantages, but I have my spies and wily ways, and was able to send him, at one point, a rather intimate and sinister memo from Spiro Agnew to Richard Nixon, on White House stationery. I dare say you can appreciate how the rich, full flavor of this will be lost to future readers.

Ah, well. [. . .]

Tony

1977

March 24, 1977 New Haven CT

[To Brad Leithauser]

Dear Brad,

[. . .] I thoroughly applaud your regimen of reading, and agree with you about the supreme accomplishment of Herbert. I don't know whether you feel that your reading of the poetry would be in any way chilled or spoiled by having it in concert with critical and scholarly commentary, but I would want to recommend A Reading of George Herbert by Rosemond Tuve (Chicago). I picked it up recently, remaindered for a dollar. It is a breathtakingly brilliant work of scholarship, humanely written, gently and thoughtfully argued, but documented beyond the possibility of dissent; and it demonstrates, among other things, with marvelous lucidity, the vast and subtle debt of Herbert to certain parts of the liturgy. That may not sound very compelling to you, but once you see it at work in the poetry you will see a great enlargement in Herbert's resonance; and some of the buried ecclesiastical metaphors (Christ as a bunch of grapes) surface with great force. In recommending Tuve I am not preferring her to Helen Vendler, whose book on Herbert I have not yet read. Nor to my own colleague at Rochester, Joseph Summers, whose book on Herbert I very much admire and have learned a great deal from. [...]

Thank you very much for writing, and keep in touch.

Tony Hecht

March 25, 1977 New Haven CT

[To Harry Ford]

Dear Harry,

We just returned from a spring vacation in Florida—where we had been invited by friends from Rochester—and I breezed into the Yale Co-op to see how things were doing, and one of the young men who works there and knows me asked if I had yet seen <u>The New York Times Book Review</u> of my book [*Millions of Strange Shadows*]. As he fished about for it he told me it was by Denis Donoghue, and I remarked that he was a critic I admired. And then I read the review as the young man stood there and watched. It was a little bit like being publicly disemboweled. The review is foolish and misses the point of the book. But the fact still is that this is <u>the one review</u> that everybody sees, and that it reduces to self-admitted failure, evasion and triviality the labor of ten years, and does so in the space of a few paragraphs. I try to tell myself that this brief review will not count heavily in the long run. But it is hard to dismiss Donoghue, who has written well on many topics, who has no visible literary axe to grind, is not part of any American literary or poetry establishment or counterculture, whose credentials seem quite unsullied. I'm feeling down in the mouth today for a number of reasons, of which the chief is that my father is rapidly losing his faculties, attempting suicide or threatening to, causing my mother and brother constant and unremitting alarm, yet they refuse to put him in a home. I found this out this morning by talking, first, to my mother and then, over her protest, to the family doctor. Though there would have been no <u>good</u> day to read that review, today was especially ill-suited for it. I am writing, not to ask for consolation, but to let you know that I have read the review, and that by the time the rest of the world turns to the Sunday paper I will have regained some of my balance, or at least I hope so. This is, therefore, not a letter that expects a reply; I'm simply grousing because I feel bad, and you are welcome to send this on to the incinerator with the rest of the junk mail.

Tony

[To W. D. Snodgrass]

Dear De,

[. . .] And speaking of being moved, I am writing to you on the very day that I'm being clobbered by Denis Donoghue in <u>The Times</u>. This may suggest to you a superb composure, but the fact is that I've had a few days to compose myself, having got hold of an advanced copy of <u>The Times</u> and having slowly and carefully swallowed my cup of poison.

The metrics of the chorus from Sophocles are in no way orthodox Greek, which I do not know. They are what I take to be a legitimately free and licensed English version of Sapphics, in no way strict either by syllable count or by accent, yet with enough resemblance to eye and ear to suggest the ancient form.

We send our love,

Tony

AEH: aeh

Daniel Halpern (1945–) is a poet and editor. Hecht's essay discussed below was never written.

May 17, 1977 Rochester NY

Dear Daniel,

Your letter (dictated, but not signed) of May 13th has served to remind me that I promised you something on Stevens; and has further served to make me focus on what I might possibly write about. And I think I've come up with a topic that might serve. Let me preface this by saying that my family and I are going off very shortly for about six weeks to Europe, and I don't expect to be able to address myself to the essay till perhaps the beginning of August. (I read, by the way, in <u>The New York Times</u>, that the government is going to send you abroad as an ambassadorial poet; very splendid indeed; congratulations.)

The topic I have in mind is: "Frost & Stevens: Styles of Reticence," and a major part of it would concern two Stevens poems, "Peter Quince" and "Le Mononcle de mon Oncle." There used to be some humorous taunting of one another that went on between Frost and Stevens when they met together in Florida, Stevens accusing Frost of writing on "subjects" and Frost accusing Stevens of writing on "bric-a-brac." But the fact is that both poets in rather different ways contrived to deal with very personal, sometimes emotionally devastating matters in their poetry. In Frost's case this is well recognized, even when he took certain precautions, and when he exerted a suitable and artistic reticence. With Stevens I think it has been less well known, or less noticed; and I think I can show something very personal about Stevens behind the "stage décor" or "bric-a-brac" of the two poems I mentioned. If you think it wrong to intrude Frost into a collection of essays so pointedly focused on Stevens please let me know; I don't want to upset your plans. But I think that the way different poets reveal and conceal themselves is an interesting one in these days of "confessional poetry," and while Frost and Stevens might at first appear to be polar opposites as poets, I think they used some of the same strategies and were urged by the same sort of tact and discretion. [. . .]

All good wishes,

Tony

In the fall of 1977, Hecht had begun work on "The Venetian Vespers," his longest poem, thus prompting this letter to William MacDonald, with its comments on John Ruskin.

September 9, 1977 Rochester NY

Dear Bill,

I suppose it was simple envy of the quality of your Polish joke that kept me from telling you in a straightforward way how splendid it is—surely the best I've ever encountered—and not only how splendid it is but the hysterical effect it continued to have on Helen and me for most of the day it arrived. Periodically we would lapse, without uttering a word, without reference to anything, into convulsions of laughter, like blithering idiots. [. . .]

With regard to S. Mark's, I've been reading Ruskin, as of course I should have done right away. After getting our eyes used to the underwater dimness of the interior he remarks, "It is the Cross that is first seen, and always, burning in the center of the temple; and every dome and hollow of its roof has the figure of Christ in the utmost height of it, raised in power, or returning in judgment." (Without meaning to quibble, I am absolutely certain that one of the domes, I think the west, or entrance, one has the dove of the Holy Spirit, not Christ, at its center.) It is true, in any case, which is Ruskin's main point, that while much attention is paid by inscription and design to the Virgin, Christ is in fact the presiding figure. But if he is here presented, as he is, whether in the domes or elsewhere, as "raised in power, or returning in judgment," may he not be called Pantokrator? What are the special conditions that permit the use of that term?

Must it be confined to buildings or images to the east of a certain meridian? I hope I don't seem to be nagging about a small point.

Ruskin is absolutely astonishing; I never read him before with any care. He has his moments of exhortation and rank evangelism, a sort of shrill and even hectoring high moral tone, reminding one uncomfortably that his father was a clergyman (I think) and suggesting that he is being weakly filial. But I find it easy enough to put those moments aside in the name of the vast variety of things that are brilliant and good and sane about him. Not least of these is that sound moral sense which condemns that aesthetic and moralistic purist who, finding an unsullied spiritual simplicity in Fra Angelico, is unable to stomach the worldly exuberance and vigor of, in his example, Rubens. (See appendix 15 of the First Book.) But even this sound, well-founded amplitude and catholicity of taste, is not in itself what impresses. What I find so striking on virtually every page is a vast knowledge—including the geological and topographical conditions that antedate all building—together with a deeply felt (I suppose there is no other word for it) "Moral" sense of the ways we live, or ought to live, or have failed to live, and the ways that these modes of living, healthy and unhealthy, worldly and spiritual, exalted or debauched, reflect themselves in works of art, and especially of architecture. There is no question but what he does [is] exactly what Ward Perkins [the Roman architectural historian] reprehended you for doing: interpreting architecture as an experience comparable to other forms of human experience. This seems to me, indeed, what all the best art historians are concerned to do; though perhaps I may confide a heresy to you. I suppose Panofsky and Wind are among the Dominations and Powers of art criticism in this century, and I admit to reading them both with fascination and delight, and of course with improvement. But their notion of iconography is essentially literary, and their approach to art is often a narrowly literary one. It may be an irony that I should be one to complain of this, and I don't mean really to complain. But reading their work has about it the kind of pleasure I get from detective fiction, in which the brilliance of the deducer or his fund of arcane knowledge is carefully and slowly played out like fishing line, and hauled in with the catch of a revelation at the end. Ruskin is simply far more philosophic, immediate, and direct, risking more and not showing off as much. Perhaps I'm just carried away by a current enthusiasm.

May all things go well with you. I hope I can make my poem justify all the ruminative pleasure I am taking in reading about Venice.

Unicus Aretinus

Elizabeth Hardwick was Robert Lowell's second wife, with whom he had a daughter, Harriet. Lowell died suddenly of heart failure on September 12.

September 13, 1977 Rochester NY

Dear Elizabeth—

I've just learned of Cal's death, and I write to say that I share a sense of the grief you and Harriet must feel.

I remember with special and vivid gratitude the kindness you and he showed me at a particularly bleak moment in my life.

Affectionately,

Tony Hecht

[October 10, 1977] Rochester NY

[Postcard: Ingres—La Baigneuse Valpincon, 1808,

Musee du Louvre, Paris]

[To William MacDonald]

Scout's honor, this is a blurb on a book I just received. The commender is Moshe Greenberg, Prof of Bible, Hebrew U. of Jerusalem. He writes: "Marcia Falk's translation of the <u>Song of Songs</u> is a very affecting and successful set of lyrics whose effect on me not once was to uncover new possibilities in the original Hebrew."

Louisa May Woollcott

December 23, 1977 Rochester NY

[To Howard Moss]

Dear Howard,

[. . .] I am not in the least surprised that you should have had at least one or two scruples about the poem ["The Venetian Vespers"], and that of these one should concern its length. Though I could not have known this for a fact, it would have been my guess that <u>The New Yorker</u> had never published a poem of this length; and of course it occurred to me to wonder what Mr. Shawn would make of a poem this long. But I felt there was a chance it might have a sufficiently intriguing narrative embedded in its midst to satisfy those perfectly legitimate expectations of the magazine's readers and editors. And I recalled also that, if I'm not mistaken, it was Mr. Shawn himself who at least once before threw all precedence to the winds by devoting a complete issue to John Hersey's "Hiroshima" report. Anyway, about the matter of length, it does not surprise me that this alone could constitute the single and sufficient obstacle to <u>New Yorker</u> publication; and I fear nothing could be done about that by way of abbreviating the poem to plausible and standard lyric size.

As for what you refer to as "the second difficulty," the "story" and your various questions about it, let me say, first of all, that I have made a small, but as I think, crucial, revision in the last two pages of the poem, which I enclose herewith. They constitute the addition of only five and a half lines, but I would like to hope that all by themselves, taken of course together with the other hints embedded in the poem, they might be enough to point the reader in the right direction. In the sincere hope that this indeed may be the case, let me ask you and Chip to read through the poem with the enclosed pages 28 and 29 substituted for the ones you have on hand, and see if they bring things into any sort of focus. Admittedly, this is not straightforward, unambiguous narrative, and the very questions you raise in your letter to me are precisely meant to be raised in the reader's mind. But I shall reserve showing my hand completely till the second page of this letter, in order to let you read the poem without any further, and I hope, superfluous, gloss.

And now, before continuing, let me say that beside the additional lines supplied herewith I have made a few changes of wording here and there throughout the poem, nowhere radical, and always in the name of clarity or the decencies of English speech. So here is the cat, let out of the bag. The narrator is a man in a deeply troubled and turbulent state of mind, whose chief torture is that his troubled mind can never be set at ease and satisfied. He is, flatly, unsure whether his father is the man the world takes to be his father, the man who disappeared when the narrator was one year old, and came back dead when the narrator was eighteen, or whether in fact the man the world takes to be his uncle may not in truth be his biological father—who, if he did not actually send his brother west to make his fortune was by no means displeased with that plan, having already cuckolded him and begotten a child by his wife, and who found it easy and convenient to keep him locked up in a distant city so that his affair might continue. Why should the narrator think this even possible? Well, first because of the uncle's inordinate grief at the narrator's mother's death, grief which remained starkly unexpressed, and perhaps unfelt, at the death of his own brother. The fact that, even at best, the uncle's explanation (for it can only be the uncle's post-facto excuses being repeated here) of why he betrayed his brother by allowing him to linger in a Toledo asylum is a cruelty and heartlessness so grotesque in itself, that the additional sexual betrayal could certainly be ascribed to the same person as being at least no more hideous a motive, and at least as understandable. The fact that the uncle undertook so specifically and particularly to "make himself a parent"—not an adoptive parent or foster parent but one with all the "forbearance" that true intimacy entails, and one who leaves everything to his son.

The son, the narrator, feels repulsed and contaminated by this inheritance, both the money and the uncertainty. And feels a terrible loyalty to the man, known as his father, who was betrayed. He therefore contrives, on the whole unconsciously, to expose himself either literally or symbolically, to all that his so-called father had to go through. He exiles himself to a foreign country where he knows no one and where he takes pains to get to know no one. (Incidentally, his early encouragement at home, obviously from his uncle, to be good at elocution and vocabulary was intended to keep him from being, as well as from ending up, like his so-called father, a step a true father might want to make to keep his son more his own and unlike someone else.) His experience in the war, in which he enlists to get out from under his uncle's roof, leads to a Section Eight, a "mentally unfit" discharge, and there are signs in the poem (recollections of someone tranquilized by a hypodermic and then straightjacketed, "trussed like a fowl") that, like his so-called father, he knows what asylum life is like. He has cut himself off from family life as his father was cut off. He has taken upon himself the penance for all the accumulated guilt, largely suspected, but absolutely unproveable, of what went on when he was a child. The very fact that he will never know the truth, all central persons in the drama now being dead, is what makes him constantly fear for his own sanity and recall the insanity of others. His doom is never to know for sure; therefore his constant attention throughout the poem to visual clarity, and his constant assertions that visual clarity, for all its clarity, is misleading: we never know the truth. Venice for him is hell. But it is an apt, a fitting hell because it is all artificial, that is, man-made, just as all he suffers from is man-made. And, of course, it is a city with all the gorgeous emblems of salvation (which for this man fail to work) as well as the emblems of worldly grandeur and success, now reduced to decline and impoverishment, like the history of the narrator's family, like the narrator's fear of death.

Okay. That's the gist of it. It is still my hope the poem has largely worked for you without your having read this far. (That last line about the wise child "who knows his own father" ought to be a dead give away.) Anyway, if you feel that my gloss supplies essentials which the text of the poem itself conspicuously lacks, or which are not sufficiently clear or not emphasized enough, I'd be more grateful than I can say if you would let me know quite candidly. I am so greatly encouraged by the enthusiasm of this letter that I feel I would be prepared to make any revisions that I could be persuaded were really to the point, if they would then satisfy you and Chip McGrath and Mr. Shawn. Please, after enjoying the finest of holidays, let me know what you think.

> With grateful good wishes,
> Tony

1978

Having lettered the word AESOPIC for the title page of the book of couplets Hecht composed in 1967 for the Gehenna Press, John Benson, of the John Stevens Shop in Newport, Rhode Island, wrote Hecht inquiring whether he would consider writing lapidary inscriptions for a "group of standing stones."

> February 10, 1978 Rochester NY

Dear Mr. Benson,

Many thanks for your letter, which I found both flattering and bewildering. After all, it isn't every day I'm invited to become part of a literary Mount Rushmore, or given the promise of such marmoreal perpetuity. Even the setting, as you sparely describe it—"10 acres overlooking the sea"—has something about it that would not be out of place in a Victorian novel of pathos and high passion.

When I think to myself of such texts as actually find themselves graven upon buildings and monuments—the pious platitudes on post offices and court houses, or else the mortuary inscriptions "That teach the rustic moralist to die"—it occurs to me that what they are likely to have in common is the convention of their sentiments (since public feelings are not to be outraged) and the brevity of their statements (since this kind of engraving must surely be the most exacting and laborious there is). All of this inclines me to wonder just what it is that this exotic invitation of yours, o rare John Benson,[4] desires of me. I am indeed curious, while reflecting, as I cannot help but do, that there is already a body of great American poetry from the past, some of it both brilliant and terse (the names of Philip Pain and Emily Dickinson instantly present themselves) that could handsomely answer your purposes. Unless, of course, your purposes were especially directed towards some immemorial anthology of contemporary American poetry. Were that the case, I should think you might perhaps be

---

[4] The wit of the transposed "O Rare Ben Jonson" (or "Johnson") is very rare indeed, the phrase appearing as the inscription, not on Mt. Rushmore, but on the slab above Jonson's grave in Westminster Abbey.

not untroubled by the qualms that must always beset an anthologist; and the dangers of misjudgments, the faults of omission or inclusion, must be vastly magnified by such ineradicable, monumental and conspicuous publication. We are prepared to forgive even maudlin sentiments on a tombstone, if only out of some civil respect for the dead and for the bereaved. But we are under no such polite compulsions when the text is obliged to stand on its own. You are kind; you are more than kind, you are highly flattering, in suggesting that I might compose, might perhaps have already written, the sort of thing that could bear such incising without mockery. Let me hear more of your plan.

Very truly yours,
Anthony Hecht

February 16, 1978 Rochester NY

[To Harry Ford]

Dear Harry,

I was, as you may imagine, filled with warm approval of the letter of outrage you addressed to Harvey Shapiro in behalf of Bill Merwin.[5] Up here we don't get advance copies of the Book Review, and so I have not yet seen the Bly review. But curiously he has been vaguely present in my mind for the last few days, perhaps because of another piece he did for the Times Book Review a few weeks ago on Carlos Castaneda. Castaneda is not, frankly, a writer who interests me in the least, but when a Bly review turns up I normally read it since I can count upon a number of splendid imbecilities that keep me humming contentedly to myself for days on end. And I had been thinking to myself after reading that review that Bly after all had something else to recommend him besides the pure amusement he almost always afforded me. In his own odd way he was very nearly a reliable critic; which is to say, I could be almost certain of liking any book with which he found vigorous fault. In that particular Castaneda review he found occasion, God knows why, to abuse C.S. Lewis, with particular reference to his autobiography, "Surprised by Joy." This is a book I had always been meaning to read, and Bly's attack, converging upon my discovering the book, in paperback, remaindered at a sale, encouraged me to buy it, and I'm now reading it with all the pleasure of which I was virtually guaranteed by Captain Bly's maledictions. [. . .]

Affectionately,
Tony

[5]Ford's letter was published in the *New York Times*, April 30, 1978. Bly's review of Merwin's *Houses and Travellers* appeared on February 5, 1978.

Ashley Brown (1923–) is professor emeritus, University of South Carolina. His essay, "The Poetry of Anthony Hecht," appeared in Ploughshares *4 (1978). His friendship with Hecht dates from the early 1970s, when the two met in Brazil.*

April 18, 1978 Rochester NY

Dear Ashley,

Your splendid essay arrived yesterday, and for some eighteen hours I have given myself up to shameless narcissism. You could not have been more generous and flattering; I could not have hoped for a more sympathetic ear and eye, or a mind more accessible. Though you were so modest as to say in your letter that you supposed I might "find something to disagree with on every page," my response to what you have written is one of uncomplicated gratitude. [. . .] If anything, I might offer you here, privately, a small confirmation of an incidental apercu of yours. You write: "One might suppose that his main reference for the tragic vision would be <u>King Lear</u>, the play which has had a special fascination for the post-war world, but it seems to be the <u>Oedipus at Kolonos</u>, the great classic of reconciliation. . . [.]" The fact is, you are right in both cases. The evidence for the voice and presence of Sophocles is there, and you have pointed to it. As for <u>Lear</u>, there is an interesting and odd anthology by Richard Howard, called <u>Preferences: 51 American poets choose poems from their own work and from the past</u>. The idea of the book was to illustrate a true and intimate connection between "modern poetry" in all its brash novelty and the traditional work from which it actually derives. The choices are sometimes interesting and thought-provoking. Auden chooses a Campion poem, as does Creeley; Dickey elects a passage from Christopher Smart, Elizabeth Bishop chooses Herbert, Ginsberg takes Wordsworth's Immortality Ode; Merwin, the ballad Thomas the Rhymer, etc. I believe I'm the only one in that anthology who elected a passage from Shakespeare's dramatic verse: <u>Lear</u> 4. 7. 44–75. I would guess that, along with <u>The Tempest</u> (which, like <u>Kolonos</u>, is a great play of reconciliation) <u>Lear</u> is the play I "know" best and most carefully; the one I have taught most. But more to the point of solid evidence, the tragic vision of <u>Lear</u> is actually present in <u>The Hard Hours</u>, in the final part of "Rites and Ceremonies." The lines, in quotation marks,

"None does offend,
None, I say,
None"?

is <u>Lear</u> [4.6.168]

[. . .]

You are right, I think, in your feeling of the modern importance of Herbert to many poets, critics and readers, and your sense that he has edged out Donne in our esteem. They are, of course, not easily comparable, and lumping them together under the rubric of "metaphysical" does not make them so. There is often something boyish, show-offy, sometimes even strident and ostentatious in Donne, and even in his fervent religious poems, which contrasts markedly with the eloquent, unposturing reserve of Herbert. We have also, of course, been richly and well instructed by the likes of Rosemond Tuve, Joseph Summers, Helen Vendler and others. That he means much to me is evident not only in the little anthology you asked for and which I enclose, but also in his central presence in "Gladness of the Best" in Millions of Strange Shadows.

To return, for a moment, to a strand that binds Lear to my work, they both touch on, not so much madness as the fear of madness. It is there in "Behold the Lilies, . . ." and "The Venetian Vespers," "Birdwatchers of America," "And Can Ye Sing Baluloo," (which has some genuine Lear eye-imagery) and perhaps elsewhere. In any case, it would justify your chosen epigraph.[6]

I am grieved by the news of Allen Tate's blindness. I had been dawdling with the idea of sending him a copy of the "Vespers," but now that would merely impose, perhaps unpardonably, upon the time and patience of Helen [Tate's wife] or someone else who would have to read aloud to him. What is saddest of all is the thought that almost as soon as he is dead everyone will suddenly feel the need to acknowledge his central importance to American poetry, and the honors which he might have enjoyed and certainly deserved in life will be heaped like tin wreaths on his grave. Meanwhile he must dwell in a Miltonic obscurity, deprived of light and notice. I should not want to write him a letter obviously generated by solicitude, which would merely annoy or offend him, and grieve his wife. Nor could I quite pretend not to know of this late declension into darkness. I would like to write, but I must find the right strategy.

The snows are at last part of the ubi sunt of Villon, but last night, for example, the temperature went down to 30, and nothing of consequence is in bloom yet, not the forsythia nor crocus, which I have seen in New York and Baltimore. We are retarded up here, but we shall come limping into spring one of these days.

[6]"What is it to be free? The unconfined/Lose purpose, strength, and at last, mind." From "The Nightingale," included in *AESOPIC*, published by the Gehenna Press in 1967, with twenty-four couplets by Anthony Hecht to accompany the Thomas Bewick wood engravings.

Many grateful thanks for all your labor over and devotion to my work; my debt and my pleasure are both greater than I can say.

Tony

[To Harry Ford]

Dear Harry,

I have now had a chance to read well into, if not all of, the three books you most recently sent me, by [John] Hollander, [Mark] Strand and [Daryl] Hine, and have read at least enough to make my thanks to you—and my general satisfaction with the high stature of Atheneum's poetry list—a substantial thanks and satisfaction. Fancy though that sentence may be it intends to convey how enormously impressed I am to get three such extraordinary volumes at once, anyone of which would be of greater moment and value than almost any book that comes my way for long stretches of time.

John's book [*Spectral Emanations*], first of all, is truly an impressive achievement, solid and brilliant, rich and varied, and everywhere firmly accomplished. I think I must have every one of his books, and have read them with care, so I have no right to be surprised by the strength of this book for which he has assembled so much from earlier ones. But, oddly, I am; they combine with the new poems to make a strong and original canon of work, an ambitious and large realm that is distinctly his. This book recommends itself for some important award; it is a major volume, not only in its author's career, but in our poetry. Please let John know of my high esteem.

Then Mark's [*Late Hour*]. The book is very moving. Certainly the equal of, possibly superior to, the last two books. I am struck by how Mark seems to have gone, in Eliot's phrase, "by the way of dispossession." The poems convey so poignantly the pain of renunciation, forced or willed, exacted or granted. In most the speaker seems mercifully mesmerized against at least some of the pain, while fully "aware" of the cost. The deprivations are both inside and out; the world itself is thinned to the fewest conditions and objects, the persons are all nameless, faceless and without employment. And as for inside: "My flesh is a grave with nothing inside." The dawn of luminous renewal spoken of on the jacket may be there, but it is still off on the edges of the horizon. In the main these poems still seem to me dazed, breathless and forlorn; and consequently very affecting. None of the verbal slapstick of "Eating Poetry," and the most earthbound poem here is the one dedicated to Elizabeth Bishop. A strong, bare, honest book.

And Hine [*Daylight Saving*], last only because I know him least, and never met him. As witty and ingenious as any poet now writing, and certainly more suave and skillful at his gymnastics than anyone since Auden. The sheer dexterity of the poems deserves acclaim. For all three, much thanks. And much praise to you and Kathleen and the House of Atheneum itself, which seems a tower of literary strength. [. . .]

Tony

June 10, 1978 Rochester NY

[To Harry Ford]

Dear Harry,

Thanks for your note about "The Short End," and for the honesty and candor of your comment. Your dismay consorts with the reaction of the three people, not counting Helen, who have seen it so far, and who have had no trouble containing their enthusiasm. It has been in the hands of Howard Moss for about two weeks and I have heard nothing. But if his reaction conforms to those I've had, I would guess that he has not yet returned it only out of embarrassment at too swift a rejection. My own confidence in it has been a good deal shaken.

But I've not completely lost faith in it. Admittedly, and indeed, deliberately, this is a different sort of poem from any I've written. You wonder, in your note, whatever gave me the idea to write it. I'm not sure I can trace its origins accurately, but I do know that after finishing "The Venetian Vespers" I wanted to do something that would balance it by dramatic contrasts: the sleazy instead of the opulent, America instead of Europe, a woman as central instead of a man. That was one of the aims. Another was to take a character almost entirely unprepossessing, a fat and slovenly drunken woman with garish and vulgar taste, and to try to win the reader's sympathy for her by the time the poem was over. That is to say, if the reader is obliged to reverse his initial sense of repulsion and his emotional bias against her, then the poem would have performed one of the tricks I'd hoped from it. And then, before the poem had taken any shape or outline, I knew I wanted to get down that desolate landscape in November, and contrast it to the stage-set dawn of the New Yorker ad.[7] I'm puzzled that the poem suggested John O'Hara to you, for to me its atmosphere seems more like Nathaniel West. But if indeed it has that mordancy, if it has the overtones of an Ensor painting, then, though it make the skin crawl somewhat, it will have worked as it should.

[7]Examples of the advertisement referred to here and in more detail in the following letter can be found in *The New Yorker*, February 15 (1966), p. 218, and October 15 (1973), p. 168.

Needless to say, it is not my ambition to continue in this vein; but I could not help regarding it as, if nothing else, an expansion of horizons.

Anyway, thank you again for your frankness, which I value highly. If opinion continues undivided about this thing, I will have to regard it as a puzzling aberration, and hope that it never takes possession of me again. Meanwhile, still waiting to hear from Howard, I've given a copy to my colleague, Joe Summers, a friend and admirer of Jimmy Merrill's and Elizabeth Bishop's. Just trying to hold out a small hope.

Best

Tony

Joseph Summers (1920–2003), scholar of seventeenth-century literature and avid reader and teacher of poetry, was Hecht's longtime colleague at the University of Rochester.

June 16, 1978 Rochester NY

Dear Joe,

It's not easy to tell you how grateful I am for your letter about "The Short End," and how heartened. If I have a grim fantasy about what the undetected onset of senility may be like, it involves my writing a poem I myself regard as very good by the standards at least of my own work, only to find that friends cough and avert their eyes, unable to tell me straight out that, like late Wordsworth and others, I've gone into obvious literary decline. [. . .] Since I pretty much expect the New Yorker to turn it down [which it did], your good letter will at least relieve me of supposing that their rejection confirms what everybody but I can see: that I've taken to blathering, and, what's worse, at length.

Your suggestions, especially the slug, are pertinent and useful, and I shall make use of them. I am, however, a bit worried about your own uncertainty concerning the end of the poem. I emphatically do not mean to be obscure or difficult, and not even, though you use the word, surrealist. What I intend, whether it succeeds or not, is this: The woman is drunk. She allows her eyes and mind to play over the New Yorker ad. She identifies with the slim, young woman in the ad, and in so doing places herself at the end of Fifth Avenue in the arms of a young man. She is, in a drunken sense, bilocated, being in her home and in Washington Square at once. She scrutinizes the image of the flame in the carriage lamp. On the literal level, she is merely isolating that image in the ad for close inspection. It seems to repeat in its hues all the colors with which, in her pillows, she has always surrounded herself, those flame colors which she seems to like. These become profoundly real to her in her scrutiny because, in her drunken state, she has set the house afire. If that much is not clear then there is still work to be done.

Of course, Joe, you may keep the poem.

Gratefully,
Tony

[To William MacDonald]

Dear Bill,

If you could without great inconvenience help me out in a matter concerning a painting I'd be much obliged. The painting is by Renoir, it's dated 1872, and called "Parisian Women Dressed in Algerian Costume." It hangs in the National Museum of Western Art in Tokyo. The best reproduction I can find of it, which leaves much to be desired, is in black and white, and appears in <u>Mnemosyne: The Parallel Between Literature and the Visual Arts</u>, by Mario Praz. There are a lot of things in that picture I can't read, partly for lack of color, no doubt from reduction in size. But in the hope that you can lay your hands on a good reproduction among your own books or the Smith archives I have a number of questions to ask. 1) With regard to the woman in the background with her back to the viewer: is she looking at a painting or a mirror? The woman left foreground is taking at least momentary notice of her in a pause during making up the central woman. If that's a mirror in the background, the woman regarding it has apparently already been made up by the same cosmetic artist, and is now admiring the effect, while the artist pauses to listen to her praise. If a picture, though little enough of it is shown, it might be another exotic, Algerian one (by Ingres? Delacroix?) and the background woman is reporting cosmetic effects to the foreground artist, who is trying to put them into practice on the central subject. 2) What is the curious, fluffy thing on the carpet beside the sandal? 3) What is the pendant that the artist seems to hold in her left hand? 4) What is the background behind the artist? We must assume that the literal setting is a Paris apartment that these women have tried to redesign to resemble a sultry harem or desert tent. 5) Am I right in thinking I see a parquet floor at the lower left?

All these bear upon a poem I'd like to write,[8] and I'd be more grateful than I can say if you could help. I report with chagrin that neither the Rochester

---

[8]"The Deodand," included in *The Venetian Vespers*.

Memorial Art Gallery nor the Art Library of the University was able to help me in any way.

We send our love,
Tony

For Robert Fitzgerald

Robert, how pleasantly tempting to surmise,
    As Auden half suspected,
That heaven and the benign Italian skies
    Are intimately connected.

And once there we shall truly be translated
    In grand Italian style
And <u>bella figura</u> flourish, who are fated
    To tarry here the while.

Amid hill towns and palaces where dwell
    The blessed of heaven's See
They shall address you as Signor Freetzjell,
    Me, Signor Hecate.

With love,
Tony

Commenting on a poem that William MacDonald showed him, Hecht was led to recall an incident from his own army experiences not published elsewhere. A version of the events recorded here exists in the Hecht archive at Emory University.

September 1, 1978 Rochester NY

Dear Bill,

I'm delighted by your poem, "Hadrian Orders the First Batavians to Swim the Danube." [. . .] The first part of it seems to me especially successful, <u>exactly</u> conveying that insufferable arrogance of high-ranking officers who, under the guise of undertaking no more than the enlisted men, show off with useless feats of strength or daring—[. . .] supremely without regard to the cost in life to others of such heartless ostentations. The smug, vain, unawareness of

Hadrian, the decent compassion of the veteran who speaks, are both clear and telling.

I am, however, less certain of the propriety of the <u>tone</u> in the last part. The propriety, that is to say, of the explicit <u>complaint</u>. After all, when a soldier signs up, he is, for the term of his service, putting his life itself on the line whenever it's called for. No doubt it can be called for foolishly, to no great purpose, merely for the convenience of the top brass. You and I both know of such behavior from our own war experiences. I myself remember a particular example. My regiment was stationed on the west bank of the Rhine, across from Cologne. The east bank of the river was fortified by a very high, immensely thick wall of reinforced concrete. Orders came down from, not merely Division, but from Corps or perhaps even from Army, to send out scouting expeditions at night in rubber boats, to reconnoiter the far side of the river. Two companies (not my own, thank God) were chosen, in both of which I had friends, to perform this foolish, pointless and costly errand. They went out at night in rubber boats, were spotted by enemy searchlights above those walls, and were ruthlessly machine-gunned in the middle of the river.

This happened not once or twice but time after time, and there was no information to be gotten, even had the enemy not fired a shot, except the fact that there was a thick concrete wall on the far side—a fact which you could tell by looking across the river in the day time. This, however, took place during our division's first three weeks of actual combat; and the speculation throughout my own company on the reason for this mindless massacre was simply that our Division Commander, who had himself never committed any troops to combat, was too scared to disobey one of his first combat orders—to conduct reconnaissance of a specified kind. It was my first real insight into the way wars are regularly waged. Outraged, however, as my feelings were then and still are, it would never occur to me, in a mild and reasonable tone, to argue with the general on what he has a right to do, on what we've signed up for, on Justice. What I guess, after all this palaver, I'm getting to is perhaps merely the excision of about two and a half lines. [. . .] Anyway, my quibble is small, and your poem is a strong and fine one. [. . .]

> We send our love,
> Tony

Gary Metras (1947–), poet, reviewer, and the editor and publisher of Adastra Press, taught high-school English for thirty-one years. In the summer of 1975, he studied with Hecht at Bread Loaf and, in 1980, received his master's degree from Goddard College.

November 13, 1978 Rochester NY

Dear Mr. Metras,

You were right in guessing that I would not remember your name nor the poems you showed me that summer of 1975. If my critical comments on those poems were harsh, as they must have been to turn you to your long poem of invective, you at least have been generous enough to characterize the comments as made with "kindly thoroughness." And indeed your letter is full of honest dignity in its account of the anger and frustration my negative reaction aroused. And I would not now be able to write you without a complex sense of embarrassment were it not for the fact that your collection of poems, <u>A Roomful of Walls</u>, seems to me so powerful and successful, so eloquent of strong, controlled emotions, that I am at the very least reassured that my coolness towards that early work did you no permanent damage, though I'm sure it caused you much pain at the time. Robert Frost, another old Bread Loafer, used to say, "It's hard to know how much discouragement is good for a man." I repeated that once to another poet, who replied, incredulously, "Why, <u>no</u> discouragement is good for anyone." But he was wrong, and Frost was right. And perhaps my coolness fired your ambition. But in hoping so I don't mean to take any credit for the very considerable achievement your collection represents. I can only congratulate you, and wish you continued success.

Sincerely,

Anthony Hecht

1979

March 13, 1979 Rochester NY

[To Gary Metras]

Dear Mr. Metras,

[. . .] With regard to your plans for entering a writing program, I have, I'm afraid, no advice to offer you except, perhaps, this: I suspect that, given the initial talent, one may learn more informally than formally from a teacher, so it is best to study with a writer one admires rather than seek out an elaborate program or a school with a fancy name. What I mean is that if I studied under Elizabeth Bishop, whose work I enormously admire, I would not expect to be instructed by her in matters of technique—which, after all I could learn on my own, or by attempting to imitate her work—though no doubt she would go over my poems with me in instructive detail. But I would probably learn more, in the end, from her appraisals of other poets, especially if those appraisals were different from my own. Why should she like X and not Y? To be able to grasp those almost-never articulated standards and modes of taste is what I think of as the most valuable kind of literary education. [. . .]

Yours,
Anthony Hecht

Hecht, who describes his friendship with Dimitri Hadzi in his letter to George Ford of October 20, 1968, collaborated with the artist to produce a fine press, limited edition of The Venetian Vespers, *published by David Godine in 1979, with etchings by Hadzi.*

March 31, 1979 Rochester NY

Dear Dimitri,

I'm delighted to hear that the work goes well on the Venetian project. As for the "sources" you inquired about, let me say that I read Ruskin's <u>Stones of Venice</u> here and there, but especially his descriptions of St. Mark's, and I have appropriated some of his language in the poem: especially as regards the initial darkness of the church when entered from the sunny piazza, and the gradual clarification of its interior as the eye accustoms itself to the muted light. Also the lines about the "dissolute young with heavy-lidded gazes of cool, clear-eyed, stony depravity" are virtually Ruskin's own words about the people who hung around just outside the church to pick up tourists. I read <u>A Wanderer in Venice</u> by E.V. Lucas, a pleasant, popular book, which supplies the names of Buono and Rustico. I had a cheap, paperback guide book, published by Scrocchi, and picked up when I was in Venice around 1948; probably long out of print, but not in any way distinguished. There is a good deal about Byron in Venice by Pete Quennell, but there seems to be no need for you to look into any of that unless it interests you. I did however, look at lots of pictures, and especially a book called <u>Wonders of Italy</u>, part of The Medici Art Series, published in Florence by G. Fattorusso. This has wonderful photographs of virtually all the mosaics in St. Mark's, as well as much else in Venice and all in great detail. I'm not sure you need any of this, but there it is.

Love
Tony

Austin Warren (1899–1986) was an author and eminent literary critic, whom Hecht first encountered at Kenyon in the summer of 1948.

April 27, 1979 Rochester NY

Dear Austin,

I've just returned home from the happy business of conferring the National Book Award for Poetry on James Merrill—a ritual I performed in the company of Elizabeth Bishop and Michael Harper—to find a copy of <u>Sewanee Review</u> [volume 87, Spring 1979] with your fine article on Auden. I thank you for it in the double sense of having first of all composed it, and then of seeing to it that the copy came my way. I have read it through with pleasure and assent. It seems to me you perform exactly the three tasks you set out for yourself— always allowing for the fact that an attempt to say "what kind of man" any- one was can never be quite perfectly realized. And in Auden's case this task is complicated by a remarkable reticence regarding his own virtues. He is the only man I have ever known who went to the same contorted pains to conceal his kindnesses from public notice the way most of us conceal our vices. You cite his famous gift to Dorothy Day ["how, looking like a tramp, like her own 'parishioners,' Auden emerged from a crowd to give her a check for $250 and then disappeared"—p. 244][9]; he must have suffered agonies when that became widely known. But the stories I have heard, all second-hand, confirm both an unusual generosity and a fanatic desire to conceal it. I've heard, for example, that after World War II he adopted, anonymously and through some agency, two German war orphans, and quite simply undertook to guarantee their up- bringing and education through college without ever meeting them. There is another story about a young man in Ischia who somehow got a fish-hook caught in his eyeball, and the physician having to be fetched by bicycle from an- other town, Auden was the only one willing and able to stay with the wounded stranger and hold his head and talk with him till help arrived. I cannot vouch for either of these representative tales, but they conform with my sense of the "kind of man" I think he must have been.

With regard to another question you raise—"how he could be at once a Christian and a practicing homosexual"—perhaps with years he arrived at the settled formula by which you explain that reconciliation, but I don't entirely

[9]A fuller version of this anecdote can be found in Humphrey Carpenter, *W. H. Auden: A Biography* (Boston: Houghton Mifflin, 1981), p. 382.

believe it, and at least have personal, first-hand knowledge that at one time it was not so. I knew him in Ischia for about a year in 1950, and once he ventured to speak candidly, movingly and briefly on this topic. Recollections from so far back are bound to be misty and likely to be distorted, but my sense of the conversation is that it began with Auden saying that in the absence of a church of his own he regularly attended the Roman Mass, and of course made his confession. There was some jest about the wisdom of seeking out a Franciscan, say, instead of a Dominican, if there were something especially burdensome to confess. It was in this context that the problem presented itself, and I remember very clearly that Auden said he took very solemnly the injunction against sodomy in Deuteronomy. He said it with such simple, unqualified force that all talk ceased for a very long interval until some altogether different topic presented itself for discussion. His declaration carried the weight it did because it was itself an open confession of spiritual unhappiness, and at that juncture in his life, as all of us who were there well knew, he was not enjoying domestic tranquility. And I can't help feeling that my recollections here are borne out by precisely the essay on [J. R.] Ackerly you cite, in which he [Auden] says, "Few, if any, homosexuals can honestly boast that their sex-life has been happy,"— which is admittedly not the same as saying it is contrary to the decrees of religion. Nevertheless, for someone like Auden I would guess there must have been some connection; why else should homosexual love be "damned" as unhappy? Not, for Auden at least, because it came under the public censure of parochial bigotry, for which he would have felt only contempt.

Finally, while agreeing with you that Auden was never an anti-semite; that, as you said, "many of his best friends, early and late, were Jews;" yet I think that in his case the point has to be made positively rather than negatively: he was not merely not anti-semitic, he was "philo-judean," and some of his friends used to remark that he regarded himself as an honorary Jew. Whether he did indeed I don't know, but somehow, and perhaps not unlike Bonhoeffer, he meant to preserve himself and his Christian faith from any taint of complicity with what happened under the Nazis. And to do more than merely preserve himself and his faith out of some sense of fastidiousness; not so much to "set himself off from the wicked" as to embrace without reservation whatever the wicked condemned. And to do so for love. I believe he was personally stung by any expression of anti-semitism wherever he found it, and it was his especial humiliation to have to take account of its expression on the part of certain poets and teachers he revered. There is no doubt whatever, for example, in my mind that he is referring to a barbaric sentiment of Eliot's when he allows the Narrator (in section IV of the part called "Summons" of the Christmas Oratorio) to say:

> . . . and the recent restrictions
> Upon aliens and free-thinking Jews are beginning
> To have a salutary effect upon public morale.

He must have known, in writing that, that Eliot might take it as a slight. And it is by no means the only such gesture in that text.

As compared with your large and generous survey, my essay on [Auden's] "In Praise of Limestone" is narrowly circumscribed. It is due in the fall, and I shall certainly send you a copy. Meanwhile, I hope you will not find any impertinence in my comments here; none, certainly was intended. And I hope, moreover, that your eyesight is happily restored.

Affectionately,

Tony

I have not been able to discover the identity of this person beyond the fact that she lived in Montana when she wrote to Hecht.

May 3, 1979 Rochester NY

Dear Phyllis Siegrist,

Your letter and accompanying poems arrived at what is for me, and perhaps for you, too, an especially busy and almost frantic juncture of the academic year; I'm up to my ears in term papers and poems from my own writing students and the hot breath of the registrar, calling in dragon-flame for my grades. So I cannot give you here what I think you may have hoped for: a detailed commentary on individual poems. I'm sorry if this disappoints you, but you were right in guessing that yours is by no means the only unsolicited manuscript that has recently come my way.

To speak generally of your work, of such work of yours as I've seen, let me say that I think you are genuinely talented, markedly gifted; though at the same time (and this is no disgrace, considering your youthfulness) your work is recognizably derivative, and excessively "influenced." At this early stage that is not in itself necessarily a bad thing; one probably always learns one's first writing skills by the sedulous aping of the styles and authors one most admires. Moreover, it is pointless and foolish to attempt earnestly to "be yourself" till you have a pretty firm sense of who you are. That "identity," in person and in writing, appears in time, and without effort, like the evolving signs of bodily maturity. But there is about your work something else that disturbs and bothers me—as I suspect it is intended to. You display what appears to me to be a "spiritual affinity" to those two shockingly self-destructive poets, Sylvia Plath and Anne Sexton; and when I say this I don't mean to say that you are as yet anywhere near as skilled a poet as either of them. I mean merely that you seem to me to be playing with some of the simple ingredients that go into many of their poems: a powerful solicitation of the emotion of pity (either for yourself or for someone else) which at the same time is hedged and protected (though never quite disguised) by a certain hardboiled stance, a posture of tough indifference. This is a combination of attitudes that can be very endearing in adolescent boys, but one is very eager to see them grow out of it. In any case, what I am talking about is more than merely a matter of literary strategy; your poems, a few of them, suggest that you are disposed that way, that you have a sort of addiction, which their (Plath and Sexton's) careers have made, if not respectable, then shockingly and defiantly successful.

One may not presume to give advice to an addict. I myself am proud of having quit smoking about three or four years ago, but it was not, as it ought to have been, out of respect for the warnings of the Surgeon General. And with regard to that hungry and understandable need to try to make something out of one's misery (and how almost sufficiently rewarding if it turned out to be a good poem!) it is a plausible, perhaps even a laudable motive. And it can be shown to lie behind a good deal of excellent writing. It's a primary force in Keats's "Nightingale" ode, and it preoccupies Herzog in Bellow's novel, when he writes, "On the knees of your soul? Might as well be useful. Scrub the floor." But that native desire to turn deficit into profit becomes dangerous when it turns to an habitual need for misery to make poems out of. For after all, poems can come out of other sources; and be made out of other ingredients than pity in a hard-boiled masquerade.

If I am right in this little, long-distance attempt at diagnosis, you are not likely to be pleased with this letter; and of course if I am wrong you are likely to feel equally contemptuous. But after all, you did send me your poems, and I have simply tried to say what I found in them. Let me, in any case, wish you well most sincerely, and hope that things may prosper for you both as a person and as a poet. And believe me when I assure you that these sentiments do not arise out of some simple-minded YMCA heartiness; I have seen a portion of the darkness myself, and have tried, fumblingly, to make something of it. But as a vocation it is a poor one at best.

Yours,
Anthony Hecht

August 9, 1979 Rochester NY

[To William MacDonald]

Dear Bill,

We just got back a few days ago, and of course I have found waiting for me your Piranesi lecture, along with some genial cards from you. I've had a chance to read the lecture through once with care, and to browse in it here and there as well before writing to thank you. It strikes me as so dense and suggestive that it should more properly be acknowledged with a long, discursive letter of thanks. I was reminded, for example, of a recent book of photographs of Freud's home in Vienna, and especially the room he used for his practice of therapy. It was filled, as no doubt you know, with ancient artifacts, most of them fragments, many of them Egyptian, as well as Greek and Minoan. His archeological interests were clearly a symbolic parallel to the dredging up of the unconscious or the buried personal past. And in Piranesi there is not only the same archeological bias, but, as you make clear, a keen interest in foundations, in unadorned underground structures and a focus which is usually looking up from below. Those cellar-ages do suggest the terrifyingly large and unsuspected dimensions of a buried and hidden life; they cast something of the same spell as the enclosed spaces (The Cask of Amontillado, The Pit and the Pendulum) in Poe. This is not to side with those who call Piranesi a romantic or drugged hallucinator—though he did consciously romanticize some of those scenes in their later states, as you point out. But for now I can only send my very grateful thanks for your rich, provocative work.

Tony

Daniel Hoffman (1923–), poet and critic, formerly taught at the University of Penn-sylvania. He is the editor of The Harvard Guide to Contemporary American Writing *(1979). His friendship with Hecht dates back to the 1960s.*

November 14, 1979 Rochester NY

Dear Dan:

Nearly a month ago I saw one of the ads for the Harvard Guide, in which I found mention of my name, so I sent off for the book. Shameless in the vanity that prompted me, I continued shameless and vain in turning first of all to see what you had said of me, and now I must report that my vanity could not have been more generously gratified. I did go on, of course, to notice what you had to say about certain others, too; buoyed by your kindness, I was prepared to let you spread your generosity widely. Yet, just, careful, perspicuous as you were in every case I examined, I returned again with increasing satisfaction and gratitude to what you wrote about my poems. Especially I want to thank you for your detailed concern with "Rites and Ceremonies." You are the only reader I have ever come across who has not stopped at noticing the debt to Eliot— Lowell remarked as much—but could see the "double-edged" nature of that allusion to him in a poem about the Holocaust. You were right in detecting the consequent complication of tone, involving homage but bitterness, and both overlaying the horror of historical fact. You are the first person to make me feel the poem is not a pretentious failure. For that, but indeed for all you wrote I send my very grateful and sincere thanks. [. . .]

Sincerely,
Tony

1980

[To Robert Fitzgerald]

Dear Robert,

We met last amid all the Roman grandeur of the White House, and you had only just launched upon an encomium about me when I must have appeared to turn my back on you and walk away. I hope that when I returned I was able to make clear what had happened. There was a gentle tap on my shoulder, it was Jim Wright's wife, Annie, saying they were leaving immediately and that Jim, who could scarcely speak, wanted to make his hasty farewells. Without so much as an apology to you I turned and went to embrace Jim, and say goodbye and wish him well. I hope you were not offended, though after the Wrights had left, and after we, Helen and I, had gone to get our coats and were remounting the stairs in order to depart by the main portico, we passed you descending, and you looked very earnestly as if you did not desire to be addressed or to acknowledge noticing us. Though you, too, tried to catch up with Jim to say goodbye, I gather you must have missed him, or so Annie has told me. The news from her is as bad as it can be. Jim, who is now in Mt. Sinai, will soon be discharged to a hospice after a second platinum treatment. He is not expected to live more than about three months. Annie is hoping for nothing more than that he may regain enough comfort and energy and presence of mind to make final revisions on a rather large book of poems. She is breath-takingly brave, and seems frankly more concerned about the effect Jim's death will have on my brother, Roger—who really has no other friend but Jim—than about herself. It leaves me wordless.

I am sorry for all reasons to be writing this letter. But I hope at least to renew contact with you. I know about your Virgilian undertaking, and have something droll to send you about that poem, but it has no place in this letter. Instead, I send my love.

Tony

April 19, 1980 Rochester NY

[To Brad Leithauser]

Dear Brad,

[. . .] If you go to Japan you cannot fail to be impressed with the enormous natural beauty of the countryside. I was there for some eight months on occupation duty at the end of WWII. What I think astonishes most of all is that Japan looks just as Japanese art leads you to believe it does, and being there seems like a magnificent and magic confirmation of an aesthetic predisposition. I had the same, dream-like feeling in Italy, where the Alban hills, the Apennines, the pines, the ilex and laurel all suddenly appeared, like props from the background of Renaissance Italian paintings, known to me through reproductions and visits to selected American museums.

I'd be interested in seeing your reviews, especially the one of Jean Stafford's stories. I knew her quite well at one time, and there are people who believe that I figure as a prominent character in one of those stories. But do not trouble to go combing through them again to try to find me. If I am indeed there I am so thoroughly bemasked as to be beyond all possibility of identification.

May all your projects prosper.

Tony

Jacqueline Simms succeeded Jon Stallworthy as poetry editor for Oxford University Press.

August 15, 1980 Rochester NY

Dear Jacky:

[. . .] Yes, a number of very appreciative reviews of <u>Vespers</u> have indeed reached me from your clipping service, seasoned, very properly no doubt, with one contemptuous dismissal to prevent me from becoming light-headed and uppity. A certain Andrew Motion (which sounds like a term in the physics of outer space) expressed his wearied irritation and lofty incomprehension in <u>The New Statesman</u>. And even among those who have praised the book generously, both in England and here, there have been stunning examples of obtuseness, for instance about "The Grapes," in which several reviewers suggested that in an interesting though not altogether intelligible way a bunch of white grapes were meant to be a symbol of mutability. I suppose, however, that one should prefer to be misunderstood by someone who regards the work favorably rather than unfavorably.

I am finishing up a "quartet," called "A Love for Four Voices: Homage to Franz Joseph Hayden," which will in no way resemble any works by The Possum [T. S. Eliot], being far more light-hearted, and, indeed, written for four voices, representing the four instruments of the string quartet and given the names (Hermia, Helena, Lysander and Demetrius) of the young lovers in <u>Midsummer Night's Dream</u>. It's a kind of masque, though not, I think, one that could very easily be performed or even set to music, there being too much text. Still, I feel I've made some headway towards a new book, and it's important to me that I should feel this since I'm not likely to get any work of my own done until the academic year concludes in spring. Give my warm and affectionate greetings to the Stallworthys.

Gratefully,
Tony

David Lehman (1948–), poet, critic, and editor, teaches at the New School and New York University.

December 15, 1980 Rochester NY

Dear David,

[. . .] I like the new poem enormously ["The Square Root of Minus One"]. On first reading, it seemed at the very least a <u>tour de force</u>, or rather a grand tour of literary monuments—which indeed it is—but it is more than that, and more serious; it's a matter of coming to terms with the Ruins of Rome, as in Ronsard and Du Bellay and Piranesi. It is, or seems to be, a choice of whether to consider ourselves the ghosts of ghosts, or the immensely favored beneficiaries of price-less heirlooms. And the final truth is that we have no choice but to become comfortable with the past.

<u>The Hard Hours</u> is a rather bleak note on which to end the semester. I, by

contrast, ended a course of mine on the Pastoral Tradition with Keats' "To Autumn." [. . .]

> With best wishes,
> Tony

1981

Timothy S. Healy, S.J. (1923–1992), Donne scholar, D.Phil. (Oxford, 1965), was president of Georgetown University (1976–1989) and The New York Public Library (1989–1992).

January 14, 1981 Rochester NY

Dear Father Healy,

Tomorrow I begin teaching "The Wreck of The Deutschland," and I'm prompted as a consequence to write to you, protracting by a little the puzzling I've done over "dandled the to and fro" [in stanza 16]. Whatever small merit this letter may have may reside in the fact that it requires no answer. I should like to add to the controversy about that very odd phrase what cannot, I suppose, be called anything like solid evidence; doubtless something flimsier than that; but evidence of a sort nevertheless. Perhaps it is already well known to you, though it only came to my notice within the past year or so.

As we know, and as Hopkins frankly admits in the poem, he was safely far away in Wales when the catastrophe happened, and his whole source of information was The London Times of December 11, 1875. [W. H.] Gardner [in *The Poems of Gerard Manley Hopkins* (Oxford)] gives the briefest and most selective citations from that article in the notes for stanza 19; in fact, only one sentence from the whole account in The Times is quoted; and there is no note citing The Times account that relates to stanza 16, the one we have been puzzling about.

There is a fairly new biography of Hopkins by a woman with the unlikely name of Paddy Kitchen, an infuriating book in a number of ways, including bad proof-reading. But it has at least the merit of presenting a good deal of that Times article verbatim. Let me copy a passage here.

"At 2 a.m., Captain Brickenstein, knowing that with the rising tide the ship would be waterlogged, ordered all the passengers to come on deck . . . Most of them obeyed the summons at once; others lingered below till it was too late; some of them, ill, weak, despairing of life even on deck, resolved to stay in their cabins and meet death without any further struggle to evade it. After

3 a.m. on Tuesday morning a scene of horror was witnessed. Some passengers clustered for safety within or upon the wheelhouse, and on the top of other slight structures on deck. Most of the crew and many of the emigrants went into the rigging, where they were safe enough as long as they could maintain their hold. But the intense cold and long exposure told a tale. The purser of the ship, though a strong man, relaxed his grasp, and fell into the sea. Women and children and men were one by one swept away from their shelters on the deck. Five German nuns, whose bodies are now in the dead-house here, clasped hands and were drowned together, the chief sister, a gaunt woman 6 ft. high, calling out loudly and often 'O Christ, come quickly!' till the end came. The shrieks and sobbing of women and children are described by the survivors as agonising. One brave sailor, who was safe in the rigging, went down to try to save a child or woman who was drowning on deck. He was secured by a rope to the rigging, but a wave dashed him against the bulwarks, and when daylight dawned his headless body, detained by the rope, was seen swaying to and fro with the waves. In the dreadful excitement of these hours one man hung [sic!] himself behind the wheelhouse, another hacked at his wrist with a knife, hoping to die a comparatively painless death by bleeding. It was nearly 8 o'clock before the tide and sea abated, and the survivors could venture to go on deck. At half-past 10 o'clock the tugboat from Harwich came alongside and brought all away without further accident."

It's a shame, and something of a mistake, I think, that neither Bridges nor Gardner cared to supply this much of the text on which Hopkins based his poem, for the article is very instructive in a number of ways. Among other things, it shows Hopkins' careful and deliberate strategy in omitting a number of sensational and sordid details: the decapitation of the sailor, the two suicide attempts, at least one of them successful. Another poet might very well have chosen to use such material as a way of indicating the panic, hopelessness of some, and the seeming malice of the elements. I suspect it was not mere "tastefulness" in its fastidious Victorian sense that prompted Hopkins to pass by these vivid details, but rather a desire not to diffuse the focus of his poem from the five heroines, and the one chief heroine, to whom he would address a prayer at the conclusion. But if The Times article is of interest in showing what Hopkins chose to leave out, I would want to point out too that there is a phrase in the article he decided to keep: "a wave dashed him against the bulwarks, and when daylight dawned his headless body, detained by the rope, was seen swaying to and fro with the waves."

The little expression, of course, was no coinage of The Times' that could have delighted Hopkins in any special way, nor is it likely that he had to read that issue of the paper to learn it. But no small part of the poem is given to that precise "spiritual exercise" in which the spirit is expected to embrace as completely as possible in the imagination of the experience, normally of The Passion, that it has set itself to contemplate. Hopkins is continually trying to make real and present, not only to the reader but to himself, the facts and particulars of that shipwreck; and all he had to go on was <u>The Times</u>. It was his job to be faithful to the facts as he found them; and my conviction that Hopkins' sense of fidelity to the facts of the nun's agony was an analogue to his fidelity to the facts of the Passion strongly suggests to me that he would have considered it wrong, frivolous and possibly blasphemous to tamper with them in either case. [. . .]

I have made a resolve not to mention the weather, which is, on the whole, unmentionable; but at least I feel vindicated in having written a rather bitter sestina about this neck of the woods.[10] When that poem first appeared some colleagues found it expressive of disloyal and traitorous sentiments. They have dropped those accusations this winter.

With cordial good wishes,
Tony

September 17, 1981 Rochester, NY

[To Jacqueline Simms]

Dear Jacky,

[. . .] I enclose, as you kindly requested, the fruits of this summer's growth. The sestina ["The Book of Yolek"] was the last to be written, and got finished just before I had to plunge into the thickets of academic chores and leave all thought of writing poetry behind. Of the other two, "Devotions of a Painter" resulted from a trip on the "Burchiello" along the Brenta Canal, while "Meditation" derives in part from a synthesis of recollected paintings (by Bellini, Carpaccio and Cima) in the Accademia of Venice. Recollected, I may add, in the superb tranquility and comfort of the Hotel Cipriani in Asolo. I have discovered since writing "Meditation" that paintings entitled "Sacred Conversation" concern a far narrower and more specific subject than I was aware of, or intended for my poem. It seems that the traditional title is applied to paintings in which certain very particular saints (most usually doctors of the church) are represented as engaged in a discussion of the Immaculate Conception, in the presence, of course, of the Madonna and Child; but the topic of their discourse is precise and

[10]"Sestina D' Inverno," in *Millions of Strange Shadows*.

limited in a way I was quite unaware of. <u>Vogue</u> will be publishing the poem in its November issue, so it's too late to do anything about my error now. Anyway, I see no reason why I may not enlarge the area of discussion for the sake of my poem. [. . .]

I send love. [. . .]

[Tony]

September 22, 1981 Rochester, NY

[To John Hollander]

Dear John,

The Yale Press, at your very kindly instruction, has sent me <u>Rhyme's Reason</u>, for which I am delightedly grateful to you, and also to them. It is a jocund and witty ancilla to your more serious and formidable <u>Vision and Resonance</u>. By a happy coincidence I was looking into that larger book of yours only a few weeks ago, and found myself full of cheerful agreement with everything I came across. Including, I may add, some of your incidental and very just comments on the, chiefly metrical, ignorance of some of the experimentalists. You and I, I think, agree about Williams; he's an immensely eloquent, instinctive poet, but when he opens his trap on any theoretical subject, from prosody to Aristotle (and he came to regard his opinions on all such topics as seer-like) he was embarrassingly sophomoric. And, it seems to me that many who have defiantly declared themselves his heirs have embraced his ignorance without possessing his talent. [. . .]

With all good wishes,
Tony

This is one of several letters to Ira Sadoff, poet, critic, and professor of English, Colby College, Maine, on the subject of diction and literary decorum.

October 22, 1981 Rochester, NY

Dear Mr. Sadoff:

Thank you for your note of inquiry regarding the diction in my poem, "The Grapes." The puzzle you and your class have raised is an interesting one, and one that various poets have undertaken to solve in various ways. On the face of it, it is absurd to think of anyone—anyone, that is, who is not supremely affected— speaking in poetry. Indeed, if poetry is conceived as deliberated, meditated, cast and recast expression, artificially contrived to seem spontaneous ("a line may take us hours maybe,/Yet if it does not seem a moment's thought,/Our stitching and unstitching has been nought")[11] it is by just so much removed from spontaneously "sincere" expression. This kind of paradox has always been present in poetry, and it might be as well to acknowledge as much. But there is more to the matter, of course.

One of the additional problems, for example, has to do with the degree of shared experience, and therefore vocabulary, of reader and writer, and this in turn touches on questions of "class" and "social status." To some of your students, "incandescent filaments" sounds like elevated diction. To people of my grandparents' generation, it was the standard advertising parlance used to describe lightbulbs, which, in one of my older dictionaries, are designated as "incandescent lamps." It had never seemed to me a phrase of special sophistication, nor has it seemed to me fruitful to confine the diction of a chambermaid to such limited expression as might be appropriate to her role in a novel by, say, James T. Farrell or Nelson Algren. In saying this I don't intend any disparagement whatever of those writers. Instead, what I mean is this: There have been a number of modern poets (doubtless your class can easily supply their names) who have with admirable strictness confined their poems to the severe and limited vocabulary that would plausibly belong to the unaffected and spontaneous speech of ordinary, unsophisticated people. This poetry inclines, even though very powerful at times, to be spare, even bleak, in expression, narrow in its emotional range, and somewhat wanting in variety.

At the other end of the spectrum, one may plausibly suppose that in all likelihood no one ever really spoke like any of the characters in Shakespeare's plays. And there is scarcely a character of his who does not rise to a pitch of eloquence if given the opportunity. The abundance and richness of Shakespeare' s world is everywhere in evidence in his vocabulary just as the starkness and poverty of Beckett's world is exhibited in his own vocabulary's parsimony.

And there are yet other factors to consider. For example, it seems to me that in a short lyric, or even a short poetic monologue (though admittedly the term "short" is indecisive) the diction ought to observe a decent consistency, and aim for some fidelity to an imagined character. But as a poem lengthens, I would claim that the poet has an obligation to his reader, whose interest must continuously be courted, to rise above what might dangerously become the pedestrian limitations of insight and vocabulary that might conventionally be assigned to a particular character. I am simply trying to make a case for a sort of flexibility here. Tennyson, aware of the problem, inclined to choose either mythic or

[11]A slight variant of W. B. Yeats, "Adam's Curse."

regal or at least aristocratic figures to speak in his poems, thereby allowing himself a sufficiently grand style. And though Browning employed characters of all classes, they all sound as if they were distinctly related to one another, the Renaissance painters and petty tyrants being cousins of the modern charlatans, and no one, in any case, being even semi-literate.

As it happens, I am just about to take up the poetry of Robert Frost in class. And we will soon be discussing "The Witch of Coös." The chief speaker in the poem is the witch herself, and early in the poem's course she says, "Don't that make you suspicious/That there's something the dead are keeping back?" But this apparently unpolished woman, later in the same poem, is able to say, "A tongue of fire/Flashed out and licked along his upper teeth./Smoke rolled inside the sockets of his eyes." While I would admit there are no exotic words employed here, the diction is decidedly more "elevated" than in "Don't that make you suspicious . . ." I am trying to argue in behalf of a special flexibility in this matter that poets ought to aim for in the name of breadth of vision, of richness and amplitude. Above all, poets should not let themselves be ruled and judged by the standards and limits of realistic or naturalistic fiction.

There is, of course, much more to the topic than I've touched on here. But, for the present, the defense rests.

Yours,
Anthony Hecht

Edward Hirsch (1950–), poet and literary critic, was appointed president of the John Simon Guggenheim Foundation in 2002. A friendly exchange between the two began with the publication of Hirsch's first book, For the Sleepwalkers *(1981).*

November 21, 1981 Rochester NY

Dear Mr. Hirsch,

Thank you very much for your kind letter of admiration and praise. I seem to remember a statement of Robert Graves's somewhere, regarding poets, to the effect that the natives of the Scilly Islands, off the coast of Cornwall, maintained a precarious living by taking in one another's laundry, and that poets contrived to survive in much the same way. And it is sadly true that if we do not admire one another's work, the list of admirers is likely to be very short indeed, and composed nearly entirely of immediate kin.

Let me wish you every success.

Sincerely,
Anthony Hecht

*For a variety of reasons, Hecht's thoughts in the late 1970s and 1980s were increas-
ingly turning toward Auden, as is suggested by the presence of multiple postscript
comments (of which two appear below) in an already long letter responding to ques-
tions by Auden scholar Edward Mendelson. Hecht's own book on Auden would
appear in 1993.*

Dec. 20, 1981 Rochester NY

Dear Ed,

I've given your letter much thought during the past few days, and this morn-
ing I realized how much I'd rather be writing to you about Auden than doing
what I ought to be doing: correcting and grading term papers and exams. And
so, with all the firmness and resolution of the self-indulgent, I've set aside my
chores to respond, and I hope you won't mind if I venture some highly question-
able speculations.

[. . .]

P.P.S.: Secrecy, an abiding excitement. It was present in the early world of
Mortmere that he invented with Isherwood; it is there in Tolkien, in Firbank,
in everything he liked. A case can be made, of course, to affirm that poetry
itself is not "communication" so much as secret or coded message—Kermode
[in *The Genesis of Secrecy*] is splendid on texts of this sort—though it is per-
fectly clear that not all poets regard poetry this way. One of the things Auden
clearly admired in the popular love songs of Cole Porter and Rodgers & Hart,
quite aside from their wit and technical virtuosity, was their ability to write
what amounted to androgynous lyrics, or, rather, sexually convertible ones.
This was purely a commercial gimmick, making it possible to pluck a song
out of its dramatic context in a Broadway musical, and allow it to be sung on,
say, a radio broadcast performance by either male or female singer with equal
appropriateness. This was done, as I said, purely in the interest of increased
revenues and broader circulation of the songs in question. But of course it had
a hidden sexual meaning for some; it was redolent of a secrecy that could pa-
rade itself in public and go undetected by all but the initiate. From the almost
indecipherable early love poems to the late reference to "the choir we sort
with," Auden liked to employ covert and devious locutions that were at once
the speech forms of the proud and the shy, the powerful and the powerless.

P.P.P.S.: Finally, as to the powerful and powerless. A related obsession of
Auden's was his concern with the idea of "the hero," with how he is to be

known, to be recognized, to be perhaps emulated. The mystery of what he was truly like goes back a long way, to those school conversations with Isherwood about "the truly strong man," and plays a part in Auden's changing ideas about T.E. Lawrence, Homer Lane and others; and of course it is relevant to specific poems. The mystery of who is truly the strong man is certainly connected with the secrecy and mystery surrounding the Incarnation, and the revelation that was made only to a selected few. In Ischia in 1950 Auden declared that the martyr, the passive hero, was the only kind of hero possible in the modern world, because all the conventions and rules of heroism of the classical and chivalric ages had been debased or eliminated by modern warfare. Nevertheless, the old heroism was something he longed for, and I find it both touching and vaguely disagreeable that he should have stipulated that Siegfried's Funeral music should be played at his death. His own kind of heroism was very far from Siegfried's, almost to the point of ludicrousness. Was there some note of self-contempt involved? Hard to say, but I doubt it; though meanings become complex and involuted here. Doubtless there was the sheer emotive power of the music itself, grand, operatic, frankly "campy" in its ostentations, the sort of thing that would please him as well as the choir he sorted with. But the possibilities of meaning beyond this point are not only numerous, they are beyond calculation, and bear at last upon his secret opinion of himself, which we will never completely know.

Best,

Tony

1982

David Bromwich is a literary scholar now at Yale University. The exchange was prompted by an essay Hecht published in The New York Times Book Review *(February 7, 1982) titled "Masters of Unpleasantness."*

February 12, 1982 Rochester NY

Dear David Bromwich,

Thank you very much indeed for your kind letter, and your generous invitation. Alas, I never seem to get to Princeton at all, and very rarely even to New York. It would be both fun and interesting to discuss these matters with you, and perhaps, in some unexpected way, the time may yet come when we can do so.

Meanwhile, let me just say that, while the topic is of course a very serious one, I thought it best, in writing for so large, miscellaneous and popular an audience as the <u>Times Book Review</u> is likely to reach, to pitch my voice safely within the range of levity. I did indeed know that it was you who had written that review [of Lawrence Thompson's and R. H. Winnick's *Robert Frost, The Later Years, 1938–1963*]; but I elected to omit mention of your name lest it be supposed either by the editors of the <u>Review</u> or by its readers that I was using one of the largest of the reviewing media to address myself to a single critic, and to air a private difference with him.

But even within the range of levity, I think what I said about the general moral complexion of poets is true: we are a touchy and easily offended lot, and this reflects the uncertainty of our place in society, and this has been true ever since the rise and popularity of the novel, the birth of journalism and Grub Street, the collapse of the patronage system, all of which began in the eighteenth century. The kind of precariousness that poets seem to suffer from is not purely financial, though of course it is that, too. But I remember Robert Fitzgerald telling me about Vachel Lindsay's suicide. He died, as you may know, in a particularly hideous way: by drinking lysol. Robert said he did this in part because of the burdens of the Great Depression (he died in 1931) but chiefly because he feared that his gift had dried up, his "inspiration" departed. Now, other men get tired and bored with other kinds of employment; sometimes they change their careers in very radical ways. But there are not many for whom their entire <u>amour propre</u> is so intimately tied to their professional careers.

There were admittedly many unattractive features to Frost's character, but in not a few ways they were the corollaries and necessary consequences of his virtues. He was a tower of strength in a badly shattered family; and while his strength did harm, there could have been no family without it. And, of course, no poetry. Not a little of his poetry is in fact about necessary selfishness, like "Two Tramps in Mudtime." Loneliness breeds defiance, and poets are far more isolated than novelists. Anyway, it was no Miltonic hubris that allowed me to accuse myself, and I have read the Thompson biography—carefully enough to notice that in Ellman and O'Clair's <u>Norton Anthology</u> they misquote Frost on Stevens as well as Stevens on Frost, and get some of their facts wrong.

I myself am in part a product of the New Critics; at least, Ransom and Tate were teachers of mine. The kind of criticism they and their friends advocated was very valuable and useful in its day as a healthy corrective against what often was no more than straight biography disguised as criticism. Many of their principles still work with certain kinds of poetry, or with the poetry of those about whom we know virtually nothing. There are, after all, poets, like Frost, whose poems are remarkably intimate, once you crack their codes. There are others who are remarkably distant and remote, and do not desire a better acquaintance with the reader. Virgil is one. To the degree that I favor any school, it would be the one that takes greatest advantage of every tool and trifle of knowledge for the best, most careful and comprehensive understanding of the text. When Empson is good, and he so very often is, it seems because he feels free enough to resort to Freud for <u>Alice</u> but also to Marx for pastoral literature, and to make keen and intelligent use of whatever he employs.

Anyway, many thanks for your letter, and I hope we may meet again soon.

Anthony Hecht

Norman Williams (1952–), Vermont lawyer and author of several books of poems, studied with Hecht in 1976 while a student at Yale Law School.

February 21, 1982 Rochester, NY

Dear Norm,

[. . .] After I wrote what was meant to be a lighthearted little essay on the place of the poet in modern society that appeared in the <u>New York Times Book Review</u> on Feb. 7th, I not only got a lot of curious mail but seven unsolicited, book-length poetry manuscripts (one of them from a psychiatrist) all asking for professional appraisals. I have not answered any of them yet. In fact, I have set all such obligations aside in order to spend time in a way that I think may somewhat surprise you. I am well into what promises to be a lengthy critical essay on <u>The Merchant of Venice</u> [eventually published in *Obbligati,* 1986]. By lengthy I mean that I have gotten twenty pages into it so far—plus four pages of footnotes—and calculate that I am roughly halfway through; though my calculation may err on the side of brevity.

I am obsessed with this essay because I am convinced that I am the only person who understands that play; and that, moreover, my essay will not simply be one more "interpretation" that can be set along side of other "interpretations" and judged either better or worse than they. What I am writing I think will prove to be unassailable and incontrovertible; and what is most astonishing is that there is no commentary on the play that comes anywhere near saying what I am saying. In other words, I believe that once my essay is published it will become an indispensible exegesis for the play, and will be beyond dispute correct; unless the disputant were to maintain that the play is the better for not being understood. It's hard to convey to you how excited I am about this. I really feel I have made a major discovery, and for the last month and a half I have been thinking about little else.

Needless to say I can't summarize my discovery here, but I can tell you that my essay begins by saying that I intend to provide answers to a set of six questions, and the questions are these:

1) The Merchant of Venice is listed in the First Folio among the comedies, but throughout a large part of the 18th century it was played as a tragedy. Modern productions exhibit a distinct sense of embarrassment and indecisiveness in their confused attempts to arrive at the proper "tone" and "intention" of the play. While it may be claimed that some of the "problem plays" are equally unsettling in their effects, none of them presents quite the same teetering history of interpretation. Why should this be?

2) The "Merchant" of the play is Antonio, who seems to have been assigned the most passive, ill-defined and generally uninteresting role in the entire play; Gratiano and Morocco are miracles of characterization in comparison. And when great actors, from Garrick and Kean to Olivier, elect to appear in the play it is always Shylock's part they undertake; never Antonio's. Macbeth, Hamlet, Coriolanus are indisputably the vigorous and potent central figures of the plays of which they are the titular characters. Why, then, should this play be named for a character who has consistently aroused so little interest?

3) What is the meaning of Antonio's line, which is also the first in the play: "In sooth I know not why I am so sad"?

4) What is the real motive behind Shylock's contract for a pound of Antonio's flesh?

5) What sort of sense are we to make of the last will and testament of Portia's father that could so perilously and capriciously bind his daughter's fate without regard to her own wishes, and according to rules of a game so apparently frivolous?

6) On what grounds if any can we accept the notion that Portia, a very intelligent but manifestly uninstructed girl, could successfully solve the legal dilemma that appears to have baffled the Duke and his court; and just what is the solution she furnishes? [. . .]

I have one other piece of news, and it, too, is a sort of surprise. I have been invited to be the next Poetry Consultant to the Library of Congress, to begin my two-year term of duty next September. But I am by no means sure I will or can accept. In due course, I'll let you know what happens. And please keep writing, even though I am dilatory about answering.

Tony [. . .]

Joseph Brodsky (1940–1996), poet and literary critic, received the Nobel Prize for Literature in 1987.

May 18, 1982 Rochester NY

Dear Joseph,

I've kept your "Winter Eclogue" at hand and have had the chance to read it a number of times, always with mounting pleasure and admiration. First of all, it is beautiful and moving in its own right—an eloquent and astonishing poem of sustained plangency and elegiac mood. It moves like a cortège. But in addition it is something of a <u>tour de force</u> in its deliberate violation or contradiction of the Virgil Fourth Eclogue from which it appears to spring. While the Virgil is all forward-looking, expectant and prophetic, yours is deeply and darkly retrospective and melancholy. And while the Virgil was famously and shamelessly Christianized, yours seems to me, by virtue of its backward-looking perspective, and its grave sadness, somehow Jewish in spirit. In other words, what I think you have done is miraculously to relate, by contrast and contradiction, the past with the future, the Old with the New Testament, lament with exultation, and all by the suggested Virgilian link in which the Roman poet serves you as he once served Dante. It is a brilliant and highly original work, and moreover, a beautiful one. I'm truly grateful to you for sending me a copy of it. [. . .]

And the whole family, in gratitude and affection, sends LOVE.

Tony

Hecht's roiled musings here about his own anger were set off by a family incident, in which, upon the death of his parents in the late 1970s and the dispersion of some of the contents of their apartment on 163 E. 81st Street, his brother Roger disposed of some books dear to Hecht.

June 24, 1982 Rochester NY

[To William MacDonald]

Honored Sir,

[. . .]

Thank you for your very compassionate, generous and understanding letter. I am happy to report that I am by now quite over the shock—and it was shock more than anything else that so stirred me. I knew at once that the loss was almost entirely symbolic, though the knowledge did not in the least diminish my Gordian knot of rage, guilt, and other violent emotions that I had thought pretty well buried for good. In fact, the chief shock was to find myself experiencing feelings that had blissfully been banished for so long, but which had once festered in ulcerous silence for years. Anyway, while I would still like to retrieve the book, and some efforts are still going forward to that end, I have been restored to calm and good spirits. Your letter was wise and thoughtful, and agreed in many of its insights with intuitions of my own. It is curious how long it takes us, how much pondering and ruthless self-inquisition, to come anywhere near understanding ourselves, and how we turn out to be the most subversive and resistant witnesses in all such inquiries. And it is no less curious that both Socrates and Freud should have thought self-knowledge was the ultimate kind. In this the two of them stand opposed to all that empiric and positivistic sciences profess to honor as the only kind of knowledge—impersonal and quantifiable. I once annoyed my Dean here, who also teaches psychology, by referring to that field as "the softest of the sciences" in a paper I was giving. When he raised his objection at the end, I merely said that by calling it the softest I meant it was the most literary. Since I was a literary type myself, he could not proceed to object, but he was not happy. Anyway, the way we disguise our deepest truths from ourselves is the subject of my poem, "Green: An Epistle," which was prompted by, first, an insight into symbiotic family ties, and later into myself. It's a better poem, I think, than has so far been noticed by those who are supposed to notice such things—except for Allen Tate, who wrote me a warm and generous detailed letter about it when I sent him a copy shortly after finishing it. It is no longer a poem that I am much interested in, though in some ways it may be one of the most personal I've written. [. . .]

Edward the Superfluous

Anthony Hecht, James Merrill, among others, for T. S. Eliot
Centennial Celebration in St. Louis, 1988
Courtesy of Emory University Libraries Rare Books and Manuscripts Division

SIX

Critic and Poet
1983–1992

IN 1982, HECHT WAS APPOINTED CONSULTANT IN POETRY TO THE Library of Congress, a position now known as Poet Laureate, following generations of eminent poets to Washington—Robert Frost, Allen Tate, Robert Lowell, and Elizabeth Bishop, to name a few he most admired. At the conclusion of his two-year term, Hecht returned to Rochester for a final year of teaching before moving permanently to Washington, where he was appointed University Professor at Georgetown. He taught there until his retirement in June 1993 at the age of seventy. About the prospects of retiring, he expressed both glee and cautious optimism: "Tomorrow shall be my dancing day, of sorts, being the beginning of my final term of teaching at Georgetown," he remarked to Harry Ford, "though as the future comes gradually into clearer focus, it may be that Evan's continued education will drive me back into the not altogether loving arms of academia."

The letters from these later professional years reflect his increasing interest in writing literary criticism and his emergence as a man of letters, generated in part by official duties in Washington, including public lectures on "Robert Lowell" and "The Pathetic Fallacy" delivered at the Library of Congress and "Houses as Metaphors: The Poetry of Architecture" given at the Folger Shakespeare Library in early 1985. Material from these lectures helped to bolster his first collection of critical writings, *Obbligati: Essays in Criticism*, published by Atheneum in 1986. This volume also included essays that had appeared in various literary journals, beginning with "Shades of Keats and Marvell" (*The Hudson Review*, 1962) and essays written in the 1970s on Emily Dickinson, Richard Wilbur, Elizabeth Bishop, and W. H. Auden. However, two long, previously unpublished essays on Shakespeare, *Othello* and *The Merchant of Venice*—the latter covering ninety pages—make up the lion's share of this book. In his final years of teaching, Hecht divided his time between two other major critical projects: *On the Laws of the Poetic Art*, delivered as the A. W. Mellon Lectures in the Fine Arts at the National Gallery in 1992 and published by Princeton University Press in 1995, and *The Hidden Law*, a lengthy critical study of the poetry of W. H. Auden, published in 1993 by Harvard University Press. And, as testimony to his continued admiration for George Herbert, Hecht edited and annotated *The Essential Herbert* for Ecco Press (1987).

Hecht's correspondence during this period documents his enthusiasm for these various critical and scholarly ventures. Readers who know little about the Shakespeare essays, for example, will be surprised by his zealous pursuit of hermeneutics in *The Merchant of Venice*, an attitude aired and defended in his earlier letter of February 21, 1982, to Norman Williams. But along with hermeneutics, there is the further subject of Hecht's poems and of Hecht as a poet, a matter of continuing focus during these years, as illuminating letters to Sandy McClatchy (August 8, 1985) and Kenneth Gross (June 4, 1987) make clear. Letters of this time also reveal a sudden flurry of interest in the history of the canzone, that most challenging of poetic forms descending from Dante Alighieri, with few modern practitioners. And once again appear exchanges with Joseph Summers, this time about the relative merits of John Donne and Ben Jonson (1985) and his own "Love for Four Voices," based loosely on *A Midsummer Night's Dream* (October 11, 1990).

The understory of these years, however, is the relative paucity of poems. In a brief note to Jacky Simms, his Oxford editor, Hecht wrote in 1988: "as for my own work, I confess with humiliation to a blockage that has gone on, alas, far too long, and which I am struggling to overcome." And, indeed, *The Transparent Man*, published in 1990, represented not only eleven years in the making, but also an uneven distribution of poems written across the years. A good number, including the title poem, date from the early 1980s and in some regards continue, in either subject matter or mode of address, the explosion of energy he experienced in *The Venetian Vespers*. I am thinking especially of "Devotions of a Painter" and "Meditation," but also of "The Transparent Man," another dramatic monologue spoken by a female, and the sestina, "The Book of Yolek," although one wants to be careful about imposing strict boundaries on a poet of strong broodings and ruminations. Still, Hecht's own confession about struggling with a writing block helps to shed light on, but not altogether explain, one of the most difficult episodes in this period: the "peculiar panic" Hecht felt over the sharp criticism Joseph Brodsky leveled against "See Naples and Die," Hecht's recently written, lengthy monologue that was to be one of the anchor poems for the new book. Although their friendship would survive this episode, the subject serves as the pointed matter of a letter written to Brodsky in April 1990; and as is often the case, the letter to Brodsky includes some valuable insights by Hecht about his own purpose in writing the poem.

Hecht would occasionally say that when he couldn't write poems, he would turn to writing criticism. One doesn't want to be altogether solemn about the alternation between these two habitual modes of thinking and practice, and regret one for the sake of the other. It is clear that, at some level, these were deeply intertwined and mutually reinforcing pursuits for Hecht, even if they didn't occur with the same breath. But the letters from this period show, too, that he was never idle. He was an incessant reader, often addressing a wide variety of subjects simultaneously, as he amusingly notes in a letter to Nicholas Christopher (March 22, 1989), and he devoted a great deal of time to helping and advising younger poets. In addition to his ongoing exchanges with Christopher Ricks, moreover, he embarked on what was to be a fruitful correspondence of many years with the literary critic Eleanor Cook on a variety of poetic matters. Hecht could even be ruefully stoical about the fate of *Obbligati* in a letter to Harry Ford of May 10, 1991. And, of course, no matter a book's fate, there was always a great jest to be had with MacDonald—in one instance over a possible list of fictitious names one might mention in a book's acknowledgments to enhance its worth (March 31, 1984).

The roughly 650 or so letters and postcards that survive from this period have their sorrows—the death of Roger is mentioned, and more than once—but the image of Hecht putting on his dancing shoes in anticipation of retirement seems somehow just and right. The ten years in Washington were full of activity, indeed distractingly so, with the several moves back and forth from Rochester. The next ten years promised to be perhaps livelier still.

As this anecdote has acquired a life of its own in the history of the Yale Series of Younger Poets, it should be noted that Hecht has conflated 1950 with 1955, when he also spent time in Ischia. Ashbery received the prize in 1956.

January 25, 1983 Washington DC

[To James Merrill]

Dear Jimmy,

[. . .] It was generous of you to take on the Yale Series, which is bound not only to be a lot of work, but filled with unexpected frustrations. An instance: When I was living in Ischia in 1950 and Wystan had the job, he invited me to help him read some of the manuscripts, and I was flattered to have been asked. I think I went to his house for lunch, and then we divided a very large pile of submissions, though it should be added that he had already gone through a lot of stuff on his own, and, of course, Yale had done its own triage and win-nowing before sending him anything. Anyway, everything I saw was wretched, and so was his batch, and finally we went through everything and nothing of merit had turned up. This annoyed him greatly, because he knew of at least one manuscript that had been submitted and which he would have liked. So he wrote directly to the young poet involved, who happened to be John Ashbery, and asked him to submit his work directly to Ischia, since the Yale winnowers had tossed him out. A cautionary tale. [. . .]

Yours,

Tony

February 9, 1983 Library of Congress,

Washington DC

Institute of Foreign Literature,

Chinese Academy of Social Sciences (CASS)

Beijing, China (PRC)

Dear Mr. Zhao:

Many thanks for your letter of inquiry about my poems. [. . .] As for suggested poems of mine that you might use in your anthology, I believe there might be some suitable shorter ones in my two latest volumes, <u>Millions of Strange Shad-ows</u> and <u>The Venetian Vespers</u>. Specifically, I think of "The Odds," "The Lull," "The Feast of Stephen," "A Birthday Poem," and "The Grapes."

As for your puzzle about the line, "A Lüger settled back deeply in its glove" [in "'More Light! More Light!'"] let me say that the poem deliberately avoids presenting the person of any of the Nazis; only their arms and attributes appear, in order completely to depersonalize them. A Lüger, you are quite right in supposing, is a weapon. It cannot do anything of its own accord, not even "settle back" into anything without somebody there to do the settling. But the reader is never allowed to see the "doer." The Nazis remain invisible, and only their gestures appear.

Sincerely,
Anthony Hecht
Consultant in Poetry

Judith Testa was professor of art history at Northern Illinois University from 1969 to 2000.

March 30, 1983 Library of Congress, Washington DC

Dear Judith Testa:

I am delighted not only by the manifest enthusiasm of your kind letter, but by your name that indicates you have a sound head on your shoulders. And of course by the fact that you are a friend of Bill MacDonald's. Curiously enough, I have seen more of him since I moved to the Washington area than at any place outside of Rome. We have known one another for many years, and I would never dream of signing any letter of mine to him by my own name. Nor would he do otherwise. This adds considerably to the market value of our correspondence when we come to assess it, since, for example, I now boast of owning rare notes in American demotic by such persons as the Emperor Hadrian and John of Cappadocia. I hope he has also told you that we are engaged in a duel to the death about who can manage to write his letters on the rarest and most difficult letter-paper that can be acquired. My current notion of real exclusiveness would be the paper of the Warden of the Regina Coeli Prison in Rome. Neither of us has come up with that as yet, though we've both made noble tries. Anyway, let me thank you again for your kind letter, and tell you, if you don't already know this, that Bill intends to settle in this area, and will begin apartment hunting in Washington in the very near future.

With best wishes,
Anthony Hecht
Consultant in Poetry

[To Mark Justin]

Dear Mark:

I have now had time to read your poems, and to think about them as well. And time, also, to think about what I could write to you that could be of any use to you. Your work is obviously very, very skillful, and if I did not fear being identified with Black Mountaineers and other literary barbarians, I might be tempted almost to say that you are nearly too skillful. By which I mean two things. First, that your meters are for the most part so neatly regular as at times to seem to govern everything else in the poem. John Crowe Ransom, in a number of essays, one on Milton and again when writing on Thomas Hardy, spoke of both poets as "roughening up" their meters, and deliberately avoiding a too perfect smoothness. Ransom wrote of this as though it had been done largely for acoustical reasons, though I suspect it was quite otherwise. Especially when something urgent or deeply personal is being written about, a metrical smoothness may impart a rather chilling distance between the burden of the poem and the polish of its discourse. For example, the opening of your poem that begins, "A great angel cries out to all the nations," might usefully be compared to John Donne's sonnet, "At the round earth's imagined corners, blow. . . ." The apocalyptic scene is the common factor, but Donne's agitated irregularity, his heated, jumpy explosiveness, carries a conviction that your own smoothness lacks. Moreover, your smoothness allows you occasionally to slip in some small feeble word, which, while not contrary to your drift, performs little in the way of function other than to keep the meters pure. If poetry is really "emotion recollected in tranquility," and if enough emphasis is placed on the tranquility, then your own musical smoothness might always be appropriate. But poetry—your own as well as others'—often tries to do other things than attain to either tranquility or meditation. If I may generalize about your poems, and I know I do so at my peril, I would say that you have a tendency to submerge, and indeed even to subvert, some of the dramatic ingredients in your poems, losing sight of the drama out of a formal scruple. The second point that seems worth noting is that you have brilliantly learned to duplicate the rhetorical complexity and syntactical sinuosity of the best of discursive English Renaissance poetry, and your fluency in this regard is admirable. Admirable, but detectably dated. Let me recommend a studious reading of the whole of "Hello, Darkness" by L.E. Sissman. He is no less skillful than you, but he has found a way through the Renaissance conventions to a modern and personal idiom.

I hope you will find these observations pertinent and useful. And I hope you will not find them disappointing or irrelevant. It was a pleasure to meet you, and to read your work, and I wish you every success.

Sincerely,

Anthony Hecht

1984

January 20, 1984 Library of Congress, Washington DC

[To Edward Hirsch]

Dear Ed:

Many thanks for your kindness in sending me both your poem and your review of the "oral biography" of Stevens. I have not read the book, and yet I would guess that "out of respect for the living" the whole truth of the matter has not yet appeared. I think it is pretty well known that Stevens rather brutally broke up Holly's marriage rather imperiously. From what I have heard, it was not the most suitable or promising of marriages, and was undertaken with an impetuosity that strongly suggests that it was chiefly an act of filial defiance. Stevens's ruthlessness in the matter (Holly had borne a son before the marriage was busted up) may well have reflected dissatisfaction with his own marriage. As for Mrs. Stevens, she seems more and more like "The Mad Woman in the Attic." There is also, in the poetry itself, more than a hint of Stevens's involvement with other women, a topic not likely to have been bandied about by any of the interviewees. In fact, I can remember reading somewhere about Stevens showing up somewhere with a young chick on his arms. All these matters would go a long way toward suggesting that we still have a good deal to learn about the poet.

And now, the poem.[1] I hope you will not mind my expressing a reservation. Your poem deliberately goes about twining and twinning the bag lady and John Clare in a way almost inextricable. Or this seems at least to be your intention. And yet for me, somehow, this pairing does not seem to work the way you want it to. The problem is that we know too much about Clare's life and motives for the journey, and too little about the bag lady's. Clare had as a motive both the desire to escape from a lunatic asylum (sufficient almost by itself) and a pathetically crazed ambition to find his long-dead first wife. The bag lady is a scrounger, but what brought her to this pass and what her hopes of survival

---

[1] Because of their shared feeling for John Clare and out of admiration for Hecht's poem "Coming Home," published in *Millions of Strange Shadows* (1977), Hirsch sent Hecht a copy of his poem, "Three Journeys," later published in *Wild Gratitude* (1986). The title of the Wilbur poem hesitatingly referred to by Hecht is "In the Smoking Car."

are we cannot guess. To make her comparable to the poet is to "poeticize" her unjustifiably, and to give her a spurious glamour that none of the particulars of the poem actually bear out. One may think of her as being very courageous; but one may equally easily think of her as one who has abandoned hope of anything more than mere degraded survival. (I think of a Wilbur poem—can it be called "Failure" in which a man, fallen asleep on a train, has comfortably "given up" the struggle with a clear sense of relief?). Obviously, you don't want us to feel that way about your bag lady, and have tried to prevent such suspicions by your appeal to the ghost of Clare. But Clare, it seems to me, is a "ringer" in this poem, at least until you can tell us more about that poor woman.

I know this is not the sort of comment you can rejoice in reading, but I felt that an honest reaction was what finally was called for, and was what you really wanted. I sincerely hope that you won't be offended.

With warm good wishes,
Anthony Hecht
Consultant in Poetry

Hecht's fascination with the canzone form would lead him to write "Terms," published in The Transparent Man *(1990).*

January 31, 1984 Library of
Congress, Washington DC

[To Edward Mendelson]

Dear Ed:

I have tracked down the formal source of Wystan's Canzone, "When will we learn what should be clear as day, . . ." You remember my asking you once if you knew how he came by it, or whether he had invented it, since it resembled no other "canzone" I had ever come across, except for those, by [James] Merrill and [L. E.] Sissman, that derived from his? Well, I wish I could take credit for this, but the information comes to me from John Frederick Nims. He writes, "Auden was clearly looking at Dante's 'Amore, tu vedi ben che questa donna. . . .' Dante's endwords in the first stanza are: donna, tempo, donna, donna, luce, donna, donna, freddo, freddo, donna, petra, petra, and in the following stanzas he permutates the words exactly as Dante had done, in a rather sestinalike way. The poem seems to be given a different number in different editions of Dante; you could find it under the first line in the index of Dante's Rime. . . . It seems the Dante poem is generally referred to as a 'double-sestina'—but that is misleading, since double-sestina is the term we generally use for poems like Sidney's 'Ye goatherd gods . . .' which has twelve stanzas instead of the usual six. Modern editors of Dante's poems have suggested that it be called a canzonesestina (sic: no space, no hyphen). . . . In De Vulgari Eloquentia (II, 13) in speaking about the form of the canzone, Dante warns against 'excessive repetition of the same rhyme,' but then adds, defensively, 'unless perhaps some untried novelty in art claims this privilege for itself. . . .' This, I myself endeavored to do in 'Amor, to vedi ben. . . .'" Nims adds, "Diehl's Introduction to his Dante's Rime says of the poem, 'Critics generally describe this poem as an etude transcendentale in pure technique; Dante himself is defensive when he mentions it. . . .' And in his Notes: 'Dante here loads himself down with chains, and critics have looked askance at the result.'"

Best,
Tony

[Washington, DC] March 31, 1984

[To William MacDonald]

My dear chap,

There is nothing, you may take my word for it, nothing whatever that so guarantees the enduring importance of a scholarly book as the choice and selective list of obligations and notes of indebtedness that normally appears in tiny print somewhere at the tail of the author's preface. Long after the reader has tired of the text, long after he has dismissed the laborious arguments put forth, he can still turn to those names with a renewed and invigorated pleasure, if only they have been chosen with flair and imagination. I have been giving much thought to this matter since I am on the point of completing a volume, not of poetry this time, but of critical prose—which will allow me, as poetry would not, a suitable prolusion and dropping of names. And I furthermore find myself still smoldering with resentment at having been beaten to the draw by Hugh Trevor-Roper, who, with an easy and familiar calm, expressed himself as obliged to Letitia, Lady Lucas-Tooth. There is a name worth relishing, and just the sort of thing that would make any work of Trevor-Roper's worth preserving, no matter how tiresome or wrong-headed (as he was, of course, about Anthony Blunt) the main body of the text might be. I have in consequence been casting about among the list of those cited by The Shorter Oxford English Dictionary, and am pleased and reassured to have winkled out the following largely neglected names: Dionysius Lardner, Vicesimus Knox, and Mountstuart Elphinstone. If one is able to convey, ever so casually, that one pals around with the likes of these, an air of worldly assurance and sophistication is imparted to

March 31, 1984

My dear chap,

There is nothing, you may take my word for it, nothing whatever
that so guarantees the enduring importance of a scholarly book
as the choice and selective list of obligations and notes of
indebtedness that normally appears in tiny print somewhere at
the tail of the author's preface. Long after the reader has
tired of the text, long after he has dismissed the laborious
arguments put forth, he can still turn to those names with a
renewed and invigorated pleasure, if only they have been chosen
with flair and imagination. I have been giving much thought to
this matter since I am on the point of completing a volume, not
of poetry this time, but of critical prose – which will allow
me, as poetry would not, a suitable prolusion and dropping of
names. And I furthermore find myself still smouldering with
resentment at having been beaten to the draw by Hugh Trevor-
Roper, who, with an easy and familiar calm, expressed himself
as obliged to Letitia, Lady Lucas-Tooth. There is a name worth
relishing, and just the sort of thing that would make any work
of Trevor-Roper's worth preserving, no matter how tiresome or
wrong-headed (as he was, of course, about Anthony Blunt) the
main body of the text might be. I have in consequence been
casting about among the list of those cited by the Shorter
Oxford English Dictionary, and am pleased and reassured to
have winkled out the following largely neglected names:
Dionysius Lardner, Vicesimus Knox, and Mountstuart Elphinstone.
If one is able to convey, ever so casually, that one pals
around with the likes of these, an air of worldly assurance
and sophistication is imparted to the work that cites them in
suitably modest small print that is always used for such
occasions.

You would be wrong to suppose that the two ladies whose seated
portraits appear above are maiden aunts of mine. They are nothing
of the sort; they are instead allegorical figures. What looks
like the fine-feathered hat of one of them is actually a nest
of serpents, and she is a Medusa-like representation of Wrath.
Her companion, wearing an overturned soup-bowl on her head,
represents penitence, and is all wet and uncomfortable, as
well as smelling strongly of New England Clam Chowder. The
work as a whole is very edifying, and I commend it to you for

Copy of original letter with elaborate letterhead, typical of the kind
used by Hecht in his exchanges with William MacDonald
Courtesy of Emory University Libraries Rare Books and Manuscripts Division

the work that cites them in suitably modest small print that is always used for such occasions.

You would be wrong to suppose that the two ladies whose seated portraits appear above are maiden aunts of mine. They are nothing of the sort; they are instead allegorical figures. What looks like the fine-feathered hat of one of them is actually a nest of serpents, and she is a Medusa-like representation of Wrath. Her companion, wearing an overturned soup-bowl on her head, represents penitence, and is all wet and uncomfortable, as well as smelling strongly of New England Clam Chowder. The work as a whole is very edifying, and I commend it to you for spiritual uplift and downdraft. [. . .]

Galla Placidia Augusta

The Consultant in Poetry (Poet Laureate) is required at the end of each year in office to submit a report of his activities and accomplishments for that year to the Library of Congress. Having composed a careful summation after his first year, Hecht decided at the conclusion of his second year to take a different approach. This report, copied in the letter below, was, in fact, submitted to the Library as an official account of his activities.

June 18, 1984 Washington DC

[To William MacDonald]

Great Jumping Jehoshaphat,

My final duty here in Washington has been to compose my Annual Report, and given the pressure of events I have made it mercifully brief—brief enough to offer it to you here.

ANNUAL REPORT

I terminate my appointment as Consultant in Poetry to the Library of Congress with a keen sense of pleasure in the two years of my tenure, and regret that they have come to an end; though I am pleased to think that the position will be ennobled and strengthened by my successor. It is an act of self-abnegation nearly heroic in proportions to relinquish the dictatorial powers over American Poetry that have been mine during the length of my term of office. One acquires, it may be said, a taste and relish for power, and grows used to it in a remarkably short time; and, Lord Acton to the contrary notwithstanding, I have not found it in the least corrupting. One may take simple pleasure in the ceremonial parades, the firework displays, the popular ovations, the devotion of literary groupies, the constant round of talk-shows and autograph seekers;

as well as in the public execution of those guilty of laxness in their meters (checked by a diligent staff of meter-maids)—a matter which, prompted by Ben Jonson's strictures on the metrics of John Donne, I am pleased to claim to have revived and put into settled practice.

Then there are what may be called the perquisites and garnishes of the job: the publishers' bribes—though some who are by nature niggardly have pleaded inflation. And, not least, there is the cringing servility of all the nation's poets, and their total conformity and abject meekness in adopting those themes and forms the Consultant designates as the official ones for the nation during his administration. During my own period as Consultant, poets were limited to writing sestinas, rondeaux and rhyme royal on the Persian Gulf Crisis, post-coital sadness, and the National Geographic Society. Deviations either in materials or forms were dealt with instantly and mercilessly, and it is with a genuine sense of regret that I turn in the boot, the rack and the official thumb-screws of office. [. . .]

I am pleased to claim that, besides driving the <u>vers librists</u> underground, virtually stamping out their pathetic journal, <u>Free Feet</u>, and infiltrating the Black Mountain School with long-haired double-agents, I was able, with the aid of my wife, to design a special garment to be worn by all recognized American poets. There is first of all the floppy, Wagnerian velvet hat, black for major poets, magenta for minor ones. Then the waterproof Inverness cape, lined in yellow silk, with a large manuscript pouch at one side. Special attention has been paid to shoes and boots, and any poet who lays claim to a variable foot is liable to immediate amputation. Reviving a vestment worn by John Skelton at the court of Henry VIII, there is, for the younger members of the Consultant's entourage, a red, white, and blue satin bowling jacket, with the name "Calliope" inscribed across the back in cheerful Day-Glo orange. These devices tend to call the attention of an otherwise comparatively indifferent public to the presence of poetry in its midst.

I can do no less than point out to my successor that anyone who takes upon himself the role of Caesar must expect the attendant risks. There were the usual assassination attempts. We had been warned that Robert Bly was planning a coup, but in fact the real danger came from another quarter entirely. A plot was uncovered in good time at the headquarters of the Concrete Poets, an underground bunker in Iowa, but the apprehended have not yet been brought to trial, so details are still confidential.

During my tenure, 62% of the nation's poets fell in love, well over half of these with themselves; 17% divorced; 24% watched five or more hours of TV a day; 31% were declared mentally unsound; and 8% failed to have their drivers' licenses renewed. This is a healthy trend, considering the wretched material one has to work with. It is, however, worth noting that not a few modern poets are quite comfortably situated, and I plan to live in luxurious retirement in Venice on an annuity furnished by about sixty of the most craven of the poets under my recent authority; and I suggest to my successor that he take similar steps in planning for what the rest homes so amiably call "the golden years."

* * * * *

Clement of Alexandria (VA)

Christopher Ricks (1933–), distinguished literary critic, has taught at Oxford, Cambridge, and Boston University, and is the author of many books, including True Friendship: Geoffrey Hill, Anthony Hecht, and Robert Lowell under the Sign of Eliot and Pound *(Yale, 2010). His friendship with Hecht dates back to the late 1970s.*

[July] 1984 Rochester NY

Dear Christopher:

Your generous gift of the volume of Larkin's prose [*Required Writing: Miscellaneous Pieces, 1955–1982*] arrived in time for me to read it with care just before we left Washington to return here to Rochester. We have bought a house there, to which we shall return after a year up here in Hither Thrace; and we stored in our new house everything it was not imperative to bring with us. The Larkin book, in consequence, is back there, awaiting our return. I'm sorry about this for a number of reasons, but chiefly because I wanted to set down some extended comments, by way of expressing appreciation, and even venturing some reservations. Sadly enough, with the book far away and the intervening time having elapsed, I find myself able to recall things only in a slap-dash sort of way. I recall my pleasure and approval of the pieces on jazz, which correspond more or less exactly with my own attitudes. I found the interviews and the sly or shy self-revelations very illuminating and informative. But I found myself feeling edgy about Larkin's style of "no nonsense bluntness" which strikes me as a mode of anti-intellectualism, and this is something I incline to distrust. It sets up its commentator (Larkin, in this case) as the sort of arbiter on just how detailed, fastidious, meticulous or formally stringent any argument is to be; and at the convenience of the commentator the argument can be curtailed with a brief sneer of "medieval hair-splitting," or some equivalent. Larkin has his equivalents, and if I had the book here I think I could point to them. It's frustrating not to be able to cite chapter and verse.

There were, in fact, two essays that were specifically delinquent in regard to the scholarship that might have gone into them: the ones on Marvell and Emily Dickinson ["The Changing Face of Andrew Marvell" and "Big Victims: Emily Dickinson and Walter de la Mare"]. Indeed, now, as I write, I recall that the Marvell essay was exasperating in just the ways I mentioned above. Larkin quotes some very sound and astute comments on a number of Marvell's richest lines, and follows with a wry "Possibly," which, in turn, is followed by a much simplified, common-sensical proposal of Larkin's that greatly narrows and diminishes the text.

Of Emily Dickinson he quotes the first stanza of J754: "My Life had stood—a Loaded Gun—/In Corners—till a Day/The Owner passed—identified—/And carried me away—" about which he says something like, "This is the very epitome of romantic love poetry." But it is not! It is, in fact, not really about love at all, as a careful reading of the whole poem would make clear. The poem is, in fact, about the painfulness of being both a woman and a fierce partisan of the Union forces during the American Civil War. She is as deeply committed as any soldier at the front (she was a close friend of Col. Higginson, who was a friend and abettor of John Brown's) but she was destined for the most secluded of lives. Larkin is wildly wrong here.

I'm a little surprised by some of my reactions as I set them down here, because I so very much admire Larkin's poems that I was prepared to believe that we would see eye to eye on literary-critical matters. And perhaps I make too much of my differences, in trying to recall the book from the dark backward and abysm of time. In any case, if I set down reservations, I hope you will not suppose I am ungrateful for your very thoughtful and kind gift. —I wonder if it will be possible to induce you and your family to visit us during your fall term in the States. Let me know what your Waltham or Cambridge (Mass) address is after you have settled down. It would be a great pleasure to meet once again.

> Affectionately,
> Tony

August 23, 1984 Rochester NY

[To John Hollander]

Dear John,

[. . .] As for your splendid distich,[2] certainly I agree, while admiring the Popean echo. While acknowledging that EP [Ezra Pound] had a major hand in the po-

---

[2]"On one of the great Moderns I'll be quite Terse:/God said, 'Let Ezra write!' and there was light Verse."

etic revolution of his days, that he was generous to many fellow artists, that he helped Yeats get rid of his early cloudiness, and that his own pleasure in hard, clear features was often a healthy and useful influence, that his interest in other cultures and literatures (somewhat neglected in those days) had a broadening and enriching effect—granting all this, I still find him, for the most part, unrewarding, when not infuriating, to read. In my crotchety latter years I find myself becoming increasingly impatient with anti-semites, and my impatience increases if, at the same time, they regard themselves as infallible prophets. Harry [Ford] just sent me a new biography of Hilaire Belloc [by A. N. Wilson], and by the time I finished reading it I was uncertain whether it was Belloc or his biographer (and rather disingenuous apologist) I most detested.

> Best regards to you and Natalie—
> Tony

[Summer 1984? Postcard: Firenze, Santa Maria Novella]
[To Joseph and U. T. Summers]
Dear U.T. & Joe—

We have a family ritual involving Robt. Herrick that may interest you. In the morning, since I am the first up, I recite loudly "Get up, get up, for shame, the blooming morn/Upon her wings presents the god unshorn," and Evan & Helen in concert respond, "Ah, shut up!" This sets us all up for the day. There's much to be said for the wine & cheese here, as well as the painting.

> We all send love,
> Helen & Tony

Sydney Lea (1942–) is a poet and editor of The Burdens of Formality: Essays on the Poetry of Anthony Hecht *(University of Georgia Press, 1989).*

November 7, 1984 (Day of Grief and Shame), Rochester NY
Dear Sydney:

[. . .] I'm pleased to think of you off in Bellagio, and I must tell you that while I have never been to the Villa Serbelloni during its tenancy by the Rockefeller Foundation, I did visit it once when it was still in private hands. The hands were those of the Princess of Thurn and Taxis. She was an American heiress named Ella, from Detroit, who had married and was widowed by the heir to the castle at Duino (she was strongly in favor of Ike for president, so you will know how long ago this was) but she was gracious enough to say that if ever she came back into her inheritance of Duino (which long since was Yugoslavian) she would invite me to stay and write poems, as Rilke had once been invited. I was gratified, but didn't hold my breath. The place in those days had thirty-two gardeners, and the chief gardener resembled Anatole France.

With warmest good wishes,
Tony

J. D. ("Sandy") McClatchy (1945–), poet, critic, and librettist, is the editor of The Yale Review *and many other works, including* Anthony Hecht: Selected Poems *(Knopf, 2011). He teaches at Yale University. In preparation for his essay on Hecht for Sydney Lea's volume, McClatchy invited Hecht to write a few paragraphs relating to his being hospitalized for depression in the early 1960s.*

December 26, 1984 Rochester NY

Dear Sandy,

I must try to answer your question, though I do so with a certain reluctance, since it's a topic I normally avoid in conversation, and touch upon only by indirection in the poems. I may say in an editorial way that I was never very comfortable about the way Anne Sexton exploited her hospitalizations and periods of dementia. I knew her quite well, but this "trait" of hers always made me feel ill at ease. It was clear she enjoyed both the attention she received from therapists and the more general notoriety of being "twelve-fingered," one of her kind. Cal Lowell was quite different, and though perhaps a little proud of his craziness at times (it became a license for recklessness in his manic moods, and seemed to him sometimes the sign of his genius as well as the frailty of his character) he only indulged it to the extent of not taking his lithium when the first manic signs of an attack came on him, chiefly because he felt so good, and, knowing that all the terrible consequences might, perhaps even must, ensue, he could not bring himself to descend from his exaltation.

Briefly, then, at the termination of five-and-a-half years of a painfully unhappy and unsuccessful marriage, a separation settlement was made, followed by a divorce, which required of my ex-wife that she live within 150 miles of New York City, so that I should be able to see the children on a regular basis. I must add that, while the marriage had been an unhappy one virtually from the start, its failure was a terrible blow to my self-esteem, and it was not I who sought to terminate it. When it was over I invested all my frustrated familial feelings on the two boys whom I saw, like most divorced fathers, on weekends, making those days unhealthily emotional, and completely without any ease or naturalness. In a way, I resented this arrangement: I had a job to perform during the week (teaching at Bard in those years) and such spare time as I had was devoted entirely to the children, who were pretty young in those days, the younger one still in diapers when all this began. So I had no private life of my own, and consequently invested too much emotional capital in the children. I was the more inclined to do so because I knew their mother to be completely irresponsible with regard to them. Then one day she told me, as I was delivering the children to her at the end of a weekend, that she had fallen in love with a Belgian, and that while I could legally prevent her from moving to Europe, as this man wished her to do, if she were forced to stay in this country she would be very unhappy, and if she were very unhappy, the children would be very unhappy. There was, of course, no argument to counter this. I had asked my lawyer, before the separation papers were drawn up, whether it would be possible for me to obtain custody of the children. He told me that it was virtually impossible, and in those days he was right. So she took the children off to Belgium, and I sank into a very deep depression. I felt no incentive even to get out of bed in the morning. I don't believe I thought in terms of suicide, but neither did life seem to hold out any attractions whatever. My doctor was worried about me, and suggested that I commit myself to a hospital, chiefly, he said, for the administration of medication. It was thorazine, which Anne took, and some other drug the name of which I no longer recall. I was there for three months, toward the end of which time I was allowed to go out during the days. Lowell was particularly kind to me during this period. The hospital was called Gracie Square Hospital, and there were some public pay phones on my floor, on which incoming calls to patients would be carried. Anyone could pick up a phone when it rang, and then page in a loud shout whomever the call was for. It was the custom of the patients to announce, in a loud and cheerful voice, on picking up the phone: "Crazy Square." Many of the patients were on electric shock; it had been agreed before I went in that I would be treated solely with medication, and this was observed. And the medication did indeed control the depression. What would have been a grim three months was, while by no means cheerful, yet remarkably endurable. The only thing I remember complaining about—it was pointless, of course, to complain about the food or routine—was the pictures. The plain bare walls were occasionally "enlivened" by framed pieces of cloth with arbitrary patterns on them, things that might have been drapes or upholstery. The chief point about them was that they were non-representational, and would not remind any patient of anything that carried an emotional burden.

Now, after all that, let me say that I really enjoyed dinner with you, and profited by your tip of the Gold & Fizdale book, which I promptly bought Helen for Christmas. She is grateful to us both. [. . .]

Tony

1985

Hecht published an appreciation of Ben Jonson's poetry in The Wilson Quarterly *19 (Spring 1995).*

[Early March 1985] Rochester NY

[To Joseph Summers]

Dear Joe,

So delighted am I with this curious correspondence about serious matters between colleagues in the same department that I felt impelled to reply to your latest quotations and observations on suitably elegant letter paper. We seem to continue in perfect agreement. You were right in supposing that I knew the passage from Jonson's Timber (I had found it quoted by Hebel and Hudson in the back of their ample anthology of Renaissance poetry) but in fact I had not read or thought about it much for years. Yes, I agree, one "winces" a bit at Jonson's tone; I very likely more than you, because he is speaking as a practicing poet, and I find myself often enough obliged to suppress sentiments analogous to his. So I find myself thinking, "Thank God he said it, so that I don't have to." There are few things that I find more unseemly than the resentful and usually envious remarks of an elder poet who feels he has been cheated out of the fame and applause he deserves. Though what Jonson says is all too often true, it is not something poets are in a position to say without appearing to have a private ax to grind. There are far too many examples of this sort of arch self-consciousness. Robert Hillyer was full of such contempt for his contemporaries, and poor John Crowe Ransom wrote a mocking commentary on Eliot's "Waste Land" (which he had the wit or grace not to republish in book form) that could not fail to remind a reader that the two poets happened to be born in the same year. Graves may have been the most reckless offender in this way, and his Oxford lectures, collected in The Crowning Privilege, contain one called "Be These Thy Gods, O Israel," which undertakes to demolish Yeats, Eliot, Pound, Dylan Thomas, and Auden. It comes dangerously close to simple vindictiveness. And yet one cannot help sympathize with any poet, even Frost, who sees his labor as lonely and largely unnoticed, and sees a lot of trumpery admired instead.

You and I admire and delight in the same details of Jonson's comments: about those who "think rude things greater than polished, and scattered more numerous than composed." <u>Numerous</u> is superb there, and reminds us that numbers is another term for poetry. Yet even as one approves of Jonson's poetic rectitude, in theory as well as in practice, one recalls his haughty remark to Drummond of Hawthornden that Donne "for not keeping of accent, deserved hanging." There is no question that the music of Jonson is more regular and clear-cut than Donne's; Jonson's poetry, though capable of a variety of paces and a diversity of moods, seems rarely to offend against what might be called a unity of sentiment: the tone, even the mixed tones, of a poem, are consistent and maintained throughout. But Donne often does something quite different and virtually opposed to this: the poems shift direction, change mood, alter as a voice alters in the course of speech. It is a more flexible range than Jonson either has or wants. And this vocal trick of Donne's allows him to be comic and serious simultaneously, to give you the impression that he's thinking as he is writing, that he is open to impulse and improvisation at all moments; whereas Jonson's poetry seems by contrast "composed" in the special sense of being plotted and planned, revised and premeditated. Both Helen Gardner and A.J. Smith (the Penguin editor) have useful things to say about Donne's versification, and make it fairly clear that in that precise regard the poet was not nearly so eccentric as modern readers with an uncertain ear, or Ben Jonson, for that matter, have claimed. [. . .]

Many grateful thanks for continuing this exchange with me.

Tony

August 8, 1985 Washington DC

[To J. D. McClatchy]

Dear Sandy,

I am greatly impressed with, and deeply grateful for, your extremely thoughtful and penetrating essay ["Anatomies of Melancholy"]. It strikes me quite simply as the very best critical piece I have ever seen about my work. Indeed, what I have seen over the years has been, by and large, so very disappointing—being either trivially superficial, or patently wrong, and usually both—that I have grown to approach the reading of any such thing with dread and depression. And I frankly admit that it was in this spirit that I opened the envelope that contained your essay. So you will understand, I hope, how genuinely delighted I am, and how surprised. [. . .]

What really impresses me is your large and compassing view of my work, your shrewd, and I think altogether sound view of it. This has nothing to do with "value" judgments. I mean to observe how keen you are in discovering a "mother" in "The Hill," a judgment that seems to me perfectly right. Indeed, your whole thesis of a union of opposites turning up in many forms seems to me right, and the right way to describe my characteristic strategies. In other words, I could scarcely be more pleased and gratified by what you have so carefully and thoughtfully done. [. . .]

Concern[ing] your astute comments on "Dichtung und Wahrheit," and the oppositions of "truth" and "art," or subjective and objective, etc: having [. . .] just finished going through the essays [forthcoming in *Obbligati*], I find that this opposition in one form or another is the principal theme that links the essays together. It is obviously central to the essay, the first in the book, on "The Pathetic Fallacy," which ought to be out any day now in <u>The Yale Review</u>. But it is present in virtually every other essay as well, and is obviously central to the very essence of criticism: how do you know when you are describing a thing accurately, as distinct from imputing to it biases and attitudes of your own? How do we get at the truth of a work of art? Or anything else, for that matter. How do we avoid "willful" or even "inadvert" mis-readings? As bald questions, these are not continuously articulated in every essay; but they are implied throughout, and they, I hope, make for a coherence I very much hope some reviewers will notice, though I suppose the chances are very poor. [. . .]

One more thing. The oppositions in the poems and essays have probably grown over the years to be a sort of technique of the imagination, a mode of apprehension. It has become firmly my own, I guess, and habitual. Whether it came to be because of my personal psychic history or not I can scarcely say. But it may be worth pointing out that it is the "dialectic" mode of Yeats, who has always been a literary hero and mentor of mine. Not only in his poems but in his prose, and chiefly in his theoretical writing (<u>A Vision</u>) oppositions lie at the center of everything. There was a time when I frankly tried to imitate Yeats's declamatory style. I wisely gave that up. But there were things in his life, as in his view of art, that chimed with my experience. He yearned to be other than he was, to become his opposite. I need no one to point out the differences between us, even apart from the question of comparative merit. He made a very public career for himself in art and politics, the sort of career from which (especially as it applies to theater) I have instinctively shrunk. But if the connection is useful to you, there it is.

Love

Tony

[To J. D. McClatchy]

Dear Sandy,

[. . .] Belated warm wishes for your birthday. Curious how a process common to us all seems so unique to each of us. At my age my greatest fear seems not to be death itself, nor physical enfeeblement, but mental deterioration, and I think the germs of that fear were laid early on. But however much I try to console myself with the assertion that this anxiety is merely a hang-up of my own, every time I forget a name, or grope helplessly for a word that refuses to come, I think of Alzheimer's disease, and imagine that I will shortly be disabled as a teacher, and will slip quickly into an ungainly dotage, a burden to everyone and to Helen especially. Naturally, I've not uttered a word of this to her. The consequence of this fear is that every time I write anything that indicates complexity as well as clarity of thought I rejoice (briefly) at what I take to be an index that my mind has not yet rotted away completely. Lately I have taken comfort in a rather intricate unraveling of the themes and meaning of <u>The Merchant of Venice</u> that will be the lengthiest of the essays in the coming book [*Obbligati*]. I'm really pleased with it because I'm convinced I'm right—and if I'm right, it means no one else has ever been right before. But also because it confirmed (for a period) a precarious self-confidence. But the writing of it, as well as the thinking it through, is already far enough behind me to count for very little. Poems, of course, work the same way; my pleasure in writing them is intense, and only slightly longer than a sexual spasm. After, they become more featureless and inconsequential than old girlfriends. I have the greatest difficulty reading any of my old poems with the excitement I know I felt around the time of their composition; and I find this terribly unnerving because I can read the early poems of any poet I admire with undiminished delight. I try to tell myself that this is because, being the work of others, they always seem to me original, whereas my own work, being the product of my own mind, is altogether too "expected." I tell myself this to cheer myself up; the alternative (that my work is really no good, and only seems so in the auto-intoxicated throes of writing, and briefly to a few generous friends) is what I avoid thinking as best I can. [. . .]

Tony

1986

Irma Brandeis (1905–1990) taught at Bard from 1944 to 1979 and was much admired by the poets who taught there, including Hecht and James Merrill. She was the author of The Ladder of Vision: A Study of Dante's Comedy *(1961). In the 1930s, she and the Italian poet Eugenio Montale were lovers, hence prompting Hecht's reference to receiving the Montale Award.*

August 28, 1986 Washington DC

My dear Irma,

[. . .] A visit to Bard on my part seems oddly remote as a likelihood. But I, too, think of you often; certainly while I was putting the book together [*Obbligati*], and on many surprising, unexpected occasions—such as a very brief trip to Milan last fall, when I became the first American poet to receive the Eugenio Montale Award. And I remember Bard in its days of primeval innocence, when it was far less gaudy than today, but when you and a few others kept it superbly lively, and a place where it was a pleasure to live and work. It cheers me to think that Mary McCarthy will be keeping company with you from time to time, and I imagine she will restore some of the ambience I remember with relish. [. . .]

Love,
Tony

1987

March 5, 1987 Washington, DC

[To Harry Ford]

Dear Harry,

This is to thank you many times over for your great kindness in sending me our correspondence from your files. I have no idea what it may be worth; doubtless nowhere near Bill Merwin's, or many another, but at least it is something I can bequeath, and which may help Helen and Evan. I have glanced through a few of the letters, and observe that they contain some juicy indiscretions regarding my opinions of certain poets and critics. Just the sort of thing that, judiciously edited, could make for a scandalously successful book. I vaguely regret the fact that I won't be around to read the reviews.

Our daffodils and crocuses, foolhardy things, are on the way up, though it was below thirty this morning. They have simply acquired habits, I suppose.

Helen joins me in sending affectionate greetings.

Tony

Kenneth Gross (1954–) is a professor of English and a scholar primarily of the English Renaissance at the University of Rochester. Hecht was responding to a draft

version of Gross's essay, which would appear in The Burdens of Formality *(1989),*
bearing the title "Anthony Hecht and the Imagination of Rage."

June 4, 1987 Washington DC

Dear Ken,

I've read over, with enormous appreciation and gratitude, your long and careful essay on my work. It seems to me that you have deserved praise on several counts. First of all, you have deftly located the strand of "rage" that runs through a number of major poems from first to last—a discovery, I may add, that no one else has made—and which is an important element in any view of my work. (It's present, of course, in a number of poems you don't mention, like "Behold The Lilies of the Field," but your essay is already of considerable length. I should add, too, that you were acute in observing that translations afford a convenient mask through which rage may be pronounced by a borrowed persona.) Secondly, your detailed remarks on particular poems, especially on "Alceste in the Wilderness" and "The Deodand," seem to me subtle and intelligent and thoughtful in all their abundant details. You have clearly read not only these particular poems with care and attention but most of my poems, and make astute use of many of them in the course of your comments. So your first venture into criticism outside the Spenserian realm is enormously impressive.

I am, nevertheless, rather puzzled that you should have found "Green: An Epistle" as baffling and opaque as you do. You seem to circle around it as though it denied entry, and was meant to keep the reader at a distance, through irony and other devices. But it's hard for me to believe that poem is as cryptic and resistant as you declare. Much of what you say about it is certainly true: it is about "growing up," though that, of course, is no simple business. It is more precisely about the familiar modes of self-deception that almost everyone employs. It is therefore about illusion or delusions, and it consequently borrows the allegorical myth of Plato's cave, transformed into a modern movie theater.

Let me volunteer a few sketchy comments in the hope that they may clear up some of your bewilderment. There are two characters in the poem, the letter writer and the person to whom he writes. Call them writer and reader, or W and R. Most of what W writes is an unattractive account of the character of R, who does not appear in the poem in his own right, so that all we know about him is at second hand. And of course the immediate question is: how reliable is W? In a poem so concerned with deception and self-deception, this is no small question.

W writes about the imperceptible development of human character, comparing this to the evolution of plant life, or even of fossil fuel and gems—a process infinitely more ancient than the development of beasts or humans. He also is writing about the fact that, by virtue of the very use of the evolutionary metaphor, we seem to affirm, whether consciously or unconsciously, a notion of progress or advance. And what this means in terms of the psyche is that we incline to see ourselves in the best possible light; and what's more, that everyone does so, including the patently wicked. We see ourselves as both the active figures who deserve credit for the initiative they have contributed towards this progress, as well as the passive and sometimes helpless victims who have heroically risen above and overcome the calamities that have been imposed upon them. (Thus the two kinds of amoebic life, active and passive, seen on the microscopic slide.)

But the Roethke epigraph is not used inappropriately. Not everyone who is persecuted is thereby made saintly, and the "new life" that begins with "lopped limbs" may have to rely on the energy of rage merely to remain "life" at all. In writing as he does, in using this "allegorical mode," in employing the vast "evolutionary metaphor," W is indicating that he is not merely describing R, but instead a large "psychic type," a kind of person not altogether so uncommon. For nearly everyone has some capacity for self-exoneration, and for viewing the past in a highly selective and self-protective way. Certain kinds of people like to see their defeats and miseries as heaven-sent mortifications of their pride, yet Freud has told us that such mortifications and repressions can be deforming, and we prefer to think of ourselves as noble rather than deformed. But deformity lies at the center of this poem. It declares that repressed malice does not make us "saints" as in the epigraph, but makes us more unconsciously cruel than overt action would. It addresses R in the assumption that, having endured a lifetime of repressed rage and malice, he mistakenly believes he has risen above them, and has attained the serenity that so much suffering entitles him to. But W maintains that this is smug and false, and that the malice has simply found new and more ingeniously "innocent" ways of expressing itself, as in "the rose," taken to be the apogee of the plant kingdom according to one version of the great chain of being. W is astute enough to see that R may envision W as being this very kind of person himself, though R is able to hold this view self-protectively, by imagining such a poem being written about W by "somebody else," i.e., not by his innocent self. In other words, the poem is about all the involution and intricacies of paranoia.

There are some other "allegorical" details in the poem. When W describes his location in "a border town" with a view that embraces both sunrise and sunset, he is placing himself at a solitary vantage from which to view the whole prospect of past and future. In this he is doubtless being self-serving—trying to sound objective and Olympian. But the poem is clearly self-reflexive: we don't know how true it may be about R (though our experience of the world tells us there certainly are such people) but it strongly suggests that W himself, for all his diagnostic skill, may be suffering from the very illness he so minutely diagnoses—as is often the way with paranoia.

Finally, I think there is a certain kinship between this poem and Auden's that begins "Since you are going to begin to-day," and which he later titled "Venus Will Now Say A Few Words." To the degree that there was any influence at all, it was almost entirely unconscious, since I did not discover the parallel until well after my poem was written. But of course I had read Auden's years before, and who can say how firmly it may have lodged in my unconscious mind?

If you can accept this account of the poem, I think you would have to agree that it is not "impersonal," as you have declared, and that it deals rather nakedly with the kind of person who is (sometimes not unjustifiably) suspicious of others, while being no less suspicious of himself. It is in fact quite "intimate," and the intimacy is hinted at not only by the fact that W claims to know R pretty well, but that they have for years entered into collusion in avoiding the topic addressed in the poem. As when people politely pretend to be friends, though suspecting one another of deep malice.

Please let me know if this clarifies the poem for you in any way. Meanwhile, let me express once again my great gratitude to you for all the thought, intelligence and work that went into your long essay. And let me add that I look forward to reading what you are going to write on <u>Othello</u>.

With best wishes,

Tony

David Mason (1954–), poet, essayist, and anthologist, co-directs the Creative Writing program at Colorado College. He studied with Hecht at the University of Rochester and wrote his Ph.D. thesis on W. H. Auden, which was co-directed by Hecht and Daniel Albright.

July 31, 1987 Washington DC

Dear David:

Thanks for your note. I agree that you should delay getting in touch with [Edward] Mendelson and [Nicholas] Jenkins until you've digested a lot of material and narrowed the focus of your inquiries enough to be able to ask some useful questions. Incidentally, a press release on new UR faculty, sent to me by George Ford, indicates that [Daniel] Albright must have a sound knowledge of music, and has written, or is planning to write, on Stravinsky. This should be of great value to you if you decide to make any use of <u>The Rake's Progress</u>. Also, Albright, who is currently teaching in Germany, must feel at ease in German literature and culture, and this was the case with Auden, too. In fact, Auden had an amusing contempt for French culture, possibly because it was so "popular." His particular partiality for Germany began in the twenties, when Berlin was famous for its libertine life; depression and inflation made everything (including sex) inexpensive to the foreign purchaser, etc. Germany, in any case, is a symbol of his generally Nordic bias, which is connected also with his love of the sagas, of Iceland, of Wagner and Goethe. There is something of the same bent in D.H. Lawrence. As for Baudelaire and Valery, you should, in time, get pleasure from reading them. There is a lovely purity to the latter that even comes across in good translations. For example, James Merrill has translated "Palme," and Howard Moss has translated "The Cemetery by the Sea." As for Baudelaire, there's an awful lot written about him, of course, and much of it is wearisome. [...] What is so remarkable about his poetry is its earnest perversity: he is serious about debauchery, not sophisticatedly witty, debonair, or self-indulgent, like Wilde, for example. And yet despite this he is able to write poems of enormous tenderness, like "Le Jet d'Eau,"[3] for example, and to write of the dispossessed, the deformed, the sick, the outcast, with a Dostoyevskyan compassion. [...]

Affectionately,
Tony

1988

The New York Public Library named several noted literary figures each year as "Literary Lions." They were celebrated at a black-tie dinner in their honor at the library, with New York society people patronizing the event. Hecht was named a Lion in 1988 and Merrill offered the Hechts the use of his apartment.

November 13, 1988 Washington, DC

Dear Jimmy,

It was wonderful being able to stay in your apartment [on 164 E. 72nd street], and the several men who manned the post of doorman all seemed to be alerted

[3]Hecht's translation of Baudelaire's "Le Jet d'Eau" appears in *The Darkness and the Light* (2001). His longstanding interest in this poem can be glimpsed in an early attempt at translation ("The Fountain"), which appears in "Uncollected Hecht," *Poetry* 198 (September 2011): 441–459, intro., David Yezzi.

to our coming and our presence, and so firmly did they seem to recognize us that I imagine you must have shown them some snapshots. Anyway, they were the souls of courtesy. And the apartment itself was luxuriously comfortable. We delighted especially in all the art work, and especially in the work of the Georgia artist [Bruce Hafley] who does huzzars with fennel shakos, and elaborations on postage stamps. And I was especially impressed by the attractive Sicilian devices you found to screen your fine cans of tomato puree.

[...] The reading [at the Morgan Library sponsored by the American Academy in Rome] with Richard Kenney went off, I think, extremely well for both of us. He read first, as was particularly respectful, and indeed [was] even reverent, in regard to me. He read some of my double dactyls as a good humored tribute, and because the form was invented at the Academy in Rome. He read wonderfully from his own work, including some new poems, and one especially funny and skillful poem about putti at the Pitti Palace. He was there with his wife and infant son, and after the reading, wife and son went home while he and a group of us were to be taken to dinner after a champagne reception at the library. The reception seemed to go on and on, so that by the time we got to the restaurant they had given away the table reserved for us. We didn't sit down to eat till very late, by which time Helen and I had largely lost our appetites, but everything was amiable if wearying.

The Lion bash was terrific. Was Mrs. Heinz your hostess as she was ours? And did you visit her mansion on East 57th St. with its paired Cranachs, its immense Bonnard, its Picasso, Renoir and other trifles? She sent a stretch limo for us, which was the more welcome because it was raining. Our table at the bash included Elizabeth Hardwick, Daniel Halpern, Robert Stone, and Roy Blount. The place pullulated with celebrities: I spotted Henry Kissinger, Bill Blass and Oscar de la Renta, while Helen noticed Jackie O. and Carolyn Roehm, to confine myself only to the non-literary types. At Mrs. Heinz's reception afterwards we had a chance to chat with the R.W.B. Lewises for the first time, and with Art Buchwald, who is a very engaging and accessible man. We had, in sum, a wonderful time.

My gratitude embraces the gift of your poem about 164 E. 72nd as not the least part of your generosity. And we both hope that you and Peter [Hooten] will be able to visit us soon again in Washington.

Affectionately,

Tony

William Maxwell (1908–2000) was a novelist and, for forty years, fiction editor for The New Yorker. Maxwell remarked in a letter to Hecht: "I remember [I. A. Rich-

*ards] saying (as we looked up at the leaves washing over us in the headlights) that
if you stood long enough in a shower-bath, it would probably be like reading* King
Lear.*"*

November 22, 1988 Washington, DC

My dear Bill:

[. . .] Your remarks about I.A. Richards left me enchanted, and mildly dazed
or bewildered for a while, until I began to think not only of his words but
of <u>him</u>, and then it all came clear. I met him a few times: at Bard College, at
Harvard, and at the Academy/Institute ceremonial, and my enduring impres-
sion was of white-maned benignity, a healthful ruddiness, and incomparable
geniality. Characteristically English, it seemed to me, yet allied to his vigor-
ous penchant for mountaineering. And then, of course, my puzzle all cleared
up. When I myself think about taking a shower, I think of the accumulating
warmth, the Turkish-bath atmosphere clouding the mirrors and beading the
tiles, a steamy world of Brazilian luxuriance, obscurely scented with fern and
mango. So that if you stood in a shower bath long enough your fingertips
would shrivel and turn leperously whitish, as would the soles of your feet. But
nothing of this kind would have occurred to, or have been intended by, Rich-
ards. Being a cheerful British stoic, he must have taken ice-cold showers from
boyhood, and it's perfectly natural that, breathing heavily and enthusiastically
under the nozzle, he would have thought, "Poor naked wretches, wheresoe'er
you are,/That bide the pelting of this pitiless storm,/How shall your house-
less heads and unfed sides,/Your looped and windowed raggedness, defend
you/From seasons such as these?" I can just hear him reciting that loudly in the
shower, as other men sing "I've been working on the railroad," and scrubbing
himself with brown soap, and possibly a brush. It is not, in any case, a text that
would present itself to the mind of either Reagan or Bush, whether showering
or not.

Your travelling around in a rumble seat, discussing hedonistic sensations with
Richards, sounds intoxicating, and reminds me that when I was in the army a
fellow soldier told me his sensual ideal was to make love to a woman and eat
spinach at the same time; when I suggested that this was awkward, and a lot of
spinach would spill on her, he didn't care. I think he also wanted Ravel's "Bolero"
in the background.

Again, my delighted and affectionate thanks,
Tony

Nicholas Christopher (1951–), poet, novelist, and translator, studied under Hecht at Harvard and is on the faculty of the Writing Division of the School of the Arts at Columbia University.

March 22, 1989 Washington, DC

Dear Nicholas,

It's amazing that anyone as fertile, industrious and productive as you are should find time to write long, newsy letters as well. I'm grateful, and delighted by all you report—or almost all: I am concerned that you have again been over-looked by the Guggenheim people. But everything else seems to be good news. You should have much pleasure with Livy. He is a writer who should be read in tandem with Virgil, even though you are reading him with Machiavelli in mind. When you write of Washington as the sin capital of the USA and then groan, "Poor John Tower," you have not come anywhere near the heart of it. Tower is Simon-Pure in comparison to our mayor, and the unwillingness on the part of everyone from the President on down to inhibit the sale of semi-automatic weapons is beyond belief.

My reading, for a number of reasons, has been more erratic than yours, and I am currently wondering whether it can be determined at what point charming British eccentricity slips into pig-headedness. I have in mind Samuel Butler, who was, to understate things badly, a great fan of Handel. Now I like Handel too, and am especially fond of Acis and Galatea. But for Butler, Handel becomes the test of all mankind. He seriously believes that music slipped into evident decline after Handel—a decline from which it never recovered. He finds Don Giovanni a bore. He declares that, to music's eternal damage, it developed from Scarlatti to Haydn to Mozart to Beethoven, omitting the healthful Handelian influence, and has suffered in consequence. In this he resembles Shaw, who made Wag-ner the test of all sensibility; a test which, I may add, I fail with flying colors. Of course, a man like Butler, who thought The Odyssey was written by a woman, and that Shakespeare's sonnets are an account of his homosexual lust for a young actor in his company named Willy Hughes, is perhaps not someone to be regarded as the measure of good sense. But I have been balancing his crackpottedness with the diaries of John Evelyn and the letters of Pliny the Younger (I told you my reading was erratic) and they are full of sound good sense. [. . .]

As for the climate, while the crocuses and daffodils are up all over the place, and it looks Easterish as all get out, still it is chilly hereabouts these days. But what o' that? We that have free souls it touches not, especially after those arctic decades in Rochester. To confess the wicked truth, Helen and I rejoice in the evening weather maps that indicate snow in Rochester while we are enjoying comparative warmth down here. Even when the weather is lousy in Washington, our spirits instantly improve at the sign of foul weather up there. There's a good poem on this topic by Irving Feldman; it's in his book called <u>All of Us Here</u>, and it's called "The Call."

Helen joins me in sending affectionate greetings to you and Connie, . . .

Tony

April 12, 1989 Washington DC

[To J. D. McClatchy]

Dear Sandy,

I have been reading randomly, but carefully, and with rich reward, in <u>White Paper</u>. Randomly, because I wanted to turn immediately to your comments that would furnish me the greatest illumination of matters still obscure to my careless or negligent reading. So I addressed myself first of all to what you had to say about Charles Wright, John Ashbery, and Adrienne Rich. As distinct, it seems to me, from all the other poets you deal with, these three I read distantly, coolly, and usually without excitement, though of course for different reasons. I found myself with you and made much more at ease regarding Ashbery, whose work I have always enjoyed in a superficial way. And I have been made more patient and perhaps even charitable towards Wright; though the Poundian technique is one I deeply distrust, employed as it has been by truly rotten poets who like to posture in the old man's mode of total omniscience and profound sensitivity. I find myself still boggling at Rich, who seems to me shrill, politicized, and narrow, and your own generous enthusiasm still baffles me. I am especially glad to see that you have written on Snodgrass at some considerable length; he strikes me as a poet once idolized with critical notice and approval, only to be dropped and disregarded as if he had never written. I feel that he did put some of his admirers to the test with the Führer Bunker poems, only a few of which worked even in parts, and which too much relied on plain, unapologetic sensationalism. Still, one of the brave things about Snodgrass was his willingness to risk big and dramatic topics. I've not yet read your long piece on him, but I assume from its length that you value him as highly as I do.

Meanwhile, of what I have read, everything gladdens, even when (as in the case of Rich) it does not absolutely compel.

With gratitude and affection,

Tony

October 7, 1989 Washington DC

[To Richard Wilbur]

Dear Dick,

[. . .] As for the other matter you mention, though I normally don't see the TLS, I was shown that infuriating Hamilton review [of your book],[4] which I read in haste, and with mounting anger, so that I don't even remember any reference to Clive James. What is perhaps most maddening about a review such as Hamilton's (which is not only bad, but unfair) is that nothing can be done about it, and the reviewee must sit there, as though bound and gagged, unable to appeal for justice. Hamilton has an obvious taste for sensationalism, a taste he was able to indulge in his Lowell biography, and which he carried almost beyond the limits of the law in his attempt to invade the privacy of J.D. Salinger. I made the serious mistake many years ago of entering into a friendly correspondence with him at a time when he was editing a literary journal that enjoyed a very brief life. One day I came across a catalogue from a rare book and manuscript dealer, listing my letters to Hamilton for sale at a flatteringly high price, and describing them as full of revelatory gossip about the American literary establishment. So when Lizzie Hardwick wrote to me to say that Hamilton was writing the biography of Cal [Robert Lowell] with her blessing, and asking me to assist him in any way I could, I was not disposed to take any initiative in the matter, and he never troubled to put himself in touch with me, which was all to the good.

His partiality for the sensational expressed itself in the review of your book in his very eccentric decision to pin the whole review, and the thrust of his judgment, on your poem about Sylvia Plath, thus setting up for himself, and for the body of readers he was counting on to share his views, a crude opposition between the raw suffering and inspired derangement of his heroine and the control of your work. Plath is almost impossible to write about these days (you did it better than most) because she has become iconic, and all kinds of crazies rally to her side as to a literary martyr. What Hamilton did was to bludgeon you with her suffering and her raving (no one seems to be aware that the "Daddy"

[4]*Times Literary Supplement*, September 15, 1989, p. 999.

poem is embarrassed enough about what it is saying to employ that "oo" rhyme so insistently as to turn the poem nearly into doggerel verse, and undermine its own seriousness). I once received the same sort of treatment at the hands of Donald Davie, who elected to review a book of mine in tandem with one by Josephine Miles, and he found a way to extol her gallant and good-humored endurance of paraplegic affliction at the expense of what he found in me as a morbid preoccupation with gloomy views and subjects.

After what amounted to the demise of Atheneum (or at last the departure therefrom of Harry Ford) in not too long a time (somewhere about May) I will be bringing out a new book at Knopf, where Harry now is settled; and they will also issue a volume called "Early Collected Poems," assembling everything prior to the new book. I am already preparing to grit my teeth and steel myself for the sort of Hamilton-Davie treatment that seems to be the standard reward for certain poets these days.

> Love to you and Charlee,
> Tony

1990

The original letter hasn't been located. This is a draft found in the Hecht archives at Emory.

[April 1990?] Washington DC

[To Joseph Brodsky]

Dear Joseph,

It has taken me a while to recover from the effect of your letter, which came as a severe blow. I never imagined you wrote out of any malice or ill-will, and I feel sure of your friendship. Nevertheless, I was reeling with bewilderment and dismay for quite some time after I read what you had written. And now [I] am still at a loss to account for your overwhelmingly negative reaction to my poem. You profoundly shook my confidence in my work generally, and in that poem in particular. And that poem is a major part of my new book.

I shall, of course, send you a short poem for the anthology you are planning. But that does not settle the matter of your views about "See Naples and Die." I suppose there is no way of altering those views, though I think you have gravely misunderstood the poem, and my intent. You complain that the "narrative" is too thin to sustain a poem of such length—which is the sort of complaint that might be made about <u>Paradise Lost</u>. I picked the comparison from Milton deliberately. My poem is intended as a <u>commentary</u> on the events in <u>Genesis</u>: the temptation, the fall, and the expulsion. It is also a commentary on the epigraph from Simone Weil. It is mainly, however, an account of the visions of paradise and of damnation that are glimpsed in the course of mundane affairs. Its speaker is one of the damned; and one who fails to understand what has happened to him. He reveals more than he understands himself, like some of the characters in Henry James or Ford Madox Ford. He is figuratively "blind," and there is irony in his pride in being a careful observer, especially when he gets cheated during the "temptation" scene. But there is no point in trying to explain what so patently failed to move or convey itself to you with any force whatever. I shall cast about for something to send you as soon as I can.

Yours,

Tony

Jennifer Snodgrass was Hecht's editor at Harvard University Press, which published The Hidden Law: The Poetry of W. H. Auden *(1993).*

August 10, 1990 Washington DC

Dear Jennifer Snodgrass,

Thanks for your careful and self-effacing letter. I am grateful for your praise, and I hope I won't seem defensive about your suggestions—chiefly the one concerning the development of a "thesis" or <u>parti pris</u> that would give the book a putative "focus," and assemble its parts as well as subordinate them properly to one another. The fact is that this is just what I am trying to avoid. There are many such tendentious books already available, each with its (often) minor ax to grind: think of the ones, for example, on Shakespeare—Shakespeare & women, Shakespeare as Tudor apologist, Shakespeare's knowledge of fairy-lore, Shakespeare and Revenge, etc., etc. There are, it should not surprise you to know, books of this kind on Auden and I want to go out of my way to avoid seeming to offer a "key" concept to which everything can be neatly tied, and which will serve to unravel all the diverse complexities and mysteries that Auden's work presents. I can, of course, see the marketing advantages of a book with such a "key" concept; it makes advertising easier, and encourages the potential reader to suppose that the multiplex problems can now be resolved with a single explanation. But I go in fear, or at least in distrust, of such a programmatic approach, just as much with Auden as I would with Shakespeare.

[. . .] I venture to say that, pleased as I am that you should write that my text has sent you "back to the individual poems with increased understanding," I take additional satisfaction in being able to claim that in almost all details my commentary differs from all those of the major commentators on Auden who have published up to this point. This, in fact, seems to me the single most interesting thing about what I have written: it corrects many fairly well-established misreadings of the poems (and the play, Dog-Skin).

This is obviously not something I can remark upon too insistently within the body of my text. But it is important to me that, for every individual poem or play I deal with, I believe I have found sounder and more persuasive interpretations than those provided by Edward Mendelson, Monroe K. Spears, Samuel Hynes, John Fuller, and several others. My differences cannot be subjoined under a single heading or "key concept," nor am I secretly engaged in trying to hold any of the established Auden critics up to ridicule or embarrassment. I am not trying simply to be different; but reading the poems one by one as carefully as I can, I am surprised and delighted to find how independent of received opinion my interpretations are. [. . .]

Best,
Anthony Hecht

October 11, 1990 Washington DC

[To Joseph Summers]

Dear Joe,

[. . .] I suspected, when I did not hear from you immediately, that there might be something of great pitch and moment that was preoccupying you, and I am concerned now for the health of you both. But before I address that inexhaustible topic, let me say in more detail how truly pleased I am by what you had to say about The Transparent Man. It could not have come to me at a more propitious moment, for I had been depressed by the Times review (as well as the Times reviewer [William Logan], who curiously regarded himself as my friend, and shortly after his faint praise was published wrote to ask me to recommend him for a Guggenheim). Anyway, your generous enthusiasm was, and remains, heartening, and I am particularly pleased by your revisionary assessment of "A Love For Four Voices." Your varying views of the "colors" of the poem perfectly reflect my sense of the curious coloration of Shakespeare's play, which, while undeniably a joyful and indeed gleeful celebration of love, is nevertheless ever so cunningly hedged about with peripheral omens and reminders of the imperfection of life. The mother of the page that Titania and Oberon fight over had died in childbirth; there are raw jokes about venereal diseases; the infidelity of the fairy couple remembers the promiscuity of Theseus and Hippolyta, with whatever suggestion this may provide regarding the future of that marriage. And indeed the very oscillations of the young couples in the course of a single night does not bid fair for the future. The "Pyramus and Thisbe" play is a joke, but a joke with a bitter taste, and there's a good deal throughout the play to remind us of our mortality. It has been my hope in some way to suggest these same glimmerings or penumbras while still keeping the poem essentially light-hearted and cheerful; and your kind comments persuade me that I've succeeded.

[...]

I shall be thinking of you, Joe, and of the operation you are to undergo on the 17th of January, which is a day after my birthday. Birthdays are curiously complicated events in these latter years, bringing me, without question, nearer to the end, but before that, and, as I now think, mercifully, nearer to retirement, which will be at hand in 1993. I find myself quite equable at the thought of it, even though it comes as what one of my Shakespeare students would describe as my "ultimate demise."

With warmest greetings to you both,

Tony

1991

January 11, 1991 Washington DC

[To William Maxwell]

Dear Bill,

A woman we saw something of when we lived in Rochester liked to claim that her greatest accomplishment in life was to quit smoking, and this was probably true. Rochester is a tranquil town, with a low crime rate. On the other hand, I cherish the same fond feelings for New York that you do, and no doubt for some of the same reasons. There are still little nooks and endroits that were the settings of a half-remembered life, and full of an obscure vitality in consequence. As regards that city I am a shameless and even dangerous conservative, and have grown to disapprove of almost all the changes that have taken place in it during recent years. This is largely because the changes have taken place behind my back, so to speak. I was born and raised in the city, as were my parents, and I can recall with simple pleasure how one day they walked me over the very route they took from their homes to their school. This was, as I said, a <u>walk</u>, and not a taxing one either. My parents seemed able to recall all the major, and most of the minor, alterations in the city during their life-times: not just the replacement of old buildings by new ones, but the changes in the smallest shops and stores. And I, too, grew to know the city on my walks in large part by the wonderful sequence of small shops, and to regret their change of ownership, but to nearly resent the interruption of that infinite variety by the occasional block of boring apartment houses that offered nothing for consideration but the names of physicians on brass plaques. The shop windows seemed to me richly and powerfully diverting, since even the same shop would vary its display from time to time. And when major innovations took place—replacing a large building with another—I was prepared to tolerate this as long as I enjoyed the privilege of watching the transformation taking place: admiring the cranes in operation, awe-struck at the huge cavity exposed in the city's depths. And perhaps because it seemed to come about gradually, there was time to accustom myself to most of such changes, though some were painful. The Depression, for my family, meant that we rather suddenly began to shop a great deal at Woolworth's—the one, I think, on Third, in the eighties. It was located, as fate would have it, right next to a children's clothing store where my clothes had come from before the crash. But then, for what seemed a long time, even my shoes came from Woolworth's, and I keenly sensed that something serious had happened, and that we had "come down" in the world. I would be asked solicitously if those wretched and cheaply-made little sandals were "comfortable," and what could I say? Certainly they were not uncomfortable, but just because the matter was so trifling they were a sure index of a decline from which I deeply feared we would never be lifted up again. It was like being an exiled Romanov. But now the changes, as I said, go on without my being aware of them, and therefore without my consent, and when I return to the city after even a moderately short absence I feel even more exiled than before—except for the fragments shored against its ruin.

The prospect, in consequence, of seeing you and Emily [Maxwell] in the grand setting of the Morgan Library fills me with the greatest and most serene pleasure.

Affectionately,
Tony

The Société Imaginaire was created in 1986 by the multinational artist Batuz.

March 18, 1991 Washington DC
[To W. D. Snodgrass]
Dear De,
It was good (and humorous) of you to send me the glossy publication about the exalted "Société Imaginaire" of Batuz' remarkable contrivance. I have not

read it all, not even all the parts of it in English, but I've read enough to know that the euphoria with which Batuz begauds and inflates his ideas (if that's what they are) are entirely alien to me. As you may know, he invited me, too, to be a party to that Berlin event, and I shrewdly declined. I had good and sound reasons for doing so: I am at work on a critical book on Auden, and did not want to interrupt the impetus of work. But I also have grown to know myself well enough by this time in my life (and high time, for that matter!) to know that the sheer elation with which Batuz envisions an immediate Utopian future is contrary to everything in my nature and temperament. The first paragraph alone of his psychedelic vision of a new world order was enough all by itself to assure me that I'd have been miserable at the sort of round-table events he so thoroughly enjoys; and his response to Arthur Miller only confirmed what I suspected all along.

The Auden work (of which I've got about 300 pages under my belt, and envision about 150 to 200 more) has entailed, among other things, reading some elementary introductory materials about the psychology of Jung, and I came across the following lively and lucid description in a book by one Frieda Fordham: "The extraverted adult is sociable; he meets others half-way and is interested in anything and everything. He likes organizations, groups, community gatherings, and parties, and is usually active and on the whole helpful; this is the type that keeps our business and social life going. . . . Extraverts tend to be both optimistic and enthusiastic . . . The weakness of extraverts lies in a tendency to superficiality and a dependence on making a good impression; they enjoy nothing more than an audience. They dislike being alone, and think reflection morbid, and this, together with a lack of self-criticism, makes them more attractive to the outer world than to their families or immediate circle, where they can be seen without disguise." There's a good deal more of this sort of thing, but this will do.

Batuz struck me as this kind of self-hypnotized rhapsode, who seriously believes (or claims to believe) that the world is at the very threshold of eternal international bliss. My tendency is to grow sullen and laconic in his presence. Mark Strand, who departed from Berlin just before you arrived, said only that he was glad to have seen some of the museums he would otherwise not have seen. I hope your visit had its real rewards.

Once again, thank you for the publication.

Tony

[To David Mason]

Dear David,

Your letter to us was elegant and welcome, and both despite the fact that much of what you had to report was dispiriting. I am thinking primarily of what you have had to go through regarding the care of your mother. But it seemed perfectly apt that you should have segued smoothly into the Persian Gulf within the precincts of the same paragraph, and continued with your views (which exactly match our own) of Bush.

Bush, and his pathetic war, and its victory parades, and all the blazing oil wells of Kuwait, the whole terrible mess has been taken by the administration as a giant photo-opportunity and campaign strategy; and in the midst of the initial rejoicing about the withdrawal of Iraqi troups from Kuwait, Bush received his highest ranking in the polls, and all the Republicans were serene in their conviction that the next election was a settled matter. Nobody seemed much concerned about the dead and the dying, the Kurds, Shiites, and Kuwaiti, or, for that matter, the flaming wells. Bush wanted only a tidy, clean little war, from which he could bring American troops back home very promptly in fulfillment of an early promise about not repeating the Vietnam situation—he continued to claim that the "Vietnam syndrome" was now and forever laid to rest by the military efficiency of his staff. The whole thing was, and continues to be, sickening. [. . .]

We send our warm and affectionate greetings.

Tony

[To Harry Ford]

Dear Harry,

David Lehman, who recently published Signs of the Times, a sort of exposé of Paul De Man in particular and Deconstruction in general, wrote me a note that runs, in part, as follows:

"I just received a letter from Donald Keene, the great scholar of Japanese literature, whom I visited in Tokyo last fall. He was writing to compliment me on Signs of the Times, and in the process he says the following, which I think will please you:

'Until I read Signs of the Times I had only one comfort—the fact that there were some people writing literary criticism that was what I always thought criticism should be—a servant of the text who helps to illuminate it. A couple of years ago I read an essay by Anthony Hecht on <u>Othello</u> that stunned me by its insights into a work that I thought I knew well. I thought that as long as even a few critics were writing so incandescently I had models to follow.'"

It's heartening to be sent tidbits of praise like this, since, on the whole, <u>Obbligati</u> may be said to have been received with stifled yawns. I still think there is much good in it, but I feel more and more lonely about this as time goes on. [. . .]

Best,

Tony

Eleanor Cook (1933–) is professor emerita at the University of Toronto, and literary scholar and critic, mainly of twentieth-century poetry and poetics.

October 16, 1991 Washington DC

Dear Eleanor,

Please forgive my tardiness in responding to your very kind invitation to contribute to the special issue of <u>The University of Toronto Quarterly</u> on the topic of "allusion." Not only is the subject endlessly rich and inviting, but the names of your projected contributors make me want to join their ranks. But prudence dictates that, with genuine regret, I had better decline. I am trying to complete a long book on Auden, and I must immediately begin another book of criticism that must be completed by next fall.

Even so, I feel not only regretful but positively wistful thinking of the topic you propose. I suppose it could be argued that all poetry (and much painting and music) is "allusive," if only because we only learn to write poetry from having read other poems, and to that degree are always in their debt, whether we like it, or admit it, or not. Moreover, "allusions" may take the form of hostility and repudiation. I've just been treating the poems of William Carlos Williams in one of my classes, and it seems to me that such a poem as "Spring and All," ("By the road to the contagious hospital") intends to be a vigorous repudiation of the standard pastoral encomium to spring, as it might be represented by, e.g., "Spring, the sweet spring, is the year's pleasant king," by Thomas Nashe, or by whole volumes of such conventions. In fact, all the internecine battles in poetry between conservatives and revolutionaries involve just such allusions on both sides. When Wordsworth writes, "Spade! with which Wilkinson hath tilled his lands, . . ." he believes he is striking a blow for poetic liberty, farm implements being regarded by "established poetic conventions" as beneath the proper level of poetic diction; but any sense of the meaning and feeling of that line requires that we be conscious of the contending forces at work. All kinds of readers' expectations may be aroused simply by the use of specific "forms," and in this way formal patterning may itself serve allusive functions.

But you have lined up a whole string of excellent poets to address these topics, and I feel confident that your special issue will be a brilliant one.

With very best wishes,

Anthony Hecht

1992

David Sofield is a poet and the Samuel Williston Professor of English, Amherst College. The Oxford "friend" alluded to is the poet and critic Jon Stallworthy. Hecht's reference to "Heaven's gate" is to Shakespeare's Sonnet 29.

June 9, 1992 Washington DC

Dear David Sofield,

[. . .] As for the lark, my "encounter" with it took place at about 9 AM in one of the meadows that surround Oxford. I had been taken by a friend whose home in that area we were visiting, and who walked through that meadow every morning on his way to his office at the university, and consequently was pretty familiar with the habits of some of the local birds. The flight of the lark is circular or spiral, rising by degrees to astonishing heights, made the more dramatic by the fact that it is a rather small bird, and, in its rise, appears so much to diminish as to become almost invisible (hence, "Heaven's gate"). Its song is not so beautiful as the nightingale's (which I have heard in Italy, and especially in Rome, where it is so much honored that it has been chosen for the signature call of Vatican Radio). What is remarkable about the lark's song is that it begins with a very extended trill, which is eventually followed by a long, sustained note, a bewildering sound inasmuch as it seems as though the bird had never drawn a breath between trill and the sustained note that follows. The effect is unbelievable. It has been surmised by those more knowledgeable than I that the circular flight is a <u>territorial</u> act, a protection of the region of the nest and exploratory quest for potential predators. The lark's eyesight must be very sharp, though it may not be as far away as its diminutive size suggests. (The nightingale, like the mocking-bird you admire, has a never-repeated sequence of notes of seemingly infinite variation and invention. Chances are that Shakespeare's nightingale was wholly literary, and adopted from texts he had read, whereas he was likely to [have] had personal acquaintance with larks). Let me add that while all these birds are lovelier in their song than your Illinois mourning dove, that bird's coo seems to me more soothing than plaintive, and ought to bespeak the powers of love.

Please send me a note signifying the suitability of April 8th for a visit, so that I can at least tack it to my bulletin board to serve as a reminder.

With best wishes,

Anthony Hecht

Alan Hollinghurst (1954–), novelist, was deputy editor of the Times Literary Supplement *from 1989 to 1995.*

August 21, 1992 Washington DC

Dear Alan Hollinghurst,

Here's my attempt to oblige you as regards your Tennyson Centenary.

If my memory is to be trusted, I believe I backed into Tennyson from an earlier enthusiasm for Thomas Hardy, a Victorian with at least a few of the same preoccupations, but with a harsher music, a sterner irony, and a more localized purview. Like many others of my generation in America, I was initially put off by my sense of Tennyson as the "representative" and "approved" Victorian poet, whom the Queen herself admired—a fact that filled me with complete distrust. (A later royal endorsement of John Betjeman's <u>Summoned by Bells</u>, which turned that book into an English best-seller, confirmed my suspicions that the royal family's taste and popular culture go pretty much hand in hand). I also remember feeling that the dramatic pretexts of Tennyson's poems were unconvincing (especially as contrasted with those of Browning and Hardy) because they seemed always at the service of, smoothed out and palliated by, an overwhelming and universally admired verbal music. The poems, accordingly, seemed to me not quite human, and the music seemed full of Romantic virtuosity, a sort of extended work of Brahms conventionalized by Elgar.

It took a long time for me to overcome this view, since Victorianism to me was over-gorgeous, repressive, and identified with the stuffiness and unimaginativeness of my own grandparents—at least those on my mother's side. I had read Eliot, Crane, Pound, Cummings and such insolent upstarts before I had really read much Tennyson, and he was in some ways exactly what they seemed to repudiate. It was Auden and Ransom who taught me respect for Hardy, and by that route I eventually made my way back to the Tennysonian domain. But it was not without a good deal of resistance. I had no taste in my youth for neo-medievalism, and Tennyson's Arthurian narratives seemed to me as artificial as the Pre-Raphaelite paintings of the same subjects: pallid, unconvincing ventures into sentimental antiquarianism. (One's literary taste probably always begins in prejudice and instinctive allegiances: I was not, however smitten, like Eliot, with Fitzgerald's Rubaiyat when young, and I came later to feel like one who had escaped exposure to German Measles or Scarlet Fever. I didn't encounter Hopkins until much later.)

It was (as I think it properly should have been) minute details that began to win me over. The softness of "night-dews on still waters between walls" enchanted and persuaded me. The specification of "between walls" was especially persuasive, for reasons at first I didn't understand, though with time it became clear that those walls guaranteed the water's stillness. The music that "gentlier on the spirit lies,/Than tired eyelids upon tired eyes" stirred me, as it were, retrospectively, because I had read Yeats' "her limbs are delicate as an eyelid." And eventually I allowed myself to be seduced by the unabashed luxuriance of the Tennysonian music, filled with all manner of predictable tricks, but none the less persuasive for all that. And eventually (helped in part by the guidance of Christopher Ricks) I was able to see what at first seemed "tricks" of diction, rhythm, metrics, music, as more than strategies: as part of a very real, eloquent, and moving drama of poetic discourse, full of an immediacy it had taken me a very long time to locate.

[Sincerely,

Anthony Hecht]

Hecht's A. W. Mellon Lectures in the Fine Arts were published in 1995 by Princeton University Press as On the Laws of the Poetic Art.

September 11, 1992 Washington DC

[To W. D. Snodgrass]

Dear De,

I'm truly astonished that the announcement of the Mellon Lectures, mailed to your Delaware address, should already have found its way to you in Erieville, though the same announcement has not yet reached my mother-in-law in Bethesda. You are right in guessing that the lectures will in due course be published as a book; that is, in fact, one of the conditions of the lectureship; so you will have a chance to find out what I had to say. With regard to the particular lecture called "Poetry and Music," let me tell you that it is a topic I am concerned with in a narrow and specific way. I will not be dealing, for example, with the musical setting of words. I will instead concern myself with what might be regarded as the musical ingredients of poetry per se: that is, all the devices a poet can bring to bear which are musical in character, and the examples I use are Shakespeare's song, "When that I was and a little tiny boy," and Hardy's "During Wind and Rain." Similarly, the first lecture, on poetry and painting does not deal with poems based on paintings or vice versa (though your own splendid poems based on painterly sources are mentioned) but rather with poems that employ painterly characteristics, and examples are offered from Elizabeth Bishop and Stevens. [. . .]

Affectionately,

Tony

Sandra McPherson is a poet and professor emeritus of English at UC Davis. Hecht's letter was in response to her query about a course she was planning on "Love and Desire in Contemporary American Poetry."

October 4, 1992 Washington DC

Dear Sandy,

Though it's hard to remember the genesis of some poems written a long time ago, I think that "The Ghost in the Martini" had, as it were, two illegitimate parents. One was Max Beerbohm, who wrote a Foreword to a reissue of his early novel, <u>Zuleika Dobson</u>, in which he announced that he had not ventured to make any changes in the book because he was keenly aware of how its young author would have resented the supervision of some elderly fogy breathing down his neck. The other parent was Mark Strand, whose poem, "The Man in the Tree," though it seems at first to have two characters, has actually, the more one studies it, only one. I once read "The Ghost in the Martini" to an audience in England which included W. H. Auden, who, after the reading was over, said that he was surprised I could get that drunk on one martini.

"The End of the Weekend" is based on an anecdote told to me by Ted Hughes at the time he and Sylvia Plath lived in Northampton, MA, when Sylvia and I both taught at Smith College, and where, it may be added, Ted was treated with chilling contempt. He applied for a teaching job there, and was told he was unqualified because he had no teaching experience.

"The Dover Bitch" started with its first sentence. I have always admired the Arnold poem on which it is based, and yet I also felt a marked impatience with Arnold's way of making love into a form of redemption and substitution for any other form of transcendent experience. Putting that much weight on human fidelity in a love relationship is to burden it beyond the limits of any lightness or carefree spontaneity. It was to make love into something grimly solemn, like

Victorian organ music, for which the word "lugubrious" could have been coined. The title of my poem was suggested to me by my friend, who at the time was also my colleague, Daniel Aaron. On the basis both of the poem and its title I have been accused of sexism, though when I wrote the poem I intended only to bring a spirit of levity and informality to the relations between men and women in the persons of Arnold's poem.

With very best wishes,
Tony

Anthony Hecht, in front of the New York Public Library, 1995
Photograph © Rollie McKenna

SEVEN

The Flourish of Retirement
1993–2004

MORE THAN TWO THOUSAND LETTERS AND POSTCARDS OF HECHT'S
date from 1993 to 2004—more than half, that is, of all the extant corre-
spondence that has come down to us, and surely enough to make for a fine
volume of its own.

One doesn't have to search far for explanations. Apart from the acqui-
sition of a fax machine in the mid-1990s, which allowed for preserving a
copy of the letter, once Hecht had concluded celebrating what he called "my
manumission and deliverance from the bonds of the academic profession" in
May 1993, he was free to devote his energies to those intellectual activities
that always mattered the most to him: "writing and the reading that is the
groundwork of my writing," as he wrote to his son Evan in 2002.

Hecht's writing was to include not just the voluminous correspondence
that marked the long, rich close of his career. He also published two new
volumes of poetry, *Flight Among the Tombs* (1996) and *The Darkness and
the Light* (2001), an introduction to the Cambridge edition of Shakespeare's
Sonnets (1996), and a substantial collection of critical essays, *Melodies Un-
heard* (2003). Even letters written in the final months of his life, although
necessarily fewer in number, brim with prospects, in spite of his being re-
cently diagnosed with lymphoma: "In fact, I had been taking notes for an

essay I would like to write," he told Eleanor Cook in a letter of August 10, 2004. "It will be called <u>De Gustibus</u>, and will concern how deeply personal, quirky and often irrational, are our judgments of taste, about which we are sometimes very defensive, and about which we sometimes feel vulnerable, residing as these judgments do in some highly private inwardness, deeply severed from what we normally think of as our faculty of judgment." Hecht did not live to write the essay, but the eighty-one-year-old poet's strong expression of intent makes clear the intellectual vigor of his later years and his undiminished engagement in the world of ideas.

The letters from this period show both an ever-widening field of correspondents and, in a few select instances, a return to the fold. Some thirty years after their initial act of collaboration on *The Seven Deadly Sins,* Hecht reunited with the graphic artist Leonard Baskin on two new collections of verse. The first of these ventures involved the elaborate twenty-two-poem sequence, "The Presumptions of Death," with death personified under various guises in the poems and the accompanying woodcuts. Initially published in an elaborate Gehenna Press limited edition, the sequence then became part of Hecht's trade book collection entitled *Flight Among the Tombs.* This project was followed by *The Gehenna Florilegium* (1998), an elegantly designed book which, like "Presumptions," was published in an expensive limited edition. The general reader will discover the sixteen "flower" poems Hecht composed for this occasion scattered throughout his last two books of poems. So, too, a number of poems on biblical themes in *The Darkness and the Light* were to be part of a shared effort between poet and artist, but Baskin's death in 2000 prevented this project from reaching fruition.

With regard to continuing and new correspondents, Hecht's greater leisure allowed further time for exchanging letters with both William Maxwell and Eleanor Cook. In the latter case, the two were especially drawn to riddles and enigmas. (Cook's *Reader's Guide to Wallace Stevens*, published in 2007 by Princeton, bears the dedication, "in memory of Anthony Hecht.") A friendship with Daniel Albright, a polymathic professor at Harvard, sparked by a mutual interest in Auden, also developed into an illuminating series of letters on Herbert and Hardy and "The Presumptions of Death" sequence. And in Garry Wills, the prolific cultural historian, Hecht discovered yet another epistolary companion. Following Hecht's response to *Papal Sin* in 2000, the exchange would grow with each new book published by Wills. During this period Hecht was also brought into contact with Hayàt Nieves Mathews, a Bacon scholar (with an unusual pedigree) residing in Italy, in response to a fan letter he received from her in 1997; and the two exchanged more than thirty letters on a variety of literary subjects. He also began corresponding extensively with Philip Hoy, the editor of Waywiser Press, in providing detailed responses that would form the core of Hoy's *In Conversation with Anthony Hecht*, first published in 1999 by Between the Lines. Hecht's friendship with the Australian poet and critic Peter Steele was a further source of pleasure in these years and indicative of a select readership from down under that included as well Christopher Wallace-Crabbe and Stephen Edgar. So, too, the letters from this period reflect friendships made with younger poets often associated with the Sewanee Writer's Conference, such as B. H. Fairchild, Joseph Harrison, Greg Williamson, Ron Rash, Daniel Anderson, and Philip Stephens.

Some old epistolary friends are missing from the letters of this period. Living in Washington, D.C., William MacDonald was no longer in active correspondence with Hecht, and both James Merrill and Joseph Brodsky had passed away in the mid-1990s. Each is eulogized in *Flight Among the Tombs*. Their absence anticipates the diminishing cast of characters enumerated in a January 29, 1999, letter to David Mason, a sentiment movingly amplified in Hecht's turn-of-the century "Sarabande on Attaining the Age of Seventy-seven," published in *The Darkness and the Light*. In 1998, however, Hecht was in touch with a companion from his earlier school days at Bard, Al Sapinsley. After a long career as a Hollywood screen writer, Sapinsley was attempting to write fiction and in desperate need of encouragement, which Hecht sought to supply in what is, in effect, a mini-essay on the value and importance of description in prose fiction and poetry, observations relevant to Hecht's own experiments with long poems. On a less urgent note, a letter to Kenneth Lynn, a biographer friend, prompted an amusing recollection of a high-school classmate and their unrequited love for a provocative young "Delilah." But Hecht's later letters, it should be said, however tinged with a sense of encroaching mortality, are never nostalgic for his earlier years, although they occasionally summon amusing anecdotes from the past to spice the epistolary present, as a letter of May 7, 2003, to Mary Jo Salter illustrates.

In selecting letters from such an abundance of material, I have attempted to capture the range of topics and variety of moods. A few letters about the poetry seem essential. By the late 1990s, in addition to the wide recognition conferred by honors and awards, Hecht had earned a special place as a poet of the Holocaust; he was asked to speak about this topic and other poems as well, including "The Feast of Stephen," and "The Venetian Vespers." The exchange with Baskin, while represented by only a few letters here, illuminates the collaborative process between two elderly craftsmen still at the top of their game. (A fuller representation of their correspondence would point to strategies of organizing the "Death" poems as well as uncovering a few poems that never made it into the final version.) As Hecht's poetry was often a response to his reading—"Late Afternoon: The Onslaught of Love" was inspired by Flaubert's *Madame Bovary*, "Sisters" by a letter to Robert Frost by his sister Jeanie, "The Darkness and the Light Are Both Alike to Thee" by the Psalms—I have included letters that represent Hecht as avid commentator in conversation with others about his reading. One further quality is sounded in the late letters that bears singling out: not just that of the involved, exacting reader, but of a person wisely seasoned in the ways of the world, who clearly trusted and greatly valued a certain view of humanity— one deeply civilized and balanced, a trust echoed in his occasional return to translating Horace in these years. In the letters, this balance manifests itself most clearly in the desire for exchanges with like-minded friends or acquaintances, and woven into this vision is a keen sense of both the ludic and the tragic nature of human affairs, the darkness and the light. A brief, late letter of April 29, 2003, to William Dougherty, a fellow soldier from the 387th regiment, might serve as an epitome of this complex sensibility so often at work in this last phase of his letter writing.

1993

May 12, 1993 Washington DC

[To William Maxwell]

Dear Bill,

Whether or not we decide to attend the annual bash—I must accustom myself to thinking of it as an "Academy" function—is yet to be determined; but Helen and I are going out to dinner tomorrow night to one of the best restaurants in Washington to celebrate my manumission and deliverance from the bonds of the academic profession—and particularly from my own local English department, years of association with which has ripened into full-blown detestation. So there is much to celebrate. I have, as you may surmise, finished grading all my term papers, and turned in my grades, and it remains only for me to clear out my office.

I should say in candor that I did not expect that I would feel this way at the end of my professional career. For by far the most part I have greatly enjoyed teaching, and have been very happy in my association both with my students and my colleagues. Former students still write and visit me, and I correspond with former colleagues at many institutions. It has taken Georgetown University to give to the notion of retirement the added glamor of serenity and gladness.

Your note about mucking around in the garden with bone-meal and night-crawlers filled my nostrils, but not with longing. Both Helen and I have black thumbs, and Nature has cursed us for this estrangement by knocking down two huge trees on our property within the space of a month. [. . .]

This comes with love from both of us to both of you.

Tony

John Whitehead (1924–1999), a self-described "Auden addict," was the author of A Commentary on the Poetry of W. H. Auden, C. Day Lewis, Louis MacNeice, and Stephen Spender (1992).

[May 27, 1993] Washington DC

Dear Mr. Whitehead,

Your letter and copious notes have been forwarded to me by Harvard University Press, and I write to express to you my deep gratitude for the receipt of them. Your scrutiny of my book was more detailed and careful than I had any right to hope for, and if there is to be a future printing I will certainly try to incorporate as many of your suggested emendations as possible. I add that, of course, I had no illusion that my text was faultless, and had myself discovered—to my great chagrin—at least a few of the errors that you also located. I only wish I could expunge or alter them all.

At the same time, you and I differ in our views of many matters—not only from one another, but from others as well. For example, I have been chidden by critics in this country for failure to take into account what they deem as incontestably Auden's "greatest work," which turns out, depending on which critic is consulted, to be About the House, The Sea and the Mirror or Homage to Clio. In your case, it is The Age of Anxiety. There is certainly nothing wrong with this diversity of opinion, and my book made no pretenses as regards covering the whole ground. Indeed, while the publishers at Harvard were nervous about the length of what I wrote, I myself wished then—and still wish—that I had gone into greater detail about the materials I selected for inspection.

There are, finally, some further topics upon which we differ. Americans are not quite so ignorant of the horrors of WWII as you seem to suppose. I myself served (in France, Germany and Czechoslovakia) in the front lines of an Infantry

Division that suffered such heavy losses (more than half the men in my company were killed or severely mutilated) that the commanding general was relieved of his command as incompetent. Furthermore, an English friend of mine [Bernard Knox] whose military career was far more daring than mine, and who was awarded the Bronze Star and the Croix de Guerre (he fought against the Franco forces in Spain, with the Maquis in France, and the anti-Fascist forces in Italy) read the book and found no fault with my views about the English attitude towards Auden's move to the United States.

With all good wishes.

Sincerely,
Anthony Hecht

B. H. [Pete] Fairchild (1942–) studied under Hecht at Sewanee and is now the author of a number of books of poems. Hecht wrote the introduction for The Art of the Lathe *(1998).*

June 7, 1993 Washington DC

Dear Pete,

I'm grateful to you for your latest letter, though saddened by the news of your various rejections. And yet, knowing your work as I do, I feel the sort of confidence in your abilities that perhaps at the moment you cannot share. The confidence of which I speak is based on a condition of objectivity, which is probably the last thing you could bring to a view of your work. And all poets, Shakespeare not excepted, are given to moments (when they are not instead extended periods of time) of grave self-doubt—

> Wishing me like to one more rich in hope,
> Featured like him, like him with friends possessed,
> Desiring this man's art and that man's scope,
> With what I most enjoy contented least, . . .

I think you are quite right to proceed along your patient course, poem by poem, adding to your work both in bulk and in development. I remember the curious anguish that went into the assembly of my own first book [*A Summoning of Stones*]. I would write a couple of new poems, and deem them better than anything written previously. So when I began to think in terms of a book I would cut out the earliest work to make room for the later, not so much out of eagerness to avoid having a book too long, but to avoid invidious comparisons (as I imagined) between early work and late. This process went on for an embarrassingly long time. Each new poem was, as it were, the death of an earlier one; so that while I always envisioned a collection of about thirty poems, the table of contents continued to change by constant addition and subtraction. I might never have published a first volume for years if I had not seen that this was a self-defeating procedure. But your work is now so firmly developed along strong and matured lines that there is probably no danger of your falling into the dilemma I found myself in. It did not surprise me, I may add, that Hopkins was as "thoughtful" about your poems as they were.

This comes to you with my warmest and most admiring good wishes,
Tony

Daniel Anderson is the author of several volumes of poetry as well as an edition of The Selected Poetry of Howard Nemerov *(2003).*

July 9, 1993 Washington DC
Dear Danny:

[. . .] Since I mentioned earlier that I have been working on the Shakespeare Sonnets, it may be worth adding that the kind of self-consciousness that modern poets invariably exhibit when the topic of literary immortality is raised was not always the emotional blight it has now become. When Shakespeare wrote "Not marble nor the gilded monuments/Of princes shall outlive this powerful rime," he was not being vain, or making a shrewd guess, or gifted with prophetic knowledge. He was echoing a literary tradition that went back to the Greeks and Romans, including Homer, Pindar and Virgil. Particularly in the era before printing, fame and the human memory of the past was conferred wholly by writers, and of these chiefly by poets, because poetry was quite simply "more memorable" than prose. To be sung about by a poet was to know that your fame would last. Hence the desire on the part of heroes in Homer, and athletes in Pindar, to be commemorated by being immortalized by bards. In our own day fame is often indistinguishable from celebrity, and both politicians and movie stars vastly prefer the second, while few desire the first, and the first rarely interests the general public, which is not interested in poetry either. There is a book on this topic that might interest you: The Frenzy of Renown, by Leo Braudy. [. . .]

All this of course may be either familiar to you or of little concern, though it all came to mind as a result of your poem. [. . .]

All good wishes,
Tony

Leonard Baskin (1922–2000) was a renowned graphic artist and sculptor. Hecht briefly describes his early connection with Baskin in the letter below to Eleanor Cook of January 9, 1997.

[Summer 1993?] Washington DC

Dear Leonard,

I've come close to clearing the decks now, and hope soon to begin on our book, about which I've been actively thinking for some time. I've finished a first draft of my Introduction to Shakespeare's Sonnets for Cambridge University Press, and once that is completed to everyone's satisfaction, I can turn to our collaboration. Almost from the first it seemed to be that Death might be conceived as a master actor or impersonator (The Presumptions of Death) and this would allow all the personages in our book to be nothing else than Death thinly disguised. The Ruskin quoted [below] seems to me possibly useful as an epigraph. Each of our characters—artist, physician, revolutionary—would be his own person but also Death in masquerade—a gigantic Carnival of death. (I seem imperfectly to remember a series of articles by Enid Starkie about a plague in eighteenth-century France which led to much wild abandon, the invention of new, lewd dances, and a general frivolity born of hopelessness.) This could be but one of the moods we might seek to create.

"[. . .] We usually speak as if death pursued us, and we fled from him; but that is only so in rare instances. Ordinarily he masks himself—makes himself beautiful— all-glorious; not like the King's daughter, all-glorious within, but outwardly: his clothing of wrought gold. We pursue him frantically all our days, he flying or hiding from us. Our crowning success at three-score and ten is utterly and perfectly to seize and hold him in his eternal integrity—robes, ashes, and sting."

John Ruskin, <u>Unto this Last</u>, Essay III, paragraphs 42–3.

Affectionately,

Tony

An expanded version of Hecht's thoughts about Time Will Darken It *appears in* A William Maxwell Portrait, *ed. Charles Baxter, Michael Collier, and Edward Hirsch (Norton, 2004).*

August 29, 1993 Bellagio, Italy

Dear Bill,

We've spent a happy week in Venice, with good weather and fine food, and we're now here in a paradisal setting, and the weather holds. While there has been plenty to do, we had the foresight to bring with us two of your novels: They Came Like Swallows and Time Will Darken It. I have read them lingeringly, lovingly, delighted as it seems to me even now by every single detail in both books, different as they are from one another. [The first] resonates with wonderful varieties of love, all of them touching. The second book is surely the more complex one, and far more demanding on the reader's sympathetic understanding. I found myself at first inclining to impatience with virtually all the major (and some of the minor) characters; and then I found I was being asked to be as tolerant and forbearing as they learned to be towards one another, and as their author found it possible to be towards them. I conceived a particular, strong initial dislike of Mrs. Potter, but gradually I saw that she was only an instance—irritating, amusing, fallible—of something that seemed to possess (afflict?) virtually all the characters in the novel: a heedlessness, a preoccupation, an inwardness of concern, of which Martha King's pregnancy (which characteristically turns her inward and vaguely allows her to feel some indifference to the rest of the world) is emblematic. It is an egocentrism that is not alien to love; on the contrary, it's what everyone uses as the basis and center of their love. But what I think made me love the book as much as I do had to do with its musical employment of three continuous and interwoven modes of discourse. Narrative and dialogue make up the first and most immediate of these. But almost equally alluring, ravishing in their clarity and symbolic weight of observation, are those passages of description—of season, weather, animals, the varying light upon furniture and rugs. They are some of the most beautiful passages of their sort that I knew, reminding me of Flaubert and Chekhov. But in addition to these two strands there is a third: a carefully weighted, infinitely thoughtful authorial voice, giving a perfect sense of control at those moments when a reader becomes anxious about the varieties of blindness and self-concern with which most of the characters are afflicted, and which in the course of the novel they manage wonderfully to overcome. This authorial voice at times reminded me of E.M. Forster's in its modest, patient sagacity. It speaks with a wisdom not shared by a novel's characters, but serving to give the reader an assurance that everything that happens participates in a design which is ordained and fitting. And indeed all the various threads of plot and character are unexpectedly woven intimately together at the end with quiet gestures of love and acceptance.

If I've rattled on so long about the second novel, this is not because I didn't care for the first, which, though simpler, is still more musical, and more direct in its lovely expression of love. It is now Helen's turn to read them both; and then I will read them again. But this is written—on an alien machine which puts every obstacle in my way—to say how grateful I am to you, and how delighted by these stunning books.

Tony

Alfred Corn (1943–) is a poet, essayist, and critic. He edited Incarnation: Contemporary Writers on the New Testament *(1990), with a contribution by Hecht, "St Paul's Epistle to the Galatians." Mrs. Edward T. Chase was director of the Academy of American Poets.*

December 2, 1993 Washington DC

Dear Alfred:

It seems to me quite profitless to pursue this line of correspondence. Your two letters make it clear that you see nothing wrong in finding fault with a speech of mine that you never heard, and that was imperfectly reported to you. You seem to feel entitled to lecture me on the topic of tolerance for minorities (a topic that was no part of my speech) and thereby to presume to some sort of moral superiority, hence my word "sanctimonious." I find this all beside the point. I have sent my introduction to Wilbur's reading to Mrs. Chase, who asked for it, and who said it would in due course be published. When and where was not specified. For the second time, I suggest to you that you would do well to read it before finding fault with it. Even in your second letter [you] write to say that if, after having read my letter "we still disagree," we could still enter into friendly and rational debate. What you persist in failing to grasp is that <u>there is no ground for either agreement or disagreement</u>. I did not make any comments about cultural minorities, which seems to be the only topic on which you have elected to take issue with me. Let there be an end to this foolishness.

Yours,
Tony

Dana Gioia (1950–) is a poet, critic, editor, anthologist, translator, co-founder of the West Chester University Poetry Conference (1995–), and former chairman of the National Endowment for the Arts (2003–2009). His acquaintance with Hecht dates back to the early 1980s.

December 15, 1993 Washington DC

Dear Dana,

Thank you for sending me a copy of your Longfellow essay, which I have read (though not quite through) with interest and with approval of your agile and flexible style. You took on a difficult assignment, and deserve commendation for your daring. You are right, I think, in feeling that it is too easy and fashionable to scoff at Longfellow, and right, as well, to compare his "popular" poetry to that of Kipling—though I would immediately add, not to that of Burns, who rejoices in a deep irony of the lower classes, a kind of pastoral and bitter knowingness; nor to Herrick, whose least efforts are classical in style and devotedly Jonsonian as well as Catullan.

Though, as I said, I have not read the essay quite through, I noted one or two things along the way that gave me pause. I hope you will not mind my pointing them out. On your p. 76 you write, "In Voices of the Night Longfellow created an influential new archetype in American culture—the poet professor. . . . Although the New Critics despised Longfellow, these poet professors were his cultural descendants. There is another side of Longfellow's version of the poet professor that has been influential." I find something disingenuous, tendentious and mistaken here, all for the sake of a petty irony involving the condescension of the New Critic Poet Professors to one who was, by your choice of language ("descendants") their forebear. But this is not strictly true. Longfellow was appointed at Harvard as a Professor of Languages, not of Poetry, and his poetic career was as independent of his professorial duties as Wallace Stevens' was of his duties as an insurance executive. By way of contrast, Ransom was appointed to his job at Kenyon, and Warren to his job at Yale precisely because they were practicing writers. At the time of Longfellow's academic career, there were few if any programs devoted to "creative writing" anywhere in the country. There were few even in my undergraduate days (the early forties) and such programs, as well as the faculty who teach them, are a fairly late growth and development, and it is faulty to trace them to Longfellow.

[. . .]

p. 82, "Longfellow, like the Elizabethan lyricists, understood that if a poet keeps the sense simple he can make music compellingly complex." I find myself filled with resistance to this collocation, and the statement itself; it grossly and dangerously oversimplifies. The subtlety, dexterity, emotional range and richness of allusion in the lyrics of Jonson and Campion, to take only two examples, is so far beyond the range of Longfellow as to be both pathetic and laughable. The writing of lyrics to be set to music does indeed require special skills and a careful sense of a limit to the complexities that can be allowed if intelligibility is to be hoped for. At the same time it is worth remembering that so densely packed and knotted a poet as Donne wrote songs, and they are very good. On the same page the lines of "The Tide Rises, the Tide Falls" need only be compared with some of the lyrics of Tennyson to see how feeble they are.

Finally, p. 84. " . . . 'Mezzo Cammin' and 'The Jewish Cemetery at Newport' (the latter surely one of the great American poems of its century. . . ." I think I might have allowed this to pass unremarked had I not recently examined the second of these poems with some care, having been assigned to read it in public. It is a poem with serious blemishes. To begin with the slightest one which is grammatical, consider the second stanza with its confusion of third-person-plural pronouns. "Their" in the first line refers to the buried Jews; "their" in the second refers to the trees. (There is another third-person-plural pronoun in the third line.) This grammatical awkwardness could easily have been avoided, and would have been by a more scrupulous poet. More seriously, consider the fifth stanza

"Blessed be God! for he created Death!"
The mourners said, "and Death is rest and peace";
Then added, in the certainty of faith,
"And giveth Life that never more shall cease."

The last line of this stanza is a totally unwarranted Christian interpolation. There is only the most fragmentary authority (based on the summoning of Saul's ghost by the Witch of Endor) for any Jewish belief in an afterlife, a belief that is almost entirely ignored in Jewish religion, but central to Christianity. The point is that if Longfellow is going to write a poem that requires background knowledge, he ought to take a little trouble about it. (The same sort of carelessness went into the composition of "The Skeleton in Armor," in which Longfellow built his poem on the slender historical supposition that both the ancient tower at Newport and the skeleton in armor found near Falls River, MA, were thought for a while to be Norse.)

But what is most distressing about the poem under discussion is the final stanza. It has about it all the cool antiquarian and philosophic remoteness of one who might be writing calmly and aloofly about the Phoenicians or Pithecanthropus Erectus. There is a vaguely regretful but supremely calm and untroubled feeling about an extinct species, bolstered perhaps by Darwinian confidence in the survival of the fittest, and assured in its sense of the absoluteness of these evolutionary laws. If one were to judge only by Longfellow's poem, one could easily assume that the last of the Jews had perished, along with their quaint faith and notions. If this poem is "surely one of the great American poems of its century," this speaks very poorly of American poetry. Happily for us we also had Whitman, Dickinson, Emerson, and some others.

I am sorry to quarrel with you in these matters, and hope you will take it in good part. This comes, for all my querulousness, with warmest Christmas greetings and best wishes for the New Year.

Tony

1994

Daniel Albright (1945–), Ernest Bernbaum Professor of Literature, Harvard University, is the author of a number of books on poetry and music.

January 4, 1994 Washington DC

Dear Dan,

I'm deeply grateful to you for the generosity of your letter, and the richness of your reaction to my poems. [. . .]

Yes, our Thano-topic is what you surmised: a rather deliberate variation on the medieval "Dance of Death." According to the traditional formula, Death invites persons of all ranks, ages and fortunes to dance with him—Schubert, Ransom, and Mussorgsky are all in this line. The idea of the "Dance," I gather, arose out of the 14th century plague of death from ergot poisoning, in which the victims went into violent seizures and epileptic fits (resembling some sort of wild dance) just before death. In the traditional version, Death remains the same indominable figure and only his victims vary, and this makes for a certain limitation in terms of a reader's expectations. It was, I felt, essential to overcome this handicap insofar as it was possible. And the result was to have Death play all possible human roles (reserving to himself only his secret, ultimate purpose). He could therefore adopt any age or sex, present himself as alluring, amusing, friendly, childlike, anything that advanced his purpose; and this would allow a great variety of "voice," however insistent the central theme, as, for example, in Lydgate's The Dance of Death.

I think you are right about Hardy being perhaps the least "debonair" of poets, and yet it seems to me that the idea of the debonair, of the insouciant, is just what he is at pains to puncture in a number of his poems, and against which his satire and irony is often directed. Nearly everyone is unwitting in Hardy, and this is not only part of the poignanc[y] of existence, but he often persuades us that this unwittingness is virtually essential to our existence, allowing us the little poise and assurance we have and without which we would instantly expire. The word "harden" at the end of the second stanza I feel sure comes directly from a Hardy poem—though not as a rhyme word. In "The Going" he writes of the moment at which, unbeknownst to him, his wife was dying, while he "saw morning harden upon the wall." That line has always had a singular power for me.

You write: "I was intrigued by the emphasis on costume in both poems: the women's coral gowns, Death's preening himself in his alb and cope." The gowns were mine, but the notion of costume probably originated in Baskin's designs. Some figures wear what amount to emblematic regalia, the archbishop being only one of these. There will be a Mexican Revolutionary with crossed bandoliers and sombrero, a circus barker with straw hat, etc. "Gowns" seems to me a rather Victorian word, suitable for a Hardy-style poem. As you say, while the Devil often adopts various costumes at will, Death normally does not; but that is exactly what we have wanted to change. Death in these poems is at least as sly and skillful as the Devil—perhaps more so, since we can outwit the Devil but not Death.

I feel just as you do about Herbert, and think him a far greater poet than Hardy; but this is precisely one of the points of the sequence: Death can adopt any number of roles and any degree of sophistication. Herbert's "musical metaphors" seemed an asset I could make use of, though I did not intend to suggest that Herbert himself is the clergyman who impersonates Death—merely that the sort of ascetic renunciation recommended in quite a number of Herbert's poems (and common enough in much Christian homiletic literature) can conveniently be adopted by Death for his own ironic purposes. [. . .]

This letter requires no answer. You are a busier man than I, now that I'm retired. But the next thing you shall get from me is my introduction to the Shakespeare Sonnets, about which I should be glad of your views. Please bear in mind that I was given a word limit. Clearly it is a topic about which I might have written at far greater length.

All best wishes,
Tony

January 30, 1994 Washington DC
[To Daniel Albright]
Dear Dan,

Thanks for your letter about the Sonnets. I'm, as always, grateful for your praise. [. . .] Let me comment, if I may, on one or two of your comments. You write, "Eliot somewhere quotes a French scholar who noted that Shakespeare used every conceivable style except the simple . . ." The Frenchman alluded to here is one M. Guizot, but the one who makes note of his views is Arnold, in his Preface to Poems (1853). This is a passage in Arnold I know quite well because I find it irritating and wrong. He describes Lear as a play in which "the language is so artificial, so curiously tortured, and so difficult, that every speech has to be read two or three times before its meaning can be comprehended." This comment fails shockingly to take account of the fact that at the dramatic and climactic moments towards the end of the play, Lear speaks with a heartbreaking simplicity that gains its power and authority precisely from its contrast with the bombast of what went before. There are few speeches anywhere in any of the plays that carry the power of "Pray, do not mock me./I am a very foolish fond old man, /Fourscore and upward, not an hour more nor less; /And, to deal plainly, /I fear I am not in my perfect mind. /Methinks I should know you, and know this man; Yet I am doubtful, for I am mainly ignorant what place this is; and all the skill I have/Remembers not these garments; nor I know not/Where I did lodge last night. Do not laugh at me; /For, as I am a man, I think this lady/To be my child Cordelia." From my point of view, Arnold and Guizot have missed the boat. [. . .]

I am, as always, very grateful to you for your thought and encouragement. [. . .]

Tony

Charles Tung, a student of Hecht at Georgetown, went to Oxford for graduate studies, when this letter was written. He now teaches at Seattle University.

February 2, 1994 Washington DC

Dear Charles:

[. . .] Now to mistier matters. I have not seen Schindler's List, and I'm prepared to believe that it is very powerful and effective. I could half persuade myself this is the case precisely because Spielberg was too young to have been personally involved in WWII, so that for him the task was one of trying to make vivid something that for most people is difficult to believe. This is the task of most theater directors, including those who direct Shakespeare. By way of contrast, though I never suffered like those who were prisoners in the camps, I did actually see one; and I need nothing to make it vivid to me. Secondly, except for Wiesel's Night, I have read no "literary" works about the prison camps that seem anywhere nearly as effective as straight reportorial accounts, because the facts themselves are so monstrous and surreal they not only don't need, but cannot endure, the embellishment of metaphor or artistic design. Please note that I am not saying what Adorno so famously said: that after Auschwitz there can be no more poetry. The right answer to that is one Mark Strand offered. After Auschwitz one can no longer eat lunch, either, but one does. What I am saying is that Homer could write unflinchingly about war because it was conducted according to certain codes that acknowledged brutality but revered heroism. Nothing of that sort obtains any more; the facts are too astonishing in themselves to be framed in a comprehensible context.

And there is another matter as well. I try as a matter of principle to avoid polemical or political poetry. Robert Frost once said, poetry comes from griefs, not grievances. Indignation is a bad foundation for any art, mixed as it always is with simple-minded self-righteousness. And nothing poets can write in the hope of being shocking can come anywhere near the actual facts. For this reason I do not much care for the engagé poems of Carolyn Forché. Poetry should not put itself in the position of trying to compete with headlines. Its power must be of another kind. W.H. Auden: "Poetry is in its essence an act of reflection, of refusing to be content with the interjections of immediate emotion in order to understand the nature of what is felt." Politically committed poetry is not interested in arriving at that understanding.

To return to another of your questions, my inability to read or write poetry during the war had little or nothing to do with its horror, at least on a conscious level; though no doubt I lived in a continuous state of fear of my life. But military training is so completely fatiguing and mind-numbing that the intelligence seems to lapse completely, as close-order drill is intended to assure. All military drills and routines makes thought both difficult and superfluous.

As for Lowell's remark that you can say anything in poetry as long as it is correctly placed, he borders on a kind of truth. Poetry ought to be able to assimilate anything, but context and scope are all-important. Hence Homer's ability to describe stomach-turning deaths and get away with it. Hence the many literary revolutions when both words and subject matter that once were deemed anti-poetic found a place in poetry; the Romantics were true revolutionaries in this way. Blake wrote of "shit," which he spelled "shite." The "pylon school" introduced industrial images where pastoral scenes had reigned. The interplay you correctly recognize between whatever we think reality is and some vision or version of it in words is always tricky, tentative, and subtle.

[...]

This comes with warmest and heartiest good wishes for the New Year,

Anthony Hecht

Frank Glazer (1915–), renowned pianist, taught at the Eastman School of Music from 1965 to 1980, before becoming Artist-in-Residence at Bates College.

February 16, 1994 Washington DC

Dear Frank,

Your dazzlingly beautiful gift of the three Brahms piano quartets arrived late yesterday in perfect condition. I had just finished some work, and felt entitled to indulge myself in some serious luxury, and I listened to the first of them. It is brilliant, and deeply moving in ways that are, admittedly, extra-musical. I first heard that quartet when I was roughly nineteen years old, during what was one of the happiest intervals of my young life. That happiness was to be cut short by the war, and for some time thereafter. And so it was both natural and easy for me to identify this music with a period in my life almost approaching bliss. And, of course, apart from these personal associations, the music is objectively lovely and eloquent in its own right. There is a shimmer to the piano part of the first movement that is like the sunlit surface of a fast-flowing stream in early spring. W. H. Auden, about whose poetry I wrote a book, and who knew and wrote about music (especially about opera and Stravinsky), hated Brahms. He said to a friend, "Perhaps my dislike of Brahms is extra-aesthetic. But whenever I hear a particularly obnoxious combination of sounds, I spot it as Brahms and I'm right every time . . ." There is, unquestionably something in Brahms's harmonies and harmonic progressions (which I happen to love) that is almost his signature, though it crops up in works of his admirers and followers, like Dvorak, for example. Arnold Schoenberg, on the other hand, whose musical tastes were far more 'advanced' than Auden's revered Brahms, and wrote of him, "The sense of logic and economy and the power of development which builds melodies of such fluency deserve the admiration of every music lover who expects more than sweetness and beauty from music." It is Auden's "extra-aesthetic" reasons that I'd like to know, but never will. It could be that he had unpleasant personal associations with his first hearing of Brahms, as I had a happy one. There's also another possibility. There are some—Bernard Shaw is an example—who feel belligerently that to like Wagner is to hate Brahms, and no compromise is possible. Shaw was absolutely intransigent on this point. My own lack of sympathy for Wagner makes it easy for me to feel that perhaps there is no meeting ground; but I would admit that I have not given Wagner a fair chance.

Anyway, I am more grateful to you than I can easily say. It was wonderful to see you and Ruth here in Washington, and Helen and I hope you will come again and stay with us for a visit.

Affectionately,

Tony Hecht

Peter Steele, S.J. (1939–2012), was an Australian poet and critic, emeritus professor at the University of Melbourne, and occasional visiting professor at Georgetown University. The elegy on Timothy Healy appeared first in Invisible Riders *(Sydney: Paper Bark Press, 1999).*

February 19, 1994 Washington DC

My dear Peter:

Helen and I were delighted to have you with us last night, and we hope you enjoyed yourself as much as we enjoyed having you with us. It wasn't until today, however, that I had a chance to examine the munificence of your gifts. To speak the truth, I have had time only to glance at the collection of essays [*Expatriates: Reflections on Modern Poetry*, University of Melbourne Press, 1985] (and to read only a few pages of the one about me. I also read the opening of the ones about Muir and Merwin, both of whom I admire, as you do.) But it is the poems that I have read with both delight and deep respect. Your elegy for Tim [Timothy Healy] I find wonderfully and persuasively moving; it may be the one which, for very personal reasons, I like best. But the others as well exhibit exactly the wit and intelligence, the agility and honesty that he would have been roused by. You seem not only to have known him well but to be very much, in your own words, "a pair of sorts." He was a man I greatly loved; and after that, or, at the same time, admired and respected and rejoiced in. At his funeral service in New York, the priest who gave the homily, and who was a very old friend from college days, remarked that none of Tim's friends was surprised that he was not canonized. This provoked a general chuckle, quite loud and uninhibited. I must have been one of the few who was silent; and more than that, vaguely hurt and offended. To be sure, Tim swore like a trooper, and he did not disguise his love of food or drink, and he knew a lot of off-color stories. He was, nevertheless, perhaps the most loving and lovable man I have known, and such failings as he had were trifles in comparison with his, as it seemed, natural capacity to love God and his fellow men and women. I can't doubt that he would have delighted in your poems as much as I do. In any case, I send you my very complex and braided thanks, as well as my congratulations on your remarkable productivity.

Affectionately, and gratefully,
Tony

April 30, 1994 Washington DC

[To William Maxwell]
Dear Bill,

I suppose you and Emmy are pruning and weeding and carrying on in a thoroughly pastoral way, so that perhaps this ought to be addressed to you out there in rural New York; but I will risk sending this to your city address.

I thought of you, and that extraordinary memory of yours which could recall all the submissions in fiction made to <u>The New Yorker</u> during the time of your editorship, as I was reading an article (in <u>The Wilson Quarterly</u> [vol. 18, Spring 1994]) about C.S. Lewis. The author, James Como (who teaches rhetoric and public communications at York College, CUNY) writes: "Upon being told how terrible it was to remember nothing, he would reply that it was worse to forget nothing, as was the case with everything he read. Of course, this declaration would be met with incredulity and demands that he put up or shut up. And so he would solicit a series of numbers from the most skeptical guest, which he then would apply to a bookcase, a shelf within that case, and a book upon that shelf. The guest would then fetch the specified volume (which could be in any one of several languages), open to a page of his own choosing, read aloud from that page, and stop where he pleased. Lewis would then quote the rest of the page from memory." There's something about this I find frightening, both in Lewis and in you. Helen and I are both moderately fairly matched with poor memories, though mine used to be reasonably good. But I have to copy things down, and even then I forget them. Whenever I read a non-fiction book I underline and make marginal notes, and even then I incline to forget everything but general outlines. For example, off and on I have been reading a book I very much like by Maurice Valency called <u>In Praise of Love</u>, which is about troubadour poetry and its gradual development into the dolce stil nuova and the Petrarchan tradition. It is full of detailed information, and more thorough-going than C.S. Lewis's own <u>Allegory of Love</u>. I've marked it all up like a student preparing for exams. But even as I do so I know it is all drifting away.

However, neither Helen nor I have forgotten we are to see the two of you at the Academy Ceremonial, and we look forward to that with excitement.

Affectionately,
Tony

Jeffrey Meyers published Robert Frost: A Biography *in 1996. He had earlier included excerpts from Hecht's essay on Lowell in* Robert Lowell, Interviews and Memoirs *(Ann Arbor: University of Michigan Press, 1988).*

September 15, 1994 Washington DC

Dear Jeffrey,

I fear that I can't be of any use to you as regards your projected book on Frost. I met him only a few times, and never knew him intimately. Our conversations were rather humdrum and unmemorable. I met Kay Morrison only briefly when she was very old—at Bread Loaf, I think. As for his influence, he continued the genre of the dramatic monologue, and was one of its best practitioners. He taught a number of poets that they did not have to write only in their own voice. In this, as well as in other ways, he performed a great service that has been badly needed in American poetry. He was also an almost solitary defender of formal poetic values during the Modernist period when formal practices were being widely trashed. [. . .]

Anthony Hecht

Denis Donoghue (1928–), prolific literary critic, who had earlier reviewed Millions of Strange Shadows *(see letter of March 25, 1977), is Henry James Professor of English and American Letters at New York University.*

December 27, 1994 Washington DC

Dear Denis,

Somehow during the cluster of holiday festivities, urged on by curiosity and delight, those very Paterian feelings, I have managed to read almost all of your splendid book on WP [*Walter Pater: Lover of Strange Souls*], and feel I want to tell you right away how brilliant, illuminating and valuable it seems to me. You have made a perfectly convincing case for him as a major Modern figure, with far more resonance to his "strange" ideas than I had ever given him proper credit for. I was, in fact, largely indifferent to him, when I was not actually repelled; and my unfairness to him resembled in some ways the doctrinaire antipathy Ivor Winters felt towards Wallace Stevens, and for some of the same reasons. I thought Pater a shallow hedonist, and dismissed him accordingly, all the while disapproving of the doctrinal severity that Winters brought programmatically to bear on the excellent work of Stevens. The three became an irritating cluster to me. I could often see how Winters came to Stevens with cookie-cutter attitudes with which he allowed himself, on haughty moral grounds, to dismiss or, perhaps more seriously, to misread the poems. And somehow, even as I was rising to Stevens' defense, I knew I was bringing the very same charges against Pater.

Pater is not a lovable figure, and you are painstaking in your effort to be just and accurate in your assessments. You have made his work and its significance much clearer to me, without, I must add, endearing it or him to me. But your examination of the very prose itself, its evasions, its assumptions, its innuendos, is masterly and immensely revealing. While this is an area I am largely unacquainted with (everyone I've read on Pater is content to describe him simply in terms of his purple passages and "art for art's sake") you are the first I know of who has attempted to do a rich justice to the work and the ideas they represent. [. . .]

Incidentally, you may not know that [Auden] took a dim view of later Stevens on what amounted to doctrinaire grounds. You'll recall, in "In Praise of Limestone," the lines that go "The poet, / Admired for his earnest habit of calling / The sun the sun, his mind Puzzle, is made uneasy / By these solid statues which so obviously doubt / His antimythological myth . . ." I had always read those lines as applying to "the generic poet." But it seems that WHA had Stevens specifically in mind, as he wrote explicitly to Ursula Niebuhr. His letter to her is contained in Remembering Reinhold Niebuhr, p. 289.

Once again, my deep thanks for a splendid and splendidly written book, with warmest holiday greetings.

Tony

Left to right (seated): Edward Simmons, Willard Metcalf, Childe Hassam, J. Alden Weir, Robert Reid. *Left to right (standing)*: William Merritt Chase, Frank W. Benson, Edmund C. Tarbell, Thomas W. Dewing, Joseph R. DeCamp
Photograph by Haeseler Studios 1908; Collection, American Academy of Arts and Letters

[April 4, 1995] Washington DC
[Postcard: *The Ten*: American painters who seceded
from the Society of American Artists in 1897]

[To Leonard Baskin]
Dear Leonard—
    You see these old men? They have grown old waiting for the books they had written to be published. When will our book appear?
                                    Love,
                                    Tony

April 20, 1995 Washington DC
[To Leonard Baskin]
Dear Leonard,
    The <u>Presumptions</u> arrived from Maine, and it is a very beautiful book. I am delighted by it and grateful for it, and rejoice in its physical existence. More of this in a moment.

First, I feel entitled to defend myself against charges of "ill-natured impatience." My several inquiries about when the book would appear were due entirely to my having no clue about what to expect, and my one sardonic postcard was no more than a reflection of this eagerness to see the final product. If I was without any guidance about what is entailed in the process of sewing and binding, or did not know, until belatedly informed, that anyone was off on safari, I can at least claim that (1) my appetite was whetted by the view you gave me of unbound proofs when I visited Mount Holyoke in early March, and (2) I had been prompted to my, as it turns out, premature expectations by your having told me yourself that I could expect the book to be completed "by the end of February or the beginning of March." So let no more be said about "ill-natured impatience."

[. . .] [T]he book is wonderful and luxurious even beyond my memory of it from that too hasty perusal in Northampton. The colored papers as well as the colored prints are gorgeous, but the black and whites are wonderfully powerful in their starkness and their mystery. A number of the prints, which before I had only seen in black and white (by "before" I mean the proofs you had sent in the mail) surprised me at finding them in color. And the color of several, most notably the Society Lady, was far more vivid than anything I had been led to expect. I know that there will be people salivating down at the Library of Congress when their copy shows up. In the meantime, I send you my very grateful thanks and warm congratulations.

Affectionately,
Tony

Christopher Wallace-Crabbe (1934–) is a poet, critic, editor, contributor of double dactyls, and emeritus professor at the University of Melbourne. Although Wallace-Crabbe and Hecht never met, they occasionally shared light verse in the 1990s. Hecht's poem is a take-off of Robert Herrick's poem to Ben Jonson, "An Ode for Him." Following in the footsteps of Hecht and other poets named below, Wallace-Crabbe gave a poetry reading at Winchester College, England.

September 13, 1995 Washington DC

Ah, Chris,
It's not amiss
That to the scores
Of youngling bachelors

At Winchester
You bring the Muse, and her
Silk finery, fine feats;
She romped with Empson, Clampitt, Keats,
And lately roused the boys
With all that artfulness your verse employs.

And, Chris,
Consider this:
Among the ranks
Of pot-wabblers, pickthanks,
She would not deign
To move or choose her train,
But crowns with sereless bay
You and good Peter Steele, S.J.,
Where her orchestral thunder
Rings through the seventh heaven from Down Under. [. . .]

All good wishes,
Tony

As a poet, Hecht received a number of unsolicited letters. I have been unable to learn more about Mr. Lord's identity, apart from the fact that he has written abusive, rambling letters to a number of Hecht's contemporaries as well. His response to Hecht's humorous letter can be found in the Hecht archive at Emory University.

December 8, 1995 Washington DC

Mr. Lord (?)

I am by no means confident that this will reach you; I've always had the greatest difficulty making out your handwriting on your return address. But I sincerely hope this finds you in one way or another, because it is meant very firmly to discourage you from sending me any further letters or enclosures.

From the first missives of yours to arrive I have been either bored or repelled by what you have written, and I rarely got beyond the first half of the first page. For quite some time now I have merely thrown anything from you into the waste basket without troubling to open it. And, of course, I realize I could go on doing that with little trouble to myself. But I feel it is unfair to you to allow you to spend as much money as you clearly do on postage. (The most recent of your missives, containing a cassette, required $1.01 in postage). The cassette, what little of it I had the patience to listen to, struck me as at least as incoherent as your written prose.

Please save yourself some money, and save me from the small task of dumping your missives in the trash.

Yours,
Anthony Hecht

December 12, 1995 Washington DC

[To Dana Gioia]
Dear Dana,

Had I not been downed by the flu, this reply to your long, kind letter would have been more prompt. As it is, with the aid of antibiotics I am enough on the mend to thank you and congratulate you and wish you well in your resettlement—though I had been pleased to think of you as something of a neighbor here in the East. The completion of your Seneca translation is splendid news, and while I won't be able to attend the Soho performance, I'm delighted for you. Work of that sort, of course, requires a dedication and withdrawal that, for all your reviews and broadcasts, must have been a different sort of existence. Thinking about the less public aspects of a poet's labors reminded me of a wonderful passage in the diaries of John Evelyn (Jan. 18, 1671). Evelyn quite literally discovered Grinling Gibbons, probably the greatest wood-carver of all time: "I was walking neere a poor solitary thatched house in our Parish . . . I found him shut in . . . I asked if I might come in, he opened the doore civily to me, and I saw him about such work, as for the curiosity of handling, drawing, and studious exactnesse, I never in my life had seene before in all my travells: I asked him why he worked in such an obscure and lonesome place; he told me, it was that he might apply himselfe to his profession without interruption, and wondered not a little how I came to find him out . . . I found he was likewise Musical, and very Civil, sober and discreete in his discourse . . ." You probably know all this. [. . .]

Tony

The book in question is Touchstones: American Poets on a Favorite Poem, *ed. Robert Pack and Jay Parini (University Press of New England, 1995).*

[To J. D. McClatchy]

Dear Sandy,

I imagine you're away now, either in England or California (I can't keep your travels straight in my memory) but I have just read your excellent little essay on Pope's "Epistle to Miss Blount," and read it not only with delight but with greatly moved feelings. Your essay, brief as it is, seems to me the best thing in the whole book called <u>Touchstones</u>. It is in many ways an odd book. I haven't read it all, and don't think I ever will; but I feel I must surely have covered both the best and the worst of it. And these "best" and "worst" fall with astonishing neatness into two distinct camps that are easy to characterize. Let me say right away that I think the "best" are, after you, Wilbur, Justice, Nims (and there may be one or two others as yet unread). The other category is more numerous, and, as I was composing it I began to think I was, as I have long been accused of being, a misogynist, male-chauvinist pig. For my list includes (in no preferential order) Linda Pastan, Maxine Kumin, Erica Jong, Clara Yu, Rosellen Brown, Nancy Willard, Chase Twichell, and (saved by the bell) Marvin Bell.

God knows when Pack first proposed this book to me (or anyone else) but he has always had a casual, informal manner about these things, and in all likelihood he simply phoned and explained what he had in mind. [. . .] In any case, when I agreed to contribute to <u>Touchstones</u> all I could recall was that I was to write about a poem that I admired and that deserved greater attention or understanding than it commonly receives. That must have been your own reaction, and Wilbur's, and Justice's, etc. However, on the back of the book it says, "here fifty-nine of America's best poets select their favorite verse by another writer and explore its influence on their own writing." It's that second clause, after the "and" that separates the "best" from the "worst" in my view. All the "worst" contributors regarded the assignment as an opportunity to write about themselves, some of them almost shamelessly. Kumin's essay, rank with self-pity, allows her to pretend she knows something about prosody, which is nearly laughable. Jong thinks she's in Shakespeare's league. All of them, in any case, begin auto-biographically, with a sickening narcissism [and seem] to come to the poem they are ostensibly writing about with some reluctance. They feel all cuddly or martyred about their past, and this is what truly moves them. Pastan on Stevens is about as vapid as you can get.

But in some ways Bell deserves a special trophy for incomprehension. It's not just that he begins with his own trifling army experience in writing about Henry Reed's "Naming of Parts." It's that there is so much about the poem he fails to grasp, not the least of this being the very clear and touching class distinction between the conscript and the staff sergeant who is lecturing. The difference would be ironically amusing (or mildly offensive) under normal circumstances: the intellectually inferior lecturing his better. But in war time, such roles are either irrelevant or reversed. And the recruit must put up with them not merely because army regulations require his obedience but because his life may depend on knowing what this well-meaning oaf is trying to impart. And all the grounds for resentment are thereby cancelled, and a new, not entirely desirable, basis for existence is established. The wistfulness of the recruit for the pastoral world of harmless nature, and the recollected world of lovers, is juxtaposed, as it was in Hardy's "In a Time of Breaking of Nations," with the familiar irony of war-time brutality.

Anyway, the book is, but for your piece, and one or two others, a silly book, eliciting the worst, the most hopelessly self-absorbed from writers who are far too self-absorbed. I confess to feeling no sympathy whatever for the state of Maxine Kumin's back, and I'm confident that there are far better ways to write about the metrics of Housman than the self-pitying one she has chosen. And it is worth adding that X. J. Kennedy writes about Marvell's "To His Coy Mistress" as if he did not know it had been written about to great effect by Eliot. Well, it's a sad performance.

On a wholly different topic, I don't expect to address the new Auden biography until after the holidays. We spoke on the phone about the conversation you had with people at Pantheon, and their decision to make no more than "cosmetic" changes in the text before they issue it here in the States. As I understand it, they will only change typos. But I would want to know whether Davenport-Hines actually believes that Poe wrote a poem called "The Bell." (That name again. It has a dying fall).

With warmest and most affectionate wishes for the holiday season and the coming year,

Tony

January 2, 1996 Washington DC

[To Dana Gioia]

Dear Dana,

[...] I was touched by, and grateful for, your enclosed copy of the [Dietrich] Bonhoeffer passage. I own, and have used in the past, <u>Letters and Papers from Prison</u>, but I hadn't looked at it for some time, and your enclosure sent me back to it, and in a timely way. I came across an entry for February 13th, 1944: "I often notice here, both in myself and in others, the difference between the urge to pass on gossip, the desire for conversation and the need of confession. The urge to retail gossip is no doubt very attractive in women, but I find it repugnant in men. Everybody here seems to gossip indiscriminately about his private affairs, no matter whether others show any interest or not, merely for the sake of hearing themselves speak. It is an almost physical urge ... It often fills me with shame here to see how rapidly men demean themselves just for a bit of gossip, how they prate incessantly about their private affairs to people who don't deserve it, and who hardly listen ... all they want to do is to talk about themselves, whether what they say is true or not." This, of course, was written in prison, and probably in the prison from which few if any had hopes of being released. [Bonhoeffer was put to death on April 9, 1945, at Flossenbürg.] It reminded me, curiously, of a passage in Chekhov, that runs, "In both men the egotism of the unhappy was powerfully evident. Unhappy people are egotistical, mean, unjust, cruel and less capable than stupid people of understanding each other. Rather than bringing people together unhappiness drives them further apart, and even where it would seem that people ought to be joined by a similar cause of sorrow, they make for themselves much more injustice and cruelty than in an environment in which people are really contented." These twinned passages resonated for me this year because I found myself particularly aware of the plight of some elderly people, one of them in a "retirement home." These people are unable, like most of the rest of us, to put aside their own troubles, largely because they can foresee no end to them. What for Bonhoeffer was prison without reprieve [or] a death sentence and for Chekhov's characters is the "egotism" of suffering, for the elderly is a stark realization that no changes for the better are any longer possible. I fear that I, too, would become fretful and self-centered under such circumstances. For most of my life I flattered myself that the kind of life I had chosen (or that had somehow been allotted to me, i.e., the life of the mind) would allow me to enjoy even a solitary existence; and that the writing as well as the reading of books could serve for a sufficient, if not the richest and most varied, existence. But this year, alas, Christmas greetings from two friends report on their increasing blindness; and both of these were men who were devoted to literature, one as an editor, the other as an intellectual and scholar. [. . .]

All good wishes,
Tony

January 10, 1996 Washington DC
[To Eleanor Cook]
Dear Eleanor,

Oh there is a blessing in this driven snow / That thickens by the minute, and it consists not merely in its beauty but in the leisure it confers. Here we are, snowbound, in a record blizzard that has made the news (to the televised extent that we are even aware of the news). No newspapers have reached us for several days, nor has the mail. We happen to be well enough stocked with food and liquor to have survived in comfort so far, though we must make a breakthrough some time. Meanwhile, I have been granted a chance to read, with some of the care and attention it deserves, your splendid essay on "methinks" and "methought."[1] I have read it not only with attention but with delight. And the delight of a kind and caliber I associate with the work of a critic I admire as highly as any—Empson. It seems to me he might have done what you have so splendidly done. Or, to word it another way, methinks it partakes of his gifts and insights.

Who knows when this letter will set forth. It's my habit to put out-going mail in our mail slot, and the deliverer picks up what we are sending when he brings what has been sent to us. But that routine has gone by the board, and I am writing in that odd hypothetical frame of mind in which Boethius must have composed his Consolation. This does not in the least diminish my pleasure in considering your work or in writing to you. I hope you will not mind my venturing some idle reactions to your essay.

As regards Eve's first reaction to her own reflected image and to Adam (PL: IV, 475–85) I have always found in these lines what seems a kind of serious comedy. Doubtless to certain embattled feminists it only confirms Milton's misogynistic nature, which makes him present Eve as vainly self-centered and

---

[1]*English Language Notes* 32 (1995): 34–46; later collected in Cook's *Against Coercion: Games Poets Play* (Stanford University Press, 1998).

self admiring. (There might, of course, be a lesbian splinter-group that would approve of Eve's preference of herself over Adam). But it may be that Milton is asking us to remember that Eve is, in effect, just born, and she therefore exhibits an infant's preoccupation with itself—hence, the "unripe judgment" of which you write.

With regard to <u>Hamlet</u>, there is an important use of "methinks" in which something nearly visionary may be intended. In 1.2.184–6, Hamlet says, "My father—methinks I see my father." Horatio: "Where, my lord?" Hamlet: "In my mind's eye, Horatio." It is a case where the idea of judgment is wholly absent.

I especially delighted in your suggestion that when Sin uses "methinks" it is parodying Milton's prose.

As for Bottom's dream, I have a theory of allusion about that dream. Bottom says "Methought I was, and methought I had—but man is but a patch'd fool, if he will offer to say what methought I had." Well, call me a patch'd fool if you wish, but I will risk a suggestion of what Bottom thought he had. My suggestion comes from <u>The Golden Ass of Apuleius</u>. As you know, of course, it's a transformation tale, a metamorphosis in which a man is turned into an ass. To this extent it is at least thematically related to what Shakespeare has done. But as you may recall, near the end of that tale a rich noble woman is overcome with lust for Lucius in his incarnation as an ass. In Robert Graves' translation, "at last she conceived the odd desire of getting to know me intimately. In fact, she grew so passionately fond of me that, like <u>Pasiphae</u> in the legend who fell in love with a bull, she bribed my trainer with a large sum of money to spend a night in my company." The implications, both as regards Pasiphae and the rich noblewoman are clear; there is not much about the general appearance of a bull or an ass to win a woman's heart, but they both have large genitals. Robinson Jeffers wrote a rather crude poem, "Roan Stallion," about just such an appetite. And so when Bottom says "methought I had," I suspect some part of Shakespeare's audience would have caught his ribald note and its classical source.

Finally, there is a lovely, visionary use of "methought" by George Herbert at the end of "The Collar," in which the voice of God speaks, or is thought to have spoken. But thought strongly enough to provoke a spoken response.

Many thanks for your essay. And also for the other enclosures regarding TSE [Thomas Stearns Eliot]. I have most recently been at work on a very short talk about the relations of prose and poetry for that outfit (Assn. of Literary Scholars and Critics) you addressed last year. They're going to meet again, this time in Boston, in late August. And another, rather light-hearted lecture (this one for a writers' conference at Sewanee) on how poets must deal with hostile criticism.

And I may shortly find myself reviewing a new (and not very good) biography of Auden. But for the present, everything has come to a blissful standstill. And so this wishes you, whenever it reaches you, a very happy New Year.

Tony

February 30, 1996 Washington DC

[To J. D. McClatchy]

Dear Sandy,

Many thanks for sending the Brodsky elegies by [Seamus] Heaney and [Paul] Muldoon. I opened the envelope boldly, and as soon as I had identified the contents I stuffed it right back again as though it were a notice for jury duty. The fact is that I am myself engaged in writing an elegy for Joseph, and I feel superstitious about reading one by anyone else till my own is finished. For two reasons that I am aware of. The first is an honest desire not to be influenced by another poet; the second is a nervous fear that my own as yet unfinished poem will suffer so greatly by comparison that discouragement will prohibit continuing. I'm not sure that either of these reasons is the real one. Since Heaney is trying to echo Auden, and I am decidedly not, that cannot be a great danger. And perhaps I could immunize myself from any danger of Muldoon in something of the same way. My poem tries (with whatever success must be judged by others) to appropriate Brodsky's own poetic resources, including extravagant personifications, metaphors drawn from time and space, many foreign settings, etc. Call it plain superstition, but I will still set aside those poems you sent until I have finished my own. [. . .]

Much love,
Tony

Eleanor Cook's comments alluded to here are from an essay published as "Fables of War in Elizabeth Bishop," in Against Coercion: Games Poets Play *(Stanford University Press, 1998), in which she also calls attention to Hecht's use of "peter out" in his poem "Retreat" from* Millions of Strange Shadows.

August 1, 1996 Washington DC

Dear Eleanor,

[. . .] I was delighted with your comments on Bishop's "Roosters," and pleased once again to be mentioned by you, though you give me more credit than I deserve, since "peter out" is no invention of mine. Like you, I've wondered how, at the end of the poem, "the sun climbs in," and have tentatively decided that, initially unseen, ("In the morning/a low light is floating/in the backyard . . .") it climbs into the scene itself, like Peter, first lost "among the servants and officers," but then singled out, "following (the first evidences of light) 'to see the end . . .'" It is Peter who is "faithful as enemy, or friend." That equivocal quality in Peter may also be said of the sun ("Shall I compare thee to a summer's day?"). Without being able to demonstrate this, I cannot rid myself of the notion that something deeply personal is being hinted at in the most delicate way in the last stanza. It might, ever so remotely, touch on some equivocal love-relationship of the poet's, who has been awake since at least four o'clock, when it was dark outside. But now with the coming light the world is about to be roused, and it may be that some partner, up till now asleep, will return to consciousness at any moment—as friend? as enemy? faithful at least in the equivocal sense that Peter, also a figure of love, was faithful as well as both enemy and friend. If this were part of the poet's intention, "to see the end" not only refers to Peter's terrible potential complicity in the crucifixion, but the possible end of a relationship between the speaker and another, unknown, unnamed, unheard, person. [. . .]

With warm greetings,
Tony

Bernard Knox (1914–2010) was a scholar of Greek literature and founding director of the Center for Hellenic Studies in Washington, D.C., from 1961 to 1985. Hecht is referring to Knox's review article "The Later Stages of Greek Drama" in Arion 4 *(1999): 155–173. Their friendship dated from the 1950s.*

September 21, 1996 Washington DC

Dear Bernard:

[. . .] Your fine and richly informative Arion article evoked a tumult of immediate reactions in my mind. The question you raise (or that [Helmut] Flashar raises) about men playing female parts in Greek tragedy reminded me that when we were in Venice this summer we saw what was called "The Greek Show" at the Palazzo Grassi. It was probably the most exhausting show I've ever seen. Among other things, there was no place to sit down as you went continuously upward from floor to floor. Every inch of wall space was devoted to commentary, floor-plans of temples and forts, conjectural reconstructions of buildings, etc., all in addition to the objects on view, which themselves were well described on labels. The show, devoted to Magna Grecia civilization, began roughly in the Iron Age, and continued into decadent Hellenistic decrepitude. The catalogue was roughly the size and weight of the Manhattan telephone directory, which discouraged us from bringing one back. But easily the most striking item in the show, the very first, the most majestic, was placed to create maximum impact at the head of the stairs to the piano nobile. Placed on a pedestal that rose about to eye level was a very large (15 feet?) figure of a well-built Greek youth (both arms broken off at the elbows, but otherwise in fine condition). He was strong, decidedly masculine, perfectly shaped, but was dressed in a diaphanous chiton or peplos that reached to his feet, designed with the finest pleating of the sort one associates with certain statues of Aphrodite, and which served only to emphasize every modeled aspect of his male body. Except for this clothing, there was nothing in the least androgynous or effeminate about the figure, which was unambiguously beautiful, though in some strange way the effect was unsettling. It was not the effect of seeing some modern man in drag, which is either comic or satiric or painful. There was no diminishment of nobility to this figure, and any feeling of being "unsettled" may well have been due to the parochialism of being a modern American. Perhaps the catalogue will make its way to the National Gallery, where you will have a chance to see pictures of the figure. [. . .]

Best to you and Bianca,

Tony

1997

January 9, 1997 Washington DC

[To Eleanor Cook]

Dear Eleanor:

I'm enormously, and suitably, grateful to you for your very kind and enthusiastic letter about the poems [*Flight Among the Tombs* (1996)]. Your heartening words were welcome for themselves, and they also serve convincingly to mitigate the effects of a moderately hostile review by William Logan which appeared in <u>The New Criterion</u>, where, along with Charles Simic, A.R. Ammons, Joseph Brodsky and some others, I was dismissed as among "the Old Guys." It's not the fact that my age is held against me that bothers me. But as I stand tiptoe upon the threshold of my seventy-fifth year I have managed to preserve the comforting conviction that my work continues to improve. Doubtless there is a self-serving element in this, and it is possibly a simple delusion, since few writers could endure if they thought they were losing their abilities. And God knows it has happened to many. Wordsworth at the end grew weak; after the <u>Quartets</u> Eliot wrote little of merit in the way of poetry. Delmore Schwartz sank into oblivion, John Crowe Ransom stopped writing, and Dylan Thomas took to drink, while Hemingway, fearing the loss of his gifts, and suspecting self-plagiarism, took his own life. The catalogue is long and depressing, so it's no mystery that most writers refuse to see their own weaknesses. At the same time, there are the heartening instances of Hardy and Sophocles. Of course, there is a built-in danger to the conviction that one is getting always better. It means that as one comes to think less and less well of one's early work, put into the shade [by] this happy progressive view, that one may be right: the early work, of which one was once so proud, may not be so good after all, and two hideous conclusions may be drawn from that. The first is that the present state of excellence may not be so great if it is merely an improvement upon what went before; and secondly, that the illusion of present merit may be just as temporary as one's view of the past. The whole puzzle does not abide much thinking on.

Let me, in any case, try to answer some of your questions. I've known Baskin since 1956, when I first joined the Smith College faculty where he was teaching. (Sylvia Plath and Ted Hughes were there at the same time.) Even in those days Leonard's interest in mortality was pronounced, in large part because his remarkable first wife was slowly dying of multiple sclerosis. In those years he was, among many other things, doing eloquent small bronze casts of hanged men. It was he who suggested that we collaborate on a Gehenna Press book to be called The Presumptions of Death. You are right in guessing that the AIDS epidemic played a part in my thoughts, and indirect allusion is made to it in the Circus Barker poem's line "Entrust yourself to the keeping of my aids ["Death the Carnival Barker"]." I had considered using "aides" or "AIDS" but settled on this compromise. (There is a Hopkins poem about Margaret Clitherow, who was pressed to death for harboring a Catholic priest.)

You are astute and right in noticing my habitual recourse to six-line stanzas. I have been semi-aware of this. It probably has something to do with rhyming patterns. A quatrain is too predictable, whether ABBA or ABAB. A quatrain with an added couplet is no more than simply that. Odd numbers of lines involve at least three rhymes of the same kind for a five-line stanza, and more with a longer one. Rhyme royal and Spenserian stanzas are either too artificial and antiquated, or they call undue attention to themselves as technical problems to be solved. That, at least, is my unconsidered view of the matter, which is susceptible to much more serious thought and discussion.

The "letter" in the middle of "Sisters" is largely borrowed, or, more accurately, adapted from the single letter in The Selected Letters of Robert Frost that wasn't written by him. It was sent to him by his sister, Jeanie, who spent most of her life in a state lunatic asylum in Maine. I've put her in a private Catholic institution for my own curious purposes, which, I will confess to you, were purely floral. Baskin and I are in the course of putting together a florilegium; he has done 15 beautiful woodcuts, and I have so far turned out about four poems to go with them. "Sisters" was composed to accompany the woodcut of Cyclamen. ("Pledge" goes with the thistle, "La-Bas" with the tulip. As you can see, I've had to be very cunning in dealing with flowers in my poems, and have taken inordinate pains to avoid Victorian valentine arrangements, pinned with golden darts. The key to writing about flowers, I find, is to approach them very indirectly. I've got one about sunflowers that has been written since the book appeared.)

The epigraph for the [James] Merrill poem is from a Palinode by Edmund Bolton that begins, "As withereth the Primrose by the river,/As fadeth Sommers-sunne from gliding fountains . . ." As for the "response" to the croupier cry in "Fortuna Parvulorum," I should confess that I am anything but a gambling man, though I once won about four or five thousand francs (when they were not worth all that much) at Monte Carlo. But you are right in thinking that I wanted exactly this "measured" reaction to the heedless risks of youth. I am very fond of the epigraph from Aristotle, which I have been cherishing for years, hoping to find an occasion for its use. [. . .]

> With very best wishes for the New Year,
> Tony

May 20, 1997 Washington DC

[To W. D. Snodgrass]
Dear De,

Warmest greetings to you and Kathy, and many thanks for the new poem, beautiful and handsomely presented.

As a stodgy old academic (long since retired) I could not help suspecting an echo of John Webster's The White Devil in your line, "Now let the mole, the vole and the fieldmouse . . ." It recalled to me that strange elegy that begins, "Call for the robin red-breast and the wren, . . ." and later goes on, "Call unto his funeral dole/The ant, the fieldmouse and the mole . . ."

I have been gripped of late with the kind of infirmities that probably belong to my age, or at least to some of my age. Back problems are the most troubling and the least susceptible to correction. I have to be very cautious about my movements, and I wear a back brace much of the time. At best this is irritating.

> Affectionately,
> Tony

Hays Rockwell was rector of St. James Parish, 1976–1991, New York City, and then succeeded to the Bishopric of Missouri. Hecht dedicated "Gladness of the Best" in Millions of Strange Shadows *to Rockwell, and he contributed his poem "Anthem," composed earlier, to the Spring Fair festival at St. James in 1980.*

May 20, 1997 Washington DC

Dear Hays,

In the more or less normal course of things I've found myself engaged in correspondence with a woman who lives in Florida and writes poetry. The first poems she sent me seemed to have merit, as well as being quirky and odd, the oddness sometimes suggesting lack of expertise, but the quirkiness a kind of Emily Dickinson, originality. I wrote her an encouraging letter, and thought that might be the end of the matter. But not long after new poems came from her. But this time accompanied by a few highly unusual biographical details. It turns out she is a deaf-mute, and I was profoundly astonished by her ability to write poems at all. This severe handicap (that's not the politically correct word these days) surely accounted for the metrical and rhythmic flaws I had noticed in her work, but upon which I had mercifully had the reserve not to remark. The next letter brought still more astonishing revelations. She has not only learned English but was currently engaged in translating a French essay by Marcel Marceau on the art of mime, a topic that meant much to her because she communicates by signs except when she writes. And then came the detail that explains why I am writing all this to you. Her name is Ann LeZotte, and her father was a roommate of yours at Brown, and is godfather to one of your boys, or at least she thinks so. She says she has met you and Linda [Rockwell] a couple of times. She mentioned this by way of belatedly introducing herself "so you don't feel I am just a crazy stranger out of the blue . . . Also, I speak so directly to people because I live in isolation, and I am a freak—there's an excuse!!!"

It is not impossible, but extremely painful, to imagine what that kind of isolation must be like. It makes one feel ashamed of any lesser complaint. And so, considering all things, we are most mercifully and fortunately well, and have little other news than that Evan celebrated the first anniversary of his domestic life with a very attractive and extremely nice young lady whom we have come to know and like a great deal.

This comes with love from us both.

Tony

Kenneth Lynn (1923–2001) was professor of English at Harvard, then of history at the Johns Hopkins University and the noted biographer of Hemingway and Charlie Chaplin. Armand Schwab was a classmate of Hecht's at the Horace Mann School, Riverdale, New York.

June 25, 1997 Washington DC

Dear Kenneth,

Your very kind and painstaking transcription of Armand Schwab's reminiscences of days I had all but forgotten about I found wryly amusing. I'm especially impressed by the accuracy of Armand's memory, though I think he gives me credit for having memorized more Browning than I'm entitled to. More amazing still, though I do remember mooning about that girl under the rustic-styled pergola, covered with vines, in Central Park, I would not, had my life depended on it, have been able to come up with her name. Those days seem to me like O'Neill's <u>Ah, Wilderness</u> [and] "The Rubaiyat," giddy innocence and blameless fatuity. What I remember of Armand is that he was particularly bright, lively, cheerful and friendly. I know I valued those qualities in him because, for reasons I myself utterly failed to understand, or, at least to admit to myself, I was anything but cheerful. As for Pat Mayer, I dimly recall her professed love of poetry, which she somehow ingeniously employed as a sexual barrier and Browning's "Last Ride Together" was consequently a great favorite of hers. If only she had known Marvell's "Definition of Love" she would have rejoiced in keeping admirers at a chaste but enticing distance. There was another girl about the same time for whom I genuinely yearned. I have no idea what her name was (is), but she aroused in me whatever could pass in those premature days as lust. She had a conventionally pretty face, but her most prominent feature, of which she was supremely aware, was her bosom. All the school athletes hung around her, and it was taken for granted that she would attend the spring prom with the captain of the football team. And yet, like Browning's Last Duchess, she had smiles for everyone, an impartiality that seemed movingly generous at the time, though I now think it was simple narcissism, and an appetite to be widely, perhaps universally, admired. She was an unashamed sexual tease, a would-be Salome or Delilah. What most provoked me about her was her open satisfaction in arousing unsatisfied yearning in almost any male in her vicinity. All these feelings about this girl and Pat Mayer were simmering at the same time we were supposed to be concentrating on Latin, French, history, chemistry and literature. As it happened, the only scholastic enterprise into which I was able to throw myself completely, and to the exclusion of any other concern, was geometry, taught by a tall, handsome, white-haired gentleman named Callahan. I greatly admired Mr. Callahan and worked very hard for him, and did well, though I was middling to bad in almost everything else.

Anyway, if you keep in touch with Armand Schwab, please greet him for me, and tell him how much I admire the reliability of his memory.

Best,

Tony

June 27, 1997 Washington DC

[To David Mason]

Dear Dave,

[…] I can understand how settling into domestic routines in Moorhead [Minnesota] may seem banal and unexciting after the adventures of the last few months, and I agree with you that at least a part of the glamour of travel is precisely that one enters a world without duties and responsibilities. This is probably always the case, though it was especially true for me when I was younger. Tourism confers a kind of magical immunity from ordinary cares; while others are going on with their lives, the tourist looks on from the sidelines and at leisure, constrained only by the limit of his funds and his time. And if you know how, you can turn a blind eye to misfortunes you encounter, and thereby preserve the tourist's privileged gaiety. But I have found this increasingly difficult as I grow older. For this reason I have never wanted to go to India, for example, where the sight of abject poverty can scarcely be avoided. It is to be seen, for that matter, right at home, on the streets of New York and Washington. It gives no joy at home, either, but seeing it abroad means that one's holiday is tainted by guilt and anguish, and since holidays are usually short, it seems worth trying to keep them as cheerful as possible. I've thought about this a long time, and, oddly, in connection with Auden. In some of what he has written he has bravely acknowledged the misery to be seen in a country he is visiting; but in other writing he manages to ignore it when that evasion serves his purpose. No doubt we all do this, both at home and abroad. But when at home we can perhaps assuage our consciences with the thought of the taxes we pay and the charities to which we make donations, while when we are abroad we are no more than privileged voyeurs. One of the reasons Helen and I are at ease in Venice is that some municipal ordinance forbids begging in the streets. (I somehow suspect that, to encourage tourism, this may be true throughout Italy, but it is a law much harder to enforce in places like Rome or Milan. Venice is also virtually free of street-crime, there being no means of hasty escape.) [. . .]

Tony

Sunil Iyengar, editor, journalist, and aspiring poet in the 1990s, is now director of research and analysis at the National Endowment of the Arts and frequent book reviewer.

June 30, 1997 Washington DC

Dear Sunil,

Thank you for your kind and courteous letter. I'm not sure I can provide you with the sort of response about how to write blank verse that you would find helpful in a truly practical way—though I have recently written a short essay on the subject for a collection of essays on metrical and poetic forms that is scheduled to be published in a year or so.

But part of any answer would be what you already suspect. As with certain familiar and conventional dance steps, you eventually find the rhythm establishing itself in some subconscious part of the mind, and it is no longer necessary to look at one's feet and keep counting ONE two three, ONE two three, etc. The body itself (in the case of dancing), a part of the mind (in the case of meter) habituate themselves to a regular pattern. Of course other factors are involved. One of them is that from early in my life I was, at first forced, and then chose, to commit a good deal of poetry to memory—and, in the English language most poetry is written in pentameter lines: all the plays of the Elizabethans; Milton; Wordsworth; Tennyson; Byron; Pope; Dryden; Chaucer; all sonnets; all sestinas, etc. For reasons too complicated to try to answer, the English language lends itself so naturally to both the iambic foot and the pentameter line that in Moby Dick Melville lapses into blank verse from time to time. And apart from the fact that I memorized a lot of poetry, I have spent my whole academic life teaching it, and returning to the same revered texts year after year. So that after a while a certain confidence is gained about line length and accentual emphasis. This is not to say that I never make mistakes; but I feel the kind of confidence that a musician must feel when he improvises on a theme. Yet, as I said, however confident I feel in the heat of composition, I always check to see if I've made any mistakes. Moreover, I have come to feel that a certain latitude is often welcome in metrical measure, and that too strict a meter can become mechanical and forbidding to a reader, so that a certain scattered number of irregularities may be welcome. These should not simply be "allowed to happen" but should be shrewdly "placed" where they are needed. The late plays of Shakespeare can be very instructive as far as this is concerned—as can both Frost and Stevens.

Good luck to you in all your undertakings.

Sincerely,

Anthony Hecht

October 24, 1997 Washington DC

[To Leonard Baskin]

Dear Leonard,

Here are the poems for the florilegium. Please remember that three poems in the sequence, "A Pledge"—thistle; "Sisters"—cyclamen; and "La Bàs: A Trance"—tulip, have already appeared in Flight Among the Tombs, copies of which you have.

Of the poems I send herewith it may be that some explanation will be useful. "Indolence" makes no explicit mention of any flower; on the other hand, mention is made of St. Matthew, and words from Matthew 6:28, "they toil not, neither do they spin," in reference to "the lilies of the field," is adapted in what ought to be an indicative way. "A Pair of Heroes" does not mention, but, I hope, describes the poppy. It may be that the most concealed one is "Secrets," fittingly enough. One of the colloquial names for the foxglove is "witches thimbles." But it is easiest simply to list the poems along with the flowers they are meant to match.

> Indolence—lily
> An Orphic Calling—sunflower
> Illumination—crocus
> Long-Distance Vision—carnation
> Witness—sea-holly
> Public Gardens—teasel
> A Pair of Heroes—poppy
> Secrets—foxglove
> Despair—marigold
> The Voice—mandrake
> Look Deep—iris
> A Fall—rhododendron

There are thirteen in all, and added to the three already published in Flight, there are sixteen altogether. [. . .]

Let me know what you think. (I'm aware, of course, that the columbine poem is something of a cheat, but I found it a stumbling-block, its name supposedly derived from a "cluster of five doves," which the blossom is thought to resemble.) Much as I've enjoyed work on this sequence, I'm relieved to be quit of it at this immediate juncture because I'm a member of the Literary Awards Committee of the Academy of Arts and Letters, and I have a formidable stack of books to read through and judge in the course of a very short time. Some are dreadful, but most have some merit, and judgment is not easy.

Best,

Tony

Laurance Roberts (1907–2002), scholar of Asian art, was director of the American Academy in Rome from 1947 to 1960. Isabel was his wife of sixty-five years.

November 13, 1997 Washington DC

Dear Laurance—

I'm deeply grateful for your kind words about the Tanning Prize. Your friendship, and Isabel's, are very important to me, and of all my happy recollections of the Academy in Rome, none are more vivid than the excursions throughout Italy the two of you conducted. I owe more than I can say to the kindness of you both.

Sincerely,

Tony

Hayàt Nieves Mathews (1917–2003) was a Scottish-born writer of Spanish descent. Her father was Salvador de Madariaga y Rojo, Spanish diplomat, later ambassador to the United States, and the prolific author of a number of scholarly and popular works and translations, including a bilingual edition of Hamlet (1949). Her mother was the Scottish economic historian Constance Archibald. At the time of her correspondence with Hecht, Mathews lived in Italy. She was the author of Francis Bacon: The History of a Character Assassination (Yale University Press, 1996).

December 17, 1997 Washington DC

My dear Hayàt,

When, unthinkably long ago, I was an undergraduate, my best college friend was named Harry Winterbottom. He was a history major, generous, warm, and with very poor eyesight, demanding eyeglasses with unusually thick lenses. He was called up for military service in World War II well before I was, and I assumed that, given his vision handicap, the army would somewhere find a niche for him that might keep him relatively safe. He wrote back to his college advisor from some camp overseas a touching and brave letter, utterly without complaint. His advisor also happened to be the college librarian, and Harry wrote that what he wanted more than anything else upon his return was to read all the books in the college library. This went right to the librarian's heart, and he allowed the letter to be published in the student newspaper, where I read it, and was charmed. It was a small college, and had a proportionately small library, but I knew that it would have taken Harry more than a normal lifetime to read all its books. But not for a minute did I doubt his desire to do it. Given the standard operating procedures of the army, I should not have been surprised when I learned that within two months of his call to service Harry was sent to the front lines and killed. I still think of him quite often, and always in regard to reading.

I would never dare to be so bold as to hope I could read all the books in even a small college library. But I used to think that once I'd retired I would be able finally to read pretty much what I wanted, and I had appointed for myself an informal but rather daunting list of books I wanted to get to. As well as death, life has its own way of altering expectations, and I've been deflected from most of my goals, but I nevertheless still intend to get around to some books very promptly, of which your life of Bacon is one. [. . .]

Love,

Tony

David Havird (1953–) is a poet and professor of English, Centenary College, Louisiana.

December 30, 1997 Washington DC

Dear David:

An interim note in response to your last letter.

1) I do know the John Rosenberg collection of Ruskin quotations.

2) As to whether I regard my work in general as an attempt to memorialize "the burning, voiceless Jews," I'm not sure I have a clear, uncomplicated answer. For one thing, I am not a concentration-camp survivor. I feel that undue indignation on my part would be a vulgar appropriation of the suffering of others for cheap rhetorical purposes and a contemptible kind of self-promotion. At the same time, I cannot help identifying with all Jews who have experienced persecution, for I have felt the effects of anti-Semitism throughout the whole of my life, though not <u>in extremis</u>, and I invariably wince at finding it widespread

in Western literature. (I have written about this glancingly in an essay on The Merchant of Venice in Obbligati, and in another on the Epistle to the Galatians, in Incarnation, a collection of essays on the New Testament, edited by Alfred Corn.)

3) Turning to [Simone] Weil and her claim that "concentrated attention" is a sacramental act, comparable to prayer, Auden claimed much the same thing in an essay in The Episcopalian that I quote (pp. 386–7) in my Auden book. But I suspect that both Auden and Weil have left themselves exposed to a peculiar and unconsidered danger, which I have tried to address in an as yet unpublished essay on Auden. The sort of devoted concentration they identify with prayer is virtually impossible to distinguish from what Hannah Arendt recognized as the banality of evil: a bureaucrat's capacity to submerge himself so completely in the paperwork details of his job that he often deliberately erases its human consequences from his thought. Much political and military jargon is widely employed for this purpose, as Orwell knew and said. The most recent one I know of is US army lingo of the Gulf War, that distinguished between "hard" and "soft" targets for bombs, the former being military installations, while the second was human beings. Technocrats are skilled at "concentration."

All good wishes for the New Year,
Tony

1998

Edward Perlman (1947–) is a poet, essayist, and faculty advisor to the M.A.s in the Writing Program at the Johns Hopkins University.

January 20, 1998 Washington DC

Dear Ed,

I will be seeing you very soon, but I'm impatient to write at once to tell you how delighted I am, and how grateful, for your really wonderful poem, sent to honor my birthday. It is a fine poem, quite apart from the fact that I have some personal connection with it, if I am capable of distancing myself from such complicit self-interest, and from the fact that it was, figuratively at least, commissioned by Helen. Its own riches resonated in my mind in unexpected ways. For example, it reminded me that once Auden, in one of his round-robin parlor game inquiries about "where and what you would like to have been if born in another era?" responded to his own inquiry (this was one of the kindest things about him; he always took part in any such cross examination along with all the others) by saying that he would like to have been a medieval monk. Most found this a surprising, as well as unlikely, declaration, coming as it did from someone the world at large regarded as libertine, but I think it was both completely honest, and something of which he was probably perfectly capable. This, after all, was said at a time when he no longer looked for any domestic happiness with Chester [Kallman], or anyone else for that matter, and principled chastity was by no means beyond him. In Donald Attwater's <u>Penguin Dictionary of Saints</u>, there's a description of the community Honoratus founded (and composed largely of other saints) in which pains were taken by the saint "that no one in this island community should be dispirited or overworked or idle." All by itself, that sounds very nearly ideal, and when you consider that the island was just off the coast of Cannes, it sounds nearly luxurious. Helen and I have made a few trips to the Italian town of Asolo (much beloved by Browning, Duse, Cardinal Bembo and D'Annunzio) and have stayed in the sumptuously appointed Hotel Cipriani, where, from the dining terrace one may look across an olive grove and cypress spires to a monastery, perched on an adjacent hill. I always remark to Helen that the monks must look across at us with austere disapproval, and she invariably responds that they doubtless manufacture their own consoling grappa. The consolations of your own terrace at breakfast time have clearly been enough to have allowed you to write this lovely poem, for which I send my enthusiastic thanks.

> With affection,
> Tony

January 21, 1998 Washington DC

[To David Havird]

Dear David,

In reply to your searching questions, let me say that the speaker of "The Venetian Vespers" is <u>not me</u>, though I have used some events in my life in the course of the poem. But most of the details I have borrowed from the lives of others, and of one man in particular. You remark that his loneliness, his "disengagement from the human race" goes hand in hand with his "looking." Just so. But then you go on to inquire, "But what should he be otherwise doing? Should he relax his aesthetic concentration and do 'real' work — minister to 'the outcasts, the maimed, the poor,' . . . etc.?" The point is that he is unable to do this, being spiritually crippled. He has been in a lunatic asylum (see Part II) and precisely because he can so easily identify with the forlorn of the world he is eager to distance himself from them. Both his war experience and his dark family secrets incapacitate him. At the same time, I agree with you that his "looking" is a moral act, and not everything he looks at is beautiful. "The great church of Health," Santa Maria della Salute elicits his admiration because of its beauty, to be sure, but also because it is dedicated to health, which he desires. He is, as you rightly say, the opposite of Ransom's practical-minded man. But this man is no believing Christian, or anything else, for that matter. He would like to believe, but he doesn't. The Madonna he speaks of in the final section he thinks of only as a Comforter, which is what certain quilts are called and what some medicines perform. He also regards himself as too old to change or to be cured. So you are right again when you suspect that "the divine presence" is absent from the poem, and that none of the intuitions of [Simone] Weil, Hopkins, Wordsworth, Shelley or Auden belong to his case. To be sure, it was I who raised the name of Weil, and called attention to her comment about "looking." But for her, as for others (for example Ruskin, who wrote, "The greatest thing a human soul ever does in this world is to <u>see</u> something and tell what it saw in a plain way") seeing is only the beginning of what could become a spiritual pilgrimage, and the speaker of the poem is too old, too set in his ways, too crippled in mind and spirit, to go further.

You are right, too, in feeling that my work as a whole is not primarily concerned with anti-Semitism. Others have suffered so much more than I that it would be impudent for me to speak self-righteously in their behalf. Ashley Brown, if it was he, was right in claiming that "Apprehensions" is largely autobiographical. As for the modern-but-not-exclusively-Jewish feeling about God's abandonment of mankind, after the Holocaust it is an understandable enough feeling, but it can be found as well in George Herbert's "Decay," and in a number of Auden's poems, as I take pains to indicate in the final chapter of my book on Auden.

All good wishes for the New Year,

Tony

Paul R. Gross (1928–) is a biologist and author of, among other works, Higher Superstition: The Academic Left and Its Quarrels with Superstition *(1994).*

January 30, 1998 Washington DC

Dear Paul,

If, as graduate dean at U or R [University of Rochester], you had to attend all commencements, and if you were there during Sproull's presidency, you will remember that the ceremonies were televised. One of the administrative worries of those days concerned the dignity of the faculty, sitting, as they were obliged to do, on stage, and vulnerably visible to the TV audience as well as all those in the Eastman Theater. Would they doze off during the almost formulaic speeches? Would they disgrace the university in the eyes of its newest graduates and their parents, to say nothing of the general television public? Concern about such matters was a keen consideration of Bob Sproull's, not to mention the TV network that did not have limitless time to allocate to such matters. Accordingly, the program was very carefully timed, particularly the speechifying part of it, the most uncertain aspect of which was the major address of a recipient of an honorary degree. All that could be done was to ask him or her in the most earnest way to try to confine their remarks to a very specific number of minutes. Most were very obliging in this, but of course, there was no control whatever about the content of the speech itself, which seemed to present the greater danger of being boring than of inciting to riot. For all the administrative worries on this point, they were quite needless. The faculty invariably seemed galvanized by whatever the speaker had to say, no matter how trite, weary or unimportant. This was because there was a faculty pool on the length of the speech. Everyone put in a buck and chose a number of minutes. Since the faculty was large, the pot was a handsome one. From the moment the speaker began the faculty were riveted, averting their eyes only fleetingly to glance at their watches. [. . .] I never won, but I was as entranced as everyone else. [. . .]

> Tutti bestorum,
> Anthony Hecht

Although modestly suggested, the "small matter" described here has the merit of offering a solution to a puzzle that has long vexed Ralegh's editors involving the sense of the second stanza.

January 31, 1998 Washington DC

[To Hayàt Mathews]

My dear Hayàt,

[. . .] I myself have indulged in conjectural emendations in a small and amateurish way.

Like Tottel's <u>Miscellany,</u> <u>The Phoenix Nest</u> was a fine anthology of poems by various hands, not all of them identified, and still open to conjecture as to authorship. One of these in the latter book seems to have been ascribed to [Sir Walter] Ralegh, and I have no quarrel with the ascription. But I <u>do</u> have a quarrel with the text of the poem, and I'm the more puzzled in that it has never been questioned by any critic, to my knowledge, nor by any editor of Ralegh. The poem is called "An epitaph upon the Right Honorable Sir Philip Sidney, Knight, Lord Governor of Flushing." It is a poem written in fifteen pentameter quatrains, rhyming ABBA. And I will copy out here the first three stanzas.

To praise thy life, or waile thy woorthie death,
And want thy wit, thy wit high, pure, diuine,
Is far beyond the power of mortall line,
Nor any one hath worth that draweth breath.

Yet rich in zeal, though poor in learnings lore
And friendly care obscured in secret brest,
And loue that enuie in thy life supprest,
Thy deere life done, and death hath doubled more.

And I, that in thy time and living state,
Did onely praise thy vertues in my thought,
As one that seeld the rising sunne hath sought,
With words and teares now waile thy timelesse fate.

I have described my "theory" about what I think is wrong with these lines to Gwynne Blakemore Evans, the Harvard Shakespeare scholar, for whose edition of the <u>Sonnets</u> I wrote the introduction. And he was good enough to say that he agrees with me. In the end, it is, I suppose, a small matter, but I am annoyed by its editorial persistence. What I propose is that the order of these stanzas is in error, and that the second ought to be the third, and the third second. This is demanded by both grammar and syntax. It is the "I," only mentioned in the first line of what passes for the third stanza, who is "rich in zeal, though poor in learning's lore," in the second stanza here. Without that first person pronoun, the stanza that regularly appears as the poem's second one has no referent, unless it were to be Sidney himself. But that stanza is full of denigration (self-denigration, as I think) and in a poem that throughout praises Sidney to the point of fulsomeness and extravagance, a claim that he is "poor in learning's lore" would be ridiculously out of place. I cannot tell you how many people have doubted this alteration I propose, while having no rational explanation for the stanzas in their canonical order. [. . .]

This comes with love.
Tony

The "Tree" referred to here is Iris Tree (1897–1968), daughter of Herbert Beerbohm Tree, and poet, artist, actress, and artist's model. Hecht probably met her sometime in the late spring of 1955.

July 25, 1998 Washington DC

[To B. H. Fairchild]

Dear Pete,

I'm first of all delighted by the news of the success of your Italian holiday, both in Rome and in Venice. Your Roman location, on the Scalinata, near the Keats house, recalls a fortunate event in my own life that I can take pleasure in recounting. Around 1955 I was living in Ischia where, in the words of Gershwin, "living was easy," and I had a very limited budget. I attended an interesting social gathering—there was a lively expatriate community there, of which Auden was only one—and I met a striking old woman, very alert and amusing, whose last name was Tree, and who modestly acknowledged a relationship to the great actor, Herbert Beerbohm Tree. She took a liking to me because I knew the Latin derivation of "egregious." (Proving the old adage that a little Latin is a valuable thing.) She told me she had an apartment in Rome that she would be leaving vacant for a month or so, while she went to London, where a play of hers was scheduled to open. (She turned up later in the course of things as an elderly British lady in La Dolce Vita.) Naturally I was delighted, not least because the Rome apartment was offered to me rent-free. But having gratefully accepted, I had no idea, until I arrived, what luxury I was awarded. Her apartment was at the top of the building right next to the Keats house, and one storey higher, so that it looked out over the Keats house at the Spanish Steps and the Piazza d'Espagna, across the city to St. Peter's dome to the west, and just about everywhere else. Moreover, very neat and small as the apartment was, it boasted a very large terrace with plants and flowering oleander—just the place for cocktail parties, which, trust me, I gave for my Roman friends. [. . .]

This comes with warmest greetings.

Tony

August 16, 1998 [postcard of the Ghetto Campo, Venice]

[To J. D. McClatchy]

Dear Sandy:

The heat here has risen to Texan heights, and the pigeons to plague proportions. John Ruskin called them "doves," which speaks volumes about his character, as well as his grasp on reality. But the wine and gorgonzola, the painting and architecture, recruit the spirits and exalt the soul.

Love to both
Tony & Helen

Al Sapinsley, a classmate of Hecht from Bard, was a Hollywood screenwriter seeking advice about writing a novel.

December 11, 1998 Washington DC

Dear Al,

That was some letter. It requires complicated response. I'll begin at the most elementary level, where I probably belong anyway, since I'm not in your league as regards the technology of writing. No discs or mice in my writing world. For poems, I start in longhand, and only slowly work my way to the typewriter, never advancing beyond that rather dated point. I'm barely out of the quill & inkstand stage of development, rather pithecanthropic, all things considered. And this may go a long way to explaining why my writing is so far removed from the playwriting, screenwriting, TV-writing world which is yours. I once began to write a novel, but I was shrewd enough to know I had no idea what I was doing, and quit in good time. But my career as a teacher, which went on for a long time, gave me some insights into the art that I have found useful, at least in the classroom.

Dialogue is indispensible, providing vigor, pace, drama, and immediacy; and is ultimately unimportant. Which is to say that no really good novel is remembered purely, or even largely, for its dialogue. The books one remembers for their dialogue are likely to be brittle social comedies by the likes of Nancy Mitford or E. F. Benson. To be sure, there is wonderful dialogue in Dickens, as there is in Dostoyevski; but this is not what we remember about them. I taught <u>Crime and Punishment</u> for years, made notes and outlines, read the critical commentaries (some of which were wonderfully illuminating) and I came to see how many descriptive elements and symbolic devices, operating subliminally, work so effectively in that wonderful book. The color yellow all by itself plays a major role in the story. Of course, in a tale that is chiefly a psychological/ spiritual drama, concerned so crucially with <u>inwardness</u>, many meanings must be conveyed by actions or descriptions, as distinguished from the very overt means of dialogue. But Dostoyevski is not unique in this regard. T.S. Eliot has been justly criticized for writing plays in which the central action is inward, and thus cannot be dramatized in dialogue. We are never shown how Beckett makes the right choice in <u>Murder in the Cathedral</u>; and this is true of his other plays.

My own heroes as fiction writers are Joyce and Flaubert. After many years, I still believe that "The Dead" is possibly one of the greatest pieces of prose fiction ever written. This, too, I taught for years, and even as I bring it up much of its non-dialogic beauty floods back upon me. So you must forgive me if I offer some reflections that may seem familiar. The first word in a narrative titled "The Dead" is "Lily." It is not uttered by any character, so it could not be incorporated into any filmic or staged version of the tale. I have sedulously avoided seeing the John Huston film, lathered in piety about Joyce though it was, because I know how much any film would have to omit. There is, of course, much dialogue in the story—a great deal more than in most of the stories in <u>The Dubliners</u>. But the chief point of almost all the dialogue is how misleading, evasive, deceitful, or even politely tactful, but always beside the point, all the talking is. (Chekhov sometimes uses dialogue the same way.) For all the near-hostilities, the mollifications, and awkward quadrilles of conversation, the truly important events, the events that carry the whole power of the story, are symbolic. Gabriel stands at the foot of the stairs, looking up at his wife as she listens to a piece of music, the lamplight brilliant upon her hair. What is happening to her and to him at that moment is profoundly tragic. But no one says anything. He simply entertains his thought. Indeed, his thoughts are the most important elements of the story, and they are not always voiced. And the last pages of the story, after all dialogue has been abandoned, are among the most beautiful in English prose. There is a delicacy, a tact, an artistry in Joyce beside which the skills of John Huston are little short of vulgar.

As for Flaubert, permit me to quote two favorable paragraphs from <u>Madame Bovary</u>:

One day he got there about three o'clock. Everybody was in the fields. He went into the kitchen, but did not at once catch sight of Emma; the outside shutters were closed. Through the chinks of the wood the sun sent across the flooring long, fine rays that were broken at the corners of the furniture and trembled along the ceiling. Some flies on the table were crawling up the glasses that had been used, and buzzing as they drowned themselves in the dregs of the cider. The daylight that came in by the chimney made velvet of the soot at the back of the fireplace, and touched with blue the cold cinders. Between the window and the hearth Emma was sewing; she wore no fichu; he could see small drops of perspiration on her bare shoulders.

After the fashion of country folks she asked him to have something to drink. He said no; she insisted, and at last laughingly offered to have a glass of liquor with him. So she went to fetch a bottle of curaçao from the cupboard, reached down two small glasses, filled one of them to the brim, poured scarcely anything into the other, and, having clinked glasses, carried hers to her mouth. As it was almost empty she bent back to drink, her head thrown back, her lips pouting, her neck on the strain. She laughed at getting none of it, while with the tip of her tongue passing between her small teeth she licked drop by drop the bottom of the glass.

Let me indulge my pedantry enough to venture three points. The descriptive elements of the first paragraph, while they might possibly be worked into a film, are almost uniquely effective as prose narrative because, as reader we come upon them in the singular sequence in which the novelist provides them, each item focused upon in its turn, and singled out by selective observation in ways a film would fail to convey as precisely "selective" and "sequential." (The film-viewer would just think: setting; details.) But it is the painstaking notice of the novelist that is at work, and films rarely give the impression of being painstaking in matters of this sort. Notice also that at the end of the first paragraph, Charles is beholding Emma, who does not know she is being observed. The author then neatly omits her discovery of Charles's presence, her rising from her seat, the formulaic exchange of greetings, and all that fluster. Finally, Emma's awkward, amused, slightly clumsy attempt to get a taste of the liquor from the almost empty glass is a touching symbol of the insatiable craving for experiences that were never hers because they were unreal and belonged entirely to the realms of her imagination.

Perhaps because I have given my time so much to poetry, I tend to live in a world of description, the very one you call your greatest difficulty. This not only fills the body of my work; it becomes what I find I most relish in other writers. Because descriptive elements often bear so rich a burden of meaning. This is as true of Hardy as of Shakespeare; of Yeats as of Conrad. I acknowledge that this is the prejudice of the poet speaking for "my nature is subdued / By what it works in, like the dyer's hand [Shakespeare Sonnet 111]." Enough pontificating. Please forgive me. It's probably due to the fact that retirement from teaching has left me without the docile audience I had grown undeservedly used to. [. . .]

Affectionately,

Tony

*Timothy Murphy (1951–) is a poet, translator (of Beowulf), memoirist, and agri-
cultural entrepreneur, who lives in North Dakota. Hecht wrote an introduction for
Murphy's second book of poems, Very Far North (2002). Hecht's "Instructions" is
an appropriately foreshortened sonnet in thirteen lines.*

January 15, 1999 Washington DC

Dear Tim:

The goings-on in this city are so depressing as to have driven me to the
following:

Instructions to a Painter for the Capital Dome

Borne up on cappuccino froths of cloud,
Two grizzled gods, beefy, contemptuous,
Should look down casually at the likes of us
Benighted taxpayers, who are allowed
To view them and their kind at stated hours,
Spouters of solecistic filibusters,
Smug, well-heeled heels of the legislative powers,
The whole to be titled <u>Venality and Greed</u>
<u>Triumphant over Merit and Common Sense</u>.
Let there be drapes of scarlet, massive reds,
Gold leaf thickly applied at our expense,
And, as baroque foreshortening has decreed,
Enormous butts and little pointy heads.

Aside from the imbecilities of the Congress (with Henry Hyde supposing
he was quoting that exemplary man, Sir Thomas More, about honoring one's
oath, when in fact he was quoting a film script of <u>A Man For All Seasons</u>; like
many others, Hyde can't distinguish between reality and Hollywood) the city
has, as of last night, been sorely troubled by an ice storm, and today not only
are the streets impassable, but water-mains are bursting everywhere, and the
trees are glistening at every tip with brilliant glazes. All this would be tolerable
from my selfish point of view except for the fact that my mother-in-law, who is
96, lives in a retirement apartment in Bethesda which is without electricity and
heat because of the storm, and unless power is restored quickly, I will have to

rescue her later today. The streets are fairly well cleared by now, but the city is still semi-paralyzed, like the minds of the Senate, along with those of us incautious enough to have watched the impeachment-trial proceedings [of President Clinton]. No doubt in Fargo you can smirk at our complaints about the weather. So I hope this will furnish you with a couple of laughs.

All good wishes,
Tony

January 18, 1999 Washington DC

[To Jon Stallworthy]

Dear Jon,

Many warm thanks to you for your Christmas card, as well as for your explosion of indignation at OUP for its abandonment of its modern poetry list. You were right to suppose I had heard about it before you wrote. The first to let me know was Jacky Simms, who phoned and was almost grief-stricken, and seemed to feel that she personally had let me down. I next learned of it from Philip Hoy, one of the editors of Between the Lines, who has "interviewed" me by correspondence, and who sent me copies of the news (and outbursts against it) that had appeared in the London press. Thirdly, came an embarrassed and embarrassing letter from one Andrew Potter ("Director, Music, Trade Paperbacks and Bibles Publishing") who sent what was in effect a "form letter" that must have gone to all the poets on the list. There was no real "explanation" for the decision, and Jacky had assured me that the list "paid for itself," and even made a profit for the press (though I imagine this was not great). I found a charming irony in the appointment of a "Bibles" director to distribute the bad news. I feel, having had time to digest the news, sorriest for Jacky herself, whose life has not been an easy one, and who now must be out of a job. Next in order, I feel sorry for those poets on the list—Porter, Enright, Wallace-Crabbe, Scupham among them—whose sole publisher was OUP, and who, cast overboard, must flounder unless picked up by some chance vessel that turns up to rescue them. Others (Brodsky, Zbigniew Herbert and I) have other resources. Still, it is a great disappointment. And not least because of the "interview" [with Hoy] I mentioned earlier. I think it's a lively and interesting one, more detailed and more thoughtful than any I've given before, and the sort of thing that ought to prompt interest in my poems. But it may be that by that time they will no longer be available in England. It was very kind of you to offer to vend my work elsewhere, but I don't want to put you to that trouble. The needs of Peter Porter, et al, are truly more urgent than mine, and it was heartening to know his work sells as well as it does. I am content to wait until fate finds me a publisher over there. [. . .]

This comes with love to you and Jill and all the long Farm Hands.[2]

Tony

January 29, 1999 Washington, DC

[To David Mason]

My dear David,

[. . .] Meditations on mortality are altogether in order for someone my age; of the family into which I was born, I am the only survivor, my younger brother having died a good number of years ago. I have begun to feel the agues and other vexations that must have afflicted Justice Shallow. And, like him, I'm aware that many of my juniors have died. Among the poets these would include Jim Wright, Jimmy Merrill, Joseph Brodsky, Ed Sissman, Anne Sexton, Sylvia Plath, Ted Hughes . . . But it is your fortune cookie that struck a special echoic note of great importance for me. On one of the last days in February, 1971, I got a Chinese fortune cookie that told me: "Nobody will mar your happy future." This seemed so admirable an omen that, whereas I normally paid no attention to these things, I packed this one away carefully in my wallet. On the fourth of March I met Helen. Some years later, when we were settled in our East Boulevard house in Rochester, Helen decided to compose a set of scrapbooks for me, of clippings and other memoranda of my life before we met, as well as after. This included that fortune cookie message, which I had kept. It also included my pocket calendar of that year, with notations of our meeting and of subsequent dating, and a "map" of the seating plan of the students in the Smith College class she took with me. [. . .]

Affectionately,

Tony

Philip Hoy, editor of The Waywiser Press, *and, among other writings and interviews, the author/editor of* In Conversation with Anthony Hecht *(1999; rev. 3rd ed., 2004).*

June 18, 1999 Washington DC

Dear Philip,

[. . .] The director of the Rochester Memorial Art Gallery [Grant Holcomb] [. . .] invited me to write a poem about one of his paintings.[3] You may remem-

---

[2]Long Farm is the name of the Stallworthy home in Oxfordshire.

[3]Hecht's poem, "The Road to Damascus," included in *Voices in the Gallery: Writers on Art*, ed. Grant Holcomb (University of Rochester Press, 2001), appears in *The Darkness and the Light*.

ber that I wrote a villanelle that turned out to be unsuitable ["Nocturne: A Recurring Dream"], but which I can still publish without reference to the Winslow Homer painting upon which it was nominally a comment. Having had to abandon the Homer, I turned instead to a painting that meant more to me as subject than as pictorial image. It's by Francesco Ubertini (known as Il Bacchiacca) and it exhibits a sort of Mannerist awkwardness that in this case I find rather off-putting: puzzles about the perspectival size of figures in foreground, middle-ground and background, among other anomalies. Anyway, the painting is about the conversion of St. Paul, his "vision" on the road to Damascus. This is a topic that has preoccupied me for a very long time, and Paul is someone I have found profoundly troubling. Some of the conjectures about him I acquired from a book I have known for many years: From Jesus to Paul, by Joseph Klausner [1944] who is particularly good about the likelihood that Paul was epileptic, and, on testimony from Dostoevski and Mohamet, what the effects of seizures are like to the one experiencing them. [. . .]

With warmest greetings,
Tony

July 12, 1999 Washington DC

[To Hayàt Mathews]

My dear Hayàt,

You and I are about to disagree on the topic you raise regarding rhyme in translation. My view has no bearing, needless to say, upon your father's translations.[4] But I have given a good deal of thought to this matter, and have compared various kinds of translations. Once you acknowledge that no translation is going to be perfect, the overwhelming problem that remains is: if perfection is impossible, what can be conveyed with the greatest fidelity? Let me quote something I said in an interview in The Paris Review some years ago, that bears on this. "In his comments on his translation of Villon, Galway Kinnell has written, 'I decided against using meter and rhyme . . . What is more expressive of a poet than his images? Yet in rhyming translations we can't even be sure that the images are the poet's . . . And I wonder, do rhyme and meter mean for us what they meant for Villon? It may be that in our day these formal devices have become a dead hand, which it is just as well not to lay on any poetry.'" I find that view utterly wrong, and for two reasons. The first is the comparatively modern heresy that the most important element in a poem is its imagery. I discuss this

[4]See head note to Hecht's letter of December 17, 1997.

briefly in the Mellon Lectures where I observe that "there is a fine body of excellent poetry, some of it of the very first class, that comes close to being devoid of imagery" and I instance two Shakespeare sonnets ("Farewell, thou art too dear . . ." and "Th' expense of spirit. . ."), Robert Frost's "Provide, Provide," the first section of Eliot's "East Coker," and Thomas Wyatt's "Forget not yet" [*On the Laws of the Poetic Art*, p. 20]. No less important, Villon was a great maker of Ballades, a difficult and demanding form: it is commonly 28 lines long, and contains only three rhyme sounds for the entire poem.[5] This is extraordinarily demanding on the vocabulary, the sinuosity, the craft and deftness of the poet, and it's easy to see why Kinnell decided to eliminate the whole problem. But no small part of our pleasure in reading a ballade consists in seeing how skillfully the poet meets this challenge. If his careful deftness of deployment of words appointed to appear at rhyming positions is surgically removed by the translator, we are being given something very diluted, and, from my point of view, unsatisfactory.

[. . .]

Love,
Tony

September 1, 1999 Washington DC

[To David Havird]

Dear David,

[. . .] I also was grateful for your comments on my poems. As to "The Darkness and the Light," I really meant by "peat" something soft, which in the dark might seem plush and velvety, as opposed to stony and hard. The speaker is not so much "observing the twilight of a day of wine, women and song" as he is observing a twilight and diminution of all that is rich and lovely, and envelopment of life in the mounting gloom and darkness. The sparks "bedded in peat" are not meant to be dangerously combustible; they are meant to have settled into a plush darkness, like fine jewels set off on a jeweler's tray of dark velvet. As for "Late Afternoon," you are entirely right to feel that the joy being celebrated is the perilous joy of that single moment in time, a moment that carries no assurance of lasting, and is therefore fragile and vulnerable in its brief duration. The "caulking" was not meant to seem ominous; just to provide a strong and distinctive smell, and not an especially romantic one. In fact, it's only her intoxicated

[5]See Hecht's own ballade, "Death the Poet: A Ballade—Lament for the Makers," collected in *Flight Among the Tombs*. The final quatrain appears on his gravestone at Bard.

elation that can somehow absorb into its bliss the oakum and fried smelts, the yelping of dogs, the creosote, the oil . . .

This comes with warmest greetings.

Tony

Hecht's letter below was written in response to the following topic for inclusion in The Yale Literary Magazine *(Winter 2000).*

"In his essay, 'Making, Knowing, Judging,' W. H. Auden offers a model for the developing writer's relationship with his early influences":

A would-be writer serves his apprenticeship in a library. Though the Master is deaf and dumb and gives neither instruction nor criticism, the apprentice can choose any Master he likes, living or dead, the Master is available at any hour of the day or night, lessons are all for free, and his passionate admiration of his Master will ensure that he work hard to please him.

"Who were your masters and why? What did you take from their projects, and how did you learn to leave those voices behind to create something distinctly yours? When you write today, are you able to read your Masters without their styles creeping back into your own?"

November 3, 1999 Washington DC

Dear Messrs. [Gregory] Tigani and [Callie] Wright,

Here are some rough answers to your three questions.

My early literary heroes were Eliot, John Crowe Ransom, Hardy, Auden, early Robert Lowell, along with John Donne, Marvell, and Yeats. Of these I personally knew only Ransom; the rest I studied and emulated at a distance, receiving, as Auden says in your quotation from him, "neither instruction nor criticism." The apprenticeship of a young poet is often a matter of servile imitation; and this is not a bad thing, if it can be controlled and overcome. Keats started out writing imitations of Spenser; Robert Lowell was imitating Milton and Marvell; Eliot imitated Laforgue; Shakespeare, in I Henry IV, in the great scene (2.4.) in which Falstaff "plays" the King, imitates these lines of Lyly's Euphues: The Anatomy of Wit, "Too much study doth intoxicate the brains, for (they say) although iron the more it is used the brighter it is, yet silver with much wearing doth waste to nothing; though the cammock [a crooked staff] the more it is bowed the better it serveth, yet the bow the more it is bent and occupied the weaker it waxeth; though the camomile the more it is todden and pressed down the more it spreadeth, yet the violet the oftener it is handled and touched the sooner it withereth and decayeth." There can not be many poets of any merit who have not seriously apprenticed themselves to masters of their own choice, and often those among the illustrious dead. There was a time when I wrote too much like Lowell imitating Milton. One gets over these early crushes. And I can now read almost any poet without danger of infection from their style. It may be added that sometimes one wishes deliberately to sound like a certain poet other than oneself, especially when translating. I have, for example, (and not in a translation) tried to write a poem that resembles the verse of the Old Testament.

> Yours,
> Anthony Hecht

Mary Jo Salter (1954–), poet and editor, taught many years at Mt. Holyoke College. She is now on the faculty of the Writing Seminars at the Johns Hopkins University.

November 8, 1999 Washington DC

Dear Mary Jo,

You were right in suspecting that I returned to a very Mont Blanc of mail: three postal bins full of the stuff, much of it, of course, to be discarded, but it took a day to sort things out before even beginning the task of answering what called for answers. I haven't yet caught up entirely. The worst of it is the bad news you come back to; two friends hospitalized one of them over ninety with pneumonia, another with kidney failure. Consequently, this will be a poor reply to your very long letter, and its congeries of many topics. There's no way I could hope to address all the questions that you raise, but I would at least venture the comment that as regards the "delayed resolution" or "delayed satisfaction" of rhyme in Herbert's "Denial" and Hardy's "A Light Snowfall After Frost," Herbert seeks purposeful dissonance in the final lines of each stanza until the last one; whereas Hardy simply withholds the gratification of consonance for a fairly long time, keeping our attention suspended, our appetite unappeased until he is quite ready to satisfy us. Take a comparable technique of "delayed" or "suspended" rhyme in Arnold's "Dover Beach." "Roar," which ends line 9, only is granted its mate in line 22, and again in line 25. That's a long interval to hold a sound in the ear's memory, waiting, either patiently or impatiently, for resolution. And, as you know, there are plenty of poems in which only some of the lines rhyme, and not always the corresponding lines of different stanzas. [. . .]

> Love to you both,
> Tony

December 15, 1999 Washington DC

[To David Mason]

Dear David,

[. . .] Tomorrow I am to be whisked to a BBC studio here in Washington, there to be interviewed by radio from New York by a young lady who is assembling a collection of such interviews, all of them about Joseph Brodsky. [. . .] The invitation gave me a chance to reread some of the poetry, and to think about it. And in the course of thinking I seemed suddenly to remember a critical essay by Empson called, I think, "Donne: The Space Man," or something like that. I've looked high and low for it, but can't come up with it. [Empson's essay appeared in *The Kenyon Review* 19 (1957)]. As I recall, it focused, reasonably enough, on the effect of the Copernican revolution on Donne's thought and imagery. And it seems to me that Brodsky is more given to imagery drawn from the Space-Time continuum than any other poet I can think of; and among his earliest poems is an "Elegy for John Donne." I would like to say something about this tomorrow, if I have a chance.

This comes with love from Helen as from me,

Tony

2000

Shirley Hazzard (1931–) is the author of many works of fiction and nonfiction, including Greene on Capri, a Memoir *(2000), to which Hecht is responding.*

February 25, 2000 Washington DC

My dear Shirley:

I've read through your Greene Thoughts with all deliberate loitering, delighting in so many things along the way, the lovely deployment of your language, the elegance, the ricercare, of composition, musical in its every aspect, the open and welcome candor about everything of importance, and not least about the prickly and even forbidding qualities in Greene himself. It is far more than a memoir; it is full of suggestive depths and seemingly casual riches that conduce to long mulling. Perhaps because I was in neighboring Ischia in the late 40s and early 50s, much of the landscape shows again with all its damp or warm authenticity, its steep inclines, vineyards, rural simplicities. Ischians used to boast, in those days, that they grew and pressed the grapes that were bottled and sold as Capresi wine, chiefly because Capri didn't have enough room for sufficient vineyards, given over as it largely was to tourist trade.

I was also prompted to think, not for the first time, of the importance of silence to some writers, though not to others. As doubtless you know, Hart Crane used to play jazz music loudly on radio and records while he was writing poems. Of all sounds that would absolutely prohibit any work of mine, music of any sort, either classical or pop, would be first. It calls attention to itself, with its own syntax, its own line of development, blotting out, for me, my own slowly developing lines of thought. Random street noise I can generally disregard, unless it is extremely loud. Conversation, of course, is impossible. I used to envy the artist, Leonard Baskin, who used to work late into the evenings, doing the most delicate wood engravings or etchings, and entertaining company, me among them, while concentratedly at work, but able to converse with guests nevertheless. Nothing of that sort has ever been possible for me.

Chiefly, of course, I was led to ponder, as all your readers will be, on Greene's extraordinary, willful, and often selfish character. I am not referring to moments of pettiness or explosive rage, though these are unpleasant enough. I'm led to mull upon his apparent need to have as his mistress a woman who is married to someone else. This cannot be set down to mere mischief. I suppose there are no end of reasons that draw people into adulterous affairs, that there's no formula, even psychoanalytic, to describe the need that compels this triangular situation. But I have seen enough of it in the course of time—have, I confess, once involved myself in such a situation—but much more often have considered the motives of others; and rarely if ever have I thought it anything but self-indulgent as well as cruel. The role of the ego in matters of love is probably the most difficult thing to account for, and perhaps except for other-worldly love, can never be kept in decent order. But in Greene's case it almost seems as though the compliant husband was nearly as essential to him as the indulgent wife. From the point of view which concerns itself with egotism, this is particularly striking. [. . .]

This comes to you with love from us both.

Tony

Deborah Garrison succeeded Harry Ford as the poetry editor at Knopf. Hecht is discussing the order and format for The Darkness and the Light.

March 17, 2000 Washington DC

Dear Deborah Garrison,

[. . .] Regarding the introduction of "Mirror" and "The Ceremony of Innocence" into the sequence, I have given the problem a good deal of thought, and have at length decided to put "Mirror" (which, by the way, The New York Review of Books has just accepted) right after "Memory" and before "Samson." It's a poem that will, without danger of weakness, break up the seriousness of the sequence in which it would find itself in the way of immediate context. "Ceremony" I think will fit well between "Poppy" and "The Road to Damascus."

As to the cover, I would like you (and Chip Kidd, if he is to have a hand in this) to consider the use of a ceiling painting by Giambattista Tiepolo of The Sacrifice of Isaac that is in the Archbishop's Palace in Udine, and is reproduced on page 203 of Michael Levey's Painting in Eighteenth Century Venice, published by Yale. It has, to my mind, these factors in its favor. 1) It is pertinent to the biggest poem in the book, 2) By virtue of its dramatic chiaroscuro it displays the "Darkness and the Light" of the book's title, and, finally, Tiepolo is a favorite painter of my wife and son as well as mine. I don't mean to sound inflexible on this point, for the painting may not be available for such use, or only after payment of an extortionate fee. There are also two Rembrandt drawings of the same subject, both to be found in Volume II of The Drawings of Rembrandt, edited by Seymour Slive and published by Dover [1965]. They are plates 471 and 530, the first in Berlin, the second in London. I am open to further suggestions on this topic.

I confess myself puzzled about your feeling that a poem dedicated to someone makes a reader feel "left out," as though the poem were meant to be understood only by the dedicatee. I've never encountered anyone before who held this view. Only occasionally are poems composed with a solitary reader in mind, as when Milton addresses a sonnet to Cyriack Skinner, or John Donne or Ben Jonson address verse epistles to friends. The far more usual modern practice is to write a poem that the poet thinks good enough to serve as a suitable homage to some friend; but the poem is almost always composed first with no special audience in mind, and the dedicatee is chosen much afterwards. [. . .]

Anthony Hecht

Henry A. Millon (1927–), dean of the Center for Advanced Study in the Visual Arts at the National Gallery (1976–2000), Washington, D.C., is the author of a number of books, including the one mentioned below.

April 24, 2000 Washington DC

Dear Hank,

Through a mail catalogue I got hold of a copy of The Triumph of the Baroque, which we had earlier admired during our residence in Bogliasco, but which only now am I able to appreciate with something like the full sense of its genuinely triumphant impact and stature. [. . .]

Early in the book, around page 61 I think, there's a beautiful color photograph of the exterior baroque brick-work of San Andrea delle Fratte, which brought vividly to mind a visit Helen and I paid to that church one especially hot summer some years ago. The interior seemed an especially cool and welcome sanctuary from the punishing outdoor temperature, and the dimness of shadow a retreat from the glare of the streets. Gradually, as our eyes adjusted, we came upon a plaque commemorating a singular event that had taken place in the church not long since. I transcribe it here in a French account, the only one I have been able to locate, though I feel sure the plaque was multilingual, and that we read the details in English.

> M. Ratisbonne, un juif, appurtenant à une très-riche famille d'Alsace, qui se trouvait accidentellment à Rome, se promenant dans l'église de S. Andrea delle Fratte pendant qu'on y faisait les préparatifs pour les obsèques de M.l de la Ferronays, s'y est converti subitement. Il se trouvait debout en face d'une chapelle dédice à l'ange gardien, à quelque pas, lorsque tout-à-coup il a eu une apparition lumineuse de la Sainte Vierge qui lui a fait signe d'aller vers cette chapelle. Une force irrésistible l'y a entrainé, il y est tombé à genoux, et il a été à l'instant chrètien.[6]

After digesting some equivalent of this, Helen and I looked at one another with something of a wild surmise, and made our way with great dispatch and delicacy out of the church. We were of course fully aware that I was not a rich man with rich Alsatian connections—something dim but persistent in my memory tells me that Ratisbonne was identified quite specifically as a "banker"—but, given the devious and acquisitive ways of the BVM [Blessed Virgin Mary], the shameless advantage that must have been taken against one who probably only entered the church to escape the heat, as we had done, it seemed best to leave. Among all its other treasures, your book will always recall my narrow escape.

Gratefully and with admiration,

Tony

[6] A rich Alsatian Jew named Ratisbone found himself one day in Rome. As he walked about the church of S. Andrea delle Fratte he noticed that preparations were being made for the funeral of M. de la Ferronays. In an instant he saw the light. Standing in front of a chapel dedicated to the guardian angel, he experienced a sudden vision of the Virgin Mary. She told him to walk toward the chapel. An irresistible force drew him there. He fell on his knees. In an instant he became a Christian.

Francine du Plessix Gray (1930–) is the author of many works of fiction, biography, and autobiography. The two friends referred to are, respectively, Helen Bacon and William Maxwell.

September 6, 2000 Washington DC

Dear Francine:

Thank you very much for sending me your thoughtful and eloquent memoir-cum-meditation on mortality. By striking coincidence, it arrived in the same mail as a new biography of St. Augustine, to whose life you make reference in your essay.

It seems to me as I approach my seventy-eighth year that I have been acquainted with death from very early in my life; and by acquainted I mean intimately acquainted. I no longer have much fear as regards my own death, though I dread the possibility of preliminary pains that may precede it. I am much more distressed by the thought of the misery my death will give to my family. I feel none of the need for the comforts of ritual grieving for others: there have been too many, beginning well before my front-line combat infantry service in WWII. I have felt no inclination to police my grief, or to formalize it through public acts of piety. But this does not mean any less respect for the rituals of mourning you so movingly describe.

Yesterday I spoke by phone with an old friend, four years my senior, a brilliant classical scholar, who is now wheel-chair-bound, suffers from an obscure neurological illness, and who said she doesn't expect to still be alive when an article of hers will be published next year. She lives now in a permanent state of discomfort, as well as disability.

At the same time, I know very well, and very deeply, that I would be at so great a loss as to be virtually paralyzed were one of those I love—my wife, or our son—to predecease me. I confess I have no psychological provisions for such a calamity. Another friend told me not long ago (being at the time over ninety) that while he would never commit suicide, he felt entitled to the option of refusing to eat. About a week after his wife died, he stopped eating, and died shortly thereafter. No doubt after a certain age, the ambitions that sustain us in youth cease to play any role in our lives, and we have to fall back upon love. And when that is gone, we are truly bereft.

Thank you once again for sending me your essay.

Tony

Garry Wills (1934–) is a prolific author and emeritus professor of history, North-western University. The passage in question can be found in Venice: Lion City: The Religion of Empire *(New York: Simon & Shuster, 2001), p. 276.*

September 17, 2000 Washington DC

Dear Garry,

I'm delighted by your fine, lively and scholarly comments on the Schiavoni Carpaccios, and very grateful to you for the gift of them. It may amuse you to know that when we first visited Venice we brought our son, Evan, with us, and he was five at the time. The city's grandeur and glamour were not at all lost on him. And one morning, pointing excitedly to Mark's lion, he cried, "Look, my name!" And there, indeed, inscribed on the open book, were the words,

PAX	EVAN
TIBI	GELIS
MAR	TA
CE	MEUS

There was one comment of yours, about St. Augustine's study, that puzzled me. You write: "It is a supernatural light that shines on Augustine's uplifted face, passing through the astrolabe (symbolically, through the created universe, from beyond it). We know this light's special character from the contrast with natural light, which enters from the opposite direction to shine on the apparatus in the recessed cabinet."

The two directions of light might conceivably be rationalized architecturally, and without recourse to the supernatural. I must hasten to say that I am not opposed to the assertion of supernatural sources of light, and in Marilyn Lavin's study of Piero della Francesca's The Flagellation, she makes what seems to me an incontrovertible case for a hidden and supernatural source of light. But in Carpaccio's painting, if we confine our sense of light initially to the study itself, the rectilinear room, and its recessed apse, all the light enters from the right-hand side where three windows admit it. This light falls on the saint's face, his habit, his hands, and crosses the pages of an open book at his feet in a downward slant. It casts a shadow of the figure of Christ on the apse's wall. And, indeed, all the shadows in the room—of the dog, the furnishings and the bishop's cope, lie to the left of the objects that cast them. If we were to think of this room as giving on an open courtyard to its left, then the brilliance of circumambient morning light would flood in from the opposite side to the little room with its pyramidal book-rack. I have never had trouble reconciling these light sources in a naturalistic way, for in Venice especially the light leaps from no single source but from a rich diffusion of reflections and refractions.

I'm a little shy about sending you my comments on Galatians, but I'll send them on later, if you really think you would like to see them. I am no scholar, or even a reader of scripture with any trained gifts or learning in the field. I wrote my essay, which was published in 1990, for a book edited by Alfred Corn, and published by Penguin Books. I was one of many laymen invited by the editor to express their views of one of the books of the New Testament. The volume itself was called Incarnation. John Updike and Reynolds Price were among the more thoughtful contributors. I suppose I would have to count myself among the more disgruntled. Though perhaps not quite as much as David Plante, a lapsed Catholic and gay rights advocate, who wrote on Romans, and held the entire Catholic Church and all its clergy responsible for the unhappiness and frustrations of his childhood and youth. Paul has seemed to me in many ways a most uncongenial and unsympathetic figure, and I have written about him in a poem I enclose ["The Road to Damascus"].

With admiring and grateful good wishes,

Tony

Philip Stephens (1966–), poet, song writer, and novelist, studied with Hecht at Sewanee Writers' Conference.

September 24, 2000 Washington DC

My dear Phil,

Thank you for the generously inscribed copy of your book [*The Determined Days*] which, I may add, richly deserves the commendations on its jacket, especially mine. I'm glad to have it, though I want you to know that at least in my own case your publisher was responsible enough to send me a copy; so I have one to offer to a suitably worthy reader when I come across one. I shall, of course, retain the inscribed one with fierce pride. [. . .]

When you write, "Any time I stand up to read the poems it feels like they were a lifetime ago, and someone else's life at that," you were right to add, "Maybe that's normal." As far as my experience goes, it is. And this is not to be regarded as a bad thing, though it is admittedly disorienting. It means that even in the brief course of, possibly a few days, between the composition of a poem and its performance in a reading, or its appearance in print, the poet himself has changed. Writing the poem was itself part of the mechanism of the change. We do alter with time, and good poets alter for the better. Pound once said that no poet was to be valued who did not change with time and this is one of the faults of Cummings, whose cute or sentimental poems are alike early and late, and there's no reliable way to tell an early from a late one.

Phil, I would be pleased to look at some of your new work. It was most considerate of you to ask in advance; not all poets are as thoughtful. In your particular case, I so much admire what I have already seen that I look forward to new work from you.

This comes with warm affection,
Tony

Dorothea Tanning (1910–2012), wife of the surrealist painter Max Ernst, was a painter, poet, memoirist, and novelist. Katharyn Aal (Katharyn Howd Machan) is a poet who teaches at Ithaca College.

October 26, 2000 Washington DC

My dear Dorothea:

Your fine card with its Maxfield Parrish painting of "The Enchanted Prince" brought to mind a poem by one Katharyn Aal, which you may not know, but which I think you might like. It is called "Hazel Tells Laverne."

last night
im cleanin out my
howard johnsons ladies room
when all of a sudden
up pops this frog
musta come from the sewer
swimmin aroun an tryin ta
climb up the sida the bowl
so i goes ta flushm down
but sohelpmegod he starts talkin
bout a golden ball
an how i can be a princess
me a princess
well my mouth drops
all the way to the floor
an he says

kiss me just kiss me
once on the nose
well i screams
ya little green pervert
an I hitsm with my mop
an has ta flush
the toilet down three times
me
a princess

We both send love.
Tony

Michael Blumenthal (1949–), poet, essayist, novelist, and peripatetic educator, was director of the Creative Writing Program at Harvard from 1983 to 1992.

October 30, 2000 Washington DC

Dear Michael,

Thank you for your letter and its enclosures. I must confess that I don't know exactly how I feel in this matter of German guilt about the Nazi era. On a simple rational level, I would go along with your argument that just as white Americans would bridle at being held guilty for nineteenth-century slavery, or the virtual extermination of the American Indian tribes, so those Germans who were born long after the Nazi atrocities do not care to inherit a guilt for something they had no part in. Reasonable enough. But it is worth adding that neo-Nazi movements have cropped up again, and they have not done so in Australia or Finland or Spain, but in Germany. To be sure, we have our native reactionary bigots, and they form themselves into organizations with pass-words and handshakes and capes and clownish hats, though no less poisonous for all that. But no one in this country, however demented, has seriously proposed reintroducing slavery as an institution. We have, somehow, gotten beyond that. Not much beyond, perhaps; but still and all, beyond that. This, however, is not the case in Germany. It's one reason I could not bear to go back there. I was there during the war, and I saw one of the camps, still filled with prisoners who were dying of typhus at the rate of 500 a day. I spoke to some of them. I have never had nightmares more terrible than my memories of those days. I am, I fear, unforgiving; perhaps more unforgiving than some actual survivors of the camps. My touchstones in this matter are Elie Wiesel and Primo Levi. To read them is to feel that forgiveness is not easily purchased, and that a culture that continues to produce neo-Nazis is one I would prefer not to confront.

As for my review of Amichai, I thank you for your praise of it. His book is not only superb, but would, all by itself, have merited a Nobel prize. For a while there, I thought I would get a lot of angry letters, not about my appraisal of Amichai, but about some of the rash theological and scriptural points I raised. (That may yet come to pass; the issue has not been out for long.) For example, the claim (which I can document) that the pun on Peter's name has given rise to Protestant/Catholic hostilities. Anyway, the book is a triumph, and I'm glad you share my view of it. I just noticed that I can fax this to you, and so this comes with warm greetings on the very day it was written.

Tony

Shawn Holliday (1969–), an English professor now at Northwestern Oklahoma State University, wrote to a number of authors, hoping to put together a collection of essays on American writers and popular music.

November 6, 2000 Washington DC

Dear Mr. Holliday,

Here's my attempt to respond to your inquiry about popular music.

I came to popular music, more specifically to dixieland jazz, rather warily and through the backdoor of classical music. Not by way of Gershwin or Copland, but from Johann Sebastian Bach. My first love (after an infantile infatuation with Tchaikovsky) went almost directly to Bach, and I treasured the Brandenburg Concerti in a 78rpm recording that featured Alexander Schneider's chamber orchestra with Rudolph Serkin. From Bach as a home base, I ventured outward to Mozart, Beethoven and Brahms, and was long content to spend my time within their royal preserves. My discovery of dixieland occurred, rather surprisingly, in Europe, and through the agency of a friend who, like me, had a fine library of classical recordings, including all the Artur Schnabel renditions of the Beethoven sonatas. He also had some dixieland records, and since we were in Paris, where American popular music was much admired and widely available, I bought some rather wonderful second- or third-hand badly scratched acetate disks of the very old bands and the earliest performers. These included Scott Joplin, Louis Armstrong, Sidney Bechet, Bunk Johnson, Earl Hines, Art Tatum, Jelly Roll Morton, and Fats Waller. And the performances that settled into a sort of canonical solidity in my auditory memory and imagination were, in no special order, "Quincy Street Stomp," "Maple Leaf Rag," "Muskrat Ramble," "When the Saints Go Marching In," "China Boy," "Stomping At the Savoy," "On the Sunny Side of the Street," "Basin Street Blues," and "Honeysuckle Rose."

With a stern purity that belongs to youthful prigs, I loftily rejected any extrinsic, non-musical valuations of music that are characterized by the commonplace expression: "They're playing our tune." Music for me was pure music, without bearing upon where or with whom I first heard it. With the passing of time and the acquisition of experience I began to make comparative evaluations of various performers, to feel that there was no perfect or ideal version of any composition, and that one could enjoy Scarlatti both on the harpsichord and the piano; just as one could approve different versions of a Scott Joplin rag. My puritanism began to dissolve, and I started to recall with gratitude my earliest encounters with particular performers or composers. In one way my tastes in popular and classical music exhibit a curious parallel: while there are great symphonies and concerti (by Mozart, Beethoven, etc.) that I am happy to listen to, in the course of time I have found myself increasingly drawn to small chamber works and solo performances, in which it is possible to take full cognizance of everything that is going on—to hear each voice independently and in collaboration with each of its partners. Similarly, a small jazz group (as opposed to the "big bands" of the 40s) allows complex satisfactions afforded by the improvised accommodations of all instrumentalists to one another, and in this resembles the classical form of "theme and variations."

When I was a schoolboy, my classmates, with whom I rarely saw eye-to-eye, were enamoured of the big bands: Artie Shaw, Tommy Dorsey, Glenn Miller, and Benny Goodman. None of these interested me at the time, though I later became fond of Goodman as a clarinetist, and I like his performances with small groups. So even my love of popular music is of a kind with my tastes in the classics: both for the earliest, and for the best established. It follows that I don't like rock or country music, or rap, bluegrass, soul, reggae or punk. My twenty-eight-year-old son is fond of a variety (the name of which I don't know) that is tuneless and wholly percussion, and, I understand from him, very fashionable. But at the age of seventy-eight, I'm content to be old-fashioned.

There used to be a radio program, originating, I think, in England, but copied in this country, and called "Desert Island Discs." Like the equivalent stumper about books, it asked what you would take to a desert island where you would be indefinitely exiled to solitary meditations, and where you could seek comfort, uplift, [and] pleasure, from a very select group of works that, above all, had to prove durable. Getting old is very instructive in such matters. I used to feel confident in my choices of Shakespeare plays, for example. But time has taught me that my views of the Shakespeare canon have altered over the years, and I have learned to detect treasures where formerly I had overlooked or under-appreciated them. This can be said more fully of music, both classical and popular. One can tire of a particular performance, even an excellent one, and feel grateful for an alternative interpretation, that brings freshness to details that were ignored or overlooked in a familiar recording. For this reason I am unwilling to put any musical performances in a preferential order.

Sincerely,

Anthony Hecht

October 26, 2000 Washington DC

[To Philip Hoy]

Dear Philip,

[. . .] I'll begin with the story I promised earlier to tell you about Don's [Donald Justice's] friend, Henri Coulette [1927–1988], who plays in it the role of the messenger in Oedipus or the Agamemnon, who reveals the great off-stage truths. As you know, I've been sorting out my papers in the expectation of selling them, and have been going through individual cartons of them to assist an appraiser. In one of them I found a postcard from Louis Simpson, in which he thanked me for agreeing to recommend him for a Guggenheim; and saying that from the vantage of his post at Berkeley he would see what he could do to get me invited out to read at several campuses in California. Years went by and nothing eventuated about such readings, though Louis got his Guggenheim. And so, after the passing of years I was living alone in quiet bachelorhood in Rochester, NY, teaching at the university when I got a phone call from one Henri Coulette, whose name I knew and whose work I admired, but whom I had never met. He had been awarded a grant to tour the country, interviewing poets about their work and work-habits, and wondered if he might visit me with a tape-recorder. I was delighted to agree, and he duly turned up, and I came over with a bottle of booze, and we sat around his motel, drinking and talking for the better part of an afternoon. I liked him a lot, and we had a number of friends and literary heroes in common. Toward the end of our meeting he confessed that he had phoned me initially with some trepidation and uneasiness. He had been teaching at California State [University] in Los Angeles, and the various California universities had formed a consortium by way of pooling their small resources to bring poets to read seriatim on their campuses from distant parts of the nation. Henri had proposed my name with enthusiasm, but

Louis Simpson, representing Berkeley, demurred. He explained that I suffered from a very pronounced speech defect, and that it would be a kindness not to expose me to public terror and humiliation that a poetry reading by me would certainly entail. Since Simpson was the only one of the group who could claim to know me personally, his word on the subject was final. Henri explained that when I answered his phone call, he was astonished and pleased to find I could talk without difficulty. [. . .]

I've written a short (700 words max) essay on Tennyson's song, "Now sleeps the crimson petal, now the white," trying to explain the pronoun "she" in the sixth line in reference to the peacock, which is male. I've sent a copy to Christopher Ricks, and will let you know what he says. I've spoken with him on the phone about it, and he acknowledges it is a puzzle he never gave attention to before. [. . .]

All the best to Evelina and to you.

Tony

December 29, 2000 Washington DC

[To Brad Leithauser and Mary Jo Salter]

Dear Brad and Mary Jo,

This comes with warm and grateful thanks for your generous gifts. The crimson heart was right out of [Richard] Crashaw, and now adorns our tree, but the CD is another matter altogether. Those Schumann trios are quite wonderful, and were unknown to me. The liner notes urge one to find affinities to Mendelssohn, who was admittedly greatly admired by Schumann. Nevertheless, I found myself feeling the rich effects of Brahms, who was another Schumann hero. I only recently finished reading a fine Brahms biography by Jan Swafford, which I can strongly recommend. Schumann, and, of course, Clara, both play major roles in the story, Schumann's particularly pathetic and moving. Lots of supporting characters, chiefly Wagner, Liszt, Chopin, but plenty of conductors and critics as well. Schumann's special brand of madness, which was suicidal, is beautifully described, and made altogether sympathetic; and this is the more striking in that one of the other presents I received this season (from Helen) was the <u>unabridged</u> journals of Sylvia Plath, a book that is nearly repellent in its narcissistic self-absorption, and has a number of quite mean things to say about me, some of them very peculiar indeed, such as the claim that I have my hair "professionally curled." She was really stark raving bonkers. She also claimed that I squirreled away my <u>Hudson Review</u> Fellowship, wishing to hoard it at a time when both Sylvia and Ted were envious, and wished they could have a grant, and felt that I was keeping such funding from some other worthy poet. It's especially galling to be calumniated from beyond the grave. [. . .]

Love,

Tony

2001

From March 25, 1943, to March 31, 1946, William Dougherty was, with Hecht, a soldier assigned to Co. C-386th Infantry Regiment, 97th Infantry Division.

January 6, 2001 Washington DC

Dear William Dougherty,

I'm very grateful to you for sending me the outline of the movements of the 97th division, as well as for your postcard with the name of C Company's first sergeant, James Hunt. The names of the women you mentioned (Nancy Clifford, Ruth Temple, Dale Thomburg) mean nothing to me, nor does the name of Fred Millard.

There used to be a conventional vainglorious boast in the army: "I'll be around to piss on your grave." It was partly a prayer for survival, I suppose; as well as a sort of Homeric boast. It is one of the reasons that reunions of old army buddies has such small attraction for me. I feel grief for a few friends who died, and no gratification in thinking I survived them, since I could have gone just as easily. There were a number of men I knew in the army whose injuries or deaths could just as easily have been mine but for sheer chance. I know this, and find it painful to think about.

With many thanks,

Anthony Hecht

January 8, 2001 Washington DC

[To J. D. McClatchy]

Dear Sandy,

Here, from the publication called <u>Crossroads</u>, issued by the Poetry Society of America (Autumn 2000, No. 55) is the imperishable item I read to you earlier today. It appears on page 11, and I copy only the first sentence of a short paragraph that serves as Preface:

<u>Collaborations</u> is a new series that explores the varied and provocative presence of artistic alliances in our culture . . .

Cinepoesia
Euphrosyne Bloom (filmmaker)
Julie Patton (poet and performance artist)

Cinepoesia is based on a series of on-going collaborations between filmmaker Euphrosyne Bloom and poet and performance artist Julie Patton. As a visual artist herself, Patton has long been interested in the material and "vegetal" nature of the written word. She believes that her handmade books, which include loose topsoil and flower petals, emphasize "the natural processes of growth and decay, and the kind of random beauty and chaos often found in nature." Her poems and books serve as catalyst and fodder for Bloom's process of handmade films, in which the reels are subjected to mold and other organic processes.

Not only would [S. J.] Perelman have liked this, but so would have JM [James Merrill] and WHA [W. H. Auden]. There's not the least evidence that this was published tongue in cheek, or with any sense whatever of its absurdity. Much of the Preface, which I omitted, is ponderously solemn, and quotes Robert Creeley on how collaboration can allow the solitary writer to escape from the "romantic vision" engendered by solitude. [. . .]

Let me know how your homily on The Future of Poetry works out.

Love,

Tony

Hecht's review of W. H. Auden, Lectures on Shakespeare, *edited by Arthur Kirsch (Princeton, 2000), appeared in* The Yale Review *89 (July 2001).*

January 10, 2001 Washington DC

[To Garry Wills]
Dear Garry,

I'm a little better than half-way through [my review of] Auden on Shakespeare, a volume that is brilliant and infuriating, not by turns but at one and the same time. It is brilliantly edited, the lectures being reconstituted from student notes, like Aristotle's [*Poetics*]. The devotion that went into this is deeply impressive.

I suspect you got mired early in the lecture on Henry VI, where he resorts, uncharacteristically, to a very tedious plot summary. This is not the case anywhere else, and indeed so much does Auden take for granted his audience's familiarity with the action of the plays, that he almost entirely slights that rather central aspect of the dramas. He is interested in the history of ideas, and the plays become little more than pretexts to discourse on generalities; more than half the lecture on As You Like It, for example, is devoted to ideas about the pastoral, with interesting references to Empson, Panofsky, Hesiod, D.H. Lawrence, Theocritus, Virgil, Lucretius, Pliny, Hobbes, Whitman, Spengler, Sidney, Milton, Lao-tse, John Gay and classic detective fiction (as opposed to the noir novels of Hammett, Chandler, and Spillane.) Only after he's gotten through all that—much of it admittedly fascinating, does he get around to Shakespeare's play, about which he does not seem to be especially pleased. He concludes by saying that civilization is a dance (his own metaphor) between the ocean of barbarism, which is a unity, and the desert of triviality, which is diverse. And who, apart from Rosalind in the play, is capable of dancing such a dance? Why, Alice in Wonderland, he concludes.

As you can see, there's something characteristically—independent? eccentric? wayward? original? zany? (and sometimes campy)—in these lectures. There's nothing else in Shakespeare criticism quite like them. Curiously, his editor in this book, the admirable Arthur Kirsch, tells us that, first, he used the Kittredge edition, and that he was familiar with the commentaries of Theodore Spencer, Granville-Barker, G. Wilson Knight, Caroline Spurgeon, and Mark Van Doren. These writers are largely (except for Spurgeon) concerned with problems of dramatic action, which Auden conspicuously disregards. It may be noted that his own plays are rather devoid of such action, and he is quite simply more interested in general ideas. If As You Like It is about pastoral ideas, Julius Caesar is about ideas of society, community and the crowd, i.e., political philosophy. One suspects that, given Auden's natural brilliance, as well as his wide range of reading, it would not be enormously difficult to locate the general topics, the clusters of ideas that lie in any given text and to enlarge upon them ad lib. And this, I think, is what he did, circumscribed by little more than the time limit of his lectures and the number of the plays.

But I have not fairly conveyed the richness of what he has done, and I hope to get nearer to that when in due course I write my review.

Best wishes for the New Year,
Tony

R. W. B. Lewis (1917–2002), distinguished American literary scholar and biographer, taught at Yale for most of his career. Hecht's musings over Brunetto Latini's placement in Hell continues, taking an Eliotic turn, in his letter to Lewis of March 4, 2002.

Dear Dick:

If you've wondered from time to time just how rude I can be for not so much as acknowledging the gift of your brilliant and lively life of Dante [Penguin, 2001], please know that I have been mightily preoccupied with the perilous health of family members for well over two months, and neither of the two imperiled ones is yet out of danger. This has entailed daily bedside vigils, and our lives have been narrowly rescheduled to an austere pattern. I brought your book to the bedside, reading it initially in snatches, but with much delight, even in the confines of a hospice. It is full of a fine vigor, and covers an enormous amount of materials with an easy flair that is admirable and everywhere persuasive.

I was one brought up in the old school of hermeneutics, the four-fold reading of Dante as of scripture, and yours is a refreshing liberation from the undeviating solemnity of that school. But your biographical approach, enchanting as it is, raises its own problems. I was struck by this especially in your account of Brunetto Latini (your pages 38–9). If Brunetto was really not homosexual; if he is placed by Dante in Hell with the sodomites simply because Dante feels a sense of rivalry and competitiveness with him, Dante, then, by your own thesis that the <u>Comedy</u> is an exercise in self-knowledge and self-confrontation, must have realized that he was himself profoundly guilty of one of the seven deadly sins. Moreover, Dante's placement of Brunetto cannot be likened to Ezra Pound's assignment of all those he despises (with a good number of Jews among them) to some inferno of his own making, since Pound clearly does not believe in his own Hell, and is merely being venomous, whereas Dante has the whole orthodoxy of the Church, the Summa Theologica, canon law, the "works" behind his condemnation. To put someone in Hell who does not belong there must surely be a sinful act. Even to put someone in the wrong circle of Hell is wicked, if you believe, and want your readers to believe, that the whole order of the Cosmos justifies eternal punishments as meted out by this design. [. . .]

With grateful good wishes,
Tony

William Pritchard (1932–) is Henry Clay Folger Professor of English, Amherst College, and the author of numerous critical works.

September 10, 2001 Washington DC

Dear Bill,

Many warm thanks for your letter, and for the praise therein. It's good to know a course on major writers begins with Ben Jonson, a poet not everywhere given his due, nor even always understood. For example, it seems not to be widely recognized that "The Dreame" is what in my youth was called "a wet dream," or, more solemnly, "a nocturnal emission." And thank you, also, for the fine tribute to Merrill, and for your kindness in placing me alongside of the elite Amherst poets [in the Amherst College *Alumni Magazine*].[7] You are right in everything you notice about "The Victor Dog," all its wit and ingenuity. And the "dog's life" to which poets are committed is beautifully tied to the bargain in "The Tenancy." But I can't help feeling (without being able to prove) that something else is involved as well, having to do with Elizabeth Bishop and Merrill, both of them devoted to their art perhaps in part because, both being childless, there was nothing else that could command so complete a devotion. Indeed, I know, as perhaps you do as well, certain writers (and other artists) who have had no children on principle, not wanting to let anything interfere with their devotion to some muse. (And the mention of "muse" reminds me that that splendid clergyman, Sydney Smith, told someone he had the most marvelous dream, in which it was revealed to him that there were thirty-nine muses, and only nine articles.) [...]

> With many thanks,
> Tony

October 18, 2001 Washington DC

[To Philip Hoy]
Dear Philip,

Congratulations on the Donald Justice volume. I put my check for it in the mail yesterday, so you should get it soon. The exchange between the two of you is wonderful, not least in its easy negotiation among the various arts Justice has mastered. So many fine things about him emerge from the interview, not least his championship of others. It is not only a heartening book in itself, but it is bound to serve the good purpose of sending readers back to look at Don's own work in poetry and prose—and perhaps music as well. There was a passage of reminiscence on page 66 that struck me as not only characteristic of Don's profound personal honesty, but a way of distinguishing him from many other kinds of poets, some good, some bad. About returning to Florida after years of absence, he writes: "I have a distinct memory of walking out onto the

---

[7] Also collected in Pritchard, *Shelf Life: Literary Essays and Reviews* (Amherst: University of Massachusetts Press, 2003), pp. 63–71. Along with Merrill, Pritchard cites Richard Wilbur, another Amherst poet (p. 68).

golf course behind our house late one night, walking our dog, and standing there looking up at the moon as it flooded the fairway with light. Very nice. I felt touched by an emotion I must have been inventing." It's that last sentence I find so persuasive. [. . .]

Best,

Tony

October 21, 2001 Washington DC

[To Peter Steele]

My dear Peter,

My complex and embroidered thanks for your gifts: the new poems and the very flattering essay. I like especially the ekphrastic poems—I recognize the Daumier, and wish I knew the Pinturicchio, an artist I greatly admire. But in all of them your lines are taut, vibrant, active, full of Hopkinsian vigor. I'm not sure I grasp "Ivory," though it reminds me of de la Tour. And your essay made me very happy, as how could it not? One detail in it especially came home to me with much energy. Of my poem "Auguries of Innocence" you write, "The 'small, un-smiling child' of the first line, who is also the 'speechless child of one' of the last stanza, summons in his silence, and is a kind of augur of the photograph's omens —is, in fact, a medium of the ominous. Untroubled himself, so far as we know, he is deeply troubling. Virgil, in his Fourth Eclogue, says, 'Incipe, parve puer, risu cognoscere matrem'—'Little boy, begin to know your mother by a smile,'" and then you go on to quote Hans Urs von Balthasar to the effect that "A baby is called to self-consciousness by the love and smile of his mother."

Now as it happens, I have been engaged in a very happy if irregular corre-spondence with the historian Garry Wills, who has written on many topics from "The Gettysburg Address," and a book on "The Declaration of Independence" to Papal Sin and a biography of St. Augustine, and a book on Venice. The biog-raphy of Augustine led him to venture a translation of his own of Book One of the Confessions, which he, for good reasons, prefers to call Testimonies. His translation endeavors to preserve the artful syntax, the balanced phrases and rhetorical skills of the original. He translates, in paragraph 8, "In time I began to smile, only in my sleep at first, and later when awake — so it was said of me, and I believed it, since we observe the same thing in other babies, though I do not remember it of myself." He provides not only the translation but a commentary, and on this passage he writes. "What Augustine first notices about the infant's activities is its smile at its mother. Folklore cynicism has recently held that this is just a twisting of the mouth to ease the escape of gas, a kind of silent burp, but researchers find that it is one of the earliest manifestations of a sign language that precedes verbal expression and is an occasion for it—as Augustine will assert [in his dialogue, Teacher, written near the end of his life.]" What you go on to conclude about the mother's smile in my poem is exactly right. [. . .]

Looking over what I have written, I notice that I failed to mention that in connection with the exchange of smiles between mother and child, Wills quotes the same line of Virgil's Eclogues that you quote.

With best wishes,

Tony

Ann Kjellberg is an editor and Literary Executor of the Joseph Brodsky Estate. Ilya Kaminsky's collection of poems, alluded to below, was an early version of Dancing in Odessa *(Tupelo Press, 2004).*

November 27, 2001 Washington DC

Dear Ann,

Here is Ilya Kaminsky's collection of poems. I hope you will think as highly of them as I do. But I shall not say anything to him about sending them to you, lest you should find them disappointing. If indeed you do find them wanting in some regard, I hope you will return them to me.

I have cast about in my mind for some publisher to send them to; but without coming up with anyone or anything, due largely to the fact that I really don't know poetry editors at publishing houses, except a very few. It seems to me that New Directions is the sort of place that might look favorably on this book, but I know no one at that firm. Nor do I know the editors at the small presses, which might also be hospitable. Any advice along these lines would be most welcome.

Ilya himself was a student at Georgetown who graduated last spring. I had long since left, having retired in 1993; but he wrote to ask if I would be willing to look at some of his poems, and in his letter he expressed a great admiration for Brodsky's work and for mine. What he showed me I thought extremely good, but somewhat hasty and uncontrolled. I invited him to visit me at home, and he proved to be a most engaging, excitable and winning young man. He now lives in San Francisco, where, I think, he has gone for a graduate degree.

I hope that between the two of us we can do something for him.

With very best wishes,

Tony

[To Tim Murphy]

Thanks for sending me the exchanges about "The Feast of Stephen" [on the EratoSphere blog site]. Much serious thought has been given to it, for which I can be nothing but grateful. Both Susan McLean and A.E. Stallings have sound insights into the sources and subject of the poem, which is about "what turns young men into basketball stars, or bullies, or Storm Troopers—and a conclusion that the three have more in common than we might like to think," as one of them said. The poem's title is meant to remind a reader of the description in Acts of the Apostles (7:58) of the martyrdom of St. Stephen, at which the Saul who would in time become St. Paul was present as a passive participant. Only the final section of the poem is clearly related to the title and the biblical passage. The first three parts merely lead up to what, at the end, becomes a lynch mob, whether of long ago or of today. I remember being struck by the fact that not a few Renaissance paintings of martyrdoms presented the torturers and executioners as vigorous and athletic young men, hateful in the glee with which they set about their task, but admirable in their physiques and sturdy bearing. I had in mind such paintings as Pollaiuolo's <u>The Martyrdom of St. Sebastian</u>, Luca Signorelli's <u>Flagellation</u>, and Caravaggio's <u>The Martyrdom of St. Matthew</u>. It seemed worth meditating on what could lead men into such barbarity. And it seemed that the competitiveness that begins early in comparatively innocent games, encourages youths to attempt to "beat" one another in sports; and it would not be too great a step from that to the administration of real beatings. Everything about domestic propaganda created by the Nazis for home consumption focused on images of nordic Supermen. The second section of the poem is full of puns, jokes that make pleasantries of what is potentially dangerous and sinister, and which appears without disguise in section III. Jokes, as Freud pointed out, are a means of concealing aggression. The seed of all these dangers lies in that "self-love" mentioned in the first section which is indifferent to the condition of others, and which is purely selfish. It is a natural state of infants, and it endures for a while, and some never abandon it, remaining cruel their whole lives. The four parts constitute an account of the evolution of the persecutor.

Once again, I'm grateful for the thought and attention you have given my poem.

[Tony]

Robyn Creswell, a frequent reviewer, was appointed poetry editor of The Paris Review *in 2010.*

December 31, 2001 Washington DC

Dear Robyn Creswell,

Thank you for your warm response to my letter, and for clearing up my bewilderment about how Sandy McClatchy came by your review [of *The Darkness and the Light* in *Raritan*]. (I hope he signs you up as a regular reviewer.)

It seems to me you are quite right in your feeling that poems don't console. I have never felt them to be consoling, in the usual sense of the word. Instead, they provide a curious kind of communion, which is what Auden must have meant when he said that our reading of literary works was a way of breaking bread with the dead. We become aware of certain kinds of intelligence, resonances of feeling, sympathetic vibrations of knowledge that speak to us from the words of total strangers, and it may be that we feel less alone—if that can be called consolation. I find this to be true of music as well as poetry. To be able to give full attention to a work of music—full enough attention to apprehend every quirk and turn, modulation and contrapuntal filigree—is to adapt oneself, in trust, to a complete coincidence with another mind, and to rejoice in the bond that has been so established. I should imagine that performers especially must feel that (all matters of technique apart) they are thinking as the composer thought when they are playing. For a large part of my own life I was very lonely, even when in close contact with others, and my experiences of music and literature were those I felt most intimately, and where I felt most sure of myself.

As for your suggestion that poetry criticism seems a willfully blinkered pursuit when considered against the backdrop of the Twin Towers and the bombings in Afghanistan, I think the only reasonable response for such as you or I would be that of Yeats's in "Lapis Lazuli." It takes the disciplines of a good part of a lifetime to command the faculties that go into the making of a good poet or a good critic, and these faculties are not the ones employed to address the calamities of existence. We should do what we have committed ourselves to doing, and do it as best we can; and if upheaval demands that we take up arms or help the wounded, we set aside our principal task until the emergency has been dealt with. Whereupon we resume what we had elected as most important to us.

This will not reach you before the beginning of the New Year, a year which must stand a reasonable chance of being better than the last; but it comes with wishes that 2002 may be happy and successful for you.

Sincerely,

Anthony Hecht

2002

January 7, 2002 Washington DC

[To Eleanor Cook]

Dear Eleanor,

Many grateful thanks for your letter about <u>The Darkness and the Light</u>. In reply to one of your questions, no, I did not have Browning's Johannes Agricola in mind when writing "Indolence," though you were perfectly right to suppose I might have. My speaker was far less a theologian/philosopher than Browning's was. But I had [in mind], apart from the generic beatnik source, a passage of Auden in his <u>For the Time Being</u>. In Herod's speech he declares that if the "rumor" of salvation by the New Dispensation is not stamped out, "Every corner-boy will congratulate himself: 'I'm such a sinner that God had to come down in person to save me. I must be a devil of a fellow.' Every crook will argue: 'I like committing crimes. God likes forgiving them. Really the world is admirably arranged.'"

As to translations, they are often things that I dwell with for the longest time. I can fall in love with a poem in another tongue, and yearn to get it into some kind of English, and experiment year after year, almost always—no, always, with a sense of defeat, since no matter what I do, it will lack important elements that made the original what it is. In this book there's a version of Charles d'Orléans' "Le temps a laissié son manteau" which I had tried at the outset to do in a version that appeared in my first book, published in 1954. Horace is a challenge, but so are almost all poets of any worth. Sometimes one must try to settle for an equivalent music. Your husband and I share a liking for walnuts at the Christmas season.

As for the war poem ["Sacrifice"], that story about the French family was a kind of word-of-mouth lore that passed among the troops in France when I was there. It was perfectly believable. Your reflections on the conjunction of "the deeply civilized and the deeply barbaric" served to remind me that a <u>TLS</u> (hence, in those days, anonymous) review of <u>A History of England</u> by Winston Churchill declared, "The whole action of history seems to prove that it is more dangerous to be intelligent than to be warlike. Culture is not only futile but, when combined with kindness, almost always actively fatal" [April 27, 1956]. This led George Lyttelton to say that he had come to agree with a certain Bishop Creighton, "who reassured an anxious seeker after truth that 'it is almost impossible to exaggerate the complete unimportance of every-thing.'"[8] [. . .]

With best wishes for the New Year,
Tony

Sherod Santos (1948–), poet and essayist, was a professor at the University of Missouri, Columbia, when this letter was written.

January 7, 2002 Washington DC

Dear Sherod Santos,

Your extraordinary letter left me virtually speechless, and it deeply moved my wife, who must be just as grateful as I am.

Having said that, I have just about exhausted my vocabulary of gratitude. Any comment of mine would now sound posturing or fatuous, though I confess that what you wrote led me to lingering ruminations about my work, as well as the work of others. Self-assessment is next to impossible, even, perhaps especially, at my age, when I behold myself, in somebody else's words, "Beaten and chopped with tanned antiquity" [Shakespeare, Sonnet 62]. The attitudes of most poets, I would imagine, must oscillate between feeling that a number of their best effects have gone unnoticed, and feeling that they have been too generously dealt with. Usually far more of the former than the latter. It is a common hope that posterity, which Emerson called bribeless, beyond entreaty, and not to be over-awed, will come to see what once was missed. I have known some particularly bad poets who have survived on the thin gruel of this hope. Even Shakespeare endured moods of doubt, in which he found himself "Desiring this man's art and that man's scope." And every poet who is not a fool must resign himself to a lifetime in this equivocal no-man's land. It is a permanently unsettled condition, sometimes, though rarely, brightened by such a letter as yours, for which I send you my deepest thanks. [. . .]

Sincerely,
Anthony Hecht

[8]*The Lyttelton Hart-Davis Letters*, ed. Rupert Hart-Davis (London: John Murray, 1978). 1.124 (letter of May 2, 1956).

Gerry Cambridge is a Scottish poet, with an interest in natural history, and editor of The Dark Horse, *a Scottish American poetry magazine, which published several of Hecht's poems. They met at the West Chester University Poetry Conference in 2001.*

February 9, 2002 Washington DC

Dear Mr. Cambridge,

[. . .] I very much like your, as you say, "uncharacteristic-sounding" quotation from Randall Jarrell: "A good critic is one who likes as much as possible as persuasively as possible." Jarrell was splendid in his enthusiasms, but I suspect most memorable in his devastations. E.g., in a review of <u>Chorus of Bird Voices, Sonnets, Battle-Dore, Unconventional Verse, etc.</u> by William Bacon Evans, Jarrell wrote, "Mr. Evans' title is almost enough for a review of his book. While ailing in Syria, he wrote songs for every species of North American bird (I am no ornithologist, but there <u>can't</u> be any more of the damn things); it has seldom been better done. This is poetry which instructs its writer and entertains its reader (the function of poetry, I have read); a missionary could hardly be more harmlessly employed. Mr. Evans is an amiable, unpretentious, and tolerant person—he appears to dislike nothing but cigarettes—and won my heart immediately: more than I can say for most of the poets I am reviewing. But then, Mr. Evans is no poet." I would have to admit that in an early phase of my own reviewing career I succumbed to the temptation to be amusing at the expense of some of the writers I wrote about. And I have not yet quite stamped out a lingering streak of Alexander Pope in me, though I try to keep it under control. [. . .]

With grateful good wishes,
Anthony Hecht

John Van Doren, literary friend of Hecht's dating back to the early 1950s, is the son of Mark Van Doren, one of Hecht's teachers at Columbia University.

February 16, 2002 Washington DC

Dear John:

I'm grateful to you for the candor of your response to <u>The Darkness and the Light</u>, which, as I think, is not much nearer to despair than some earlier volumes of my poems. But you are right in singling out that timbre, or tone, or atmosphere, as dominant. I'm not sure how this is to be explained. It may be part of my metabolic make-up. In terms of William James's temperamental categories in <u>Varieties of Religious Experience,</u> I recognize myself as sharing many of the views and feelings of those he calls "Sick Souls." It might also be that my experience and reading have contributed to this. It occurs to me that of all Shakespeare's plays <u>King Lear</u> is the one I have been and continue to be most moved by. It is probably the bleakest of the plays, the most unconsoling. During the years I taught Shakespeare I always gave strong emphasis to a detailed examination of that play.

With specific regard to the poem called "Witness," it undertakes a task I attempted once before in a poem called "Poem Without Anybody," written in memory of James Wright. Both poems eliminate all human presence. The attempt is to avoid at all costs any employment of the pathetic fallacy, which is not an easy thing to do in poetry. A world from which human compassion, tenderness, sympathy has been removed is the external universe of Lear, as of not a few poems by Hardy. And of some classical drama. A psychoanalyst might not wrongly discover materials from my childhood to account for this posture; but in the end it is shared by a small number of others who see the world somewhat as I do. The attempt to see life steadily and see it whole permits no parti pris. I find this also in Frost's "Design."

At my age I must expect a few elements of feebleness to creep in, and my arthritic discomforts are among these. They are still with me. And now my eyesight is weakening. But in most regards I am well and cheerful.

This comes with warm greetings to you and Mira, and with best wishes.

Tony

This letter continues a discussion with R. W. B. Lewis begun in Hecht's letter of August 26, 2001.

March 4, 2002 Washington DC

Dear Dick,

Thumbing about in Helen Gardner's book on Eliot's <u>Four Quartets,</u> I came across something that bears upon your book on Dante, and our correspondence about it. In the last of the <u>Quartets</u>, "Little Gidding," Eliot puts in a very moving and eloquent passage in a species of <u>terza rime,</u> in which, instead of linked rhymes he alternates masculine and feminine endings. In this passage, which is set at night in bomb-scarred London, Eliot, in an early draft, comes upon "a familiar compound ghost" of uncertain identity, of whom, in this early draft, he inquires, "Are you here, Ser Brunetto?" This was destined to be changed to "What! Are <u>you</u> here?" John Hayward, to whom Eliot showed early drafts of these poems, "queried the disappearance of Ser Brunetto," Gardner reports, and she continues, "Eliot replied that this was necessary because of the change he had made in the speech of the 'dead master.' There were, he said, two reasons:

"The first is that the visionary figure has by now become somewhat more definite and will no doubt be identified by some readers with Yeats though I do not mean anything so precise as that. However, I do not wish to take the responsibility of putting Yeats or anybody else into Hell and I do not want to impute to him the particular vice which took Brunetto there. Secondly, I wished the effect of the whole to be Purgatorial which is much more appropriate."

As you can see, Eliot seems to have been far more scrupulous about consigning people to Hell than Dante was in regard to Brunetto, if your surmise is right.

We've had a remarkably warm winter that has been followed by an icy spring, with temperatures in the 20s.

All good wishes,
Tony

April 22, 2002 Washington DC

[To Dorothea Tanning]
Dear Dorothea,

While on the face of it the current scandals of the Catholic clergy are plainly horrifying, I find myself also amused by the continuing revelations, which for all their gravity share with the Enron mess a certain hilarity. In today's <u>Washington Post</u> there is an article about a pharmacist in Kansas City who, for ten successive years, watered down expensive drugs taken by some 4,200 people with very grave illnesses, in order to "pocket hundreds of dollars per dose." The patients being cheated were suffering from AIDS, among other terrible diseases. The pharmacist, one Robert Courtney, did this to pay more than $600,000 in taxes "and fulfill a $1 million pledge to his church." Why, it's enough to give religion a bad name. The Enron team were just straightforward crooks, misleading employees and investors, etc. But to endanger the lives of the innocent, or to corrupt them <u>in the name of the church</u>—it makes little difference which church; I suspect that Courtney was some brand of protestant—seems somehow more wicked, perhaps because the villains of the story are usually given to sanctimonious postures. Pascal: "Men never do evil so completely and cheerfully as when they do it from religious conviction." Tomorrow the Pope is to meet with the American cardinals, and one fears that the burden of their discussion will tend toward cleansing and protecting "the church" as an institution, whatever the cost to those families who were betrayed, including boys driven to suicide. [. . .]

It may amuse you to know that while we were gone I received voice mail from someone calling to congratulate me on a review of a book of mine in the <u>New York Review of Books</u>, which was accompanied by a David Levine cartoon portrait. The caller declared that the cartoon was very unattractive and looked just like me.

Love,

Tony

Harold Bloom, eminent literary critic, has taught for many years at Yale University. His friendship with Hecht dates back to 1971.

October 18, 2002 Washington DC

My dear Harold,

I learned around the time of the Bollingen anniversary festival that you were slated to undergo (or else had just undergone) coronary by-pass surgery. I suppose you are now still in the hospital, and things are moving along according to a schedule that is wholly in the hands of others. So this letter, wishing you a full and carefully paced recovery, being sent to your home, will await you there in the dark along with accumulated mail-order catalogues and utility bills. It invites no answer; it comes simply as a greeting from one who has gone through roughly the same experience.

As your senior in this procedure by a mere matter of weeks, I can tell you that recovery is slow and more draining of energy than you may have expected. I found it fatiguing even to read for very long. And as for writing, it took some time before I could compose more than a single letter a day. I'm only slowly now getting beyond that stage, but not far beyond it. On the positive side, however, I went through a long stretch, not yet altogether passed, during which every waking moment was a continuous Emersonian astonishment at the reality of everything around me—a new-born, born-again delight full of quiet, secret rejoicing. This feeling overrides all the bad news in the headlines—which is certainly very bad. And it is, perhaps, profoundly selfish in its willful blindness to anything beyond itself. I suspect that it teaches nothing much about mortality. At least in the course of my life I've come near enough to those dangers not to regard this one as a novelty.

While still in the hospital I had a small cassette-player, and was able to listen to Mozart, Haydn, Schubert and Beethoven any time I wished. I found this very sustaining; and it also served to block unwelcome noise from elsewhere. Only yesterday I spoke on the phone to William Merwin, who is to undergo major surgery this very day in Honolulu, and he, too, has fortified himself with a selection of recordings. I earnestly hope your recovery will be as tranquil as mine, which, though somewhat frustrating by dint of a lack of energy to do as much as I would like to, or feel I need to, is still something to be savored richly and gratefully—and slowly.

With affectionate wishes for your recovery,

Tony

2003

Jonathan Post, a former student of Hecht and professor of English at UCLA, was preparing to give a talk for the John Donne Society on the subject of the aubade, a subject dear to Hecht, as his late "Aubade," written in 2004, reveals.

January 25, 2003 Washington DC

Dear Jonathan,

This will seem a shamefully tardy response to your fax of the 14th, but I can explain that the day before you sent it we departed for a ten-day, visit-cum-birthday celebration to New York, where we have acquired a splendid three-and-a-half room pied-a-terre, and where I turned a graceful, if graying, eighty. There was a fine party that included Sandy, Richard Howard, Shirley Hazzard, Mark Strand and Maria Brodsky, and a very good time was had by all.

And now, to the aubade. You mention Bishop, Larkin, Empson & Snodgrass. MacNeice wrote one six lines long; Wilbur wrote "A Late Aubade," which is quite wonderful. There's Pound's "Alba" and there are dawn songs in some of the later Cantos. It may be worth informing your learned audience that "in France the term is applied also to the performance of a military band in the early morning in honor of some distinguished person" (Britannica). There is also, famously, that scene in Romeo and Juliet in which they debate about whether the birdsong they've heard is a lark or a nightingale. There's another antithetical one by Baudelaire, called "L'Aube Spirituelle," as well as one called "Le Crepuscule du Matin," which I have translated as "The Ashen Light of Dawn," in my most recent book of poems. The trouble is that I know perfectly well that there are others evading the reach of memory. Two more just occurred to me: Auden's "Prime" from his canonical hours sequence, and Wilbur's "Love Calls Us to the Things of this World." So I haven't altogether disgraced myself.

This comes with love to you and Susan.

Tony

Jeff Balch is a freelance writer in the Chicago area. His interpretation of Hecht's poem can be found in Jewish Currents *(September 2007).*

February 11, 2003 Washington DC

Dear Mr. Balch,

In an interview (book-length) with an Englishman named Philip Hoy, and published by Between the Lines in 1999, I replied to a question about "The Book of Yolek" in roughly the following terms: There were a number of sources: my having seen Flossenbürg was certainly one. (Flossenbürg was a concentration camp annex of Buchenwald).[9] There was also a memorable photograph, one of the most famous to survive from the Warsaw ghetto. It's of a small boy, perhaps five or six, wearing a shabby peaked cap and short pants, his hands raised and a bewildered, forlorn look on his face as he gazes off at something to the side of the camera, while behind him uniformed, helmeted soldiers keep their rifles trained on him, as one of them looks directly at the camera without the least expression of embarrassment. But of course I did a lot of reading about the Holocaust. There were many books, but one in particular proved helpful to me. It's an Anthology of Holocaust Literature edited by Jacob Glatstein, Israel Knox, and Samuel Margoshes. It contains, among other moving and terrifying, even stomach-turning accounts, a piece by Hanna Mortkowicz-Olczakowa which bears the title "Yanosz Korczak's Last Walk." Yanosz Korczak was a famous Jewish educator in Poland who, having been ordered to lead the children of an orphanage where he taught to an assembly point from which they would be taken to death camps, refused to part from them, knowing, as they did not, where they were headed, and went with them to their deaths. Among these children were "little Hanka with lung trouble, Yolek who was ill . . ." As you will notice, I recalled this account imperfectly, and gave the bad lungs to Yolek instead of little Hanka. But apart from such explicit sources, I found myself meditating on the sestina form itself, without reference to any particular subject matter. I was thinking about how various sestinas I knew operated. And it occurred to me that because of the persistent reiteration of those terminal words, over and over in stanza after stanza, the sestina seemed to lend itself

[9]Although Hecht occasionally refers to Flossenbürg as an "annex" of Buchenwald, his precise use of this term is unclear since the two camps were geographically many miles apart. In the week before Flossenbürg was liberated by the Allied Forces on April 23, 1945, however, the camp had housed seven thousand prisoners from Buchenwald, according to the timeline provided by the U.S. Holocaust Museum. This association may well have persuaded Hecht, interviewing the prisoners, that the two camps were more closely affiliated than was actually the case. My thanks to Diederik Oostdijk for this suggestion.

especially well to a topic felt obsessively, unremittingly. And when this realization fell into one place with the other preoccupations aroused by my reading and that remembered photograph, I had the materials for my poem. The poem's epigraph is Martin Luther's German translation of words from the Gospel of John 19:7, which in English reads, "We have a law / And by that law he must die." In the Gospel this demand is attributed to the Jews who sought the death of Jesus. As my epigraph, it constitutes the German justification of killing children, Yolek among them.

Best wishes,
Anthony Hecht

Ronald Schuchard is the Goodrich C. White Professor of English at Emory University and the author of many critical studies.

April 27, 2003 Washington DC

Dear Ron:

I'm very grateful for you for sending an offprint of your essay on Eliot and anti-Semitism, together with various responses to it, and your own reply to the others. The entire collection is riveting to read, and I send my warmest thanks.[10]

It arrived at a time when I am preparing some notes towards a lecture on Keats, about whom the charge of anti-Semitism has never, so far as I know, been raised. I'm not being entirely facetious when I write this. Even Empson, who admired Eliot almost without reservation, was able to admit that a "defense" was called for. The Horace Kallen friendship and the letters between the two men seem to me a major new element of undeniable importance; and it is to be hoped that with time more such evidence will turn up. But with regard to the question of when Eliot might first have learned about what was happening to Jews in Germany, and your quite plausible conjecture that while he was revising After Strange Gods he could well have been utterly unaware of their plight, it cannot be that he was altogether innocent of such knowledge in 1936, when that deplorable review of The Yellow Spot: The Outlawing of Half a Million Human Beings was published in The Criterion. Mrs. Eliot affirms that he did not write it, and I'm prepared to take her rather tardy word on the matter. But as the journal's editor, he could scarcely have been unaware of its brief and dismissive contents. Indeed, the chances are good that he chose [Montgomery] Belgion to

---

[10] "Burbank with a Baedeker, Eliot with a Cigar: American Intellectuals, Anti-Semitism, and the Idea of Culture," plus replies, appeared in the journal *Modernism/modernity* 10, no. 1 (January 2003).

write the review, and would have had a rough sense of how Belgion would react to the volume. Certainly, as editor, he published it, and it is morally repulsive.

My own feelings about the matter are very complicated. As my essay indicated, Eliot was my first master and guide, my touchstone and literary parent. He was so for a number of my actual teachers, such as Allen Tate and Austin Warren, the latter a virtual Eliot acolyte for whom Eliot's slightest opinion was cherished with reverence, not excluding High Anglican positions and disdain for Milton. It is hard to come to terms with such a mentor when elements of anti-Semitism seem unmistakably to appear in his poems and essays. Denis Donoghue has long felt indulgent towards Eliot, since they both take their religion very seriously, and that factor overrides all other considerations.

There is another puzzle about the notorious passage in the Virginia lectures, where Eliot recommends that "The populations should be homogeneous . . . What is still more important is unity of all religious background . . . etc." Eliot gives the impression that he is proposing a novel experiment, but it was put into practice long ago in Spain, with terrible consequences. The fall of Granada in 1492 ended more than 200 years of civilized rule under Muslim government which gave patronage to art, literature and science, attracting many learned and skilled men to its court, resulting "in a brilliant civilization of which the Alhambra is the supreme monument," according to the Britannica. Granada's fall marked the end of a Spanish culture in which "Islamic, Spanish and, indeed, Judaic strands had been inseparably intermingled for centuries," writes Lisa Jardine in Worldly Goods. What Spain got, after driving out the Moors and Jews, was the Inquisition, and an impoverishment of its culture. [. . .]

Tony

April 29, 2003 Washington DC

Dear William Dougherty,

I want to thank you for your diligence and hard work in tracking down the members of C Company of the 386th Infantry Regiment. I'm grateful to have this list. But I am puzzled and saddened that so few names have stuck in my mind. Of those few, I can offer one or two comments. Joe Hastings received the Congressional Medal of Honor. He was a machine gunner in the heavy weapons platoon, and he was killed in Germany. Ferrante got a purple heart. A bullet grazed his forehead. He was very lucky. Godsell was a sergeant; a short, stocky man. Geist knew German, and served as interpreter for regimental brass. And unless I'm mistaken, Zeigler was a second Lieutenant. But what was the name of our captain, an over-weight regular army man who was not popular with the troops? And what was the name of our First Sergeant, who put in the Captain's name for a Silver Star, which he got for action on a day when he was behind the lines with dysentery? I am most haunted by the memory of a young soldier who, like me, must have been no more than a pfc. He was tall, blond, good-looking, and stood beside me in formation at some German town we had captured, as we waited to be assigned to work details by some sergeant. Many had already been assigned and had gone off to their tasks. Of the few who remained, this soldier was assigned to locate the town's water supply. He left the formation to address his task. And I was still standing there waiting for an assignment when that soldier returned on a stretcher, borne by two medics, having lost a leg to a booby trap. He looked at me with an expression of infinite sadness, and I immediately realized that but for accidents of fate it might have been me who had been assigned that job. Apart from those already named, I think I remember Gambill and Wilk and possibly Herrington, but no one else.

Again, many thanks for your hard work.

Anthony Hecht

May 7, 2003 Washington DC

[To Mary Jo Salter]

Dear Mary Jo,

Thanks for your marvelous book, <u>Open Shutters</u>, and the wonderful Ligurian setting to which the title poem refers, and which fills me with nostalgic happiness as you recall it to me. And thanks for everything else in your fine book, which I have read with pure delight. Your poem to Sarah M. Lyon ["Deliveries Only," which includes the epigraph "for Sarah Marjorie Lyon, born in a service elevator"] reminded me that once, at the American Academy in Rome, at a very grand cocktail party at the Villa Aurelia, the director, Laurance Roberts, brought me to a corner of the room to introduce me to an English poet named Hugh Chisolm. He was moderately famous; I was utterly unknown. And, alas, the only thing I could remember about him (though I suppose I must have read some of his poems, which made little if any impression upon me) came from an item about him in the "Talk of the Town" section of <u>The New Yorker</u>, where it was reported that he was born in an elevator at the Plaza Hotel in New York. Mr. Roberts presented me to him, and stood aside, perhaps expecting something electric or magical to take place at this encounter of two poets. But the only thing I could think of to say was: "Is it true that you were born in an elevator of the Plaza Hotel?" He said briskly, "Yes," and turned away to resume talking to someone else. [. . .]

With warm affection,
Tony

2004

David Slavitt (1935–) is a translator, poet, and author. His appreciative note was about Hecht's collection of essays: Melodies Unheard: Essays on the Mysteries of Poetry *(Baltimore: Johns Hopkins University Press, 2003).*

February 10, 2004 Washington DC

Dear David:

How very kind of you to write as warmly and generously as you did about my essays. I'm deeply grateful, and I mean that sincerely. Such "tributes" are few and far between.

I have mused upon your inquiry regarding Housman's choice of "nighing" rather than "nearing." It led me to look over his Collected Poems, and I was struck by the highly unstatistical suspicion that, while we commonly think of Housman as using simple, straightforward diction, he is also given to archaisms: "The God that glads the lover's heart," for example. To be sure, Hardy is still more enamored of archaisms, and in "In Tenebris" he began, "Wintertime nighs." In the "Epithalamion," Spenser wrote "Now day is done, and night is nighing fast./Now bring the bride into the bridal bowers." It's not inconceivable to me that Housman might have wanted to echo Spenser's marriage hymn for brutally ironic purposes. But the fact is that "nigh" according to OED entries was quite widely used from about the 1200s on. I have long thought the Hardy poem very moving, and it gives special emphasis to "nighs" by putting it in a rhyming position, so that the first stanza reads,

Wintertime nighs;
But my bereavement-pain
It cannot bring again:
Twice no one dies.

Once again, let me thank you for the generosity of your letter.

Best,
Tony

One of a number of letters Hecht wrote to The Washington Post, *this letter was never published.*

February 17, 2004 Washington DC

[To the Editors of *The Washington Post*]

Today's issue of the [*The Washington*] *Post* carried a front page article on Mel Gibson's film, <u>The Passion of the Christ</u>, that continued on to page 11 and was written by Caryle Murphy and William Booth. Towards its end it states, "One of the most sensational moments in the version of the film that has been screened in previews is a line from the Gospel of Matthew, in which the mob calling for Jesus to be put upon the cross shouts out, 'His blood be on us and on our children!' Often called the 'blood libel' quote, it has been interpreted in the past to call down rage and blame upon the Jews in the centuries-long tradition of Passion plays."

This is mistaken. The quote from Matthew is accurate, but the long-standing "blood libel" is altogether separate from the Gospels, and dates instead from the Middle Ages. It first surfaced in 1144 in the city of Norwich, England. Its premise was that "once the Jews had crucified Jesus, they thirsted for pure and innocent blood. Since the formerly incarnate God was now in heaven, the Jews aspired to the most innocent of the believers, i.e., the children, the tender Christians. As a result of this reasoning, the season of the most libels or charges of ritual murder was that of the Passover festival, which was close to the time of the Passion of Jesus," as Haim Hillel Ben-Sasson writes in <u>The History of the Jewish People</u>, Harvard University Press, 1976. Many such medieval claims were made, one of them by Geoffrey Chaucer in his poem <u>The Canterbury Tales</u>, one by Bernardino da Feltre in 1475. One of the putative motives ascribed to Jews for the murders of children was that 1) they needed Christian blood as an essential ingredient for their Passover bread, and 2) that it was a means by which they could free themselves from a tell-tale Jewish stench, <u>foetor Judaicus</u>, which was said to afflict them, and to which Martin Luther refers in 1523.

Yours,
Anthony Hecht

April 12, 2004 Washington DC

[To Dimitri Hadzi]
My dear Dimitri,

Helen and I were deeply distressed to learn (as we did from Judy Millon) of your hospitalization for a clinical depression. I was, if possible, the more distressed for having gone through such a hospitalization myself at one time. So I know that nothing could be more irrelevant than glib advice to cheer up, delivered with scoutmaster optimism. The hospital where I was treated was so concerned about the potential suggestivity of any "art" on its walls—posters, reproductions, etc.—that, determined nevertheless to decorate the bare walls of the place, they put up framed swatches of upholstery fabric, which were unlikely to touch on any sensitivities of any patients. The news about you was the more distressing because, when last we spoke, you were full of enthusiasm for the Athens subway project. But, as I said, I know how destructive to one's self-esteem such depressions can be. Right now I myself have been trying to deal with a not completely latent anxiety, due to the combined facts that a) I haven't written any poems of consequence for more than a year, and b) I'm scheduled to go off to an Italian villa to write in mid-May, and already fear that I may not be able to come up with anything. I have no firm way to deal with this, except to remind myself that I've often felt this way in the past, and have nevertheless, by some kind of miracle, come up with something totally unexpected. There's a beautiful poem by George Herbert, called "The Flower," which bears directly and persuasively on the kinds of fluctuation you and I are both subject to. Ask Cynthia if she can find a copy of it to read to you. It's one of Herbert's best known poems, so it should not be hard to find.

    This comes to you with our combined love and admiration.

Tony

P.S. I enclose a copy of the Herbert poem.

July 1, 2004 Washington DC

[To Philip Hoy]
Dear Philip,

    I don't wish to complicate your life unduly, and I know you will be granted only a few minutes during the panel discussion; but after thinking about your topic, I made a hasty check of my published poems and find that there are a number of others that draw significantly on prose sources. There are, for starters, all the poems with biblical topics, including "The Feast of Stephen," based on the Book of Acts. But in addition there is "More Light! More Light!" which is indebted to a book called The Theory and Practice of Hell by Eugen Kogon; "Lizards and Snakes" on the autobiography of Mark Twain; "The Book of Yolek," on "Yanosz Korczak's Last Walk," by Hanna Mortkowicz-Olczakowa; "Sisters" on a letter to Robert Frost by his sister, Jeanie; "The Life of Crime" on an account of a pickpocket in Henry Mayhew's <u>London Labour and the London Poor</u>; and "A Certain Slant" on a story by Chekhov.

This fax will be followed by a new poem ["Menassah ben Israel"], also based on a prose text, in this case a book called <u>Rembrandt's Jews</u>, whose author [Stephen Nadler] I can't identify because the book is in New York. It's a poem I wrote this spring in Bogliasco, and Sandy [McClatchy] will bring it out in <u>The Yale Review</u>, in winter, I think. I thought you might like to see it.

Best,

Tony

August [17?], 2004 Washington DC

[To William Pritchard]

Dear Bill,

I'm grateful to you for your several favors: 1) the kindness of your note about my work, 2) your shrewd and just essay on Hardy (about which more in a moment), and 3) your ruminations on style as applied to Jane Austen.

I think you and I must be very close to perfect agreement on Hardy, and certainly we like the same poems pretty much for the same reasons. I am, however, ill-at-ease with Larkin's (in my view) heavy-handed mode of distinguishing between the poetry of Hardy and Yeats, even as it applies to his own work. As for the objection of Orwell to the line of Yeats, "Or that William Blake," there may be something slightly arch about the word "that," and yet it could be justified by saying that Yeats's emphasis is meant to single out "that William Blake/Who Beat upon the wall/Till Truth obeyed his call," as distinct from, say, the William Blake who wrote, "Can I see another's woe/And not be in sorrow too?" Anyway, if there is undeniably something histrionic about Yeats's posture towards death, etc., a posture of braggadocio, a defiance, a curious lack of grace, clearly Hardy's is, as you justly point out, far more circumspect. But what troubles me is that this should be an argument of Larkin's who is himself so unpleasantly self-commiserating, so off-puttingly sorry for himself, e.g., "Home is so sad," "Breadfruit," and a number of other poems in which he laments how his childhood was "unspent." My point is that it's not as though there were only three options: Yeats, Hardy, and Larkin. But as for Hardy, what you have to say is fine and right. (I, too, admire the triolets.)

I am glad to learn you are not planning to retire, and that this is with the approval of your doctors. I, on the other hand, retired long since, and my doctors are by no means so sanguine. I've been diagnosed with cancer, and have already undergone the first of six sessions of chemotherapy that, when complete, will not only leave me shorn but carry me into late November. I mention this partly to explain something about a poem of mine I enclose ["Declensions"]. It was not written with prophetic vision; it is merely the meditation of an eighty-one year old.

As for the vulgarities of Ms. Sedgwick [Eve Kosofsky Sedgwick], they are all of a piece with two papers given at a 1989 MLA meeting: "Desublimating the Male Sublime: Auto-erotics in Melville and William Burroughs" and "'The Pea that Duty Locks': Clitoral Imagery and Masturbation in Emily Dickinson."

All best wishes,
Tony

August 10, 2004 Washington DC

[To Eleanor Cook]
Dear Eleanor,

Many thanks for splicing observations of mine into your fine and learned essay on Enigmas.[11] I feel very proud to be thus cited. And thank you as well for the postcard reproduction of the David Milne painting, who seems to bear a family resemblance to Maurice Prendergast.

I have, I regret to say, some distressing news to impart. I have been diagnosed with cancer [. . .] and it has taken me and my wife completely by surprise. In fact, I had been taking notes for an essay I would like to write. It will be called De Gustibus, and will concern how deeply personal, quirky and often irrational, are our judgments of taste, about which we are sometimes very defensive, and about which we sometimes feel vulnerable, residing as these judgments do in some highly private inwardness, deeply severed from what we normally think of as our faculty of judgment. I suspect that [Jacques] Maritain's startling and irrational dislike of Dürer—"We may draw in this connection a particularly instructive lesson from the great and noble illusion—and failure—of those masters of the Renaissance, especially Albrecht Dürer, who believed that a superior knowledge of the Mathematical laws of form and of the world of geometrical proportions would enable the artist to attain beauty in its unique and definite type (as if beauty were not a transcendental) and to encompass its essence in their work." Creative Intuition in Art and Poetry, p. 171n. This neo-Thomist terror of the rigors of mathematics as applied to art is amusing, since no notice is taken of the very many Renaissance artists, Piero della Francesca, Alberti,

[11]The essay referred to here later appeared as "Enigma as Masterplot" in Eleanor Cook, *Enigmas and Riddles in Literature* (Cambridge University Press, 2006).

Leonardo, Palladio, Serlio, who wrote treatises on the demonstrable relation of beauty and numbers. But they, of course, were good Catholics, while Dürer was a wretched Lutheran. Was Maritain aware that his doctrinal biases were showing? Hard to say. I've assembled an interesting list of quirky opinions, along with speculations on why they were adopted. But I will have to put that aside for the present.

With affectionate good wishes,

Tony

ACKNOWLEDGMENTS

THIS BOOK WOULD NEVER HAVE BEEN POSSIBLE without the extraordinary dedication and efforts of Helen Hecht. During the more than five years it has taken to uncover, assemble, and edit her late husband's letters, she has been an indefatigable researcher, the most generous and tireless of correspondents, and a patient and acute reader of almost every phrase that appears in this book. Along with the careful attention she paid to her husband's letters, I am especially grateful for the improvements she made to the general introduction to the letters and the prefatory matter for the individual chapters. Although final responsibility for the text, including the selection of letters, rests with the editor, it would misrepresent the process to suggest that combing through the correspondence was not, at almost every stage, a shared venture. I might only add that this venture had its origins for me many years earlier when I was a graduate student in a specially memorable seminar that the recently and happily remarried Hecht taught at the University of Rochester in the spring of 1972 on William Butler Yeats and Theodore Roethke. The seminar marked the beginning of a friendship that continued until Hecht's death in 2004.

Editing the letters has not only deepened my knowledge of the person and poet I long admired; it has allowed me to realize anew the many acts of generosity and encouragement he characteristically accorded others. A good number of these individuals have been instrumental in the creation of this volume. J. D. McClatchy has been an indispensible and sagacious resource at every stage of the project, as has been my UCLA colleague and friend Stephen Yenser. On more than one occasion Christopher Ricks, when asked, graciously added his editorial expertise and vast textual knowledge to his general enthusiasm for the project. For offering encouragement and advice along the way, I also want to acknowledge Daniel Albright, Robert Bagg, Gregory Dowling, Stephen Edgar, B. H. Fairchild, Kenneth Gross, John Hollander, Ann Kjellberg, James Longenbach, David Mason, Russ McDonald, Sandra McPherson, the late Barbara Packer, William Pritchard, Peter Sacks, David Sofield, Willard Spiegelman, Mark Strand, and Richard Wilbur. At a crucial moment, John Irwin helped the project gain momentum when he offered to publish a sampling of the letters in the *Hopkins Review*. The sharp eyes and thoughtful minds of my UCLA English Department colleagues Albert Braunmuller and Stephen Yenser (again) lent a finishing touch to the whole. The work also benefited greatly from the efforts of two intrepid research assistants at UCLA, Tina Ta and Claire Byun.

For responding to specific queries, some of considerable length and intricacy, it is a pleasure to acknowledge Colin Burrow, Jean Claude Carron, Elisa Harkness, Adam and Lisa Hecht, Michael Heim, Edward Hirsch, Raymond Knapp, Kathleen Komar, Ivan Majdrakoff, Cameron McCauley, Michael North, Margaret Rosenthal, Chris Van 't dack, Irving Weiss, Stephen Werner, and Claire White. For many kindnesses while overseeing our visits to the Hecht archive at Emory University, Kathy Shoemaker deserves special mention, as does Elizabeth Chase, Catherine Fernandez, and the former director of Special Collections, Stephen Enniss, now at the Folger Shakespeare Library, and his wife, Lucy Enniss. The Schuchards, Ron and Keith, graciously extended the hospitality found at the library into the surrounding academic community at Emory.

Philip Hoy has been, from the beginning, a keen and helpful advocate of this project, as he is of all things related to Hecht. On difficult questions of inclusion, Evan Hecht served admirably as unofficial consultant. I am also grateful to Diederik Oostidijk for his perceptive comments especially with regard to Hecht's war letters, and to Mary Jo Salter for always enlightening conversations about poetry and life. In her capacity as the librarian of the Grace M. Hunt Memorial English Reading Room at UCLA, Lynda Tolly was frequently asked to reprise her role as artful tracker of the most arcane references. Jeanette Gilkison continues to be the unflappable, non-pareil of English department administrators. Grants from the Robert Woodruff Library at Emory and from the UCLA Academic Senate helped to fund research necessary for the completion of this book. I am grateful as well for the advice and direction offered by my editor at the Johns Hopkins University Press, Greg Nicholl, and my copyeditor, Maria denBoer. Grant Rosson did a superb job proofreading and preparing the index.

Susan Gallick, my companion and adventurer in this and all other things, never tired of participating in conversations about a poet and person she too knew and admired. We both thank Helen Hecht for her generous hospitality and years of friendship.

Special thanks are due to the following for graciously supplying copies of letters used in this book.

Institutions

Amherst College Library: letters to Richard Wilbur. *Anthony Hecht Papers: Manuscripts, Archives, and Rare Book Library, Emory University*: All letters to Dorothea, Melvyn, and Roger Hecht; copies and drafts of letters to numerous others. *Brown University Library*: letters to Austin Warren. *Dartmouth College Library, Rauner Special Collections*: letters to Philip Booth. *Georgetown University Library*: letters to Timothy J. Healy, S.J. *Harry Ransom Humanities Research Center, University of Texas at Austin*: letters to Anne Sexton, William Arrowsmith, Elizabeth Hardwick. *Houghton Library, Harvard University*: letters to L. E. Sissman. *I Tatti Library, Florence, Italy*: letter to Laurance Roberts. *The Library of Congress*: letters to Mark Justin, Gary Metras, Judith Testa, Y. H. Zhao. *Milne Special Collections, University of New Hampshire Library*: letter to Donald Hall. *New York Public Library*: letters to Daniel Halpern, Howard Moss. *Oxford University Library*: letters to Jacqueline Simms Flursheim, Jon Stallworthy. *Princeton University Library*: letters to Allen Tate. *Smith College Library*: letter to Newton Arvin. *Special Collections, Leeds University Library*: letters to Philip Hoy. *University of Chicago Library*: letter to Karl Shapiro. *University of Delaware Library, Newark, Delaware*: letters to W. D. Snodgrass, Donald Justice, Bill Read. *University of Rochester: Rare Books and Special Collections*: letter to George H. Ford. *Washington University Libraries*: letters to James Merrill, Howard Nemerov, Mona Van Duyn, Jarvis Thurston. *Yale Collection of American Literature, Beinecke Rare Book and Manuscript Library*: letters to Joseph Brodsky, Alfred Corn, J. D. McClatchy, Robert Fitzgerald.

Individuals

Daniel Albright; Daniel Anderson; Lisa Baskin for the letters to Leonard Baskin; Harold Bloom; Michael Blumenthal; David Bromwich; Ashley Brown; Beatrice Cazac for the letters to Hayàt Mathews; Nicholas Christopher; Eleanor Cook;

B. H. Fairchild; Alan Frost; Deborah Garrison, Hecht's editor at Alfred A. Knopf; Dana Gioia; Frank Glazer; Kenneth Gross; Paul Gross; Cynthia Hadzi for the letters to Dimitri Hadzi; Donald Hall; David Havird; Daniel Hoffman; John Hollander; Richard Howard; Philip Hoy; Sunil Iyengar; Sydney Lea; David Lehman; Brad Leithauser; Valerie Lynn for the letter to Kenneth Lynn; William MacDonald; David Mason; Kate Maxwell for the letters to William Maxwell; J. D. McClatchy; Sandra McPherson; Edward Perlman; Jonathan Post; William Pritchard; Christopher Ricks; Hays H. Rockwell; Ira Sadoff; Mary Jo Salter; Sherod Santos; David Slavitt; David Sofield; Jennifer Snodgrass, Hecht's editor at Harvard University Press; Kathy Starbuck for the letter to George Starbuck; Peter Steele, S.J.; Philip Stephens; U. T. Summers for the letters to Joseph Summers; Dorothea Tanning; Charles Tung; John Van Doren; Claire White; Ella Whitehead for the letter to John Whitehead; Norman Williams; and Garry Wills.

INDEX

Page numbers in bold indicate a brief biographical note on the subject.

Hecht, Anthony, poetry of: "Adam," 103; *AESOPIC*, 168, 171; "After the Rain," 134, 152; "Alceste in the Wilderness," 72, 85–87, 88, 225; "And Can Ye Sing Baluloo," 171; "Anthem," 284; "Apprehensions," xviii, 3, 23, 133, 134, 158, 293; "The Ashen Light of Dawn," 335; "At the Frick," 71; "Aubade" [2004], 13, 335; "Aubade" ["A Deep Breath at Dawn"], 94, 98; "Auguries of Innocence," 325; "La Bàs: A Trance," 283, 288; "Behold the Lilies of the Field," 23, 171, 225; "The Bells," 118; "Birdwatchers of America," 171; "A Birthday Poem," 206; "Black Boy in the Dark," 133; "The Book of Yolek," 4, 23, 190, 205, 336, 342; "The Ceremony of Innocence," 308–309; "A Certain Slant," 343; "A Choir of Starlings," 96, 99; "Chorus from Oedipus at Colonos," 155; "Circles," 102; "Clair de Lune," 102, 104; *Collected Earlier Poems*, 234; "Coming Home," 209; "La Condition Botanique," 94–95, 104; *The Darkness and the Light*, 72, 102, 228, 249–251, 302, 304, 308–309, 328–329, 331–332, 335; "The Darkness and the Light are Both Alike to Thee," 252; "Death the Carnival Barker," 282; "Death the Poet: A Ballade—Lament for the Makers," 304; "Declensions," 344; "A Deep Breath at Dawn," 23, 98; "The Deodand," xv, 23, 175, 225; "Despair," 288; "Devotions of a Painter," 205; "Dichtung und Wahrheit," 134, 222; "The Dover Bitch," x, 104, 118, 245–246; "The End of the Weekend," 245; "A Fall," 288; "The Feast of Stephen," 23, 206, 251, 327, 342; *Flight Among the Tombs*, 72, 249–251, 281, 288, 304; "For James Merrill: An Adieu," 283; "The Fountain," 228; *The Gehenna Florilegium*, 250, 288–289; "The Ghost in the Martini," x, xvii, 132, 140, 245; "The Gift of Song," 104; "Gladness of the Best," 133–134, 171, 284; "The Grapes," 135, 187, 191, 206; "Green: An Epistle," 132, 135, 146, 200, 225; "Hallowe'en," 95; *The Hard Hours*, xii, 73, 101–103, 118,

126–127, 131, 136, 143, 170, 187; "Heureux qui, comme Ulysse," 126; "A Hill," 104, 119, 222; "Illumination," 288; "Imitation," 104; "Indolence," 288, 329; "'It Out-Herods Herod, Pray You, Avoid It,'" 102; "Japan," 23; "Je n'ai pas Oublie," 118; "Late Afternoon: The Onslaught of Love," 252, 304; "A Letter," 103, 104, 121, 122; "Life of Crime," 342–343; "Lizards and Snakes," 143, 342; "Long-Distance Vision," 288; "Look Deep," 288; "A Lot of Night Music," 134; "A Love for Four Voices," 187, 204, 236; "The Lull," 206; "Matisse: Blue Interior with Two Girl—1947," 72; "Meditation," 190, 205; "Memory," 309; "Menassah ben Israel," 343; "A Message from the City," 103, 123; *Millions of Strange Shadows*, xiv, 3, 131, 133, 140, 155, 158, 161, 171, 190, 206, 209, 279, 284; "Mirror," 308–309; "'More Light! More Light!'" 23, 104, 119, 142, 207, 342; "The Nightingale," 171; "Nocturne: A Recurring Dream," 303; "The Odds," 133, 206; "Once More, With Feeling," 329; "The Origin of Centaurs," 104; "An Orphic Calling," 72, 288; "Ostia Antica," 102; "A Pair of Heroes," 288; "Peripeteia," 132; "Persistences," 23; "A Pledge," 283, 288; "Poem Without Anybody," 332; "Poppy," 309; "Praise for Kolonos," 155; "The Presumptions of Death," 250, 252, 270–271, 282; "Proust on Skates," xvi; "Public Gardens," 288; "Retreat," 279–280; "Rites and Ceremonies," x, 23, 72, 127, 170, 185; "The Road to Damascus," 302, 309, 313; "A Roman Holiday," xvi; "The Room," 127; "Sacrifice," 23, 329; "Samson," 309; "Samuel Sewall," 72, 104; "Sarabande on Attaining the Age of Seventy-seven," 251; "Seascape with Figures," 72, 76; "Secrets," 288; "See Naples and Die," 205, 234; "Sestina D' Inverno," 190; *Seven Against Thebes*, 140, 143; *The Seven Deadly Sins*, 114, 250; "The Seven Deadly Sins," 104; "The Short End," 173–175; "Sisters," xvi, 252, 282–283, 288; "Songs for the

Ravel, Maurice, "Bolero," 230
Read, Bill, letter to, 142–143
Reagan, Ronald, 230
Redon, Odilon, 61
Reed, Henry, "Naming of Parts," 275
Rembrandt van Rijn, 309
Renoir, Pierre-Auguste, x, xv, 229;
"Parisian Woman Dressed in Algerian Costume," 175–176
Rice, Philip Blair, 73, 74–75
Rich, Adrienne, 232–233
Richard, I. A., 229–230
Richard I of England (Coeur de Lion), 41
Ricks, Christopher, 205, 215; letter to, 215–216; mentioned, 244, 319
Rilke, Rainer Maria, 218; "Cornet," 62; "Ein Märchen vom Tod," 99; "Das Stundenbuch," 62
Roberts, Laurance: 289; letter to, 289; mentioned, 91–93, 106, 289, 339
Rochester, New York, 134, 153, 171, 205, 215, 232, 237, 302. See also University of Rochester
Rockwell, Hays, 284; letter to, 284
Rodin, Auguste, 144
Rodziński, Artur, 57
Roethke, Theodore, 226; "The Lost Son," 154; "Praise to the End," 154
Ronsard, Pierre de, 187; "Contre Denise, Sorcière," 96
Rosenstock, Dr. Joseph, 57
Rosenthal, Elsa, 71, 92, 94
Rosenthal, Ray, 71, 92–93, 94, 96
Rouault, Georges Henri, 85
Rousseau, Henri, 53
Rubens, Peter Paul, 164
Ruskin, John, 163–164, 290, 293, 296–297; The Stones of Venice, 163–164, 179; Unto This Last, 256

Sadoff, Ira, 135, 191; letter to, 191–193
Salinger, J. D., 233
Salter, Mary Jo, 134, 251, 306; letters to, 306, 319–320, 339–340; "Deliveries Only," 339; Open Shutters, 339
Sanders, Ed, 138
Santayana, George, 73, 146
Santos, Sherod, 330; letter to, 330
Sapinsley, Al, 13, 251, 297; letter to, 297–299; mentioned, 75–76

Scarlatti, Domenico, 231, 317
Schnabel, Arthur, 316
Schneider, Alexander, 316
Schoenberg, Arnold, 265
Schopenhauer, Arthur, 37, 39
Schubert, Franz, 261, 334
Schuchard, Ronald, 337; letter to, 337–338
Schumann, Clara, 319
Schumann, Robert, 319
Schwab, Armand, 285–286
Schwartz, Delmore, 281–282
Scupham, Peter, 301
Seneca, xiii, xiv, 273
Serkin, Rudolph, 57, 316
Serlio, Sebastiano, 345
Sewanee, 151, 278
Sewanee Review, The, 114–115, 180
Sexton, Alfred ("Kayo"), 121–122, 124
Sexton, Anne, xiv, 103, 120, 127; letters to, 120–126; mentioned, 183, 218–219, 302
Shakespeare, William, xi, xii, xiv, 13, 22–23, 204; mentioned, 16, 27, 36, 53, 57, 128, 135, 156, 192, 231, 235, 237, 242, 254, 255, 263, 274, 278, 288, 299, 318, 321–322, 330, 332
Shakespeare, William, plays of: As You Like It, xii, 322; Coriolanus, 198; Hamlet, 20, 23, 29, 33, 52, 66, 198, 278; I Henry IV, 305; II Henry IV, 302; Henry VI, 321; Julius Caesar, 49, 322; King Lear, 23, 27, 170–171, 230, 263, 332; Macbeth, 128, 198; The Merchant of Venice, 197–198, 204, 291; A Midsummer Night's Dream, 132, 150, 187, 204, 236, 278; Othello, 82, 204, 227, 241; Romeo and Juliet, 335; The Tempest, 133, 170
Shakespeare, William, poetry of: "The Phoenix and the Turtle," xiv; Sonnet 29, 242; Sonnet 53, xiv, 158; Sonnet 55, 255; Sonnet 62, 330; Sonnet 87, 304; Sonnet 129, 304; "When that I was and a little tiny boy," 245
Shapiro, Harvey, 169
Shapiro, Karl, 72, 85; letter to, 85; mentioned, 36, 94
Shaw, Artie, 317
Shaw, George Bernard, 231, 265; Major Barbara, 139

Shawn, William, 21, 48, 165, 168
Shelley, Percy Bysshe, 293
Sidney, Philip, 295, 322; "Ye goatherd gods," 210–211
Siegrist, Phyllis, 135, 182; letter to, 182–184
Signorelli, Luca, *Flagellation*, 327
Simic, Charles, 281
Simms, Jacqueline (Jacky), 186, 204; letters to, 186–187, 190–191; mentioned, 301
Simonides, 139
Simpson, Louis, 104, 133, 138, 145, 158, 318–319
Sirota, Leo, 57, 59–60
Sissman, L. E., 102, 145; letter to, 146–147; mentioned, 210, 302; *Dying: An Introduction*, 154; "Hello, Darkness," 208; *Pursuit of Honor*, 154
Skelton, John, 214
Skinner, Cyriack, 309
Slavitt, David, 340; letter to, 340
Smart, Christopher, 170
Smit, Leo, 71, 96, 99
Smith, Sidney, 324
Smith College, 80, 101, 104, 113, 114, 115–119, 124, 132, 143, 150, 155, 175, 245, 282, 302
Snodgrass, Jennifer, 235; letter to, 235–236
Snodgrass, W. D., 133, 152; letters to, 152–153, 162, 238–239, 244–245, 283; mentioned, 138, 232, 335; "Heart's Needle," 154; "The Marsh," 134, 152
Société Imaginaire. *See* Batuz
Socrates, 200
Sofield, David, 242; letter to, 242–243
Sophocles, 156, 162, 282; *Oedipus at Colonus*, 155–157, 170; *Oedipus Rex*, 318
Spears, Monroe K., 236
Spencer, Theodore, 322
Spengler, Oswald, 58, 322; *Decline of the West*, 12, 64
Spenser, Edmund, 305; "Epithalamion," 340; *The Shepherd's Calender*, 145
Spielberg, Steven, *Schindler's List*, 263
Spillane, Mickey, 322
Spofford, William, 116
Spurgeon, Caroline, 322

Stafford, Jean, 186
Stallings, A. E., 327
Stallworthy, Jon, ix, x, xx, 104, 127, 186; letters to, 127–128, 160, 301–302; mentioned, 187, 242
Stanislavski, Constantin, 53
Starbuck, George, 138; letter to, 138; *Works: Poems Selected from Five Decades*, 137
Starkie, Enid, 255
Stars and Stripes, 20, 22, 46, 52, 53, 54, 67
Steele, Peter, 251, 266; letters to, 266–267, 325–326; mentioned, 272; *Expatriates: Reflections on Modern Poetry*, 266
Stein, Gertrude, 66
Stephen, Saint, 327
Stephens, Philip, 251, 313; letter to, 313–314; *The Determined Days*, 313–314
Stevens, Wallace, 157, 162–163, 196, 209, 245, 259, 269, 275, 288; *Harmonium*, 62; "Le Mononcle de mon Oncle," 62, 162; "Peter Quince at the Clavier," 62, 162
Strand, Mark, 239, 264, 335; "Eating Poetry," 172; *Late Hour*, 172; "The Man in the Tree," 245
Stravinsky, Igor, 228, 265; "The Rake's Progress," 228
Suetonius, 96
Summers, Joseph, 133–134, 174, 204; letters to, 174–175, 217, 220–221, 236–237; mentioned, 161, 172, 174
Summers, U. T., letter to, 217
Swafford, Jan, *Johannes Brahms*, 319
Swift, Kathryn, 20; letters to, 40, 57, 62–63; mentioned, 39–42, 44, 46, 54, 61
Switzerland, 82, 108–109; Zurich, 74

Taine, Hippolyte, 53
Tanning, Dorothea, 314; letters to, 314–315, 333–334
Tanning Prize, 289
Tate, Allen, xii, 70, 71, 90, 101, 103, 132; letters to, 90–91, 95–97, 99, 114–115, 118–119, 151; mentioned, 86, 91, 94, 171, 196, 200, 338; *The Fathers*, 118
Tate, Helen, 171

Tate, Jim, 138
Taylor, Eleanor Ross, 70
Taylor, Peter, 70
Tchaikovsky, Pyotr Ilyich, 316
Tennyson, Alfred Lord, 159, 192–193, 243–244, 260, 287; "Now Sleeps the Crimson Petal," 319
Testa, Judith, 207; letter to, 207
Theocritus, 322
Thomas, Dylan, 220, 282
Thomas Aquinas, Saint, *Summa Theologica*, 323
Thomas the Rhymer, 158, 170
Thompson, Lawrance, 145
Thurston, Jarvis, 133, **157**; letter to, 157–158
Tiepolo, Giambattista, *The Sacrifice of Isaac*, 309
Times (London), 188–190
Times Literary Supplement, 132, 233, 329–330
Tolkien, J. R. R., 194
Tottel, Richard, *Tottel's Miscellany*, 294
Tree, Herbert Beerbohm, 296
Tree, Iris, 296
Trevor-Roper, Hugh, 211–212
Trilling, Lionel, 75, 128
Tung, Charles, **263**; letter to, 263–264
Turner, J. M. W., 83
Tuve, Rosemund, 172; *A Reading of George Herbert*, 160–161
Twain, Mark, 342

University of Iowa. *See* Iowa Writers' Workshop
University of Rochester, 116, 131, 133, 141, 150, 152, 159, 161, 174, 175–176, 203, 227, 293–294, 318
University of Toronto Quarterly, 241
Untermeyer, Louis, 62
Updike, John, 313

Valency, Maurice, *In Praise of Love*, 267
Valéry, Paul, 228; "The Cemetery by the Sea," 228; "Palme," 228
Van Doren, Mark, 70, 331; letter to, 331–332; mentioned, 322
Van Duyn, Mona, 133, **157**; letter to, 157–158; mentioned, 150, 153–154
van Gogh, Vincent, 40, 53

Vasari, Giorgio, "Life of Michelangelo," 89–90, 95
Vendler, Helen, 161, 171
Verrocchio, Andrea del, 82
Villon, François, 171, 303–304
Virgil, 197, 199, 231, 255, 322, 325–326; *Eclogues*, 199, 325–326
Vogue, 78, 80–81, 102, 191
Voltaire, 57

Wagner, Richard, 228, 231, 265, 319; "Siegfried's Funeral March," 195
Wallace-Crabbe, Christopher, 251, **271**; letter to, 271–272; mentioned, 301
Waller, Fats, 316
Walther von der Vogelweide, 96
Wanning, Andrews, 120, 149
Wanning, Pat, 120
Warren, Austin, 180; letter to, 180–182; mentioned, 338
Warren, Robert Penn, 153, 154, 259; *Audubon: A Vision*, 154; *Brother to Dragons*, 154
Washington, D.C., 203–205, 207, 213, 215, 229, 231–232, 252, 266, 286, 300–301, 307
Washington Post, 333; letter to the editors of, 341
Webster, John, *The White Devil*, 283
Weil, Simone, 235, 291, 293
Weiss, Anne and Irving, 71, 96
Welles, Orson, 71, 82
West, Nathaniel, 173
White, Claire Nicolas, **126**; letter to, 127
Whitehead, John, **253**; letter to, 253–254
Whitman, Walt, 261, 322
Wiesel, Elie, 316; *Night*, 263
Wilbur, Richard, xi, 70, 88, 101, 133, 204, 324; letters to, 88–89, 151–152, 233–234; mentioned, 94, 96, 106, 210, 258, 274
Wilbur, Richard, works of: "Castles and Distances," 88; "In the Smoking Car," 210; "A Late Aubade," 335; "Love Calls Us to the Things of this World," 335; *New and Collected Poems*, 233; "Sensible Emptiness," 88
Wilde, Oscar, 228; *The Importance of Being Earnest*, 136
Wilder, Thornton, 153–154

William the Conqueror, 41
Williams, Norman, 4, **197**, 204; letter to, 197–198
Williams, Oscar (anthologist), 87, 89, 94
Williams, Polly, 87
Williams, William Carlos, 191, 241; *Paterson*, 154; "Spring and All," 241
Wills, Garry, 250, **312**; letters to, 312–313, 321–322; mentioned, 325–326; *Papal Sin*, 250, 325
Wilson, A. N., *Hilaire Belloc*, 217
Wilson Quarterly, The, 73, 138, 146, 220, 267
Wind, Edgar, 164
Winterbottom, Harry, 289–290
Winters, Ivor, 269
Wordsworth, William, 22, 24, 174, 241, 281, 287, 293; "Ode: Intimations of Immortality," 170; "To the Spade of a Friend," 241
World War II, x, xii, xviii, 17, 24–59, 63–65, 67, 114, 127–128, 142–143, 176–177, 186, 253–254, 263–264, 311, 315–316, 320, 336–339; atomic bomb, 49–50, 58; Auschwitz, 264; Holocaust, 23, 185, 251, 289–290, 293, 336–337; Nazi regime, 22, 42, 45, 56, 181, 207, 315, 327; Pacific theater, 46, 51; Russia,

49–50, 56, 58; Warsaw ghetto, 336. *See also* Germany
Wright, Anne, xix, 185–186
Wright, Charles, 232
Wright, Frank Lloyd, 54
Wright, James, xix, 185–186, 302, 332
Wright, Richard, *Black Boy*, 78
Wyatt, Thomas: "Forget Not Yet," 304; "They flee from me," 96

Yale Literary Magazine, letter to the editors of, 305–306
Yale Review, 222, 321, 343
Yale Series of Younger Poets, 206
Yale University, 126, 134, 148, 153–154, 259
Yank, 48–50, 55
Yeats, William Butler, 62, 89, 114, 157, 217, 220, 222, 244, 299, 305, 333, 343
Yeats, William Butler, works of: "Adam's Curse," 192; "Lapis Lazuli," 328; "A Prayer For My Daughter," 95; *A Vision*, 222

Zagorin, Perez, *The Court and the Country*, 144
Zorina, Vera, 99
Zukofsky, Louis, 154